THE POLITICS OF KINSHIP

A typical scene in Tongaland: men repairing a seine net (*mukwao wa passe*) on the beach

THE POLITICS OF KINSHIP

A STUDY IN
SOCIAL MANIPULATION
AMONG THE LAKESIDE TONGA
OF MALAWI

by

J. van VELSEN

Professor of Sociology
University of Zambia

Published on behalf of the

INSTITUTE FOR AFRICAN STUDIES
UNIVERSITY OF ZAMBIA

by

MANCHESTER UNIVERSITY PRESS

© 1964
Published by the University of Manchester
at THE UNIVERSITY PRESS
316–324 Oxford Road, Manchester M13 9NR

Distributed in the U.S.A. by
HUMANITIES PRESS, INC.
303 Park Avenue South, New York, N.Y. 10010

First published 1964
Reprinted 1971

ISBN 0 7190 1023 3

Printed in Great Britain by Butler & Tanner Ltd., Frome and London

FOREWORD

THERE are, as far as I know, at least five distinct and separate peoples called 'Tonga' in the Central African region. Two are well-known in ethnographic literature. Junod's *The Life of a South African Tribe* is about a patrilineal people in Mozambique who are part of the Southern Division of the Bantu. Dr. Colson's researches (*Marriage and the Family among the Plateau Tonga, The Social Organization of the Gwembe Tonga, The Plateau Tonga of Northern Rhodesia: Social and Religious Studies*) concern a matrilineal people of the Central Division of Bantu who both live on the plateau north of the Zambezi River in Northern Rhodesia and on both of the banks of the Zambezi River and Lake Kariba. A third group live on the lower Zambezi area in Mozambique south-east of Tete. These people, as far as I know, have never been studied intensively but from what scanty information we have they appear to be like the Sena. A fourth group, also unstudied, live in the Sabi valley in Southern Rhodesia and appear to be one of the Shona-speaking peoples. The fifth group are the people that Dr. van Velsen describes. They are a people in Nyasaland who, as a result of this book, will soon become as familiar to social anthropologists as the other two 'Tonga' peoples of Central Africa.

Nyasaland, as compared with Northern Rhodesia, is relatively poorly studied ethnographically. There have been at least eight full reports and many shorter studies and articles published on the peoples of Northern Rhodesia in the last twenty-five years. In Nyasaland on the other hand, in the same period, we have had Godfrey Wilson's study of the Ngonde (*The Constitution of Ngonde*. Rhodes-Livingstone Paper No. 3), Dr. Margaret Read's studies of the Ngoni of the Central and Northern Provinces (*The Ngoni of Nyasaland, Children of Their Fathers*) and my own work on the Yao (*The Yao Village*). Therefore, for this reason alone and were his report an ethnographic account of the Lakeside Tonga only, Dr. van Velsen's book would have been welcome.

But Dr. van Velsen's book is a good deal more than a descriptive account of the life and customs of the Lakeside Tonga. It is

v

also a substantial contribution to social anthropological theory. There are certain features of the social institutions of any tribal people which an anthropologist can reasonably expect to find when he does fieldwork among them. He can expect them to have a fairly clear-cut kinship system which organizes them into social groups. He can expect to find certain rules and customs governing the way in which land is acquired and disposed of. He can expect to find customary arrangements through which marriages are contracted and the rights and obligations of the spouses and children towards each other formally established. He can expect to find a variety of tribal office-holders—headmen and chiefs—whose positions are marked by clear-cut duties and responsibilities and whose office is embellished with some ceremony and circumstance. He can expect to find a series of ritual practices in which the salient values of the society are dramatized and expressed or religious performances which reflect the fundamental unity or divisions in the society.

Dr. van Velsen could find little of all this. The Lakeside Tonga matrilineally-biased kinship system provides little basis for the formation of local groups. Dr. van Velsen found that it was almost impossible to find out the exact legal status of a relationship between a man and a woman living together as husband and wife; the constitutional position of the chiefs was similarly ill-defined and their offices lacked traditional sanctions. It was often difficult to tell who the village headman was, and where there was a recognized headman he usually could wield no authority over his 'subjects': his office 'appeared to lack substance and sanction'. Every free-born Lakeside Tonga man in fact considered himself to be the equal of any chief or headman. Land was plentiful and, as against what happens in other parts of Central Africa, unless it was being actively cultivated it could be taken up without the formal permission of the village headman. There were few public ceremonies or rituals in which, as Dr. van Velsen puts it: 'social and political relationships and values are re-asserted and re-enacted for the inquisitive anthropologist'. There was no trace at all of ancestor worship or other traditional religious practices.

This apparent disorganization of the Lakeside Tonga is probably related partly to the fact that they are a people with a history of considerable tribal admixture in the past. In addition they were one of the first people in Nyasaland to come under the influence of European missionaries. Nowadays they all profess to be Christians, wear European-type clothing, use Western material culture in their daily lives and as many as seventy per cent of the active males may be absent at the labour centres of Southern Rhodesia and South Africa at any one time. They present, in short, little of the appearance of the well-integrated, uncontaminated tribal societies which emerge from the pages of many of the earlier and even contemporary anthropological monographs. From the point of view of a conventional anthropological study they present an unexciting prospect.

As if this were not difficult enough, Dr. van Velsen found also that he could not use the sort of field-work techniques which his colleagues had found feasible. He could not, for example, write down a genealogy of a village in public as most other fieldworkers had found possible in other parts of Central Africa. It was impossible for him, or for interviewers on his behalf, to conduct a straightforward village census—a procedure which has been one of the standard techniques of fieldwork amongst other peoples in Central Africa. The Lakeside Tonga were such individualists and were so concerned that the information which Dr. van Velsen might acquire might be used against them that any direct approach of this sort was out of the question. In fact Dr. van Velsen reports that his best information concerns those villages which he knew well but in which he himself did not live.

The social life of the Lakeside Tonga thus appeared from the outset to exhibit no regularities, no pattern which could be made the starting point of an analysis. But this very lack of apparent order set the problem for Dr. van Velsen for, as he points out in his opening paragraphs, observers of Lakeside Tonga social life in the past have presented two contradictory accounts of it. To some the Tonga were 'conceited and truculent, undisciplined and fond of intrigue', or 'a degenerated, heterogeneous rabble, who were difficult to handle'. But at the same time to others they were 'peaceful and friendly', or 'at heart an innocuous people'. As Dr. van Velsen puts it: 'On the one hand we are told that the Tonga are factious, rift with jealousies and plagued by disputes; on the other hand they are said to be peaceful and with a striking absence of violence despite their "undisciplined state".' 'It is clear', Dr. van Velsen goes on, 'that these visitors to Tongaland were struck by an apparent anarchy but many, if not most, could not help

noticing some semblance of order.' Dr. van Velsen's aim, therefore, was to describe how this apparent anarchy was in fact
ordered.

This 'apparent anarchy' of the Lakeside Tonga is not unrelated
to another striking characteristic of these people. Numerically
they are a relatively small group—some 60,000—yet in proportion to their size they have played a prominent part in the commercial and political life of Southern Africa. Almost from the
earliest days of the British campaign against the slave-trade in
Nyasaland the Tonga became the mainstay of the military forces.
They began migrating in search of wage employment as early as
1886: by 1894 Sir Harry Johnston could report that annually some
1000 to 2000 Lakeside Tonga were coming to the Highlands to
seek work on the estates as porters, 'steamer boys' and that-they
formed the bulk of the 'irregular police' at European stations
there. This trend continued so that, as Dr. van Velsen puts it:
'they have produced more than their fair share of trade union
leaders, politicians and "white collar" workers including many
in senior positions in the African Civil Service and abroad. According to one official report the Tonga people "seem to have
achieved a monopoly of many of the best jobs in South Africa".
Whether true or not, this opinion represents the reputation of the
Tonga who are widely known as a go-ahead people.' [1] Dr. van
Velsen argues that the success of the Lakeside Tonga in industrial
and commercial and government positions arises partly from their
initial advantage in education because it was amongst them that
one of the first successful mission stations started operating in 1879.
But it also stems from the consummate skill the Tonga have in
manipulating social relationships—a characteristic which reflects
the social system in which they live.

It is not surprising that Dr. van Velsen initially had some
difficulty in presenting an account of the social system of these
people. His difficulty, however, stemmed largely from the inappropriateness of the analytical model he set out to use. Anthropologists trained in British universities and who went into the
field shortly after the 1939–45 War did so in the hey-day of structuralism. Those of us who worked in Central Africa, for example,
found that we were greatly stimulated by the structural approach

[1] van Velsen, 'The Missionary Factor among the Lakeside Tonga in Nyasaland', *Rhodes-Livingstone Journal*, xxvi (1960), p. 21.

and that it undoubtedly deepened our understanding of Central African peoples. But we also found that the model did not altogether fit the social systems of the people we were studying. Gluckman's introduction to the 'Lamba Report' signposts the thinking at this stage, for here he debates whether the concept of 'lineage' could rightly be applied to the material we had collected among the Lamba and concludes that it could not.[1] This was before Barnes, Colson and I had been into the field. Two years later we could confirm this. Colson's work among the Plateau Tonga had shown that, like their namesakes the Lakeside Tonga, they were a people with a highly flexible social system. Barnes's work among the Ngoni had shown similarly that a good deal more than agnation was involved in the processes of segmentation and fission. My own studies of the Yao approached more closely the structural model but even here I was forced to conclude that Yao social structure was not 'organic' in the sense that Tallensi society was.

Dr. van Velsen started his training in anthropology at Oxford in 1947 when it was the centre of structuralism, and he was undoubtedly very greatly influenced by it. By the time he came to analyse his Tonga material in 1955 however he found certain difficulties in fitting his observations into a structural model. Several other younger anthropologists were having similar difficulties at the same time and were attempting to deepen our understanding of various social systems by supplementing their structural analyses with additional material. Worsley, for example, found that he could deepen our understanding of Tallensi kinship by examining their economic life in greater detail than Fortes had.[2] Lewis was showing that Somali segmentation could be understood better in terms of the disposition of man-power rather than in terms of the regular separation into lineage segments.[3] As Dr. van Velsen points out, the structural stage was a necessary phase in the development of anthropological theory.

[1] Mitchell and Barnes, *The Lamba Village: A Report of a Social Survey*, School of African Studies, University of Cape Town, Communication 24 (n.s., 1950).

[2] Worsley, 'The Kinship System of the Tallensi: A Revaluation', *Journal of the Royal Anthropological Institute*, lxxxvi (1956), pp. 37–75. For a revaluation of Tallensi political relations, see Sommerfelt (1958).

[3] Lewis, I. M., *A Pastoral Democracy*, London. Oxford University Press for International African Institute (1961).

The structure of a society in these broad terms is an abstract model or paradigm which is essential to our understanding of human actions. But the next stage in the development is to show how exceptions and variations ignored in the process of delineating a structure are accommodated within it in reality.

The need for this kind of study has come in the first instance from those societies in which the structural principles are not salient as amongst the Plateau Tonga or the Lakeside Tonga. Barnes has noted the same need in ethnographic studies in New Guinea where he talks of the inappropriateness of the African models in the study of the peoples of the Highlands. By 'African models' here he refers to those studies of the Nuer, Tallensi, Dinka, Bedouin and Tiv—peoples characterized by highly organized lineage systems.[1] Barnes's description of New Guinea Highlands societies, however, with the change of 'patrilineal' to 'matrilineal' could easily apply to the sort of society Dr. van Velsen describes in this book.

In fact Lakeside Tonga society is, as Barnes, following Firth, expresses it, 'highly optative',[2] and Dr. van Velsen argues that it is only by seeing the way in which people build up social relationships or withdraw from others in order to gain specific social, political or economic ends that one can understand them. In particular he examines the way in which the Tonga utilize their manifold kinship links for political manœuvring—hence the title of the book. The same sets of social relationships may serve different interests at different times and the same people may be involved in new social relationships as their interests change. In other words social relationships are more instrumental in the activities of people than they are the determinants of them. This leads to an ever-fluctuating network of links and cross-linkages and it is the interaction of these counter-balancing cleavages and alliances which in the end contribute to the stability of Lakeside Tonga society.

Dr. van Velsen found that for a long time he could not fully comprehend the nature of this social interaction in terms of shifting interests. He describes that it was only when he came to consider in detail the course of events leading up to and following

---

[1] Barnes, 'African Models in the New Guinea Highlands', *Man*, lxii (1962), pp. 5–9.
[2] Barnes (1962), p. 7.

the death of a child in a village in which he was staying that he was able to understand: 'how people are caught up in and restrained by a network of cross-cutting relationships and allegiances'. He goes on to say that: 'each individual within his or her own personal network acts now within one set of interests and now within another'. In order to be able to study the process through which people select some of a wide range of possible relationships in order to achieve their ends we must observe people in a variety of social situations. We can then analyse the behaviour of the individual in terms of the factors which constrain him to choose a particular mode of action in one situation and a different in another. This process is what Dr. van Velsen calls 'situational analysis'. It is a development of the case-method approach in anthropological studies which has characterized several recent Rhodes-Livingstone studies. Barnes has characterized the use of the 'case-method' in anthropological studies by suggesting that in earlier anthropological accounts:

ceremonies, rites, legends and myths were reported at great length, while the groups and relationships were outlined in static terms. By contrast many monographs contain only highly selected accounts of ceremonial behaviour but include long and complex case histories involving a large number of individuals whose relationships to each other are of consequence for understanding their actions. In other words a shift has been made from describing the constitution of a society to showing how it works. The difference between the two periods can be seen by reading an early and a recent monograph in succession. Whereas an early report such as Spencer and Gillen's classic . . . may remind us of a church service with elaborate symbolism and ceremonial but few distinctive roles, these later works suggest instead a Russian novel, with a host of characters whose changing positions relative to each other and to the external world constitute the plot.[1]

The development of this approach has been traced by Gluckman. He refers to it as the 'extended-case method', thereby emphasizing its essentially diachronic nature. Gluckman believes that 'the problems which are emerging and which involve the basic problems of the endurance, stability and different types of change in a

[1] Barnes, 'Social Anthropology in Theory and Practice: An Inaugural Lecture', *Arts: The Proceedings of the Sydney University Arts Association* (1958), pp. 47–67.

social system existing in space-time can only be tackled through the use of the extended-case method'.[1] This book supports this contention.

It is important thus to distinguish 'situational analysis' from what some people call 'the case method' but which is in fact only what Gluckman calls 'apt illustration'. Leach apparently fails to do this in a recent reference to 'the case history method'.[2] The way in which Malinowski uses case material in his accounts is quite different from Dr. van Velsen's 'situational analysis' and certainly 'situational analysis' can in no way be compared with the way in which Frazer used 'case material' in his works. The material is not presented merely 'to illustrate a particular theoretical principle' as Leach seems to think it is, but rather it is an integral part of the analysis of the social structure. The point is that the extended-case method can only be used *in conjunction with* a statement of the structure of the society for it deals essentially with the way in which individuals are able to exercise choices within the limits of a specified social structure. The extended case is not merely an excerpt from the fieldworker's note book. It is an edited extract designed to show the way in which the variations excluded by the necessary process of abstraction are in fact contained within the structure. The anthropologist therefore studies the social structure of a people by whatever means available to him over as large a part of the society as he can manage. He carries out his village censuses, he collects his genealogies, he attends ceremonies and social occasions, he listens to court cases and tribunals, he talks to the people and he consults documentary sources where these exist. Where he can, he presents data in quantitative form, for the extended-case method is in no way a substitution for quantitative methods of study. This use of 'case material' is different from that proposed by sociologists some twenty-five years ago when a controversy arose between antagonists some of whom advocated 'case study' methods and some 'statistical' methods as if they were mutually exclusive alternatives. Situational analysis is supplementary to, not competitive with other methods of studying a social system. An excellent modern exam-

[1] Gluckman, 'Ethnographic Data in British Social Anthropology', *The Sociological Review*, ix (1961), pp. 5–26.

[2] Leach, *Pul Eliya: A village in Ceylon*, Cambridge University Press (1961), pp. 11–12.

ple of the combined use of quantitative, observational and extended-case methods is in Turner's study of the social processes in Ndembu villages.[1]

The fact that the 'case method' or 'situational analysis' is not a substitute for but a supplement to conventional structural analysis is a point apparently missed by Eggan when he raises the question of the typicality of the cases used in the analysis.[2] The typicality of the material is irrelevant since the regularities are set out in the description of the over-all social structure. In a sense the more atypical the actions and events described in the case history, the more instructive they are, since the anthropologist uses case material to show how variations can be contained within the structure.

While the need to incorporate 'optation' is greatest in our analyses of relatively unstructured societies such as the Lakeside Tonga, it is also essential in the study of more highly structured societies. Barnes points out that there is a world of difference between the abstract accounts of the lineage system of the Nuer and Evans-Pritchard's account of actual social relationships 'on the ground' as in *Marriage and the Family among the Nuer*.[3] Leach has expressed a similar point of view. 'In my view', he writes, 'an anthropological structural analysis which appears comprehensive in that it narrowly defines *all* possible relationships is wrong in some rather fundamental way.' He continues: 'I postulate that structural systems in which all avenues of social action are narrowly institutionalized are impossible. *In all viable systems there must be an area where the individual is free to make choices so as to manipulate the system to his advantage.*'[4]

The theoretical significance of this book therefore lies in its description of the way in which social relationships are manipulated to the personal advantage of individuals involved in them. The inchoate nature of Lakeside Tonga social structure forced this 'optative' aspect of social relationships on to Dr. van Velsen's

[1] Turner, *Schism and Continuity in an African Society*, Manchester University Press (1958).

[2] Eggan, 'Ethnographic Data in Social Anthropology in the United States', *The Sociological Review*, ix (1961), pp. 19–26.

[3] Barnes (1962), p. 5.

[4] Leach, 'On Certain Unconsidered Aspects of Double Descent Systems', *Man*, lxii (1962), p. 133. Original italics.

attention but he has been able to draw the wider lesson from his experience and thereby focus our attention on the extent to which optation is an element in *all* social systems. This book raises the whole question of avenues of social action alternative to those institutionalized in structural systems. This is a step forward in the study of social systems since it demonstrates one way in which the structural model can be elaborated to make it reproduce social reality a little more closely. And the closer the fit of theory to reality the better it is.

CLYDE MITCHELL

Salisbury,
  September, 1963

CONTENTS

Cases

Genealogies

Maps and Plans

Tables

Plates

PREFACE

IN common with many other peoples the Tonga say that 'a chief without people is no chief': a man with a title but without a measure of popular support is in a helpless position. How similar is the position of the sociological fieldworker who is so dependent on the co-operation of the people whose institutions he wants to study. The Tonga, like any community suddenly finding an intruder in their midst, naturally regarded me with a good deal of suspicion, particularly since I did not fall within any of the known and accepted categories: neither missionary, nor teacher, trader nor administrator. Suspicion was enhanced by the fact that I arrived in Tongaland at a time of considerable political tension. The idea of a Central African Federation had aroused, and was later implemented against, a good deal of popular opposition. As a result, my quests for genealogical and other information often took a course very similar to that described by Professor Evans-Pritchard in a well-known passage in *The Nuer* (p. 12). That in spite of these unpropitious conditions I found so much generous hospitality and friendship and as much co-operation as I did, makes my debt of gratitude even greater.

I cannot, of course, mention individually all those who helped to make my stay in Tongaland a most valuable experience (academically and otherwise) but there are some people to whom I feel particularly indebted. It was Mr. Mtalika Banda who, after a prolonged initial period of frustration, helped me to break at least some of the ice. Chiefs Guru and Mlenga Mzoma used their influence by the lakeshore to get the reason for my stay accepted. The former, moreover, in spite of considerable opposition both from within and outside his village, permitted me to build a temporary house by his own hamlet, whilst Chief Mlenga Mzoma hospitably welcomed and lodged my research team, thus carrying on the tradition of an ancestor who, nearly a century previously, warmly welcomed the first European visitor in that area: Dr. David Livingstone. In the hills it was Chief Kabunduli who introduced me to his people and offered me hospitality in his hamlet.

Among others who showed much generosity (material and otherwise) and shared with me their local knowledge I particularly want to mention Messrs. Charles Kalimba and Champion Zimba, constant aids and companions, Mlita Phiri, Ababu Msumba, Ringstead Banda, Stand Kaunda and his wife Nyavula. And also Mr. and Mrs. Patel, of Chinteche, Mr. and Mrs. M. M. V. Leonard and Mr. and Mrs. I. T. Nance; their doors, too, were always open to myself and the family. I hope that some at least of the rich experience I gained of Tonga life and, indeed, of human nature is reflected in this book. I also gratefully acknowledge the ready assistance I received from various officials, high and low, at the District H.Q. in Nkata Bay in my search for contemporary and historical information in journals and files.

For a few weeks towards the end of my stay in Tongaland I was joined by a research team from the Rhodes-Livingstone Institute. The team consisted of Messrs. E. Tikili, H. D. N'gwane and L. Bweupe. The purpose of their visit was to provide me, through a survey of several villages, with more extensive, quantitative data on demography, labour migration, family budgets and other problems. In spite of their persistent efforts, the yield was not as large as we hoped for. This was due not only to the suspicions of the people who were reluctant to be interviewed—which was perhaps not unnatural under the circumstances—but also to factors inherent in Tonga society which I mention later in the book. However, the data the team did manage to collect have proved most useful, particularly in relation to my study of the problem of labour migration which I hope to publish separately in the near future. I want to record my thanks for the team's very valuable assistance.

I also gratefully acknowledge the generous support of the Rhodes-Livingstone Institute. In view of the regrettable and, alas, increasing tendency towards research grants for a year or even less, I have become even more aware of the generosity and wisdom of the Institute's policy prevailing at that time. After an initial period of preparation, including library research, at Manchester University, I lived in Tongaland from May 1952 until October 1953. I then spent another six months at Manchester writing a preliminary account and clarifying my ideas in seminars and discussions and returned to the field for a second period from June 1954 until October 1955. The final 'write-up' was also done at Manchester. All this was done under the auspices of the Rhodes-Livingstone Institute.

My description of the Tonga scene refers to the situation as It was at the time I left Tongaland, except where explicitly stated to the contrary. I have, of course, not been able to discuss whatever developments may have taken place in Tongaland as a result of the constitutional changes of August 1961 in Nyasaland.

Like other tools, the tool of analysis needs constant sharpening. I found many 'whetstones' among my colleagues at the Rhodes-Livingstone Institute, Manchester University and the University College at Salisbury. I particularly want to mention Professor Max Gluckman, Dr. I. Cunnison, Professor Mitchell and Mr. A. Sommerfelt. From my many discussions with them and many others, drawing on their experience, I gained a greater insight into my own material.

Sociological research necessarily involves an element of intrusion into people's private lives. Furthermore, the kind of analysis which I have used in this book necessitated detailed narration of events involving specified actors. I have therefore disguised the individuals concerned through fictitious names. However, the names used in this book are fictitious only in that they do not belong to the actors concerned: I have tried to maintain local colour by using as substitutes other Tonga names: biblical, vernacular and clan names. I have used names of the different categories of names in roughly the same proportion as they are in reality. And kinsmen bearing the same names have been given the same names in this book too. To make it easier for the reader to follow the actions of the principal actors over a period of time, I have entered their names in the index.

Particularly in view of the increasing interest in ethno-historical and replication studies, the use of fictitious names may be a very real handicap to future research workers. However, a copy of this book with the real names has been deposited with Manchester University and could be made available after consultation with the author.

The village genealogies record all the members of the villages concerned (including those who were working abroad at the time and were considered by their fellow villages as only temporarily absent) and also the odd person who lives elsewhere but figures a good deal in village affairs. On the skeleton genealogies which accompany descriptions of particular events, the reader may find the occasional individual who will not be found on the main genealogies. The explanation is that such persons appear in a particular case but not in the rest of the book and do not belong to the villages under discussion either.

The village plans and the sketch map are not to scale. They are intended only to indicate the relative position of clusters, houses and other features of the villages.

J. v. V.

SYMBOLS USED IN THE TEXT

I have used the following symbols and combinations of them wherever I have abbreviated kinship terms.

M—Mother	B—Brother
F—Father	Z—Sister
D—Daughter	S—Son

In the genealogies the number of the house on the village plan is shown thus: (1); (LM) denotes: Absent Labour Migrant. When a person appears on a village genealogy without either symbol, he or she is domiciled in another village.

In the text, references to the genealogies are given by the initials of the village, the letter of the generation column, and the number down the column. Mul. for Mulombwa; Map. for Mapalassie; Kam. for Kamanga; Chin. for Chinyafwa; Mba. for Mtomba; Mz. for Mzenga. E.g.: (Map. C 2).

Hereditary names denoting titles of political offices are printed in small capitals to distinguish them from personal names.

NOTE ON THE SITUATIONAL ANALYSIS

MOST of British anthropological writing of the last twenty or thirty years has been (and much still is) within 'the structural frame of reference . . . which gives us procedures for investigation and analysis by which a social system can be apprehended as a unity made of parts and processes that are linked to one another by a limited number of principles of wide validity in homogeneous and relatively stable societies'.[1] This passage sums up the salient features of the structural approach. Firstly, structural analyses are primarily concerned with relations between social positions or statuses rather than with 'actual relations of Tom, Dick and Harry or the behaviour of Jack and Jill'.[2] There is clearly a preference for abstractions as against the particulars on which these abstractions must necessarily be based. Indeed, Radcliffe-Brown emphatically rejects the particular (which he appears to equate with the unique) behaviour of Jack and Jill as unsuitable for an 'account of the form of the structure', even though it 'may go down in our field note-books and may provide illustrations for a general description'.[3]

A second characteristic feature of structural analyses is the assumption—and perhaps necessary assumption—of homogeneity. A third feature is the concern with the stability of the society or community studied.

This structural frame of reference has produced many important results which have provided the subject with a firm foundation. This applies particularly to such pioneering studies as those on the Tallensi and the Nuer which were the first detailed descriptions of the morphology of societies where order is maintained without specialized governmental institutions. If some of the younger generation of anthropologists are beginning to doubt the

---

[1] Fortes (1953), p. 39, presents us here not only with a valuable interpretation of the structural literature up to 1935 but also with a survey of the developments leading up to the structural analysis. Barnes (1958) and Gluckman (1961) also cover the history of modern anthropology but from a somewhat different angle and including the more recent developments.

[2] Radcliffe-Brown (1952), p. 192.

[3] *Loc. cit.*

adequacy of the structural approach, this is only a measure of its very success: the foundations are so firm that subsequent workers feel sufficiently confident to continue building on them.

Structural analysis aims at presenting an outline of the social morphology; consequently there is a marked emphasis on consistency so that variations are ignored in its abstractions.[1] This outline is reduced to 'a limited number of principles of wide validity' from which the rough edges and loose ends have been removed. But as Schapera has pointed out: 'culture is not merely a system of formal practices and beliefs. It is made up essentially of individual reactions to and variations from a traditionally standardized pattern; and indeed no culture can ever be understood unless special attention is paid to this range of individual manifestations.'[2]

Norms, general rules of conduct, are translated into practice, that is, they are ultimately manipulated by individuals in particular situations to serve particular ends. This gives rise to variations for which the writer does not account in his abstractions. He may not consider these variations particularly relevant and he will therefore not state that they exist or explain how they fit into his frame of general principles of wide validity. Alternatively, he may mention that there are variations but ignore them as being accidental or exceptional. In this way, too, variations are not fitted into the structural framework. However, labelling this category of observed data 'exceptional' or 'accidental' does not solve the problem for, after all, they occur within, and are part of the same social order which the ethnographer has set out to study and describe.[3]

There have been indications of a reaction to the structuralists' over-emphasis on consistency and the formal rule. One way in which this reaction has expressed itself has been to over-emphasize actual behaviour: particular events and relations are treated as

---

[1] Cf. Radcliffe-Brown (*loc. cit.*): 'the general or normal form of this [structural] relationship [between mother's brother and sister's son is] abstracted from the variations of particular instances, though taking into account those variations'. He does not make it clear how such variations can be and are incorporated into the general norm.

[2] Schapera (1938), p. 29.

[3] Cf. also Turner (1957, p. 232): 'Thus apparent exceptions to statistical regularities obtained from genealogical data on village fission prove themselves regularities within a wider system of social relations.'

unique and there is a reluctance to relate them to a general frame of reference.[1] But this ignores the fact that the social anthropologist is concerned with people who live and act within a certain social order and whose actions must therefore have some reference to established norms of conduct. Ideal norms of conduct and actual behaviour are necessarily closely interconnected. Thus Devons argued in a debate on 'myth and reality' in politics that 'any satisfactory view of politics must comprehend both, contradictory though they are. We get a misleading view if we attempt to explain the reality of political behaviour exclusively in terms of one or the other. The reality is a complex interaction, admittedly not easy to disentangle or to explain.'[2]

There is now a growing desire to show how actual, observed behaviour fits into the structural frame of 'a limited number of principles of wide validity'. We need to know more about the variations in actual behaviour, the confusion and conflicting events[3] which occur within the same frame of values. As a result an increasing number of writers are answering Malinowski's call for 'the imponderabilia of actual life'[4] with co-ordinated accounts of the actions of specified individuals. There is a 'shift away from the collection of statements about the customs and the details of ceremonial behaviour to the study of complex social relationships' with the consequent 'emphasis on actors rather than informants'.[5] Thus records of actual situations and particular behaviour have found their way from the fieldworker's notebooks into his analytical descriptions, not as 'apt illustrations'[6] but as a constituent part of the analysis.

I shall call this way of presenting ethnographic data 'situational analysis'.[7] By this method the ethnographer not only

---

[1] See e.g. Bohannan (1957).

[2] Devons (1956). 'Myth' here refers to a formal rule of conduct (e.g. a legal rule or a rule in the statutes of a society or club) which may be ignored in practice although theoretically it is still valid.

[3] Some structural analyses mention their occurrence but do not analyse them: cf. Evans-Pritchard (1940a, p. 138): 'political actualities are confused and conflicting. . . they are not always . . . in accord with political values'.

[4] Malinowski (1922), p. 18.

[5] Barnes (1958).

[6] Gluckman (1961), p. 7.

[7] This term may be more suitable than 'case method' or 'extended-case method' (Gluckman, 1961) because 'case' has been used with so many different

presents the reader with abstractions and inferences from his field material but he also provides some of the material itself. This should put the reader in a better position to evaluate the ethnographer's analysis not only on the basis of the internal consistency of the argument, but also by comparing the ethnographic data and the inferences drawn from them. Particularly when several or most of the actors appear again and again in different situations, the inclusion of such data should reduce the chances that cases become merely apt illustrations. I am not implying that ethnographers working with a structural frame of reference do not have any accounts of actual situations in their note-books or did not publish any. Rather, as I have indicated before, the difference would appear to lie in the fact that structural descriptions do not give us a series of connected events to show how individuals in a particular structure handle the choices with which they are faced—as individuals are in all societies. Indeed, Radcliffe-Brown's statement (quoted on p. xxiii) appears to indicate that he is not concerned with this problem.

When case material is presented in the form of apt illustrations, the reader cannot easily assess the relevance and aptness of those illustrations and hence he has no check on the degree of selection of the published material. Naturally, any author will always have to apply a certain amount of selection for the sake of intelligibility. But I would suggest that in a situational analysis, incorporating co-ordinated case material, the reader is in a better position to examine for himself the basis and validity of the author's selection. Moreover, if the reader does not agree with the ethnographer's selection or interpretation of the material, he will be better equipped to attempt a different interpretation or to test different hypotheses because he will have more material to work on. Thus an author using situational analysis is more exposed—he has put more cards on the table. The reader's position is more like that of the reader of an historical work who can go back to the documents and check up on the author's interpretations and conclusions.

So far I have been discussing the general question of the analysis

---

meanings. I have already referred to the very different analytical context in which Bohannan uses his 'cases'. Richards (1939) writes about 'cases' in the sense of life histories. The use of 'case method' in social welfare work is different again. Turner (1957) calls his cases 'social dramas'.

and the presentation of the problem of the relationship between actual behaviour and generalized description. And I have expressed my own preference for the situational analysis which seems to offer better opportunities for integrating the accidental and exceptional with the general than does the structural analysis. If this can throw more light on, and give greater depth to, the total process of social life in clearly structured societies, I would argue that this approach is inescapable, if one has the same ends in view, when describing an unstructured society like that of the Tonga. Where the agents in the system are not so much corporate groups as individuals interlinked through continually changing alignments in small and often ephemeral groups, one cannot talk meaningfully about exceptions.

When I left Tongaland after a three years' stay, I could see the main outlines of their social and political system. But I had not perceived the integrative factors amongst this welter of small groups with their opposed interests and apparent lack of unity although order was clearly present. To put it more colloquially, I had not found what made this society 'tick' in spite of so much dissension. It was not until I began to analyse my records of disputes, in courts and elsewhere, that I received my first clues. I saw the same individuals or small groups—appearing in different or even in the same situations (cf. 'Meya's Death')—adopt different roles and align themselves with different interests. It was particularly the analysis of my data connected with Meya's death which made me understand how people are caught up in and restrained by a network of cross-cutting relationships and allegiances. Each individual within his or her own personal network acts now within one set of interests, now within another.

In this study I have built my analysis of the systematic features, the typical norms and values around particular social situations of which 'Meya's Death' is the central case. I have thus juxtaposed ideal rules of behaviour and actual practice. My aim has been to describe the Tonga social system by the same process whereby I gained my own insight.[1] I have therefore aimed at making the cases integral parts of the analysis and not apt illustrations.

---

[1] My experience accords largely with Colson's descriptions of the Plateau Tonga. My first understanding of how that equally unstructured society functions came with reading her account of how a conflict case was settled: Colson (1953).

I have argued that the situational frame of reference is well suited for unstructured societies like the Tonga. I now want to return briefly to Fortes's summing up of the structural approach which I quoted at the beginning of this Note. Fortes limits the suitability of the structural frame of reference to 'homogeneous and relatively stable societies'. This limitation should perhaps be related to that method's emphasis on consistency. The characteristic feature of both unstable and non-homogeneous societies or communities is variation: variations over time in the case of the former, and in the case of the latter synchronic variations as between constituent parts of the society or community. I have remarked before that situational analysis is a method of integrating variations, exceptions and accidents into descriptions of regularities. This method of analysis might therefore be particularly suitable for the study of unstable and non-homogeneous societies and communities.[1]

One final point on the question of typicality. Throughout this study I have presented my analysis, which is based mainly on five villages, as an analysis of the Tonga village in general. Although I have good reason to believe that this is so, I realize that I have not produced the evidence to support this assumption. Turner solved this problem very successfully in his work on the Ndembu.[2] He alternates sections presenting a general outline of the society whose typicality is stressed by a wealth of numerical data, with sections containing intensive descriptions of actions involving the inhabitants of a small number of villages.

My own quest for numerical data was not very successful. Tonga reaction to attempted surveys, involving as they did questioning people with whom I had had very little if any personal contact, was such that I had to abandon the idea. I found that, in general, I could expect information only from persons with whom I had had prolonged and close personal contact. Indeed, that is why I had to restrict my intensive enquiries to a few limited

---

[1] Mitchell (1960) has argued this very convincingly with regard to 'the study of social relationships in plural societies' (p. 32) where we are clearly 'not dealing with an integrated cultural system but with one in which quite disparate systems of belief may co-exist and be called into action in different social situations' (p. 19). Mitchell (1957) and Epstein (1957) are examples of the application of this method of analysis.

[2] Turner (1957).

areas. Moreover, as I shall discuss later, information on, for instance, the precise legal status of many marriages (*viz.* whether they were formal or informal) cannot generally be obtained in casual interviews. However, although in this study most of my material comes from five villages, I also lived for longer or shorter periods in other villages. The reasons why I have largely limited my descriptions to these five villages are, firstly, because I wanted to limit the spread of the description in order to be able to give it greater depth. Secondly, my data from these five villages are more systematic and co-ordinated since they were collected in the latter part of my fieldwork.

Thus for my general outline of Tonga social morphology I have drawn upon my total field experience although most social situations which I have presented are set in the five villages. I am therefore personally satisfied that the picture which I present is that of the Tonga village in general and not just that of five particular villages. On the other hand I am not unduly concerned about the typicality of my account for the whole tribe. My main concern was to understand and represent the system of social and personal relations in units of 'common participation in the everyday political economic, and social life'.[1]

[1] Fortes (1938), p. 62. Gluckman (1961, p. 14) has also hinted at the possibility 'that we shall have to abandon the concept of a society altogether, and speak of social fields'.

CHAPTER I

INTRODUCTION

The Problem and Fieldwork Method

EVER since their first contact with missionaries, administrators and other Europeans, the Tonga have had a reputation with these visitors for being 'intelligent but truculent . . . and difficult of management';[1] 'quarrelling amongst themselves . . . [and] mutual jealousies and ambitions [which] kept the country in a fever of unrest';[2] 'conceited and truculent, undisciplined and fond of intrigue';[3] 'the most prominent of all the tribes [in Nyasaland] both for intelligence and disputes';[4] 'a remarkable people, highly intelligent and having a degree of independence seldom encountered elsewhere in Africans'.[5] This is but a small selection from many similar comments. Apparently for one administrator their individualism and independence became too 'difficult of management' judging from his *cri du cœur* that the Tonga were 'reduced to a state of individualism . . . not restrained by any customs or respect or thought for their neighbours . . . a degenerated heterogeneous rabble who were difficult to handle'.[6] Such a sign of frustration is exceptional; it is much more usual to read that the Tonga are 'peaceful and friendly'.[7] Indeed, a Resident in 1937 had this to say: 'The Tonga have an intense ambition which takes them to the top when abroad. It is a source of wonder how they contrive to exist peacefully in such undisciplined state. But their salient characteristic is that, although great talkers, they seldom resort to anti-social action or indeed political action of any sort. They are at heart an innocuous people, vide the absence of serious crime.' [8]

Thus on the one hand we are told that the Tonga are factious, rift by jealousies and plagued by disputes; on the other hand they are said to be peaceful, with a striking absence of violence despite

---

[1] *Handbook* (1910), p. 8.   [2] Livingstone (1921), p. 186.
[3] Murray (1932), p. 220.   [4] Debenham (1955), p. 117.
[5] *P.C. Report, 1947*, p. 38.   [6] District H.Q. files of 1930's.
[7] Jack (1901), p. 140. Other writers have expressed similar opinions.
[8] District H.Q. files.

I

their 'undisciplined state'. It is clear that these visitors to Tongaland were struck by an apparent anarchy: but many, if not most of
them, could not help also noticing some semblance of order. The
aim of this book is to describe how this apparent anarchy is in fact
ordered.

Even the most casual observer soon discovers that although
there are chiefs (*mafumu*, sing. *fumu*) with hereditary titles, their
constitutional position is ill-defined and traditionally the office
lacks sanctions. More intensive study reveals a very complex
network of overlapping relationships between individuals and
small groups. These relationships are generally expressed in terms
of kinship so that a discussion of the political system has to be
preceded by an analysis of the kinship system. The latter will be
found in Chapters II, III and IV whilst the remaining chapters are
concerned with Tonga politics.

In the system of kinship values there is a bias towards matrilineal descent and matrilocal residence. At the same time the ties
between a person and his or her father and the latter's kin (*viz.*
the patrilateral kin) are also important and persist through at least
two generations. Patrilateral links, which tend to weaken matrilineal links, are further strengthened by the fact that marriage is
invariably virilocal (the wife takes up residence with her husband)
so that the children tend to have a real personal bond with their
patrilateral kin. My data will show that there are many discre-
pancies between formal values and actual practice. This applies
particularly to marriage, which is very difficult to define in practice although not in theory; in other words it is difficult to determine the precise legal status of a particular union of a man and a
woman apparently living together as husband and wife. This
situation is confusing not only to the anthropologist but also to
the Tonga themselves. Indeed this very confusion is one of the
striking aspects of their inter-personal relationships and much of
the first part of this book centres around a discussion of marriage.
The principal characteristics of marriage are public marriage
negotiations and certain payments from the husband's group to
the wife's group as proof thereof. I call these payments *marital
debts* because they set up debt relationships, in one way or another, between the two parties. I classify marriages as *formal* and
informal according to whether or not they were preceded by
public marriage negotiations. I will show that many relationships

are maintained if not created by marital debts. Marital debts are a
ready source of disputes, both in courts and elsewhere, and in the
course of them other problems and relationships, for example of a
political nature, are likely to be scrutinized in public; indeed it is
likely that it is these non-marital problems with which the parties
to the dispute are most directly concerned. The network of
relationships created by marital debts is further widened by the
high rate of divorce.

I proceed by way of general statements encompassing both the
structural regularities and the exceptions. These anthropological
abstractions are based not so much on informants' statements of
general rules (which may be abstractions in themselves) but rather
on more or less detailed descriptions of actual events and situations. In fact, my analysis, not only of the kinship system but
throughout the book, is built around an account of the situation
created by the death of Meya, a young girl in the house in Mapalassie village where I was living at the time. Thus the case material
in this book is not merely illustrative of my theoretical abstractions;
it is the very basis of these abstractions and forms an integral part
of a situational analysis.

In the second half of the book I discuss how the Tonga utilize
their manifold kinship links for political manœuvring. By politics
I mean those activities which, on the part of an individual or
individuals, result in leadership within and control over particular
groups, or which, in the case of competition between groups,
bring leadership and control of one group over others. These
groups may be structured or un-structured, permanent or ephemeral; they may operate within a structured framework or in a
loose, fluid context. But whatever the context and however
constituted, whilst they function they function for the promotion
of particular interests. These interests may be those of the leader
alone, or of the leader and some or all of the members of each
group. The personnel of these interest groups vary over longer or
shorter periods. Moreover, depending on the interests which are
the rallying point and the motivation of the activities of the
groups and/or their leaders, the same individuals may be members
of several differently oriented interest groups. Consequently,
individuals who are co-members in one interest group may belong
to opposing groups in regard to other interests. Political relationships are those through which political activities are conducted.

c

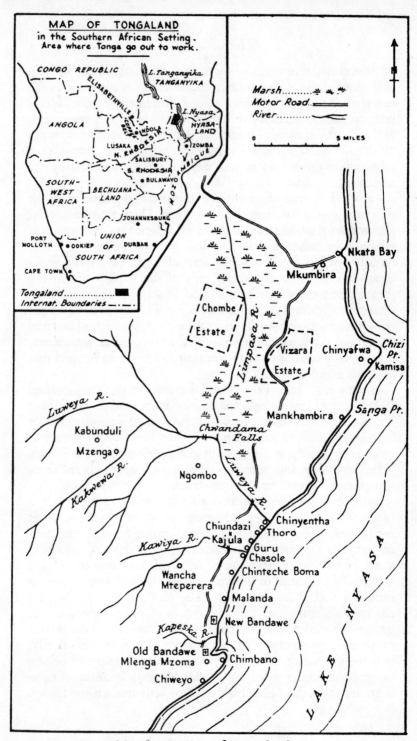

MAP I.—Section of Tongaland

NOTE: Union of South Africa is now Republic of South Africa.

In the literature 'politics' and 'political relationships' are usually defined (if at all) with reference to territorial groupings and/or the integration and integrity of tribal, national, clan or smaller units. Thus 'politics' becomes equated with government. In my view such definitions would suit the term 'political system' rather than the term 'politics'.[1] My descriptive definition of 'politics' includes government and all other activities directed towards territorial and/or tribal unity—or national, or clan, or any other similar structural unity. But to confine the term 'politics' to this type of activity would seem unduly to restrict a term which is universally used, both in literature and speech, with a very much wider meaning. Although I agree that in scientific writing one has to use terms with a greater degree of precision than in everyday speech, I feel that definitions should not so far depart from well-established meanings that they define away what could and should be potential problems of great comparative interest.[2] After all 'politics' in this restricted sense is only one aspect of the term as it is widely used. In its wider sense politics also includes activities on a different and sometimes very much smaller scale. For instance, minority groups (linguistic, ethnic, nationalist, cultural, etc.) within nations, or pressure groups[3] or many other differently recruited, constituted and oriented groups, may all engage in politics without reference, necessarily, to territorial integrity or national, tribal or clan sovereignty. There may be other interests, for example economic, which are satisfied by action *through* and not necessarily *within* the political structure.[4] Moreover, we may speak about academic (or trade union, or church) politics. By this we mean manœuvring for the creation and/or the control of certain groups for the attainment of particular goals which may be significant only within a particular context—academic, trade

[1] Even in such a highly centralized political system as that of the Lozi the territorial factor plays a very minor role: cf. Gluckman (1951).

[2] Cf. Radcliffe-Brown (1940), p. xiv: 'It would doubtless be possible to find a definition of the word 'state' such that we could say that certain African societies . . . are states while others are stateless societies. This does not help us to solve our problems.'

[3] Defined by Eckstein (1960, p. 9) as groups which 'pursue collectively common political aims (by means other than attempting themselves to govern)'.

[4] For similar conceptions of 'politics' see e.g. Sommerfelt (1958), pp. 174-5, and Bailey (1960), pp. 10-12.

union, church and so forth. It would seem that all these differently oriented activities have something in common which would justify calling them 'politics', even though these activities may fall entirely *outside* the political structure. Indeed, through my study of Tonga politics I have gained a greater understanding of such widely different phenomena as the acephalous United Nations Organization and small scale, ephemeral pressure groups.

Politics in this sense (colloquially perhaps better known as 'jockeying for position' or 'politicking') is a very dominant feature of Tonga society. With particular reference to headmanship I describe in Chapters V and VI how leadership is acquired: not so much through formal, constitutional channels but rather through skilful manipulation of personal relationships (which are generally expressed in terms of kinship) within an elastic framework of formal values. These political relationships are *expressed* in terms of kinship but I will show that the system of kinship is not identical with the system of political relationships. In other words, similar genealogical relationships may have different significance depending on the particular context within which the kinsmen are interacting—for example whether they live in the same village or not. I hope to show that kinship *in abstracto* has little meaning; it should be considered within a specific context, that is, in relation to specific interests.

In these chapters I will also discuss the significance of the Tonga headman whose office appears to lack substance and sanction; his position is rather that of a leader. He has not much to offer his followers: even the distribution of land in the village is beyond his control *as* headman. But he can make an important contribution towards peace in his own or another, related, village by co-ordinating the different and often conflicting interests of individual villagers who are generally linked to many different groups, villages and individuals outside the village.

I will also briefly discuss the role of the headman in the Administrative system, whose aims and methods are in some ways antithetical to those of the Tonga. It will be clear that in spite of this Tonga traditional values may be supported by (amongst other factors) the Administration, notwithstanding the latter's frequent complaint that the Tonga political system is difficult to handle by and to incorporate into the Administrative system.

Interaction between the Administration[1] on the one hand and tribal politics and government on the other hand is often either largely ignored in the literature[2] or described with an over-emphasis on the impact of the Administration on tribal politics and without sufficient attention being paid to the reverse process.[3] Among the Tonga power and authority are diffused; there is no semblance of a governmental hierarchy. Ever since its arrival in the area in 1897, the Administration has been engaged in attempts to fit the Tonga political system into its own hierarchically organized system. This has given rise to conflicts. But on the other hand both groups, the Administration and the Tonga, have always been primarily interested in the conservation of law and order.[4] For this reason interaction between them has generally shown the characteristics of a compromise between two different political systems. It has certainly not been a matter of the unilateral impact of the Administration upon the Tonga tribal system.[5]

I am aware that several of the problems treated in this book have been discussed by other writers. And I have approached my own problems in the light of these previous discussions in the hope that this will facilitate comparison. However, in the present study I am primarily concerned with the political aspects of kinship and the position of the headman among the Lakeside Tonga. I have therefore omitted (with a few exceptions) explicit comparisons with similar ethnographic and theoretical problems found elsewhere in the literature.

Colson reports a very similar situation among the Plateau Tonga in neighbouring Northern Rhodesia.[6] She writes about

[1] When referring to the Colonial administrative system I will use a capital initial, Administration, to distinguish it from administration in the general sense of the management of public affairs, government.

[2] See e.g. Fortes (1940, 1945) and Evans-Pritchard (1940*a*, 1940*b*).

[3] See e.g. Busia (1951); Barnes (1954).

[4] In the last few years the Administration has shown signs of abandoning this 'conservative' policy for a more active welfare policy along local government lines. However when I left Tongaland it was still too early to see the effects of this change.

[5] For a more detailed historical account of this mutual influence see van Velsen (1961).

[6] It seems historically fortuitous that these two peoples have the same name: there appears to be no historical link between them.

the headman there that: 'His authority is largely determined by his personal qualities, and not by a norm of headmanship.'[1] My principal aim has been to examine 'on the ground' how social and political relationships are maintained and how political cohesion, if any, is achieved in societies like these where so many values are seemingly unsystematized. I have tried to examine in some detail the apparent paradox of the peacefulness of the area and the prominence of individualism and the lack of sanctions in the hands of the headmen.

Since the structural regularities I could use as a starting point were few and the 'exceptions' to generally stated norms were many and baffling, I could hardly work with general statements from informants. There are, moreover, among the Tonga few public ceremonies (e.g. ritual) at which social and political relationships and values are re-asserted and re-enacted for the inquisitive anthropologist. And although the deviations, in practice, from what general rules there are were many, these deviations did not appear to be in open defiance of generally acknowledged rules and norms. On the contrary, they seemed to support those rules and norms. I therefore wanted to know not only what the formal rules and norms were and what the practice was, but also how norm and practice were related to one another. It was for all these reasons that I had to rely on my own observations of a great number of social situations and detailed analyses of them. For this book I have chosen my cases as much as possible from the same five villages so as to present a more integrated picture of the villages concerned. Moreover, the *dramatis personae* are largely the same, although the situations in which they appear as actors are different.[2] This may put the reader in a better position to assess the significance of each case than if the actors were anonymous or if each case had different actors.

In order to test their typicality I intended to support my findings from the intensively studied villages with quantitative data gained in more extensive studies (surveys) of a larger number of

[1] Colson (1951*b*), p. 118.
[2] As a result, details concerning particular persons and the situations in which they are involved are spread throughout the book. This applies especially to the key personalities in my analyses. I have tried as much as possible to link up the different parts of particular sequences of events by cross-references in footnotes. I have also included the principal actors and events in the index.

villages spread over a wider area. However, it proved impossible to carry out my surveys in a manner sufficiently systematic to make the quantitative data statistically acceptable. The majority of the Tonga were for various reasons reluctant to discuss with me, in public as well as in private, genealogies and other matters.[1]

Although their suspicions and the reasons they gave are in themselves of some sociological significance (see, for instance, p. 254 below on slave descent), their refusal to co-operate in this respect handicapped me in my search for numerical data. For similar reasons discussions in public or private of many other subjects and events was also impossible with the majority. This meant that although I attended a large number of public discussions, for instance court cases, and ceremonies such as 'shavings' [2] and the installation of a headman, in many different villages, it was generally impossible to obtain the necessary detailed background information, such as the genealogical relationship between the participants or other specific information on particular events or persons. The required information was not difficult to obtain if events took place in the village where I was staying at the time or a village where I was well-known through personal contact or where some of my small circle of personal friends happened to know the participants. Thus it is that I have a great many data related to villages other than the five which are the main subject of this book. But these data are not sufficiently systematic for presentation in a situational analysis.

Although I received much of my detailed information (as against statements on general rules of behaviour) from a relatively small number of informants, I was invariably able in one way or another (but generally not through discussions in public) to cross-check it. It is perhaps no coincidence that in the three areas where I lived for long periods, the most co-operative informants often lived not in the village where I was based but in neighbouring ones. People in my own village were generally not as forthcoming with genealogical and other details lest they rouse the suspicion of

---

[1] It is interesting to note that the attempt of the Government, in 1937, to take a census in the Protectorate had to be abandoned among the Tonga because their 'continued opposition . . . made progress . . . impossible'. The Tonga were apparently the only people in the Northern Province to put up this resistance: see *P.C. Report, 1937*, p. 50.

[2] The discussions after a funeral: see p. 109.

some of their fellow villagers of having supplied me with information which they thought I should not have.

I made my first acquaintance with the Tonga language and social system in GURU's[1] village on the northern bank of the Kawiya River. This was my base for well over a year. Apart from what I learned from the inhabitants of this village themselves I also received much information from one person in particular who lived close by in another village. This information was most useful as an addition to and a check on what I learned at GURU's. This person was one of the leaders of the Phiri faction whilst GURU had a similar role in the Kapunda Banda faction. For various reasons my data for GURU's village are less complete than those for the other villages and that is why I have not based the present study on GURU's village.

The Kapunda Banda–Phiri rivalry[2] is limited mainly to the Tonga living south of the Luweya River. I therefore wanted to study an area outside the orbit of this rivalry. With the help of a good introduction I enjoyed the hospitality of Mapalassie village for some eight months. It was whilst I was staying with the parents of Meya that her dramatic death occurred after a long wasting illness. Here again I learned a good deal about people and events in Mapalassie and closely related villages from persons in a neighbouring village which is itself closely associated with the villages of Greater Kamisa; I never lived in this village but I spent much time there.

Mapalassie and GURU's are both lakeshore villages. In order to obtain a more comprehensive knowledge of Tonga village life I wanted to live for a while in the hill area. Moreover, I wanted to see whether life in the village of a Native Authority differed at all from that in other villages. So I next stayed for about half a year in KABUNDULI's village which is some twelve miles over broken country or some five hours' walk inland. KABUNDULI is generally considered by the Tonga as the traditionally leading headman among the Phiri headmen, most of whom live in the hills. The present KABUNDULI is a young, Livingstonia-educated man. He

[1] See p. xxii for the use of small capitals for names.
[2] See p. 15 *et passim*. Note that in Tonga a consonant followed by *h* is aspirated. The two main sounds in this connection are: *ph*, as in Phiri, which is not pronounced as in *phoney*, and *th*, as in CHINYENTHA, which does not sound as in *think*.

does not seem to have the same strong leading position as his pre-decessor; this is not entirely due to his age. He had been losing control over the comparatively large village of his predecessor and by the time I went to stay there its disintegration was nearly complete. His village was adjoining a much larger village in which KABUNDULI's court house was situated, but as a headman he had no control over that village. Again, I received as much and sometimes more information on particular points from persons in a village where I was not actually staying.

Thus the villages for which I have detailed and integrated data represent three different areas but the choice of the particular villages was fortuitous. My periods of residence in these villages were not continuous. Whilst staying in one village I would maintain contact with the other two villages. Moreover, I also visited and sometimes stayed for short periods (varying from one or two days to a fortnight) in many other villages.

Habitat

The Tonga live in one of the 'pockets' of broken lowland, marked and surrounded by mountains, on the western shore of the northern half of Lake Nyasa. Tongaland is encircled by Mtoghame mountain in the north, the Vipya range in the west, and the Kuwirwe and Kwandama mountain ranges in the south. The country is broken by the high ridges of the foothills of the Vipya. It has a few large rivers and numerous perennial streams. There are many deep valleys with steep, thickly forested walls; the country as a whole is also well-wooded. With this ubiquitous supply of water and wood for domestic and building purposes and without extremes in the quality of the soil,[1] there are no natural, ecological foci for human habitation; there are thus no natural barriers to the spread of villages.

There is a strip of flat land along the lake in the shape of a wedge: its thin end is a few miles south of Nkata Bay and it gradually broadens southwards. The largest concentration of villages is along the lakeshore in a strip about a mile wide. Consequently the distance between lakeshore villages is on the whole less than in the hills where one may find a conglomeration of villages a mile or more away from the next.

The neighbouring tribes are: the patrilineal, cattle-keeping

[1] See Pryor (1938).

Siska who live in another 'pocket' to the north; the cattle-keeping Tumbuka-Ngoni[1] in the hills to the west; and the matrilineal Chewa to the south. Other neighbours, but across the lake, are the inhabitants of Likoma and Chizumulu Islands. Particularly on the edges of Tongaland there is much intercourse with the surrounding tribes and there the social and cultural differences are blurred. The language of the Tonga (*chi Tonga*) is distinct from those of the neighbouring tribes.

Population

The Nkata Bay Administrative District contains the Tonga, the Siska and the Islands of Likoma and Chizumulu, apart of course from a few Tumbuka-Ngoni villages in the west and some Chewa in the south where the Dwambazi River is the District boundary.

The official estimate of the District's *de jure* population (that is, including Tonga living abroad but still registered for taxation purposes on their villages' census) is 68,391.[2] On the basis of taxation figures for different areas I estimate that the *de jure* Tonga population is about 50,000 and the *de facto* population somewhere between 40,000 and 45,000. The population of the hill areas constitutes probably something like 20 per cent of the total Tonga population; the remainder live near the lake. The overall density of population on the basis of the official population figure of 68,391 is 35·7 per square mile. This is lower than the figure of 55·5 (in 1945)[3] for the whole of the Protectorate and among the lowest in the country.

A large proportion of the men (but relatively few women) spend longer or shorter periods 'abroad' (i.e. outside Tongaland), mostly in the industrial centres of the two Rhodesias and the Republic (formerly the Union) of South Africa. As a general rule the men leave their families behind in Tongaland. I estimate that at any one time about two-thirds of the adult men are absent and

---

[1] These people are a mixture of the original Tumbuka and the Ngoni invaders of the middle of last century. I do not know to what extent the mixture is complete or whether there are still distinct groups of Ngoni. That is why I refer to the inhabitants of the hills in the west as Tumbuka-Ngoni. The Tonga variously call them Tumbuka or Ngoni; this depends partly on the context. They are said to be patrilineal. Cf. Read (1956).

[2] See *P.C. Report, 1953*, p. 39.

[3] *Census Report 1945.*

that the ratio of adult men to women lies somewhere between
1 : 2 and 1 : 3.[1]

Economy

The staple crop of the Tonga is cassava and has been since at
least the last quarter of the last century. The cultivation of cassava
requires comparatively little hard labour and can be done (and
often is done) entirely by women. Thus the chief Tonga export,
labour, does not adversely affect their subsistence food production
or their domestic economy in general. This means that the income
derived from the export of labour is a net income: no part of it
has to be spent to make good the loss of labour, but the total is
available for expenditure on goods and services above subsistence
level.[2]

Cassava is normally served as a thick porridge (*nsima*) together
with a side dish of relish (*dendi*); to have to eat *nsima* without
dendi is considered the epitome of misfortune and I have never
observed it. Indeed, it should not be necessary in view of the
wide range of ingredients used for the preparation of relish. The
least appetizing relish, never offered to visitors, is made of the
leaves of the cassava plant[3] which are available for most of the
year. Some other vegetables used for *dendi* are: various wild
plants (including mushrooms) found in the forest and elsewhere
and such cultivated vegetables as beans and peas. Some of these
are rated higher than others but all are rated higher than cassava
leaves. The favourite relish consists of meat or fish and this is the
kind of *dendi* which every hostess strives to offer her visitors.[4]
Tonga, except for the rare individual, do not keep cattle. Occasionally a beast is slaughtered which has generally been bought and
brought down from the Tumbuka-Ngoni area farther inland;[5]

---

[1] A more detailed discussion of the problem of labour migration with special
reference to the Tonga is in preparation; a short survey appears in van Velsen
(1960).

[2] See van Velsen (1960).

[3] Tonga often refer to the usefulness of cassava: ' We eat the roots; we plant
cuttings of the stem; and we use the leaves for *dendi*.'

[4] The procurement of vegetables is the responsibility of women but the
provision of meat and fish is generally in the hands of men although women,
too, sometimes catch fish in the rivers.

[5] The meat supply at Nkata Bay, the District HQ, is rather more regular
because of a larger number than elsewhere of people with a regular cash income.

this meat is sold for cash. Meat from game, goats or sheep is equally rare; chickens are the usual stand-by on festive occasions and for visitors. In practice the ideal relish consists of fish and in many contexts the two are spoken of as synonymous. For *dendi* in general and fish in particular are more than just food: they may symbolize well-being. For instance, to care for someone is often expressed as keeping that person supplied with *dendi*, i.e. fish. Similarly, a phrase such as 'So-and-so is doing well; he always has *dendi*' does not only refer to the fact that that person always has a side dish to go with his main dish (*nsima*)—everybody is in that position even if it is only cassava greens—but the implication is that he always has fish with his meals. Later I will refer to the general principle that at least one man should stay with the women of the hamlet whilst the other men of the hamlet go abroad.[1] The role of those who stay in the hamlet is often described in terms of having to find the *dendi*, that is, fish, for the households of their hamlets. We will see that in fact there are also other, social and political, reasons for this arrangement which are equally important. In any case, there are many months in the year when no fish at all is caught because of prevailing storms. But just as pastoral people tend to express their values in terms of cattle, so the Tonga evaluate many of their norms with reference to fish.

There are a few cash crops of minor importance, for example rice and some maize are exported out of the District; of the little tobacco and millet grown some is sold internally. There is little economic differentiation between the lakeshore and the hill areas. Most of the tobacco and millet are cultivated in the hills. On the other hand the lake area is better supplied with fish, some of which finds its way to the hill area.

There has been very little development in the District. In the early years of this century the African Lakes Corporation opened two rubber estates (Vizara and Chombe) which were still in production in 1955.[2] There used to be two or three planters with small estates but they have long since disappeared, partly, apparently, because of the difficulty and cost of transport. The Administration does not employ much labour apart from some

[1] See p. 71.
[2] Some two years after my departure the Chombe estate was bought by another firm which has converted it into a tea plantation.

clerical staff, and some casual labour for the roads and lately on the development of Nkata Bay. Much of this labour comes from the Tumbuka-Ngoni area.

Consequently opportunities of earning money locally are few. Moreover local wages are low when compared with urban wages and particularly with the wages which many Tonga seem to earn in towns in the better jobs. In addition money earned locally has relatively less value because of the more restricted range of goods available in the local stores compared with those in the industrial centres.

Roads are few in the District and practically the whole of the hill area and even most of the flatter lakeshore area cannot be reached by car or lorry.

History

Although the tribal identity of the Tonga is now considered obvious by themselves and by other tribes, all available evidence points to a heterogeneous origin of the people who now call themselves, and are called by others, Tonga.[1] The beginnings of the genesis of the Tonga nation probably lie in the last decades of the eighteenth century or the early part of the nineteenth century. This was the period of the penetrations of ivory trading groups from across the north-eastern shores of Lake Nyasa, and the (consequent?) tribal movements in the northern parts of what is now Nyasaland. Some groups settled in Tongaland.

It appears that the Tonga people are an amalgamation of at least four different groups: the Nyaliwangga whose home area is TIMBIRI's area around Chikwina and who may be the oldest inhabitants of Tongaland; KABUNDULI and his followers, known among the Tonga as the Phiri, who settled in the hills around the upper reaches of the Luweya River; the Kapunda Banda who settled by the lakeshore, south of the Luweya, and who may have been a Chewa offshoot entering their present habitat from the south; MANKHAMBIRA and his followers (including, probably, KANGOMA) who are said to have come from across the lake with guns.

Traditionally there has always been competition between the

---

[1] For a fuller discussion of the Tonga past up to the arrival of the Livingstonia missionaries see van Velsen (1959*a*).

Phiri and the Kapunda Banda factions for ascendancy in the
lakeshore area between the Luweya and the Dwambazi Rivers.
This rivalry has persisted up to the present and much of the
modern struggle for power in this area is still in terms of the
KABUNDULI (representing the Phiri)—Kapunda Banda rivalry. But
although this struggle is generally cast in terms of the traditional
KABUNDULI—Kapunda Banda alignment, this is not a rigid cleav-
age and there are Kapunda Banda who support KABUNDULI and
Phiri who side with the Kapunda Banda.[1]

The process of coalescence of the various groups into the Tonga
nation was speeded up in the third quarter of the nineteenth
century through the external pressure of the Ngoni. The Ngoni
under MBELWA, who were one of the Ngoni groups which had
fled northwards from the attacks of the Zulu king Shaka, finally
settled near Ekwendeni in the middle of the last century. The
Ngoni subjugated the surrounding tribes and raided their areas.
Many Tonga who had been living in small scattered villages came
together in a few large stockaded villages or *malinga* (sing. *linga*);
there may have been some smaller *malinga* too. The four stockades
known from tradition and from travellers' accounts are: the *linga*
of MANKHAMBIRA and KANGOMA by the Chinteche River, just
north of the mouth of the Luweya River; MLENGA MZOMA's *linga*
by Bandawe; CHAVULA's in the Matete valley just south-west of
Bandawe; and CHINYENTHA is also said to have had a *linga*, just
south of the Luweya, but his was probably not built until after
the Tonga revolt against the Ngoni.

Although one of the main objects of the Ngoni raids was the
supplementation of their own food production it does not seem
likely that they found much in the way of food in Tongaland.
The Tonga have never had herds of cattle and their staple diet is
cassava which, unlike cereal crops, is not harvested and stored at a
certain time of the year but left in the ground until required for
consumption.

Another objective of the Ngoni raids was the supplementation
of their manpower by incorporating into the Ngoni tribal struc-

[1] Not all people called Phiri belong to the Phiri faction, neither do all people
called Banda belong to the Kapunda Banda faction. Phiri, Banda, like other
names such as Mwase or Nkhoma, are surnames rather than descent names: see
p. 44. I have discussed the possible historical origin of this factional rivalry and
its significance at present in van Velsen (1959*b*) and (1961).

ture aliens from the raided tribes. I have no evidence that the Ngoni sold their captives directly to Arab slave traders, although the possibility must not be ruled out. As a result of the Ngoni raids (and perhaps other factors) there were groups of Tonga living with the Ngoni. According to tradition several Tonga distinguished themselves as captains in the Ngoni armies. The state of bondage in which the Tonga lived in Ngoniland did not last more than about twenty-five years for the earliest captives and proportionately shorter for the later captives. The distance between the home country of the Tonga captives and their Ngoni residence was at the most a three or four days' walk and it seems that there was regular contact between the Ngoni-Tonga and their kinsmen at home. Thus the Ngoni-Tonga never became wholly integrated with the Ngoni people like those tribal groups who had been absorbed into the Ngoni system in the earlier stages of the Ngoni wanderings and who had therefore been separated from their own tribes through time and space.

This contact between the Tonga in Ngoniland and their home area must have facilitated their escape from their Ngoni masters: in the middle of the 1870's the Ngoni-Tonga rose in revolt and decamped to the lakeshore where they were received in the *malinga* and elsewhere. The pursuing Ngoni were routed in the battle of the Chinteche River by MANKHAMBIRA's stockade.

It is a curious fact that the end of the Ngoni dominance over the Tonga should have coincided with the arrival of another foreign element into Tonga life: it can only have been one or two years after the rebellion that Dr. Stewart, in 1877, and Dr. Laws, in 1878, walked through the area in search of a new site for the station of the Livingstonia Mission.[1] They were not the first Europeans to visit the Tonga; Livingstone and Young had visited their shores in 1861 and 1875 respectively, but their calls were short and they had no intention of staying permanently or exploring the hinterland.

As a result of these explorations and perhaps of MLENGA MZOMA's friendly and 'gentlemanly' attitude to Livingstone[2] and later

[1] There seems to be no connection between the Ngoni defeat and the arrival of the Europeans.

[2] Livingstone (1865), pp. 377–8. For a more detailed account of the arrival and settlement of the mission in Tongaland see van Velsen (1959*b*).

missionaries, the Livingstonia Mission of the Free Church of Scotland moved, in 1881, from Cape Maclear[1] at the southern end of the lake to Makusi Hill, generally known as Bandawe, near MLENGA MZOMA. The headquarters of the Livingstonia Mission later moved farther north and established Livingstonia, but the Bandawe station remained; in 1926 this was moved about three miles farther north to a site called Tipula but it retained the name Bandawe. In 1945 all European staff were withdrawn from Bandawe (partly because of the unhealthy climate) and the station was put in the charge of an African minister.

In the first six years the missionaries became involved in the tribal politics of the Tonga and the Ngoni in spite of the missionaries' determined policy of non-involvement. At one stage, in 1887, the situation became so insecure for the mission that they were prepared to abandon the station but eventually peace came to the area and the missionaries remained at Bandawe. From there they also extended their influence to Ngoniland and even as far as the Luangwa valley, in what is now Northern Rhodesia.

The mission, under Dr. Laws, attached great importance to education, not only as a means towards creating a 'Bible-reading and Bible-loving people': Laws considered education for its own sake a prerequisite for the general enlightenment of the African. He also emphasized the importance of manual and industrial training. These ideas found an eager reception among the Tonga. It is recorded that within half an hour of announcing his intention of opening a school, Laws had enrolled forty pupils.[2] The number of pupils grew steadily to 1330 in 1889. Laws was very successful in conditioning the Tonga to take their place in the new system of values which the Europeans had brought to their country and to Nyasaland in general. Within a few years the flow of Tonga workers to southern Nyasaland had begun. There, and later in other parts of East, Central and South Africa, the Tonga secured valuable contacts for the better-paid positions, and a reputation for being an intelligent and progressive people.[3] Tonga are now found in most parts of Southern Africa, even as far afield as Okiep and

---

[1] The station at Cape Maclear was abandoned for political and health reasons.

[2] See Livingstone (1921), p. 189. See also van Velsen (1959b).

[3] Cf. Bell (1938, p. 97): '. . . the Atonga, the most progressive tribe in the country, by their skill and intelligence can earn high wages abroad. . . .'

Port Nolleth on the Atlantic coast, and in the (erstwhile Belgian) Congo.[1]

Another effect of the activities of the mission at Bandawe was that Christianity is now the generally accepted religion in the area, although there are many other denominations and sects besides the Presbyterians. One rarely finds a Tonga who professes to be *kubwaru* (non-Christian; lit. outside). Most meetings (including political meetings, for example, of African Congress) are now opened by prayer. There are practically no traces left of the religious beliefs of the last century; female initiation ceremonies have ceased.

Finally, the mission was instrumental in introducing the British Administration into the area. In 1888 Mr. (later Sir Alfred) Sharpe recruited 180 Tonga for the North End War against the Arab traders. Mr. (later Sir Harry) Johnston remarked that: 'the Tonga were from the very first the allies of the white man in his struggles against the Arab and Yao slave traders.' Later the Tonga together with the Yao formed the core of the King's African Rifles (the K.A.R.) in Nyasaland. But in more recent years few Tonga have been recruited for the K.A.R. because the Tonga consider that they can earn better wages and have more freedom in industrial employment. Similarly, no Tonga are recruited by recruitment agencies such as the Witwatersrand Native Labour Association which engages labour for the gold mines. There are many Tonga employed by the mining companies, but they prefer to go to South Africa independently and to work for the mines as locally engaged labour in white collar jobs, rather than as underground miners on an eighteen-month contract which, they feel, restricts them too much in their choice and period of employment. They also consider the wages too low.[2]

In 1889 and 1894 the British concluded treaties with some Tonga headmen; certainly in the first and probably in the second treaty too, the mission played an important role as intermediary. In 1897 the first Administrative post was established in Tongaland, at Nkata Bay, which provided a good anchorage

[1] The first African I talked with on my arrival in Africa was a Tonga waiter in an hotel in Cape Town.

[2] It is significant that the Tonga use the same verb for joining the army, the police and signing a contract for indentured labour in the mines: *kujoin*, i.e. to join.

D

although its immediate surroundings were thinly populated. Within a few years, after some unrest in the Bandawe area, the District Headquarters (generally known as the *boma*) moved to Chinteche Boma[1] which is the centre of a much thicker population and is situated about eight miles north of the old Bandawe site. For a while Nkata Bay remained a sub-station with a few African police and a rest-house. Later it was the Provincial Headquarters for some years, but it seems that for some time before 1950 Nkata Bay was vacated altogether by the Administration. In 1950 the District headquarters moved back to Nkata Bay, leaving behind at Chinteche Boma (which is still known by that name among the Tonga) a small police detachment under an African corporal and a small hospital (30 beds) under an African hospital assistant.

British Administration

In the early years of the Administration in Nyasaland there was no clearly defined policy regulating its formal relationship to the political systems of the tribes administered. It seems certain, however, that at least in the West Nyasa District, as it was then called, the Administration in practice made use of the agencies of tribal rule. This situation became more formalized with the District Administration (Native) Ordinance of 1912 which was applied to the West Nyasa District in 1917[2] and provided for the appointment of Principal Headmen. Although this ordinance 'in no way intended to revivify or perpetuate government by native chiefs',[3] the appointments in this District clearly illustrate the tendency of the Administration to rule through what it considered to be the headman of standing in the tribal system. The five Tonga headmen who received recognition were: MANKHAMBIRA; MKUMBIRA; GURU, KABUNDULI and MLENGA MZOMA.[4] In theory Principal Headmen were meant to be executive agents of the Administration rather than headmen working within the Administrative

[1] Chinteche Boma should not be confused with Chinteche River, the site of MANKHAMBIRA's stockade where the Ngoni were defeated in the 1870's.

[2] For a short historical survey of the Administration in the Protectorate, see Murray (1932), pp. 126 *seq.*; also van Velsen (1961).

[3] Murray (1932), p. 130.

[4] The three other Principal Headmen in this District belonged to different tribes. In Chapter VI, I discuss the connection between tribal politics and the Administration's appointments.

system and reinforcing it with their status and authority in the tribal system.[1] I will show that at least some of the Principal Headmen were selected not so much for individual qualities but for the traditional and political standing of their titles. The Principal Headmen were not given any powers of jurisdiction and all cases, including matrimonial disputes and questions connected with deceased estates, were supposed to be heard in the Magistrate's court. It seems, however, that cases continued to be settled in the villages and that the Principal Headmen in fact assumed powers of jurisdiction. This must have been inevitable since presumably one or even two European Magistrates would not have been able to cope with all the disputes which should have been referred to their court at the Boma. This situation was regularized in 1929 with the Native Courts' Ordinance which granted Principal Headmen limited powers of jurisdiction. But 'these measures, however, did not extend to the formal grant of powers to the Principal Headmen to administer their areas by virtue of any traditional or inherent right'.[2]

Although the Principal Headmen remained in theory the executive officers of the Administration, deriving their authority entirely from it, neither in effect nor in theory was the Administrative system in those days one of 'direct rule'. Hailey defines the method of 'direct rule' of which the classic example, according to him, was found in British India, as a system 'in which the agency of local administration was an indigenous Civil Service, recruited by and drawing its authority entirely from Government, and possessing no authority derived from native custom or traditional status'.[3] Indeed, there had been a persistent tendency towards

---

[1] *Administration* refers to the system of civil administration in force in the Protectorate, with branches in the Districts and Provinces. The Tonga use the word Boma with reference not only to the District or other headquarters of the Administration but also to the Administration itself or the Government, including its non-administrative departments, e.g. the Agricultural and Educational Departments. In this sense Boma has the connotation of non-Tonga, non-traditional agencies of administration: see e.g. pp. 219-20. Except where some specificity is required I use Boma in this sense, which is very similar to the English usage of 'the Government' when referring to some anonymous governmental agency or the Government itself. I also retain the abbreviations D.C. and N.A. which are more commonly used than District Commissioner and Native Authority.

[2] Hailey (1950), II, p. 26. [3] *Ibid.*, II, p. 27.

'indirect rule' both in theory and practice. According to Hailey there has never been an African indigenous Civil Service on the Indian pattern and therefore no 'direct rule'. But he divides the procedures followed in the different British colonies into two categories. 'The first comprises those which normally make use of agencies deriving their authority entirely from statutory enactment or from their appointment as executive instruments of the Administration. The second group comprises the territories normally employing agencies which, apart from any powers they may derive from statutory enactment or appointment, bring to the service of the Administration an authority derived from their traditional status in their community.' [1]

The latter method, which we may call 'indirect rule', was officially adopted in 1930, but it was not put into practice until the enactment in 1933 of the Native Authority and Native Courts Ordinances. Under the new Administrative system the powers of the Native Authority were vested in traditional chiefs or headmen. In line with the new policy the District boundaries were altered to correspond as closely as possible with ethnic groupings. In the West Nyasa District[2] this meant that some Chewa headmen in the south and Henga headmen in the north were included in other Districts and henceforth the District contained the Tonga, forming a large majority, Likoma and Chizumulu Islands, and one or two small groups of patrilineal people (including the Siska) in the north.

Whereas in the rest of the Protectorate the new Native Authority powers were vested in individual headmen or chiefs, among the Tonga this was impossible.[3] They could not agree who was the most senior headman and should therefore receive Administrative recognition, except in the area of the hills, which is regarded as the traditional home of KABUNDULI and his followers (the Phiri); KABUNDULI who used to be the Principal Headman there was appointed the N.A. of the hilly inland area. The remainder of the Tonga, mainly those near the lakeshore, came under a N.A. which was vested in the Atonga Tribal Council. The A.T.C. consisted of 32 headmen, including the previous Principal Headmen, MKUM-

[1] Hailey (1950), IV, p. 9.
[2] Later known as the Chinteche District and since 1950 as the Nkata Bay District.
[3] Cf. *Native Affairs Report, 1933*, p. 6.

PLATE I. (*a*) The headman (centre) discusses a village matter. With him are (right) a neighbouring and closely related headman (classificatory 'son') and (left) the latter's son. Like many men attending court, a discussion, or meeting at the *mphara*, or simply relaxing, one (right) is knitting a net. The man sitting slightly apart comes from another neighbouring village. Although he is distantly related to the others, the matter under discussion was not directly his concern

(*b*) Native Authority KABUNDULI (centre) and some of his headmen

BIRA, MANKHAMBIRA, GURU and MLENGA MZOMA, who now lost their position of superiority *vis-à-vis* the other 28 headmen in the A.T.C.; they have never forgotten this 'degradation'. This 32-headed council did not work satisfactorily, at least not as an executive organ of the Administration, and in 1947 it was split up. MANKHAMBIRA was appointed N.A. over the area north of the Luweya River except for a few headmen who wished to dissociate themselves from him and claimed closer ties with the people south of the Luweya. The latter area (traditionally the area of the Kapunda Banda) could still not agree on the selection of one headman to be appointed N.A. and the powers of the N.A. were temporarily vested in the D.C. This situation was ended in 1951 when after a vote by the Administrative Headmen of the N.A.—D.C. area KABUNDULI received more support than any of the other candidates for the N.A.-ship over this area. Thus KABUNDULI became N.A. over the lakeshore area south of the Luweya as well as over the hill area; this is the position at present. Apart from a few Kapunda Banda headmen who supported KABUNDULI, the majority of them have never given up their campaign against KABUNDULI and for a Kapunda Banda N.A. in the lakeshore area.

The present Administrative bureaucracy of the District consists of the headquarters, i.e. the Boma at Nkata Bay and its local representatives in the area. The Boma is generally staffed by two European Administrators, the District Commissioner and an Assistant District Commissioner. These two officers represent Central Government, which is located in Zomba, in executive, judicial and legislative capacities. They also represent specialist departments which do not have their own officers stationed in the District. There is an agricultural officer intermittently in the District and some years ago there was a forestry officer for a few months. There are a few African forest guards and agricultural demonstrators in the District; they are employed by their respective departments and not by the Native Authorities. Up to 1953 the D.C. was also in charge of a detachment of African constables in the District but since then a European police officer has been stationed at Nkata Bay. As there is little economic development in the District, in practice the Administration is largely concerned with the maintenance of law and order. The D.C., as Magistrate, hears in first instance civil and criminal cases of a certain category; the majority of these cases concern tax defaulters. He also hears appeals from the District Appeal Court, though such appeals are few.

The D.C. is also chairman of the District Council which in addition contains the five N.A.'s of the District, two of whom are Tonga, each with a councillor or other supporter, and four members nominated by the D.C. This Council is divided into education and finance committees. The Council controls the Federated Native Treasuries of the District, but it has little autonomy because effective power lies largely in the hands of the representatives of Central Government and its revenue is small.[1] The Council also constitutes the District Appeal Court which acts as a court of first instance for cases·involving a N.A. and as a court of appeal for cases from the courts of the N.A.'s.

The Administration delegates some of its executive, legislative and judicial powers to the N.A.'s. But in practice the N.A.'s, also, are mainly concerned with the maintenance of law and order. Although formally they have powers to create new taxes and sources of revenue and thus to initiate an active policy of local government and welfare, in effect their rule tends towards the conservation of the _status quo_ of tribal values. The principal exception is the attempts of headmen with Administrative recognition (either as N.A. or as Administrative Headman) to impose their authority upon other headmen. As for the general lack of active welfare policies, the main causes are twofold. Firstly, in this strongly egalitarian society the N.A.'s, who derive their executive authority from the Administrative system and not the traditional system, are in a weak position _vis-à-vis_ their subordinates, particularly the headmen. The latter are most likely to consider themselves (and to be considered by others) as the equals of the N.A.'s in the tribal structure. Consequently, the N.A.'s, realizing their limitations, do not desire to extend the field in which they may have to impose their executive authority beyond a minimum of administrative matters. Secondly, the N.A.'s lack, both in their personal and in their official capacity, the financial and

---

[1] Its total revenue in 1955 was £8,911 of which £4,524, or more than half, consisted of a share of the hut and polltax levied by Central Government. Total expenditure for the year was £7,550 of which £3,842 was for personal emoluments, i.e. mostly for the N.A.'s and their personnel. See _P.C. Report 1955_.

economic resources which might underpin their political status
and executive authority, and provide the means for more development. This should be seen in the light of the lack of resources and
development in the District in general; the principal source of
income of the District is export of labour, the proceeds of which
are beyond the control of the N.A.'s, whilst at the same time the
absence of manpower is bound to hamper development and im-
provement plans.[1]

The Native Authority bureaucracy consists of two different
categories of officials. Firstly there is the departmental staff: the
court and tax clerks, the sanitary *capitaos*[2] and the court messengers who act as policemen with limited authority. Except for
the messengers and probably the sanitary *capitaos* (I am not certain
about them), the appointments of the other members of the
N.A.'s departmental staff have to be approved by the D.C. The
clerks are in practice under direct control of the D.C., irrespective
of whether they are employees of the Protectorate Government
or the N.A.[3] These appointments are, both in theory and in practice, personal appointments and are not hereditary. Secondly there
are the political and executive appointments which are in theory
also personal but which tend to be considered hereditary, as I will
explain later. These appointments, too, require the ultimate
approval of the D.C. The officials in this category are the Native

[1] E.g. it is a general complaint of the Administration that the Tonga resist
measures against soil erosion, e.g. contouring of gardens. One cause of this
resistance is that most schemes require extra male labour, which is largely
employed outside the area. Whilst the men and women still in the area can
keep their relatively uncomplicated subsistence agriculture going, it is very
doubtful whether they could produce the extra labour needed for additional
tasks.

[2] This Portuguese word for 'foreman' is generally used by Tonga and Europeans. The sanitary *capitao's* main task is to ensure that the villages are clean and
that every hamlet has a pit latrine. Whatever his formal authority, in practice he
has very little. Tonga villages are not particularly dirty; and as regards his power
to make people dig pit latrines, neither he nor any other official whether
African or European has so far had much success in enforcing this rule when
villagers are for one reason or another not inclined to comply with it.

[3] The ultimate appointment of the court clerk lies in the hands of the D.C. in
Council (i.e. the District Council) and not with the N.A. This strengthens the
position of the clerk who might otherwise be in a very difficult position; he
holds the key of the safe of the N.A. treasury and pays the members of the
N.A.'s bureaucracy and the N.A. himself, and he is likely to be under great
pressure by demands for unlimited advance payments.

Authorities and subordinate Native Authorities (generally referred to as N.A. and sub-N.A.) and the Administrative Headmen. The selection of these officials is generally made within the framework of tribal politics. I will show that this applies to a certain extent also to the court councillors, although strictly they are not executive officials within the Administrative system.

The two Tonga N.A.'s, KABUNDULI and MANKHAMBIRA, each have a number of sub-N.A.'s; the sub-N.A.'s each have their own area of jurisdiction. Each of the N.A.'s also has an area under his own direct control, without a sub-N.A., or to put it differently, an area in which the N.A. is his own sub-N.A. The N.A. and the sub-N.A. each has his own court, granted by court warrant, with messengers and court clerk. The court warrant of the N.A. gives him jurisdiction in a larger category of civil and criminal cases than the warrant of the sub-N.A. The N.A.'s court is a court of first instance for the N.A.'s own area and it acts as a court of appeal in relation to the courts of his sub-N.A.'s. Although the N.A. is the superior of his sub-N.A.'s in the Administrative system, there is a distinct tendency both on the part of the N.A. and of his sub-N.A.'s to consider each other as equals. Each court has one, and sometimes two, paid councillors, whose main duty lies in the court; he is generally a headman.

At the bottom of the Administrative hierarchy, below the level of the sub-N.A.'s, come the Administrative Headmen. These are headmen whose titles may, traditionally, be equal, or even superior to the titles of the headmen who have been appointed N.A. or sub-N.A. The Administrative Headman keeps a copy of the *buku*[1] in his house; on it are listed all males of taxable age within the village of which he is in charge as Administrative Headman. I will call this Administrative unit an 'Administrative village' to distinguish it from the village in the traditional tribal political system—the latter village I will continue to call 'village'. An Administrative village almost invariably contains more than one traditional village. Similarly I will call the headman with Administrative recognition 'Administrative Headman' to distinguish him from the ordinary headmen (of whom he is one) in the traditional political system. Since all Administrative officials, including the N.A.'s, are headmen within the tribal political

---

[1] *Buku* (book) is the Tonga term for the tax register (or tax census). I will call it *Book*.

system, they are therefore all, in a sense, 'Administrative Headmen'. But I will reserve this term only for those at the bottom of the Administrative hierarchy; the other officials I will refer to by their respective positions in the Administrative system.

The main responsibility of the Administrative Headman is to preserve law and order and to keep his Book up to date. He is not supposed to make any alterations in his Book but he should supply the relevant information to the tax clerk who will then alter the register accordingly. For instance, the Administrative Headman should inform the authorities which boys in his Administrative village have reached taxable age, or which labour migrants have returned from abroad and are due to pay tax. These are unpopular duties, and the failure to report tax defaulters to the authorities is a standard complaint of European Administrators, not only against the Administrative Headmen but against all the tribal agencies of the Administration, including the N.A.'s.

In the following study I will analyse some of the causes of the general failure on the part of the tribal agencies of Administrative rule to exercise their statutory authority.

CHAPTER II

THE VILLAGE

General Description

THE Tonga on the whole live in small clusters of huts scattered through the bush and the forests, among the rivers and streams and by the lakeshore. The size of these settlements varies from one hut or house to a collocation of two dozen dwellings (which is exceptional), but the average size is somewhere between two and six dwellings. I will call these separate clusters of huts *hamlets*. As I will suggest later, groups of hamlets interact in such a way that one may call them villages: but to the external observer Tonga *villages* do not have the obvious physical appearance of villages, *viz.* a collocation of dwellings clearly marked off from other similar units of habitation. In fact along parts of the lakeshore the population lives in a string of seemingly uncoordinated clusters which are generally within hailing distance of one another. In the hills the situation is slightly different. As one gets farther inland, more than a mile or so from the lake, the population becomes less concentrated and the distance between one group of hamlets and another may be greater. But here, too, villages as political units are not easily discernible for a stranger.

In my analysis of the forces which are at work in tribal politics I shall start from the hamlet. A hamlet is not a fixed unit, either as regards its site or its genealogical composition, and it does not persist through time. We shall later see that a village is a confederation of hamlets. Although villages are structurally, as well as physically, difficult to distinguish, they are important in Tonga life. Ambitious men are anxious to attract a following and to lead a village, and there are few other openings for ambition. An analysis of intrigues within the village and between villages is essential for an understanding of Tonga political life. Every kinship relationship and marriage is involved in these struggles; and although they are petty struggles to the outsider, they are the stuff of politics for the average Tonga.

The Tonga do not have different words for the hamlets and villages which I distinguish in this study, although in practice they

28

do distinguish between them as political entities. The Tonga call all settlements *muzi* (pl. *mizi*) and it depends on the context whether this word refers to a hamlet of one hut or to a large village of one hundred huts, or for that matter, to Johannesburg, London or Chicago.[1] Their expressions for 'hamlet leader' and 'village headman' show the same flexibility: *fumu* (pl. *mafumu*) can refer to either office. Indeed any Tonga who can claim a freeman's status in a village can and will say: '*Nde fumu ine*' (I am a headman, or chief). In fact the word *fumu* or its abstract counterpart *ufumu* (headmanship, chieftainship) is sometimes used as synonymous with freeman (*munangwa*, pl. *anangwa*) as opposed to slave (*kaporo*, pl. *akaporo*).

The villages on which this analysis is for the greater part based are Mulombwa, Mapalassie, Kamanga,[2] Chinyafwa and Mzenga. Although I have data from other villages where I stayed, only for these five villages are my data relatively complete; I will use information from other villages to supplement them when necessary. Although these five villages are representative of the bulk of the Tonga villages, we will come across relationships between these villages and non-Tonga areas. This is not because they are peripheral: it is a feature common to many Tonga villages.

Although the Tonga tend to refer to a village or settlement in general by the name of the person pre-eminently associated with it, I will refer to villages by the names of the localities. The names of the localities are often derived from the name of a river or any other feature of the neighbourhood. Analysis of the names of these five villages shows the essential vagueness with which this sort of settlement is indicated (one might almost say, hinted at). This adumbrative feature is also reflected in the composition of the village and the position of the headman.

Mulombwa, Mapalassie and Kamanga used to be one village under KAMISA on the lakeshore, a few miles north of Sanga, the Native Authority headquarters of MANKHAMBIRA in whose area these villages lie. But KAMISA's village is in the process of splitting up into three 'independent' villages.[3] People at some distance from

[1] Chicago is prominent in Tonga lore.
[2] These three villages form a cluster generally referred to by outsiders as KAMISA's village. Due to the scale of the map I could not mark them separately.
[3] It will be clearer later on why it is difficult to speak of Tonga villages as 'independent' units. 'Splitting up' here refers to a redistribution of political

KAMISA may still refer to these three villages as KAMISA's villages, and the inhabitants themselves may do the same when they are away from home.[1] Those who know, and the inhabitants themselves, are more likely to use the names Mulombwa, etc.

Mulombwa[2] is the village which still contains the matrilineage which is now associated with KAMISA, and the locals sometimes still call this village KAMISA. KAMISA is an Administrative Headman and Mapalassie, Kamanga and Chinyafwa come under his authority in that capacity. It is said that KAMISA was on this site before the Ngoni wars of the third quarter of the last century and has been there ever since, apart from a short period of shelter in MANKHAMBIRA's stockade.

Mapalassie[3] is mainly inhabited by descendants of some immigrants (a few of whom are still alive) from the island of Likoma which lies to the south-east of Mapalassie, near the Portuguese shores of Lake Nyasa. Their arrival around the turn of the last century seems to be connected with the end of the Ngoni threat in this area. The apparent leader of this village is Mussa Chirwa, generally referred to as Mudara.[4] As he is one of the surviving immigrant founders, this village has no inheritable name yet; but it is likely that his name, Mussa, will become the title associated with this village.

As for Kamanga village, this has as yet neither a locality name nor a title-name; its process of political separation from KAMISA's village has not gone as far as in the case of Mapalassie. When the other inhabitants of Greater Kamisa[5] talk about this village they may say 'at Kamanga's' (*kwa Kamanga*) or 'by the lake' (*ku nyanja*[6]). Kamanga is the surname of several of the men in this

---

authority in the lineage concerned—the secession is political and not geographical.

[1] They may not even mention the name KAMISA but say that they live at Chisi or Sanga, two well-known capes nearby.

[2] The name for a local tree which produces good timber.

[3] I have come across two other settlements called Mapalassie, which seems to be a corruption of the Afrikaans word for farm: *plaas*, or its diminutive *plaassie*.

[4] Mudara means literally 'an old man' but it is often used as a personal name.

[5] I use 'Greater Kamisa' to avoid the cumbersome 'the villages which are offshoots of KAMISA's village'. Greater Kamisa thus includes Mulombwa, Mapalassie, Kamanga and Mtomba's hamlet.

[6] Whilst the other hamlets of Greater Kamisa are all a little distance inland, one of the three hamlets of Kamanga village is right by the lake.

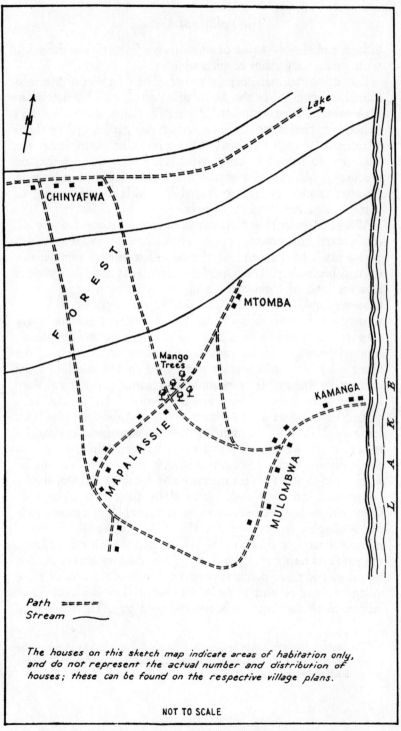

MAP II.—Sketch map of Greater Kamisa and Chinyafwa

village, and also the name of a headman a few miles to the south
with whom they claim patrilateral links.

I am not certain whether the rather isolated hamlet of Mtomba
should be included in the Mapalassie complex of hamlets or in
Mulombwa. Informants at Mapalassie claim that Mtomba's
father, who came here as a slave, was given a garden by Donald of
Mapalassie (Map. B.13.) But at Mulombwa they claim that it was
KAMISA who helped Mtomba with land.[1] This question has no
practical significance in everyday life; and during my residence in
Greater Kamisa no crisis occurred in which the ownership of
Mtomba's gardens became an issue.

Whilst Mapalassie and Kamanga have only comparatively recently started the process of political secession from KAMISA, Chinyafwa has been independent of KAMISA for much longer, if not
since its beginnings. The bond between KAMISA and Chinyafwa is
that the land of Chinyafwa is said to have been excised from
KAMISA's land as a *chisoka*[2] payment at the death of an earlier
KAMISA's wife who was the 'sister' of MAKALAMBA. Since this
MAKALAMBA is said to have been the mother's mother's mother's
mother's brother of the present incumbent of that name, the
event may have taken place some time in the middle of last
century or before. It is possible that some generations were
omitted from the genealogy which I recorded, but it is unlikely
that additional generations were interposed. Although the present
leader of Chinyafwa is a matrilineal descendant of MAKALAMBA, he
is not often referred to by that name but generally by his own
name, Nyali Kaunda. His land does not border on the lake and he
shares a net-shelter with the men from Mulombwa and Mapalassie.

The area inhabited and cultivated by these four villages of
Greater Kamisa and Chinyafwa covers about half of a square mile
and is roughly rectangular. On this stretch of the lakeshore the
hills come straight down to the lake so that there is no flat land;
the terrain is rather rocky and stony. The country here is broken
by ridges and three perennial streams. Much of the area of these
villages is covered with trees and its western limit is a large forest
infested with monkeys, baboons and wild pigs. There are very

[1] Cf. also p. 285.
[2] The name Chinyafwa may be derived from *nyifwa*, death. The *chisoka* is the
compensation which, in certain circumstances, a husband used to pay on his
wife's death to her kin: see p. 117, n. 1.

few villages in this forest; and after a two to three hours' walk from Greater Kamisa one reaches the Vizara rubber estate of the African Lakes Corporation. There are always a few men, women and children from Greater Kamisa or Chinyafwa employed on the estate as unskilled labour. These villages form part of the chain of villages spread along the lakeshore which I mentioned above.

Mzenga village is in the hills to the west of Greater Kamisa with whom it has no special relationship. The layout of the village is very much like that of the villages by the lakeshore: there are four hamlets which are clearly separated from one another. The village contains a church of the Free Church of Scotland (Livingstonia) Mission.[1] In common with most villages in the hills it has no gathering place such as a net-shelter[2] where men meet socially whilst mending or knitting nets, as in the lakeshore villages. Nearer the Tumbuka-Ngoni area villages tend to have men's shelters where the men meet and often have their meals; by the lakeshore men do not usually take their meals at the net-shelter.

Many of the hamlets which together form the villages are set apart as distinct local units. They are surrounded by gardens. Most houses have adjacent gardens although many people may have gardens elsewhere in the village as well. And in between the hamlets there may occur a clump of trees, a mango grove, high grass or a deep gully with a stream. All these features tend to give the hamlets an appearance of independence. Neither the hamlets nor the villages are built to any sort of pattern. In any case most hamlets contain too few houses to form a rectangle or circle as is common in other parts of Africa. The Tonga hamlets or the villages have no focal point such as the Tumbuka-Ngoni men's shelter where the males take their meals together or where they spend the evenings round a common fire. Although the men of one hamlet, or those of two or more hamlets, may drop in on one another and stay for a meal, this is not a routine practice amongst set groups of men. Nor do the men of hamlet or village meet

[1] This mission is now part of the Church of Central Africa Presbyterian (C.C.A.P.) but the Tonga still used to refer to it by its original name.

[2] There is practically no fishing in the hills except for a few months in the year when they catch salmon-like fish, the *sanjika*, which are running up the rivers to their spawning grounds.

regularly in the evenings either by one another's houses or at some central meeting-place. On the whole, life with its daily routine revolves around the individual households. This applies to both men and women. But the men of Mulombwa, Mapalassie and Chinyafwa do meet on the beach by their net-shelter. Sometimes the men from Kamanga may join them there; but in general they meet by their own net-shelter near Kamanga's hamlet by the lake, referred to before. The Tonga word for a net-shelter is *khumbi* but this refers only to the structure. If the net-shelter is also the place where men often sit together they will call it an *mphara*, which is the term for any congregation of a typically male character. Thus it refers to any group of men wherever they meet, be it by a net-shelter or under a tree. *Mphara* therefore also means a court or any other *ad hoc* meeting of men trying to decide a specific problem, for example discussions at funerals or divorce. Finally it is also the word for a house where only men sleep—this may be a boys' dormitory or the house of a bachelor.

When men are thus gathered, informally, it is difficult if not impossible for an outsider to deduce from the men's behaviour or seating who are the hamlet leaders, or the village or Administrative headmen: in this respect too there is no obvious focal point. This is true not only for the villages of greater Kamisa but for Tonga villages in general. The obvious exceptions are those leaders whose authority is based not only on political status but also on a dominating personality, as for instance in the case of MLENGA MZOMA whose position I will discuss later on. Milton Saka, whose role in the Phiri-Kapunda Banda conflict I will describe below, is an example of a man who commands respect by the force of his personality, in spite of his inferior political status.

Genealogical Composition

Tonga desire to establish their own hamlets. There is enough land and water to allow them to do this. The result is to be seen in the great number of very small hamlets. In Table I, I have broken down the five villages into their component hamlets with the number of houses in each hamlet, and we see that the average number of houses per hamlet is 2·5, ranging from hamlets of one house to one hamlet of six houses.[1] A hamlet is a cluster of houses

[1] I am here concerned with the composition of hamlet and village. For their social and political significance, see Chapter VI.

separated from other clusters. This separation is sometimes not very clear.

TABLE I

Number of Houses per Hamlet

Village	Total no. hamlets	Houses per hamlet						Total no. of houses
		1	2	3	4	5	6	
Mapalassie	8	2	5			1		17
Mulombwa	9	1	1	4	1	2		29
Mtomba	1			1				3
Kamanga	3		1		1		1	12
Chinyafwa	5	3	1	1				8
Mzenga	4		2	2				10
Total	30	6	10	8	2	3	1	79

The genealogical composition of the hamlets varies a great deal. One may find, for instance, a patricentric group in the father's village or a matricentric group of a widow with her children, from one or more husbands, in her own or in her late husband's village. The hamlet may be a localized lineage group of minimum depth, *viz.* the present leader of the lineage and a sister's daughter and son; this is, as we shall see, the minimum personnel required for the perpetuation or the beginning of a localized matrilineage. And, again, the hamlet may be the home of an elementary family or an extended family with a married son and his family. This variation in the choice of residence arises from the Tonga rule: '*wana banangwa*', the children are free, i.e. to follow either the father or the mother. This rule is often quoted with reference to divorce. Although it is a fact that a Tonga if he so chooses can build a house and cultivate a garden in either his mother's or his father's village, when we analyse the ties of the adult members of the five sample villages to their present place of residence we see that the majority of them reside matrilocally.

By matrilocal residence I mean a person's residence with matrilateral kin. This may—but need not—be the place where his or her mother actually lives or used to live. Similarly, a person's matrilocality is not necessarily his or her *mother's* matrilocality: it may be *her* patrilocality. Patrilocal residence is residence with patrilateral kin; what I have said about matrilocal residence applies *mutatis mutandis* to patrilocal residence.

E

The Tonga village is composed of generally small kin groups attached in various ways to the headman or another villager. Some villagers may claim a direct or primary link with the headman either as his children or through membership of the headman's matrilineage, that is, the dominant matrilineage.[1] Others may explain their residence in a particular village by reference to a primary link with the leader of the hamlet where they live, or with another person or group in the village. And it is only through such intermediate links that they are ultimately (and generally not matrilineally) attached to the headman. Residents of this category have what I will call secondary or tertiary links with their village.

For instance, Elton (Mul. D 3) at Mulombwa has, through his mother, a matrilateral primary link with the hamlet where he lives with his maternal grandmother Nyambayaya (Mul. B 22). In other words he lives at Mulombwa because that is where his mother lived (when she was not living virilocally) and died; Elton's father lives in KANGOMA's village nearby.[2] Elton's mother, Estere (Mul. C 12), was herself living with her patrilateral kin and her ultimate link with the village was through her father's father who was a member of the then dominant matrilineage at Mulombwa.[3] According to Tonga norms Elton's ultimate link with the village is patrilateral and his status is therefore that of a 'son' (*mwana*, pl. *wana*).

In this context the term 'son' refers to a person's political status in a particular village—the relative political status of the same persons may be different or even reversed in another village.[4] Although in practice the distinction is not always clear-cut, the term *mwana* is also used in the sense of classificatory 'son' or 'daughter'; in this sense it has an essentially genealogical referent.[5] In this context I will continue to use 'children', 'son' or 'daughter'. But in its political context I will translate *mwana* as *village son* (*daughter, child*) or *son*, etc., *of the village*, following Tonga idiom.

[1] See pp. 140, 185 *seq.*

[2] For further details about Elton's position at Mulombwa and his role as acting headman, see pp. 207, 232.

[3] See p. 203 for the history of the headmanship at Mulombwa.

[4] See e.g. p. 146 and Case 16, p. 233.

[5] Apart from its primary meaning of young person and parents' offspring of either sex, *mwana* is also the term for a particular category of cross-cousins: see p. 142. It will be seen that cross-cousins of the subordinate category are referred to as *wana* (children) by cross-cousins of the superior category.

In contrast, I will refer to those who are matrilineally linked to the village as *owners of the village* or *village owners*.[1]

The situation then is that the members of a village belong to two categories: those who are matrilineally related to the village, i.e. the owners of the village, and the rest, i.e. the children of the village.[2] This latter category can be further divided into patrilocal residents whose ties with the village are patrilateral throughout (for instance headman's children and his sons' children as in the case of Chimbaza's (Map. B 1) children at Mapalassie), and those villagers whose links with the village do not follow either line. The latter can be either matrilocal or patrilocal residents according to my classification; but they are all village children. Elton at Mulombwa is a case in point: he is a village son whom I have classified as a matrilocal resident; his link with the village is through his mother's father's father. Similarly Elias, also at Mulombwa (C 18), who lives in his father's village and who is also a village son even although his father lived matrilocally and was matrilineally related to the village. Thus Elias has a patrilateral primary link with the village but a matrilateral ultimate link; he is therefore a village son. To sum up; unless a villager is matrilineally related to the village, he or she has the subordinate status of village son or daughter (or slave).

In writing of a person's link to 'the village' instead of to 'the village headman' I am following Tonga idiom. The Tonga, when indicating status in the village, generally refer to the village and not to the village headman. Moreover, they tend to mention not only primary links but also ultimate links. To quote the case of Elton at Mulombwa (D 3) again, his primary and ultimate links with the village would be described (for example in court or conversation) as: 'Here is the patrilocality of his mother',[3] probably

---

[1] For detailed discussion of political ranking see pp. 140 *seq.* and Chapter V. Although *mwana* in a genealogical context refers equally to mother's child and to father's child, when used as a term of ranking it indicates subordination in analogy with the patrilateral relationship only.

[2] I am ignoring for the moment villagers of slave descent whose ties with the village are of a different character. See Chapter V.

[3] *Kunu kwe kuchirumi cha anyinao*, lit. 'here is male side of his mother'. The root *rumi* means *male*; with the prefix *chi* it means *that which pertains to the male*—the female counterpart is *chikazi*. In a genealogical context *kuchirumi* and *kuchikazi* refer to a person's male and female side or his patrilateral and matrilateral links.

followed by: 'but his own [*viz.* Elton's] patrilocality is in KANGOMA's village [where his father still lives]'. But for the fact that Elton's maternal grandmother Nyambayaya (Mul. B 22) is of slave status, the speaker might well round off this information by indicating the matrilocality of Elton's mother.[1] It should be noted that the reference is not to the name of the headman or his title, or to the name of the founder of the village, but simply to 'here' (*kunu*), that is, the place, the village.

TABLE II

Classification   Adult Male and Female Residents

Village	Matrilocal	Patrilocal	Virilocal	Total adult residents
Mzenga	5	8	5	18
Mulombwa[1]	12	10	13	35
Kamanga	2	3	6	11
Mapalassie	15	6	9	30
Chinyafwa	8	1	3	12
Total	42	28	36	106

[1] This includes Mtomba hamlet where the respective figures are: 0, 2, 1, and Total Residents 3.

Table II gives the residential links of the adult members of the five villages with which this book is mainly concerned. Since it is generally his primary link on which a person bases his claim to residence in the village (apart of course from virilocal wives), I have in this table classified the villagers by their primary links. (I should repeat that a villager's ultimate link may be the same as his primary link, for instance in the case of members of the headman's lineage or of his children and his son's children.) It appears that of the 70 residents who claim some sort of right[2] to reside where they do, 42 or 60 per cent have matrilateral primary links.

[1] To do so in this case would be tantamount to revealing publicly Elton's slave descent and this would cause trouble for the speaker if Elton or his kinsmen heard about it.

[2] Excluding wives married into the village but including residents of slave status claiming apparently fictitious rights. These figures refer only to people whom I found actually resident in the villages; villagers residing abroad at the time have been excluded.

A similar picture emerges when we classify the links between hamlets and the village: seventeen out of twenty-eight or some 60 per cent of the hamlet leaders claim a matrilateral link with the village.

TABLE III

Classification of Links between Hamlets and Villages

Village	Total no. hamlets	Matrilateral links	Patrilateral links	Unknown[1]
Mapalassie	8	6	2	
Mulombwa	10	4	5	1
Kamanga	3	2	1	
Chinyafwa	5	3	2	
Mzenga	4	2	1	1
Total	30	17	11	2

[1] The hamlets whose relationship with the village I could not trace are those of Mtomba at Mulombwa, and of Nyaulanda and her sisters at Mzenga.

I have included in Table III also the hamlets of the village headmen themselves. For, as mentioned before with regard to individuals, political relationships are assessed with reference to the village rather than the headman. In any case successive headmen are likely to belong to different hamlets.

There are two unrelated hamlets, without genealogical links with the village in which they are situated; these are the hamlets of Mtomba at Mulombwa and of Nyaulanda and her sisters at Mzenga (Mz. C 11). Both hamlets are inhabited by descendants of former slaves without kinship ties with the village.

Table II does not give an accurate picture of the extent to which the Tonga follow their mothers. For this we have to break down the numbers of patrilocal residents into those who live with their mother but in their father's (i.e. their mother's husband's) village and those who still live with their father after their mother has gone back to her own village. Table IV shows that of the 28 people living patrilocally nine, or 32 per cent, are living with their mother but in their father's hamlets; at least some of them are likely to move to their mother's village if the latter leaves her husband's village, or when she dies. Finally, those who are still living with their widowed father may also move off to their

TABLE IV

Numbers of Patrilocal Residents Living with their Mothers

A	Mother alive and still living virilocally Father dead or alive		9
B	Mother divorced and back in own village—father alive	2	4
	Mother dead Father alive	2	
C	Mother and father both dead— no living parental tie in village		15
	Total Patrilocal Residents		28

matrilocal village when their father dies. I found only four people living patrilocally with fathers who themselves also live or had lived patrilocally. If we add to the 42 people who live matri-locally (see Table II) the nine people who are living with their mothers, albeit in their fathers' hamlets, we see that 51 people or 72·8 per cent of the villagers (excluding wives living virilocally) live with their mothers or in their mothers' hamlets. We will see later that the Tonga also assume that children who stay on with their widowed mothers in their fathers' hamlets do so because of the mother and not because it is their father's hamlet. Of the remaining 27·2 per cent who have not followed their mothers many have not much choice.[1]

The figures show that although there are people living in their fathers' hamlets, there is a distinct preference for settling in the mother's village. Seminal descendants in hamlet or village have a right to stay and cultivate land, but their status carries disabilities when compared with that of matrilineal descendants.

[1] See p. 269.

CHAPTER III

KINSHIP AND LOCALITY

IN later chapters I will describe the very limited authority of the headman and the indefiniteness of the village as a corporate unit. Here I want to deal with the factors which promote cohesion in a larger field than the village, so that we can view the lack of cohesion in the village against a background of tribal cohesion.

The social unity of the Tonga is mainly based upon relationships between individuals or small (not necessarily localized) groups of individuals. These relationships, which fulfil different functions—political, economic, or emotional—are based upon claims of kinship. Ideally, for the Tonga, it is matrilineal descent that matters, and hence their stress on inheritance and succession to office by matrilineal kinsmen. But we will see that patrilateral kinship also creates ties which unite individuals. Indeed, since wives live virilocally, the village where most people grow up is their father's village. Even as regards office, there are situations in which men can expect more in their patrilocality than in their matrilocality. And I have mentioned already that the number of adults who live patrilocally form a significant exception to the ideal rule that people reside matrilocally. Factors of locality and patrilateral kinship militate against the exclusive importance of matrilineal kinship and thus promote the spread of a person's interests and relationships in various directions over a wide area. There is no concentration of power and authority in any one particular local or kinship group.

I will first deal with the unifying effect of various local and kinship ties within Tonga society at large. In the next chapter I will describe Tonga marriage as the source of most inter-personal relationships. Among the Tonga, marriage is not only a social institution: it is also—and always—a political institution. Political power is diffused and marriage is the main agent of this diffusion.

Matrilineal Descent

The Tonga distinguish between two primary categories of kinsmen: *kuchikazi* (lit. on the woman's side) and *kuchirumi* (lit.

41

on the man's side).[1] Kinsmen 'on the woman's (*viz.* mother's)
side' are all those to whom one is related in one way or another
through one's mother; I will call them matrilateral kin or, for
short, matrikin. Similarly, kinsmen 'on the man's (*viz.* father's)
side' are all those to whom one is related in one way or another
through one's father; I will call them patrilateral kin or patrikin.
Within the category of matrikin they further distinguish—not by
specific terms but rather descriptively—between on the one hand
what the anthropologist would call matrilineal kinsmen, *viz.*
people who are considered to be related by descent through
females only from a common ancestor or ancestress; and on the
other hand all other non-matrilineal matrikin, including one's
mother's father and *his* matrikin. The Tonga do not conceptualize
the obverse among patrikin, *viz.* a category of kinsmen related
through males only. Indeed, co-operation in one form or another
between persons on this ('agnatic') basis hardly occurs beyond the
two-generational span of grandfather-grandson. However, I did
come across the odd case of corporate action (including common
residence) based on what would be called 'agnatic' kinship in
another society where agnation is the recognized mode of
descent.[2] I will call such kinship links seminal. The following
diagram summarizes my categorization of kinsmen: it partly
follows Tonga usage.

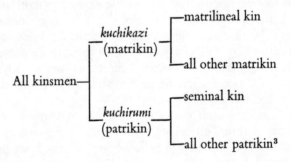

[1] See p. 37, n. 1.
[2] The seminal descendants of Amuziteni in Mzenga village are a case in point:
cf. pp. 61, 144.
[3] The Lakeside Tonga do not have a specific term for father's matrilineage
comparable to the *bashanaushi* of the Plateau Tonga (cf. Colson (1951), p. 142).
But they can of course describe this group as: the matrikin of my father
(*wakuchikazi wa ada*).

The Tonga use a variety of words and phrases to indicate kinship. Some of these words are not exclusively kinship terms; they are also used in other contexts. There is, for instance, the word *mtundu*, which literally means 'sort' or 'kind'; or the phrase *weneko weneko pe* which is difficult to translate but means something like 'relatives only' or 'all one family'.[1] The term *abali* may mean anything from acquaintances to matrikin. The Tonga also use the Chewa term *banja*.[2] None of these or other phrases refer to a specific group of kin; they acquire meaning only in context and they are generally used to set 'us' apart from 'them'. The groups involved in this antithesis may be of any size or composition and need not even be kin groups but, accompanied by a wide sweep of the hand, may refer to a whole village.

Other words refer exclusively to matrilineages but they, too, generally lack precise definition. To this category of kinship terms belong *mbumba*, *fuku*, and *khamu*, which are all three specifically kinship terms; whilst *be* (lit. breast), *nthumbu* (lit. womb), and *nyumba* (lit. house) are metaphors which are also used in their literal sense. With the exception of *mbumba* all the other terms are interchangeable. The group to which they refer is clear from the context only when they point a contrast to other similar groups.

Mbumba always refers to a man *vis-à-vis* his sisters, either classificatory or real, or his sisters' daughters, that is, to those of his female kin who are likely to perpetuate the matrilineage which he represents. The *mbumba* do not represent a specific corporate group.[3] This would in any case be rather difficult among the Tonga where women marry into their husbands' villages. It is

---

[1] The form *mwene* indicates: close association, identification, ownership. *Mweneko* (pl. *weneko*) may mean 'owner' but in a phrase such as *weneko wa nyifwa* (*nyifwa*: death) 'the close kin of the dead person' would more accurately convey its meaning than 'the owners of the dead'. Similarly, *mwene charu* is usually translated (also in official documents) as 'the owner of the land' although the phrase does not primarily convey the idea of ownership but rather that of historical identification with a particular area of land. A slightly different aspect of the idea of close association or identification is found, e.g. in *mwenumu*: *mwene* plus *umu*, i.e. 'within' or 'in here'. The question 'Where did such-and-such a thing happen?' may be answered by '*Mwenumu*', i.e. 'In this very [house, where we are now talking]'.

[2] According to Read the Chewa use it to mean 'family': see Read (1956), p. 133.

[3] In contrast to the Yao: see Mitchell (1956), p. 145. The Tonga use the term *mbumba* rather more loosely than the Yao.

much more usual for a man to refer to his sister as *mzichi* (pl. *azichi*) which is the reciprocal term for siblings, real or classificatory, of the opposite sex.

The other terms, *fuku*, *khamu*, *nyumba*, *nthumbu* and *be*, are practically synonymous, although the last three tend to be used for smaller matrilineages of less depth. *Fuku* and *khamu* are generally used for large groups of people who claim common matrilineal descent from a legendary ancestor or ancestress, or at least someone in the past whose name is rarely remembered. *Fuku* and *khamu* are generally translated as 'clan' by Administrators, missionaries and English-speaking Tonga when they present Administrators with written or verbal histories of their own villages and headmen's titles. (These histories are often meant to prove the writer's or narrator's traditional political seniority and, therefore, his claim to precedence in the Administrative system: see p. 307.)

Tonga say that there is a certain, limited, number of clans (*fuku* or *khamu*)—e.g. the Banda, Phiri, Mwale, Manda, Chirwa, Longwe, Nkhoma and Saka—many of whose names also occur among surrounding tribes and even the Yao;[1] and that each of these clans has its own area. It may be that there was a time when the Tonga had clans,[2] that is, corporate and exogamous kin groups; and that these *fuku* were localized to a certain extent, but there is no evidence to support this view. At present all that remains is the word *fuku* and the clan names. Although some will say that they belong to such-and-such a *fuku* or *khamu*, others do not know and may even give their *chiwongo*[3] when you ask them for their *fuku*. Others maintain that a man inherits his *fuku* from his father. In short, Tonga ideas about clans seem to be vague and they may merely represent hazy memories of an earlier period and organization; there are no traces now of *fuku* or *khamu* as corporate units.

I will use the term 'matrilineage' for all groups of kinsmen who claim matrilineal descent from a common ancestor or ancestress. The span of these matrilineages as operative groups varies a great deal and there is also little regularity in their composition: whilst

[1] See Mitchell (1956), p. 71.

[2] Considering their heterogeneous origin I think this is very unlikely.

[3] The Tonga word *chiwongo*, which I translate as surname, is borrowed from Ngoni where the term is *izibongo* which means praise name: see Read (1956), p. 205.

some matrilineages may contain all the descendants of the women of each generation, others may contain only some of the descendants of some of the women in a particular generation. One of the reasons for this irregularity is, as I will describe later, that in many situations matrilineages are operative groups only in relation to a particular locality.[1]

The names Banda, Phiri, Longwe, etc., which at one stage may have been clan names, are now used as *viwongo* (sing. *chiwongo*) and they are the names by which people are generally addressed or known. The majority of the people adopt the surname of their father[2] but this is by no means a hard and fast rule because a person may adopt a grandfather's surname or that of another kinsman, or for that matter any surname. A person does not necessarily adhere to one surname in his or her lifetime, nor is he or she necessarily known by only one surname.

People also bear first names (*zina*, pl. *mazina*) but it is considered bad form to address a person by his *zina* except in the case of children and headmen who are addressed as Bwana[3] KAMISA, Bwana MAKALAMBA, etc. Children will often call one another by their surnames, but it is a sign of growing up when the adults begin to call them by their surnames. At various stages in their youth people adopt new *mazina*.[4] Often the first names of adults are known only by their close kin. Even among close friends and between parents and adult children the first name is practically never used in address but may be used in reference. This was probably different two or more generations ago: when collecting genealogies I was struck by the fact that the reverse happens in the case of ancestors—they are often remembered by their first names only and not by their surnames (assuming that then, as now, people had both).

The hereditary name and title of a headman is also called *zina*

---

[1] See e.g. p. 144.

[2] Women have the same surnames but with the prefix *nya-*. Thus if a man is called Banda, his daughter may be called Nyabanda. This applies to all surnames except Kamanga and Chirwa whose feminine counterparts are Kanyaso and Nyalongwe—very occasionally one comes across a woman called Nyachirwa.

[3] The English equivalent of *bwana* is Sir, or Mr. when used with the person's name.

[4] This happens without any ceremony except for the first name-giving of a newly born child which is accompanied by a minor ceremony.

and not *chiwongo*. The name of every male Tonga who is a freeman and has full civic rights in some area is potentially the *zina* of a headman,[1] *viz.* if he can gather sufficient followers—matrikin and others—around his matrilineage and can establish his political independence. Hence *zina* acquires the pregnant meaning of *ufumu* (chieftainship) and *munangwa* (freeman). The simple phrase 'I have a name' indicates, to those who can understand, that the speaker is a freeborn man without civic or political disabilities and thus a potential chief. And if one enquires whether so-and-so is perhaps a slave the negative answer often is simply: 'What, he? He has a name', i.e. he has a potential claim to a title either in the village where the discussion takes place or somewhere else.[2] Thus *zina*, *ufumu* and *unangwa* (freeman status) are closely related concepts. They correspond to the individualistic character of Tonga society because the ultimate aim of most Tonga is to have their own hamlets or, to put it more generally, to found their own independent localized kin groups. The natural corollary of this ambition is the desire to prevent kinsmen or other residents of hamlet or village from transferring their residential allegiance. The competition between the matrikin and the patrikin in attracting their kinsmen is an aspect of the same problem.[3]

The Tonga distinguish between inheriting a name which is also a title to office, and adopting the first name or surname of a grandparent, parent or other relative. Adoption is expressed by the verb *kuto* (to take) or even *kuhara* (to inherit, in general). The phrase *kurgha zina* (lit. to eat the name) refers exclusively to succession to the name and title of a maternal uncle or other matrilineal relative.[4]

One can very rarely trace back a hereditary name, or for that matter any genealogy, farther than about four or five generations from the youngest adult of the matrilineage concerned. Patrilateral ancestry is frequently not remembered at all beyond the grandparent generation. A genealogical depth of four to five

---

[1] Cf. the case of Mussa at Mapalassie on p. 30; also pp. 211 *seq.*

[2] Cf. Charles's rhetorical question about Elton's *zina* on p. 208; also pp. 201–3.

[3] Cf. p. 84. This conflict is clearly illustrated in Case 9, pp. 149 *seq.*

[4] *Kurgha* gives the act a certain finality—it is for instance also used for someone who has appropriated and used up another person's money (e.g. a loan or a share of the bridewealth).

generations would put the ancestresses of the larger matrilineages in about the second half of the last century. And as I have shown elsewhere[1] there are very strong reasons to believe that the Tonga are an amalgamation of various tribal offshoots which coalesced at the time of, and perhaps because of, the Ngoni invasions in the middle of the nineteenth century. Many of the villages which are now by the lakeshore were founded by people who at one time or another came from farther inland or from elsewhere; many came some time in the second half of the last century as a result of the pressure of the Ngoni from the west. Consequently most villages have been on their present sites for only two or three generations.

When recording genealogies it was noticeable that the earliest remembered ancestor or ancestress was generally also the founder of the localized matrilineage, i.e. the person who originally associated the group of his or her descendants with the land on which they are living at present. Thus Tonga genealogies, particularly with regard to past generations, tend to be genealogies of localized kin groups. It is they who have most interests in common (including land) and are therefore the effective corporate kinship unit. By and large, historical genealogical links of a localized matrilineage with other areas (including the village its founder came from) are structurally not very important and fall victim to 'structural amnesia'.[2]

The Tonga attach great value to a long historical association (from time immemorial) of the localized matrilineage with its present site. In view of the comparatively short history of the Tonga and the upheaval caused by the Ngoni invasion, it is not surprising that this ideal is not often realized. However, the prevalence of genealogical amnesia helps to obscure this conflict between the ideal and the reality; in a sense, of course, the association between matrilineage and present village does go back to 'time immemorial'. This characteristic of Tonga genealogies obscures differences not only between kin groups but also between individuals. Those Tonga who have a doubtful ancestry (e.g. slave antecedents) or whose association with their present habitat is not

---

[1] See van Velsen (1959a).

[2] See Barnes (1947), p. 52. Also Cunnison (1956) for a parallel situation among the Luapula peoples. Some Tonga headmen acknowledge that their ancestors came to the present site from elsewhere but they cannot trace their genealogies back into their areas of origin.

of long standing have every reason for not remembering or wanting to remember genealogical details which would expose their political disabilities.

Immigration and 'Foreign' Relationships

The immigration into Tongaland of small tribal groups which were amalgamated into the Tonga tribe, and the Ngoni raids which drove groups of Tonga to the areas of neighbouring tribes (for instance, the islands of Likoma and Chizumulu), have created 'foreign' relationships which are still operative. There is still a good deal of contact with and immigration from the surrounding tribes—the process of amalgamation is still going on, and not only at the periphery of Tongaland. For instance, the people of Chinyafwa still have regular contacts with Usiska[1] where several of the present Chinyafwa inhabitants were born and lived before settling at Chinyafwa, e.g. Siddely (Chin. D 6), Nyamphato (E 3) and even the headman Nyali (F 4). Nyali and Siddely came here after their fathers had died in Usiska. Nyamphato, who is now a very old woman, was fetched from the north a few years ago by Nyali. He also collected his mother Nyamwaya (E 1) and his sister Lucy (F 1) who both died at Chinyafwa and are buried there. The following case illustrates how important 'foreign'—inter-tribal—contacts may be.

CASE 1: NYALI FETCHES A SUCCESSOR FROM DEEP BAY

About three years ago Nyali went up north again, this time to bring his sister's daughter Mary (G 3) and the latter's small brother Gorogo back to Chinyafwa.[2] The reason was that Nyali was worried by the fact that there was then not one matrilineal descendant of the senior line (*viz.* the descendants from Nyali's mother) of the matrilineage at Chinyafwa or even in Tongaland. Mary is married to a Henga and has had four miscarriages so far. As soon as Nyali heard that she was preg-

[1] The country of the Siska which borders on Tongaland in the north. Among the Siska titles, land and cattle are inherited patrilineally. Firewood, water and land are short and soil poor compared with Tongaland, and it is said that gardens are bought and sold for cash. The Siska consider themselves more akin to the Henga, their northern neighbours, than to the Tonga. Their language, too, is more like that of the Henga than the Tonga.

[2] Their language still shows unmistakable traces of their native chiSiska.

nant again he went to fetch her from Deep Bay because, he told me, it was her husband's people who had caused her to have all those miscarriages. Moreover, although he did not expect to be able to keep her at Chinyafwa indefinitely, he wanted this child to be born at Chinyafwa so that it 'will always remember its mother's village and later return there'. The argument he used in his discussions at Deep Bay with the kinsmen of Mponera, the husband of Mary, was that Mary's father Nguru (also a Henga) had never paid any bridewealth for Mary's mother Lucy. Nyali says he asked those Henga:[1] 'Where is the go-between you sent in the matter of Lucy's [i.e. Mary's mother's] marriage, and to whom did you send him with the money? You did not send anybody: do you then expect to keep all her children as well? Do you think she is a dog which you can just take and breed with?' From the way he told me about his discussion it was clear that although he had gone to Deep Bay ostensibly to get the bridewealth for his sister, in fact he conducted the affair in such a way that he made sure that he would not get the bridewealth since that would loosen his hold on his sister's children. To quote further Nyali's account of what he said to the people at Deep Bay: 'I am not looking for *chuma*.[2] You may give me money now, perhaps even as much as £30, but this may all be spent in a few days and in the meanwhile the children will be yours and I will have lost them. No, I am looking for children.' And he related how he emphasized that he is a Tonga; that the Tonga say that 'children are free'; and that he wanted to show them that he is a Tonga by asking for a small sum only and not the much larger bridewealth which is customary among the Siska and which gives the father a considerable degree of control over his children. Nyali wanted to have the status of Lucy's children cleared up whilst he was still alive. It was necessary to establish, before he died, the fact that these children had an *asibweni* (maternal uncle) and that therefore their mother came from such-and-such a place. Otherwise the children's paternal kin might think that their mother came from some unknown place and was

---

[1] As I was not present at the discussion I have to rely on Nyali's account of it. Even allowing for some partiality, the arguments he says he used at least show his motives which are of course conditioned by Tonga principles of kinship and marriage. I understand that both Nguru and Mponera were present or represented at this discussion.

[2] *Chuma*: wealth, bridewealth. Whilst bridewealth among the Tonga is in the region of £6–£12 or sometimes even £15, the Siska, Henga and Tumbuka pay cattle or the equivalent in money, which makes their bridewealth considerably more costly.

brought to Deep Bay as a slave and that therefore the children, too, were only their slaves. All Tonga are always 'looking for children'; but the reason why Nyali was particularly keen on getting his uterine sister's daughter was clearly expressed in his own words: 'If Mary does not produce a daughter, or if I were to lose her to Deep Bay, that would be end of my "house". I would then have to give the "name" to Dorosia or to Rabeka Nyaphiri.' These two women are the only possible successors at Chinyafwa at present. Dorosia (G 5) is a young woman, but as the daughter's daughter of Nyali's mother's younger sister she belongs to a junior *nyumba* (house) from Nyali's point of view. As for Rabeka (E 13), she is even farther removed from Nyali's matrilineage, which at present is the dominant one at Chinyafwa, because she merely has assumed links with Chinyafwa.

Mary's arrival at Chinyafwa is not just a case of immigration: her move had been engineered by Nyali in an attempt to secure the succession for his own matrilineage. The movement between Chinyafwa and Usiska is not only in one direction—some people who used to live at Chinyafwa are now in Usiska. Nyali and some of those who moved out are in a particularly advantageous position: at Chinyafwa they can claim the full status of matrilineal descendants of the founder of the village; and if their fathers are Siska they also inherit status as members of a village in Usiska.

A similar situation prevails at Mapalassie where all the members of the village of about fifty years of age or over were born on Likoma island.[1] At about the beginning of the century Mussa came from Likoma with his son Chimbaza (Map. B 1) and some

---

[1] Likoma lies about fifty miles south-east of Greater KAMISA and a few miles from the Portuguese coast. It is the headquarters of the Universities Mission to Central Africa who settled on this island for much the same reasons as the African inhabitants; to evade the Ngoni, and the Yao raiders on what is now the Portuguese mainland. Both Likoma and its immediate neighbour Chizumulu are now very heavily populated with the result that food is often short and they have to buy it from either the Portuguese or British mainland for cash or sometimes fish. Firewood almost invariably comes from the Portuguese mainland. The inhabitants of the two islands are variously referred to by the Tonga as *waku Likoma* (those of Likoma), or as *waku mwera* or just *amwera* (those of the south-east—*mwera* literally is the name of south-eastern storms). They do not seem to have a specific tribal name. There is a possibility that they closely resemble, or indeed are, the autochthones of this part of the lake. Their language is Chinyanja and the Tonga say that there 'children are not free' as among the Tonga but always 'belong' to the maternal uncle. There are many

of the children of Mussa's 'sisters' Lena (Map. A 2) and Mzake
(Map. A 3). A few of the children of Mzake and Lena stayed behind on Likoma; but a few others who were born at Mapalassie
returned to Likoma, and some of those came back again to Mapalassie. The people at Mapalassie say that their ancestors belonged
to KAMISA's matrilineal kin but retreated to Likoma when the
Ngoni began to raid into Tongaland—unlike KAMISA himself who
took shelter in MANKHAMBIRA's stockade. When the wars were
over KAMISA[1] went to Likoma because 'he remembered his *abali*
[kin] who had gone there and he wanted them to come back',
which they did.

The latest arrivals from Likoma are Albert (Map. D 4), and Jeni
(Map. D 7) and Nyamphande (Map. C 5). The last was born and
bred on Likoma where Ndazakale (Map. C 4), who says that she is
his cross-cousin,[2] met her and married her. Jeni and Albert were
both born in Tongaland but went to Likoma as children, grew
up and married there, and have recently returned to Mapalassie
where they now intend to stay. Foness (Map. C 2) was born in
Tongaland, in her father's village, but she went back to Likoma
where she lived until her husband died and then came to Mapalassie, about fifteen years ago. Thus we see that the bonds between
Mapalassie and Likoma are still strong and the contacts frequent
as indeed one might expect, considering that so many inhabitants
of Mapalassie, including Mussa the headman, were born there.
There may not necessarily be a causal connection between the
fact of Mussa's reticence or loss of memory as to his own descent,[3]
and the fact that he settled on KAMISA's land (which all acknowledge) and is now the leader of a separate village. In other words
this need not be an example of 'structural amnesia': but the least
one can say is that it is an interesting coincidence.

At Mulombwa it is said that at some time in the past KAMISA
had a 'brother' Mukhumpha who settled and lived on Likoma and

kinship ties between these islands and the Tonga, especially those by the
lakeshore.

[1] Not the present KAMISA but one of his predecessors: cf. p. 203, n. 2.

[2] See p. 233.

[3] Although he is old and deaf it still seems strange that he should not have
known who his mother or grandmother were, especially since he showed quite
a good grasp of kin relationships in other contexts. I never managed to elicit
much information on this point from other Mapalassie people, except that
Mzake and Lena were his 'sisters' without being told the exact relationship.

F

a 'sister' Nyankhata who settled and lived on Chizumulu. As no further details are known this seems nothing more than a rationalization of the already known fact that there are links, of kinship or otherwise, between KAMISA and those two islands. There are no recent and frequent 'foreign' contacts at Mulombwa such as we saw at Chinyafwa and Mapalassie. I have good reasons for assuming that Nyambayaya (Mul. B 22) and Nyajula (Mul. B 32), who are both very old women, originally came from a place outside Tongaland, somewhere to the west, and that they came to their present village as slaves. The main characteristic of the status of a slave is his comparative isolation: he is cut off from the group of kin from whom the freeman expects and receives support.[1] The Tonga say that such a person is 'alone', i.e. he has nobody to back him up, or in Tonga idiom, 'has nobody behind him',[2] *viz.* no maternal relatives. This is illustrated by Nyali's remark that he wanted to show the paternal relatives of his sister's children at Deep Bay that the children do have a maternal uncle, lest the paternal relatives might think that the children 'come from nowhere'.

In Kamanga village there are no signs of foreign immigration to any significant degree. Both Apakhati (Kam. C 1) and Chiwato (Kam. C 12) claim relationship through their maternal grandfathers with KANGOMA who was one of the great warleaders in the stockade of MANKHAMBIRA. At Mzenga village, too, there are no kinship relations with other tribes except for the descendants of Chindoko (Mz. C 4) who are still in the village.

These 'foreign' links are not a matter of sentimental attachments only; they have practical aspects, too. For instance, Nyali considered his sister's daughter and son at Deep Bay as possibilities for filling a gap in his dominant matrilineage at Chinyafwa. By bringing his sister Lucy and his mother's sister Nyamphato to his Tonga village he was trying to build up a following with these two women, not only as individual followers, but also as mothers of other potential resident matrilineage members. At Mapalassie the descendants of Mzake also hope to strengthen their position with the support of Albert who recently came over from Likoma. Before Albert's arrival there were only female descendants of

[1] See p. 254 on slaves.
[2] This phrase is generally accompanied by a gesture of the speaker of pointing at his own back.

Mzake at Mapalassie as all the male descendants had gone abroad.[1]
KAMISA, too, drew on his matrikin on Likoma as followers. But it
seems that by doing so he also let in the Trojan horse, because
Mussa and his Likoma people are now in the process of separating
themselves from KAMISA, and taking with them the land on which
they are living and which was given them by KAMISA.

The Tonga can afford to attract immigrants from outside
Tongaland because their resources of land, water and firewood
are more than adequate. It so happens that these resources are
inadequate or at least scarcer and not as evenly distributed among
many of the neighbouring tribes. The Likoma people moreover
have even fewer local opportunities than the Tonga for earning
cash by casual labour for paying tax or other purposes. Although
there are not many openings for casual labour in Tongaland there
are at least the Vizara and Chombe rubber estates, the Boma and,
till 1953, the various undertakings of the Colonial Development
Corporation. All these casual labour opportunities happen to be
within commuting distance from Greater Kamisa. I once found at
Mapalassie two young boys from Likoma who had come over for
a few months to earn some cash. They were staying with relatives
whilst working at Vizara. When they had collected enough
money for a few pieces of clothing and some ready cash they
returned to Likoma.

Marriage and Inter-Village Cohesion

There are many kinship ties which stretch across the hamlet or
village boundaries of localized matrilineages, and even across
tribal boundaries. Every person is the centre of a set of patrilateral and matrilateral kinship ties radiating over large areas and
intersecting with similar sets of ties radiating from different
centres. The contacts between individuals, hamlets and villages
which are generally based upon or rationalized as kinship bonds
vary in intensity according to geographical propinquity. The
closer the interacting units live together, the more frequent and
varied the contacts.

A regular point of contact between two hamlets, either within
the same village or in different villages, is a married woman who
lives virilocally but maintains her ties with the hamlet from which
she married. Obviously the distance between a woman's marital

[1] 'Abroad' in this book means 'outside Tongaland'.

village and her home village affects the extent of her contact with
her home village. Nyalongwe (Map. B 12) who came from near
Bandawe (about 20 miles or a day's walk south of Mapalassie),
and Nyamphande (Map. C 5) who comes from Likoma, do not
go home as often as, say, Nyamwale (Chin. F 5) who comes from
Mapalassie (Map. C 10), or Hope (Map. C 13) who lives only
about two hours away from Mapalassie. The last two women are
often seen at Mapalassie. Many of the married women, and especially those who married nearby, cultivate a garden at their
home village as well as the garden which every woman works in
her husband's hamlet. They do this so that they will not be without a garden in case of divorce, and also to give their children a
stronger claim if they should want to settle in their mother's
village later. The fact that his mother never had a garden at
Mapalassie makes it more difficult for Ndazakale (Map. C 4), who
has moved out of his father's village, to settle at Mapalassie.[1] For
children have a prior claim on the *chikweta* (garden which is still
in use) or the *masara* (garden which is no longer being tilled) of
their parents. Children may claim a garden from either father or
mother or both.

Even if married women do not hoe a garden in their home
village or go there regularly for visits, they never lose contact
with their homes.[2] In all the crises in a woman's life she will get in
touch with her home either by going there or by having a message
sent there to her own kin who can then come and visit her. The
crisis may be illness, a quarrel with her husband, birth or death of a
child.[3] And conversely her people at home will keep their 'child
who is married somewhere else' informed of the crises at home, so
that the woman can attend funerals, births and illnesses there. In
this way each of two villages not only keeps well informed about
events in the other village, but the woman's kin watch carefully

[1] See Case 10.
[2] Although in most cases a woman's home village is her natal village this is
not necessarily the case. It may be the village where she grew up or the village
where her mother went at a later age. Again it may be her father's village as in
the case of Nyaulanda and her sisters (Mz. C 11). That is why I continue to use
the word 'home' which is admittedly rather vague: but it does indicate that
every woman, except a slave wife, has a place outside her husband's hamlet or
village to which she *belongs* and which for her carries the same values as the
English equivalent 'home'.
[3] See Case 9, p. 149.

what happens in the woman's marital village to see if it is likely to affect the woman or her offspring. Thus their interest in her bride-wealth—or that of her daughters—gives the patrikin and matrikin of the married woman a vital interest in the affairs of the village where she is married.

In general[1] no woman, nor indeed any person, is ever lost sight of by either his patrikin or his matrikin. But this is most readily observable in the case of women, because it is especially the woman who, by marrying out, is often physically removed from the proximity of those who are most likely to protect her interests and, by extension, the interests of her children, who only partly belong to their father's village. The very facts of a woman's removal from the village which represents her greatest emotional and legal security, and her comparative isolation in a 'hostile' [2] environment, are of vital importance. Her comparatively defence-less position in her husband's village directs the attention of at least two groups of people to her marital village: her matrikin and her patrikin. And since the last two groups of people generally live in separate villages, the virilocal wife's 'plight', which needs scrutiny and support, links three villages sharing at least one com-mon focus of interest. Each of these three villages contains wives drawn from several other villages, and each is at the same time the 'home' of wives who have married out into different villages. Even if later a woman returns with her children to her home vil-lage, her ex-marital village will still have a special tie with her home village. This tie exists through her children whose paternal village it is: part of the bridewealth may go there in the case of daughters, or contributions to the bridewealth can be expected from it in the case of sons. Although there are special advantages attached to membership of a matrilineage, paternity too is of great social importance.[3]

[1] There are exceptions, e.g. people of slave extraction or foreigners from distant tribes: see Chapter V on slaves.

[2] Women very often talk as if they consider themselves in uncongenial sur-roundings in their husbands' villages where people treat them as 'only a daugh-ter-in-law'. The women complain that a husband, backed by his kin, would exploit and treat his wife as a slave and consider her children as completely in their power. But, fortunately, so women argue, the woman has her relatives 'behind her' as protectors to whom she can run; or she can send for a brother to come and help her. Cf. Case 9, p. 149.

[3] See Chapter IV.

Local Association and Kinship Bonds

Marriage creates bonds which extend beyond village or other geographical boundaries; it creates a common focus for individuals or groups who may be spread over a wide area. But there are also activities or events which are shared by groups of villages or individuals because they are all situated in the same area; they create bonds of local affinity. One such event is a funeral, which most adults of the neighbouring villages attend. Many of them sing and sleep together at the lyke-wake[1] on the night following the death; and they help in washing the corpse, carrying it to the grave and preparing the grave. They also attend the inquest[2] and other legal discussions following a death. Besides those who attend because they live in the same locality and knew the dead person, the matrikin and the patrikin in more distant villages also have to be informed so that they can take part in the funeral or at least the 'shaving' ceremony.[3] Here again the exception is the case of the dead slave whose social personality tends to be extinguished at death. A slave's principal function in the village is his or her procreation on behalf of the lineage group in whose care and power he or she is.

A wedding[4] is another occasion which attracts the inhabitants within the neighbourhood of the village. A big wedding with its attractions of girls, gambling, beef and dancing is an event all like to attend. The catchment area of a wedding is much larger than that of a funeral because a wedding draws not only the people (mostly young people) from a wider area around the bride-groom's village, but also many people from the bride's village attend. A wedding is important in that it brings together people

---

[1] Watch kept at night over dead body: see Oxford English Dictionary.

[2] See p. 109.

[3] At the end of the inquest and legal discussions and as a sign of their conclusion some of the closer relatives of the dead person are shaven: see p. 109.

[4] The *zowara* is a big affair with the bride in white and many of the guests in their finery. A bull is slaughtered and the meat sold to wedding guests together with portions of rice or cassava porridge and tea. There is dance music by an accordion player with band and often traditional dancing and drumming as well. An important attraction is the gambling with playing-cards called *juga*, a corruption of 'joker'. A much less ambitious wedding is the *mtimba* in which the bride generally does not wear white. It is the lack of beef which deprives the *mtimba* of a *zowara's* main attraction and this results in a much smaller attendance and hence the absence of the other activities such as gambling and often dancing.

PLATE 2. (*a*) A *malepenga* band on its way to a competition. The dancers wear white and have hats with ostrich plumes. The drums are modelled on the European military drum, with a skin on either side

(*b*) Another band, practising. Note the trumpet-like *malepenga* made of gourds with holes covered by membranes made from spiders' nests

from many different localities and may thus produce lasting contacts or friendships—among the Tonga, too, weddings may beget weddings. But the most important links between the bride's and the bridegroom's villages and kin are created at the marriage discussions preceding the wedding.

Apart from these interactions between neighbouring villages which are occasioned by and centred on some specifically organized activity, there are also casual visits between friends and relatives who live in close proximity.

Fishing, too, is a local rather than a kinship activity. Most fishing activities are centred on the village, whose menfolk share one net-shelter which is also their *mphara* (men's gathering-place). Individuals who live inland in another village may be regular visitors to some net-shelter, often on the basis of friendship with one of the members of the lakeshore village.[1]

The activities discussed so far bring people together and make them interact on a local, rather than on a kinship, basis. None of them is associated with specifically organized groups and none of them draws its participants from a prescribed area.

Although Administrative units, such as Administrative villages or Native Authority areas and courts, are clearly defined *local* units, they are not corporate units; there are no occasions on which all members of, say, an Administrative village act as a corporate body. Nor do any of these *units* as such create ties between its inhabitants.

There is, however, one activity, the *malepenga*[2] dance, which is clearly organized on a territorial basis.

Each dance group, called a *boma*,[3] comprises the men (mostly young) from a number of villages which are often separated by a river from the group of villages comprising another *boma*. This territorial division is rigidly maintained: if a boy lives in the area of one *boma* but would prefer to play in a neighbouring *boma*, he is

[1] See also p. 282.
[2] This dance is widespread over the whole of the Northern Province of Nyasaland and possibly also known in the Central and Southern Provinces. In the Northern Province it is known as *malepenga* to Africans and Europeans alike and I retain the word. I do not know its derivation or whether the dance is called after the instrument or *vice versa*; a *malepenga* is a trumpet-like instrument made from a hollowed-out gourd.
[3] Derived from but not to be confused with Boma, i.e. Administrative Headquarters.

told: 'Either you come and live here and you can dance in our *boma*, or you stay where you are and you help your own village in their *boma*.' The villages constituting one *boma* may be strongly opposed to one another in other respects. For instance, the village of Thoro[1] is a stronghold of the Phiri, and as such the political adversary of the Kapunda Banda villages surrounding it. Thoro and some Kapunda Banda villages nevertheless constitute one *boma*. The *malepenga* dance is a compromise between mime and group-dancing of men only imitating infantry drill. It has some similarities with the *kalela* dance of the Copperbelt in Northern Rhodesia:[2] participants create in the form of play the political offices, occupations and professions of the Europeans which on the whole are not open to Africans. Dance groups (*boma*) enter into competition with both neighbouring and distant groups.

Although the significance of local contiguity is not always as obvious as in the case of the *malepenga* dance group with its explicitly territorial organization, it is nevertheless an important factor in most activities and relationships. One of the themes of this book is the continuous interaction of kinship and local ties in most social and political situations. I will describe how the relative importance of these two factors may vary from one situation to another or, indeed, within the context of one and the same situation, depending on the respective positions and aims of the individuals or groups concerned.[3]

Distance tends to affect inter-personal relationships. Every Tonga is the centre of manifold patrilateral and matrilateral kinship bonds. These in turn link him to many other people who live spread over a large area—some of them live well beyond the area within which the individual moves in the daily business of living. Frequent contact with local kinsmen on the other hand deepens the kinship bond despite the fact that at the same time it increases the chances of friction. The Tonga do not concentrate their attention exclusively on local kinsmen, for there are situations in which bonds with more distant kinsmen will be useful. For instance, a traveller will call upon kinsmen *en route* for shelter

---

[1] See Case 14, p. 223.   [2] See Mitchell (1957).
[3] See e.g. Case 9, pp. 149 *seq*. There one kin group (the Mzake group) in a dispute at Mapalassie takes up a position which alternates between identification, on a village basis, with the interests of the collateral but rival Lena lineage, and support of the interests of people of a distant village on a kinship basis.

and food. Labour migrants do not necessarily choose their travelling companions from local kinsmen, and once in the labour centres they often rely on relatives for information about jobs, or help during unemployment or illness. Similar help may also be sought in Tongaland by people who live a long way from their place of employment but have relatives who live in a village nearby. When Meya, one of the small daughters of Nelly (Map. C 14), had to undergo a course of treatment at Chinteche hospital she went to stay with Adi (Map. D 9) at the latter's husband's village near Chinteche. Similarly, Chiwato's (Kam. C 12) two sons of his present marriage are staying with their father's divorced first wife who lives near their school at Bandawe.

The lack of relatives at strategic points may sometimes be overcome by institutionalized 'friendship' or *ubwezi* but not every 'friendship' [1] is entered upon solely for economic or political reasons. For instance, two Tonga who meet for the first time abroad may seal their casual friendship with *ubwezi*. I was told that they then inform their respective kinsmen at home and urge them to visit one another. On the other hand Tonga say that people who live in the hills without relatives by the lakeshore on whom they can depend for fish, will try to overcome this handicap by creating a quasi-kin relationship through 'friendship'. I was not able to verify this.

Such calls for assistance from geographically distant kinsmen or quasi-kinsmen show that a person's needs cannot all be satisfied within the area where he habitually moves. An even more significant example of this was the case mentioned above (see Case 1) of Nyali who had to go outside Tongaland in search of a successor to his title at Chinyafwa. I recorded two other similar cases. The one concerns the GURU title of Kawiya village,[2] and the other the KAMBAWE title of Mzenga village. In each case the successor had been called from another village where he had been living with

---

[1] *Mbwezi* (pl. *abwezi*) in general closely corresponds to our 'friend' with all its gradations from casual to emotional attachment. Friendship in its specific sense of a 'pact' will be written thus: 'friendship'. I actually observed only one pact of 'friendship', and I received reliable information about two other 'friendships'; I do not know whether other instances of *ubwezi* about which I heard referred to 'friendship' or not. 'Friendship' bonds do not appear in reality to be as important and permanent—at the present day, at any rate—as the Tonga say they are and should be.

[2] See p. 64.

his patrilateral kin. The KAMBAWE succession is described in Case 2.

CASE 2: *KAMBAWE* CALLED FROM HIS PATRILOCALITY[1]

Kamoti at Mzenga (Mz. D 8) told me that when his father Yaphet's predecessor died a long time ago, there was nobody at Mzenga who could succeed him. So the people from Mzenga went to Chipaika village[2] where Yaphet was living with his father NGOMBO who is a well-known headman. NGOMBO's wife Alikita (Mz. B 5) 'came from Mzenga'.[3] This is Kamoti's story: 'When the people from Mzenga came to NGOMBO to ask for his son Yaphet to succeed to the name as there was nobody left at Mzenga, NGOMBO said: "All right, you go." When afterwards Yaphet visited Chipaika village, NGOMBO would say: "My son has come. He is now no longer Yaphet but he has the *ufumu* [headmanship] of KAMBAWE." All people then knew that he, Yaphet, was indeed a *munangwa* (freeman), on both sides. The people in NGOMBO's village knew of course that Yaphet's father was a freeman and the fact that Yaphet had been called to an *ufumu* on his mother's side meant that his mother was free too. If NGOMBO had refused to let Yaphet go, then the people of Mzenga would have asked NGOMBO: "Why do you refuse? Is he not *munangwa*? And if he is *munangwa* here [i.e. in NGOMBO's village] how can you refuse to let him go to his mother's village? Would *you* want *your* house to die out? You must let him go: it will give you honour too."[4]' Thus Yaphet went to live at Mzenga where he had never lived before. Kamoti and his brother Godfrey were both born at Chipaika before Yaphet moved to Mzenga

---

[1] See Genealogy No. XIV.

[2] Chipaika is about six hours' walk from Mzenga. Especially in the hilly and rocky parts of Tongaland mileage does not give an accurate idea of the real distance for the Tonga who still inter-communicate almost entirely by walking due to lack of roads or paths which can be cycled. I therefore give the walking time wherever it is appropriate.

[3] *Watua ku Mzenga*, literally: she comes from Mzenga. The present tense implies: Mzenga is her and her uterine descendants' home. Consequently when she is said to 'come from Mzenga' that does not necessarily mean that she was actually at Mzenga at the time of her marriage; it may merely mean that Mzenga is her matrilocal 'home'. For NGOMBO see also p. 296.

[4] Note the importance of having a home 'on both sides', that is, to be 'free on both sides'. Cf. Nyali's remark to the same effect, pp. 49–50; see also p. 237.

where he died. Their mother Egenes came from Chiwana[1] and she also died at Mzenga. Godfrey has taken up residence at Chiwana but Kamoti intends to stay at Mzenga.

Another example of the pull of kinship asserting itself against local relationships is the departure from Mzenga, in 1952, of the group of seminal descendants of Amuziteni (Mz. C 10), who were living at Mzenga, and moved to Chalaunda.[2] Chalaunda is the patrilocality of Amuziteni. As far as I could make out Amuziteni was born in the stockade of CHINYENTHA by the mouth of the Luweya[3] where many of the people around Chalaunda took refuge during the Ngoni raids. Amuziteni grew up, lived and died at Mzenga; all his seminal descendants, who moved away in 1952, were born there and had lived there all their lives. I have not been able to discover why Amuziteni should have been living at Mzenga which is certainly not his matrilocality. It seems likely that his status at Mzenga was that of a slave. Nor do I know the reason why they all moved when they did. It is possible that their move is connected with the strife and discord which are breaking up the unity of the village and which arise from the dispute over the succession to the KAMBAWE title. The quarrels started before KAMBAWE (Yaphet) died as an old man in 1953 and are still causing bitter and open enmity in the village.[4] The fact remains that Amuziteni's seminal descendants all moved together[5] from Mzenga, where they seem to have had the status of slaves, to Chalaunda where they could claim the status of village sons.

Apart from the moves of Mussa and his matrilineage[6] and the group of Amuziteni's seminal descendants, I have no records of such large-scale moves of localized kin groups. I have however observed or collected reliable evidence of individuals or a single household moving from one village to another or from one hamlet in the village to another hamlet within the same village. Most of these moves involved widows returning from their marital to their own village or hamlet. The relatives of a widow's

---

[1] By the lakeshore and about a day's walk from Mzenga.

[2] Chalaunda is about a day's walk from Mzenga and at the inland edge of the flat strip by the lakeshore and south-west from Chinteche.

[3] See van Velsen (1959*a*), pp. 113–17.   [4] See pp. 195 *seq.*

[5] Including Ros (Mz. D 20), the wife of Lenox; she died at Chalaunda in 1955.   [6] See pp. 50–1.

late husband, that is, the patrilateral kin of the dead man's children, always try to keep the widow in her virilocal village, which is the patrilocality of her children. But the widow's matrikin want their kinswoman and her children to return to their matrilocality.[1] In the majority of the cases the widow does return to her home village.[2] The desire of widows to return 'home' is so strong that it is also found in women who married into a village which is only a few hundred yards from their own, or who married into a different hamlet within the same village.

Elinara (Map. B 14) and Lizzy (Map. C 16) are examples of this. Elinara was married to Yakobi (Chin. E 4) at Chinyafwa but at his death returned to Mapalassie. Lizzy was married to Msorowa (Map. C 23) and at his death returned from his hamlet (hut 2a) to her own hamlet (hut 6), a distance of fifty yards across a trickling stream; both hamlets are in Mapalassie.

This pull of the matrilocal village is also felt by children living patrilocally, particularly after their father has died. For instance, Ndazakale (Map. C 4) and Abandolo (Mul. C 7) both moved from their fathers' villages to their mothers' soon after their fathers' deaths.[3]

The reverse can also be observed: the pull of a person's patrilocal village. At Mapalassie Nyankhamoza (Map. C 7), Nyadalo (C 9) and other 'mothers'[4] of James (Map. C 12), who has been away in South Africa for many years, became worried about James's daughter Jenetti who lives with her mother in another village not far away. Jenetti had had a nasty ulcer on her leg and had been ailing for some time. Her 'mothers' (Nyadalo, etc.) were saying that the child was being neglected in her mother's village, and that nobody took the trouble to find her the right medicine, and that she really ought to be fetched to Mapalassie so that *they* could show how one should care for one's sick child. They also upbraided John (Map. C 11): they said that as he was a particularly close friend of James he ought to show more interest in the girl, give her some money to buy some tea and sugar and help

---

[1] Cf. Case 9, pp. 149 *seq.*   [2] See Table VI and p. 113.

[3] It is only a coincidence that Abandolo (Mul. C 7) moved to Chiberi village (a few hours' walk) which Ndazakale left to come to Mapalassie. See also the case of Waison who is planning to leave his father's village in order to settle matrilocally at Chinyafwa; p. 102.

[4] For explanation of this classification see p. 143.

her with medicine. They told John that if necessary he should bring her to Mapalassie, or at least help her to 'remember' Mapalassie by emphasizing that she would always be welcome there and be sure of assistance. In fact, John told me that he had already agreed with Jenetti's relatives that, as soon as he had a wife living with him, he would pay them the *ndrama za kulela* (the money for the upbringing[1]) and then Jenetti would come and live at Mapalassie.[2] John considers it his duty towards his 'brother' James to get James's child to Mapalassie where she might have been living now if James had not been abroad; James used to live at Mapalassie before he left for South Africa.

Although it is very unlikely that Jenetti will ever move from her mother's village to Mapalassie—especially as her father, James, is not even there—the incident shows that the patrilateral pull is always present. In the cases of Mary of Chinyafwa,[3] KAMBAWE (Yaphet), Amuziteni's descendants, Ndazakale, etc., the pull of kinship was strong enough because people did leave one village and went to another.

Most Tonga have a choice between a number of villages where they can settle, that is, they can in fact transfer their loyalty and domicile from one village to another. Their choice is influenced not only by kinship considerations but also by economic, political and other factors. For instance, Kamoti at Mzenga said that although his brother had changed his domicile from Mzenga (his father's village) to his mother's village, he himself preferred to stay because Mzenga is the place where he grew up and where he knows the people. Although he did not mention it, other motivating factors are that Kamoti as a church elder and as a councillor in KABUNDULI's court occupies a position of influence and power which he owes to a certain extent to being the son of the late headman KAMBAWE (Yaphet). Moreover as a councillor he has a regular income of £2 10s. per month. He also grows tobacco for sale and engages in petty trade. He would lose all these advantages by moving to his mother's village: he might carry on his trade there but he would not be able to grow tobacco.[4] Sons often

---

[1] See p. 104.
[2] I do not know what happened in the end because this incident took place shortly before I left Tongaland.
[3] See Case 1, p. 48.
[4] Tobacco is grown only in the hills, not near the lakeshore.

seem reluctant to leave their father's village where they have grown up and where they have become members of a local community apart from being members of a kinship group.

The present GURU was also called from his paternal village to his maternal uncle's village to succeed to the latter's name; his paternal village is about a day's walk south of his present village. He often complained that he did not like it at Kawiya where he lives now, because he felt alone as he had not grown up with the people there. This was partly his rationalization of another feeling of loneliness: he lived with only his two childless wives, the sister of his senior wife with her children, and an aged barren 'sister' of his own. His senior wife and her sister were foreigners of the Bisa tribe. At one time he had had great hopes that he would be able to persuade a uterine nephew and 'heir apparent' to come and settle with him. He built him a good house in anticipation and, possibly, as an additional attraction; but the nephew never came. A man and especially a headman depends for his influence and authority in the village in the first place on the prestige and support he derives from his own hamlet and/or from close relatives such as sisters, nephews and children. It is therefore clear why GURU felt lonely: he lacked a strong hamlet of his own. Nor did he enjoy powerful backing from other kin, because he was the only member of the GURU dominant matrilineage in the village amongst several sons and daughters of the late GURU whose status was that of village children.[1]

Struggle for Dependants

There are two main factors which influence the establishment and maintenance of personal relationships between Tonga: locality and kinship. Preference for a particular locality may influence a man's choice of the kinship bonds which he wants to utilize and manipulate; or, to put it differently, preference for a particular locality and, for instance, its economic advantages (like Kamoti's preference for Mzenga) can be expressed in terms of kinship. These two principles of association are therefore not necessarily opposed. Kinship relationships have a multiplex

[1] In Chapter V, I discuss the often strained relationship between a nephew who has succeeded to the headmanship and the patrilocally resident children of the late headman: see p. 237.

character and may be the basis for a variety of activities.[1] One of the elements in the multiplex relationships based on kinship is the potential bond of common residence: although a man can exploit kinship bonds for many ends, one of the most important of these is to persuade his kin to settle with him in his hamlet or village, thus swelling the number of his dependants. I call that aspect of a kinship bond which is expressed in and reinforced by common residence 'local (or residential) allegiance'.

In later chapters I will argue that although matrilineal and other kinship ties form a normal basis for co-operation between individuals and groups however far apart they may live, the most frequent contacts covering the widest field of action take place within the localized kin group, which is generally the localized matrilineage. It is within this group that kinship bonds are utilized to the full, especially in the political field. This kin group is also the starting point for the man who wants to be a *fumu* (headman or chief), that is, who desires his own village of which his own matrilineage will form the nucleus. Hence the attempts of hamlet leaders and village headmen to persuade kinsmen to settle with them. And in general they receive kindly and eagerly any newcomer to hamlet or village, irrespective of whether they are patrilateral or matrilateral kin;[2] as stated before, in theory people are free to settle with any group of kinsmen.

Kamoti at Mzenga once said: 'A man with a lot of money will have a big village because a lot of people will follow him, both sons and nephews.' It is not only money which attracts followers and thus increases the prestige of village and headman which in turn tends to attract followers. There are other factors too, for example, proximity to the lake, the main road and other amenities, and the status and personality of the headman. We have already discussed many of these, and I will discuss other factors below in relation to the mobility and residence of individuals.

A Tonga headman or aspiring headman need not depend solely on the procreative capacity of the village to build up a following: he has many *abali*[3] living in all parts of Tongaland and abroad

---

[1] See Chapter IV.

[2] Ndazakale's difficulties in trying to settle at his matrilocality may be explained by the imminent struggle for succession at Mapalassie, see Case 10, p. 190.

[3] This Tonga term and its English equivalent 'relatives' share the same vagueness and lack of precision.

who may one day come and live in his village. This speculation
about a kinsman's future residence applies especially to those who
are working abroad. Two or more villages may be equally confident that a certain labour migrant will settle with them and not
in another village. The man may be expected to settle in one
village because he used to live there before he went abroad and is
still on their tax register. Another village may also expect him to
settle there on his return because it is his matrilocality, whilst the
village where he used to live is the village of his father who has
died in the meanwhile. Labour migrants are considered villagers
in absentia and continue to count as potential cultivators of land.
Conversely labour migrants (even those who have been away for
many years) expect their kin in Tongaland to be the guardians of
the village and of Tonga society in general and to hold the land
in trust for them.

The obverse of one village attracting kin is another village
losing them. A village is always in danger of losing some of its
members, particularly those who live patrilocally and widows in
their late husband's village.[1] Although these people, who are village sons and daughters-in-law respectively, have no authority
in the village, the owners of the village are careful not to rub
this in, and generally treat them as equals in order to avoid giving
them any reason for departure. Kamoti, who is a village son at
Mzenga, once told me about a quarrel he had had with Waison
(Mz. D 18) who belongs to one of the two matrilineages at
Mzenga.[2] He said that he told Waison: 'Do you think that you
can treat me as if I were just anybody? Don't you know that
I am KAJANDI[3] and that I have my mother's village where I can
go if I want to? And if I go your village will be reduced to
nothing.' But Kamoti did not leave Mzenga, for reasons stated
above.

A good deal depends therefore on whether the headman, with
the support of other members of the dominant lineage, manages
to keep the village together; and this again depends on his personality, his authority in the village or hamlet. Mzenga, which has
been the scene of open disunity and strife for some years now,

[1] Cf. the case of Amuziteni at Mzenga and other instances on p. 61.
[2] See Case 11, p. 195.
[3] According to Kamoti this is a title which he could claim in his mother's
village. For a more detailed discussion of the question of titles, see p. 211.

shows definite signs of slow disintegration. It is more than likely that the departure of Amuziteni's descendants was connected with the atmosphere of open conflict. Wellington's (Mz. D 26) adultery with Lede (Mz. E 1) immediately became part of the succession quarrel;[1] and it ended up, to everybody's surprise, in KABUNDULI's court. Here was a married woman herself (and not her cuckolded husband) suing her lover in a public court although she was not even pregnant and although both lived in the same village. All these features were very unusual for an adultery case and many people in and outside the village, including Kamoti, commented upon these strange happenings, and expressed shock at this airing of dirty washing outside the village! People were saying: 'See now what happens in a village without *chimango* (unity) and spoilt by *sanji* (jealousy, strife).[2] Ah, you wait: soon there won't be anybody left in this village.' As a matter of fact, Wellington, who was at a mission school, was expelled from school on account of his adultery and, as often happens, to get away from it all he went to Johannesburg. The last I heard of Lede was that she wanted to go to Chipaika where her paternal grandmother, also called Lede (Mz. C 1), came from. Her 'younger father' Samu (Mz. D 3) who had just come back from Rhodesia returned there again within one or two months of the court case. The other men in Samu's hamlet, Tadeyo (Mz. D 1) and Akwenji (Mz. E 4), have also gone abroad: Akwenji came back again for a few months the following year. The fact that all the men in this hamlet are away is not necessarily exceptional but in this context it may have some significance because it often happens that a trip

[1] See Case 11, p. 195; Case 5, p. 98, and Genealogy II.

[2] *Chi-mango* is derived from *ku-manga*, to tie, and thus *chimango* is 'what is tied together' or unity. It is a very important concept and frequently used—its absence is a very serious state of affairs, one that is asking for trouble, as in this case. An even more important concept and a word that one may hear at least once a day is *sanji*. Tonga translate it as 'jealousy'; indeed, they have adopted the English adjective 'jealous' as a noun into their language. *Sanji* can also mean strife, undue ambition, in short any act or state of mind which may cause open tension and conflict between people. One might almost say that *sanji* also stands for conflict itself because when people observe or hear of a conflict or quarrel between other people their first reaction may be to shake their heads and say 'Sanji pe' (only jealousy). *Sanji* conveys a strong sense of opprobrium: '*sanji wabaya wanthu*', i.e. *sanji* kills people, *viz.* it is the end of everything. But the killing may also be meant literally because *sanji* is considered one of the main causes of sorcery.

G

abroad is considered the only escape from a difficult situation.[1] Also within a few months, Waison, who had only been back from South Africa a short time, suddenly died; and of course his death was ascribed to sorcery which is believed inevitably to accompany any such conflict. His widow, who might have stayed on, went back to her own village immediately after the 'shaving'.

The following case is another example of how strife within the village can lead to the departure of its members, particularly when there is no leader present to hold the village together.

CASE 3: CONFLICTS AT CHINYAFWA

Chinyafwa village at one stage was also in danger of losing its residents. When Nyali went to Southern Rhodesia in 1939, Chinyafwa had a fair population by Tonga standards; certainly it had more residents than there are now. Nyali stayed in Rhodesia until 1952 without a break and when he went home he found that the numbers had gone down considerably. This loss of people was partly due to death, but also to emigration without any compensating immigration. One of the people who left Chinyafwa and went to Usiska was Adamu (Chin. E 12) whose younger brother later followed him. Both belong to a junior matrilineage at Chinyafwa and in Tonga idiom they are therefore owners of the village (*weneko*) at Chinyafwa. Adamu used to have quarrels with Siddely (Chin. D 6) who lives patrilocally at Chinyafwa and is thus a son of the village. He also suffers another disadvantage: his mother was a Bisa slave, so that Siddely has no alternative home in Tongaland. But he could, of course, return to Usiska, his patrilocal home.[2] It seems that Adamu would say to Siddely: 'What are you doing here? You had better keep quiet, you have no authority in this place, you slave.' Whether he actually used these words I do not know, but this is the sort of thing he might have said if they had a quarrel. It would have been up to Yakobi (Chin. E 4) to smooth out the difficulties, but he was an ailing man at the time. And as one might expect in a situation like this when parties to a dispute are not or cannot be brought together, one of them moves out of the village. The reason why Adamu moved, rather than Siddely, although the former has

---

[1] Elton at Mulombwa (Mul. D 3), acting as KAMISA, had had a quarrel with some of the villagers. His reaction was: 'All right, I do not want to act as KAMISA any longer and I will go to Salisbury and get myself some nice clothes instead.' Here, too, a conflict over succession was in the background: see p. 207.

[2] See p. 48 and Case 8, p. 133.

the stronger claim at Chinyafwa, probably lies in the fact that Adamu and his brother had Siska fathers and would therefore be able to settle in their father's village. Although the same applies to Siddely, the difference is that Adamu and his brother have wives who are also from Usiska so that by going north they would not run the risk of losing their children, who in fact are with them in Usiska. Siddely, on the other hand, married a Tonga and the marriage, after about forty years, came to an end round about 1950. But even before the divorce his wife Nyasanga (Chin. D 7) had been living most of the time in her own village as Siddely spent most of his life working abroad. All the children of this marriage and many of the grandchildren are living with Nyasanga. Siddely has made many efforts to induce some of his children and/or grandchildren to settle with him but so far without avail.[1] If Siddely went to Usiska he would almost certainly forfeit any chance of having at least some of his progeny living with him. Siddely is now an old man of about seventy and in spite of the three daughters he has begotten and his twelve grandchildren he is still living alone— a great misfortune for a Tonga.[2] Siddely remarried, this time with a woman from Likoma, but there are no children of this marriage and it is most unlikely that there ever will be any to make up for his loss of the children of his previous marriage. He is a somewhat cantankerous and quarrelsome old man which may well be the effect of this frustration and of the fact that in Tonga eyes he has not much status as he really *is* a slave, as Adamu said. As for the quarrel between Siddely and Adamu, it is likely that in the absence of a pacifying agent it came to such a pitch that one or the other had to move. Since Siddely would lose everything if he moved out, he was determined to stay and it was Adamu who emigrated.

Nyali (Chin. F 4) blames the exodus on Siddely (Chin. D 6): he

[1] When a few years ago one of his daughters died in Johannesburg Siddely, in spite of his age and the cost of the journey, immediately went to Johannesburg to collect his grandchildren and bring them back to Tongaland. By thus showing that he loves his children and grandchildren and that he knows his duty as a father and grandfather he obviously hopes to oblige his wife and his children and to prove that they would not be neglected if they came to live with him.

[2] The Tonga express their horror of such a prospect by saying: 'A person without children dies of jiggers', or 'Who is to close your eyes and your mouth when you die?' Although other people too can take the jigger parasites out of your feet or close your eyes and mouth they are duties ideally performed by one's own children.

says that he himself would have been able to prevent it if he had been there. Whether that is so or not, the fact is that he immediately started his drive to get some of his *matrikin* back to Chinyafwa.[1] And although he intended to go back to Rhodesia he has given up the idea for the time being because he is afraid that if he goes whilst Siddely is about ('He cannot keep the peace and look after the village') soon nobody would be left at Chinyafwa and certainly nobody of his own dominant lineage.

The attempts Chimboza (Map. B 1) says he made in the middle of the 1930's to get his father Mussa back from Que Que in Southern Rhodesia to Mapalassie should be seen in the same light. Mussa had gone away to work in Rhodesia soon after his arrival with the others from Likoma and he had been abroad for about fifteen or twenty years without a break. It is possible that there was trouble brewing between Lena's and Mzake's matrilineages over the leadership[2]—the sort of strife which might easily lead to residents leaving the village. Mussa was the only one who would have authority over both the matrilineages. At that time the two lineages had not yet been re-linked by the cross-cousin marriage of Ziba (Map. C 3) and Nelly (Map. C 14); Mussa himself was the first link, since he is the 'brother' of both Lena and Mzake.

It is because of this fear that a village may become empty or hamlets (the potential nuclei of new villages) disappear, that Tonga men do not like to leave a hamlet or a village in the charge of women only. It is true that the women in the village have great influence and that their support is of vital importance to the headman. For the women are the ones who really produce the children whilst 'the men only beget them', as the Tonga often say.[3] This crucial importance of the women is illustrated by such expressions as '*ako choko, ako wana*' ('get hold of the widow and you have the children', although this is not always so because 'children are free'); and in practice it was illustrated by the trouble Nyali took to get his sister's daughter Mary (Chin. G 3) from Deep Bay to Chinyafwa.[4] The importance of the women is enhanced by the fact that many men are away in employment abroad: women may find themselves in the position of guarding interests which otherwise would have been looked after by male relatives. For instance,

---

[1] See Case 1, p. 48.   [2] See Case 9, p. 149.
[3] Cf. Nyamwale's remark to that effect in Case 9, para. 26.
[4] See Case 1.

the marriage of a brother who has gone abroad and left his wife behind may be left in the care of a sister; one often comes across women suing their sisters-in-law in the courts, on behalf of their brother, for adultery or desertion.

However the influence of the women is generally exerted informally, behind the scenes, because it is the men who are formally the carriers of authority. One is often told that such-and-such a woman is the 'real owner of the name' but it is very rare for her also to be the executive of that title; this is left to a man who 'only walks' (*watenda waka*), i.e. he is the one who represents the title in the courts or on other public occasions.[1]

Hence Tonga labour migrants try to organize their trips abroad so that there will always be at least one man left per hamlet, who is expected to represent in public the interests of the hamlet. Moreover a man is more likely to get fish for the women of his hamlet than the women themselves; indeed those hamlets with women only (e.g. Elinara, Map. B 14) generally complain of their lot in terms of not having fish rather than in terms of being without a male spokesman.[2]

Thus labour migrants are reluctant to leave their hamlets

TABLE V

Average Number of Men per Hamlet

Village	No. of men in the village	No. of hamlets
Mapalassie	8	8
Mulombwa	13	9
Mtomba	1	1
Kamanga	4	3
Chinyafwa	3	5
Mzenga	5	4
Total	34	30

[1] Cf. pp. 216 *seq.*: the KAMISA-ship at Mulombwa rests securely with Nyachenga but she never acts as KAMISA in public and the executive duties have been carried out by a succession of men of whom Elton is the latest. See also p. 218: Nyali always talks about Mary as 'the owner of Chinyafwa [or: the name]', but he also brought her brother Gorogo down from Deep Bay because he will be what one might call the executive officer of the matrilineage, as Nyali is now.

[2] See p. 14 and Case 9, p. 149, where Nyamwale complains about the absence of male spokesmen.

entirely without men. Table V shows a total of 34 men for thirty hamlets. A comparison of the village plan with the genealogy also shows that the men are fairly evenly spread over the hamlets. This policy is often explicitly stated by the Tonga. Ziba at Mapalassie (Map. C 3) frequently complained that he was obliged to go about in old clothes whilst his brothers and the other men of the village were earning a lot of money with which they could buy decent clothing. The answer to the obvious question why he, too, did not go away, was that he had often expressed the wish to do so, but that both the people in the village and his relatives abroad did not want him to go, because who would then look after the women and the village? His brothers said that they would help him with money to compensate him for loss of earnings, because Ziba was helping them by keeping the village together. 'But,' Ziba would add, 'those were only promises to keep me here—they rarely send me any money or clothes or sometimes only a little bit.' [1]

Albert (Map. D 4), who is going to settle at Mapalassie, gave as his reason the fact that 'there are no men left at Mapalassie'. There are of course several men present at Mapalassie and even the founder of the village, Mussa, is still alive. But what Albert really meant, although he did not say it explicitly, was that there are no males of Mzake's (Map. A 3) matrilineage who can act as spokesmen, [2] because all the men now in the village belong either to the collateral matrilineage of Lena (Map. A 3) or they are only village sons at Mapalassie, e.g. John and Peter. The latter are patrilaterally linked to the village and their political status in the village is that of 'sons' (*wana*) of the village or, as I have called them, 'village sons'.

It is noteworthy that it is the hamlet which is taken as the basis for the organization of the export of labour: the aim is to have at least one adult male per hamlet and not per village. A Tonga likes to think of his hamlet as the nucleus of a potential village. [3]

[1] A frequent complaint of those who stay at home 'to look after the village' and the reason why the male members often take it in turns to go abroad. Ziba, however, has never been away at all, while many of his male kin have been away practically all their adult lives.

[2] This lack of spokesmen who could speak with authority on lineage matters (sons do not have that authority) was obvious at the discussions after Meya's death.

[3] See also pp. 34–5 and 46.

Summary

Most Tonga have two sets of kinship ties: patrilateral and matrilateral. I purposely use the more inclusive *matrilateral* rather than *matrilineal* because the Tonga distinguish in the first place between kin on the father's *side* and the mother's *side*—the latter may and often do include mother's patrikin. I mentioned the case of Elton (Mul. D 3) at Mulombwa who has close ties with and lives with his mother's patrikin.[1] However, matrilateral—especially matrilineal—kinship carries greater weight, is more frequently utilized and has generally a wider span. I rarely observed the utilization of seminal kinship of greater span than that of a group of descendants of a common grandfather. The group of seminal descendants of Amuziteni at Mzenga is exceptional in its span of four generations.[2] In contrast, it is by no means unusual to find close co-operation among or common residence of members of matrilineal groups of four or more generations' depth.

Although matrilateral kinship is on the whole of greater importance than patrilateral kinship, both sets of ties are used. It depends on the circumstances which ties are utilized. Thus, although as a general rule Tonga 'follow their mother', some adult Tonga live with their father. In the case of Siddely and Adamu at Chinyafwa we saw that their choice of residence was not solely determined by their genealogical status either at Chinyafwa or in their patrilocal village in Usiska. Other factors also influenced their choice, particularly the proximity to the home village of their respective wives and, connected with this, the probability of their children taking up residence with them.

Geographic, economic, political, personal and other factors all influence a person's choice of residence, his relationships with his kin and, in general, the use he wants to make of potential kinship claims. In other words, from a wide circle of nominal kinsmen a person selects, guided by such factors as I have just mentioned, those kinsmen with whom he wants to associate in particular fields of action. For instance, in Kamoti's case it was largely his personal economic and political position at Mzenga (established before his father's death) which influenced him to stay in his father's village whilst his brother went to live in his mother's village. When a particular selection of kinsmen has been made for specific purposes, contact with other kinsmen is also maintained since a

---

[1] See p. 36 *et passim.*   [2] See p. 61.

person may want to utilize these ties later. For instance, the present GURU[1] bought a large *chilimira* net which unlike many other types of net needs a fairly large crew of about a dozen men: it is cast in the middle of the lake near submerged rocky outcrops. There are not many of those places; and those which are known 'belong' to certain people who claim the monopoly of fishing there. Since GURU did not know of any such rocks near Kawiya village, he decided to go to his father's village where he had been brought up and whence he had been called to succeed to the title at Kawiya. He said that people in his father's village knew of some rocks and that moreover he would find it easier to get the men there to help him than at his present village Kawiya, where they were 'too lazy'. The present GURU and the late KAMBAWE are also instances of the special relationship between headmen and their sister's sons who are potential successors but who are not living in their maternal uncle's village.

It is one of the essential characteristics of a freeborn Tonga (*munangwa*) that he has many kinship links outside his own hamlet[2] which may provide him with alternatives for present economic, political or residential arrangements if need be. When they felt it necessary to make use of such an alternative, the seminal descendants of Amuziteni left Mzenga and associated themselves with another set of kin in another village. Similarly a man who is a drinking and quarrelsome nuisance will find another village when he is chased away from his present village. On the whole the loss from one village means gain for another; by attracting kinsmen from other villages one can increase the numbers in one's own; and, more important still, one can fill a crucial gap in the dominant matrilineage which cannot be filled by breeding locally. I have mentioned the case of Nyali, who brought Mary back from Deep Bay, and the cases of KAMBAWE and GURU who were called from their fathers' villages to take the place of their mothers' brothers.[3]

Thus a Tonga has a set of kinship ties converging on him and, conversely, radiating from him; and these ties link him with several other villages and hamlets which may be several miles' or hours' walk away from his own. These sets of kinship ties may be different for the individual members of a sibling group; they

[1] See p. 64.   [2] Cf. p. 259.
[3] pp. 48, 60 and 64 respectively.

are bound to be different for the members of a hamlet and *a fortiori* for those of a village. For, since marriage among the Tonga is characterized by frequent divorce and serial monogamy[1] (apart from some concurrent polygyny), one group of siblings may be linked to different villages. Uterine siblings with different fathers are obviously linked to different patrilocal villages; this applies *mutatis mutandis* to seminal siblings from different mothers. The different patrilateral relationships which uterine sisters may have become clearly observable at their marriages.

Married women live virilocally and they bring at least three villages into interaction: their marital, patrilocal and matrilocal villages. The exceptions are slave marriages and intra-village marriages, but these are not frequent. Divorced women who remarry are, moreover, linked to more than one marital village. The role of married women in interlinking villages will be discussed more fully in the next chapter.

Finally there are the economic, social or other relationships which are not based upon kinship but which through a 'friendship' pact become quasi-kinship bonds.

Gluckman writes[2] that among the Barotse most relationships between individuals have a multiplex character; the relationships do not cover a single activity in the lives of the persons concerned but they embrace several, if not most, of the activities of the people, *viz.* political, economic, social, recreational, etc. The same applies to Tonga relationships, particularly to those between members of the same village: the mere fact of physical propinquity makes it likely that the same people interact in different fields of action.

In the Tonga utilization of kinship bonds the element of choice is important. Whilst a man may be in regular contact with only a certain number of his kin, he will not neglect all others, since he may need them later; he may occasionally visit them or attend their funerals.

The maintenance of wide networks of kinship ties is essential in a society like that of the Tonga. There are no apices, ritual, political or otherwise, to which the Tonga owe common allegiance and which would thus help to unite Tonga individuals and

[1] By serial monogamy I understand a condition whereby a person has experienced several marriages but has only one spouse at any particular time.
[2] Gluckman (1955*b*), p. 19.

villages into larger units. Instead, each Tonga is the centre of a network of kinship ties which is different from, but will partly overlap with, those of other Tonga: even siblings are likely to have different kin, certainly when married. And it is these intersecting kinship bonds which link individuals to other individuals, and to hamlets and villages other than their own.

The Tonga are generally classified as a matrilineal people because matrilineal ties are on the whole of greater importance than patrilateral ties. Nevertheless, paternity is also of some significance. Apart from emotional and moral bonds, patrilateral kin play an indispensable role in, for instance, the financial transactions which are part of a marriage. Because of the high rate of divorce, patrilateral attachments diversify the kinship ties of uterine siblings. Moreover, because of the everlasting bonds between father and child and the economic and other interests which a father has in the marriages of his children, the marital ties between the children's mother and her husband(s)—and his (their) kin—are never broken, and after divorce some of the marital ties are perpetuated through the children.[1]

These factors—importance of paternity and a high divorce rate—ensure a wider spread of an individual's relationships over a larger area and with a greater number of people than matrilineal ties alone would provide. Consequently the interests of even closely related individuals, who are members of the same lineage and/or residents of the same hamlet or village, will be focussed in the same lineage or local group in some situations; in others their interests lie in different lineage groups in different parts of Tongaland.

These diversified but partly overlapping networks of relationships explain the apparent paradox of the tribal integration of the Tonga despite their fiercely individualistic character. This paradox elicits comments from casual observers such as: 'They [the Tonga] claim to be a tribe, but their claim rests solely on the fact that they have accepted a common name. They have no true tribal organization. The head of each clan claims entire independence. They may be said rather to be a tribe in the making. At present there is no indication of any desire for that unity that characterized most tribal systems evolved for the purposes of

[1] For contrast see description of the position of the Yao father: Mitchell (1956), pp. 163, 185.

defence. It will be interesting to see what sort of tribal organization develops as the result of modern conditions.' [1] The writer's remark that the Tonga have no 'true tribal organization' is obviously occasioned by the fact that the Tonga are not integrated within the framework of a political hierarchy; he overlooked their integration through a complex network of intersecting and cross-cutting relationships.

There are very few relationships solely based on common residence. Indeed the *malepenga* dance group is the only association of individuals where membership is determined by the coincidence of living within certain geographical boundaries. Most other relationships are at least partly based on kinship, and like all kinship ties they have a tendency to assert themselves against local association and in spite of geographical separation. This does not mean that kinship ties are not related to or influenced by locality. People, and especially kin, who live together are more likely, for instance, to visit one another socially or to collaborate in hoeing parties and other activities.

This mutual reinforcement of local and kinship ties is also illustrated by the fact that married women want to maintain their links with their home village. Many wives who have married away cultivate a garden in their home village so as to be prepared for the eventuality of divorce or widowhood, or with an eye on the future residence of their children. Later[2] I will discuss the case of Ndazakale (Map. C 4) who has just moved from his father's village to his matrilocal Mapalassie. But since his mother never lived there or had a garden there, Ziba (Map. C 3), who does not want him at Mapalassie for political reasons, is trying to keep him out on the grounds that he has no *masara* (old gardens) of his mother on which to settle. This is in spite of the fact that genealogically Ndazakale has exactly the same status at Mapalassie as Ziba.

As in the case of Kamoti at Mzenga,[3] children who stay on in their father's village despite their inferior political status there, often do so partly because that is the only place where they are thoroughly 'at home': they know the ecology of the area with its game, fish, medicinal herbs, etc. But they are also intimately acquainted with the local inhabitants, their weaknesses, their

[1] *Census Report, 1931*, p. 23.
[2] See p. 190.

strength, and their ambitions and they know where lie the centres of effective power and influence. As I mentioned before, kinship status alone does not necessarily confer power or position, but it provides a framework within which one can manipulate economic and political factors, and people, to some specific end. Effective political power and influence do not necessarily or exclusively rest with those who are genealogically and thus constitutionally entitled to it (e.g. in Ndazakale's case).[1]

As a result of the latitude which the kinship framework provides for manipulation, and of the importance of local association, a person's loyalty to a village is not a foregone conclusion or an unalterable fact. At the same time the size of a headman's following (i.e. his kinsmen or quasi-kinsmen residing in his village) influences a headman's political status. Tonga say: 'A name alone does not make a chief, it is people who make a chief'—a man with a title is nothing if he has no following. This gives almost any villager (except slaves who have nowhere else to go) a lever to exact fair treatment from both the headman and the other villagers; he can shift his residence and allegiance if dissatisfied. Thus a headman must keep the peace in his village, and promote the welfare of his villagers: moreover, by doing so, he may attract yet more followers.

[1] Cf. also Milton's position at Thoro and *vis-à-vis* the KABUNDULI-ship: pp. 224–6, 245–6, and 250–1.

CHAPTER IV

MARRIAGE

MARRIAGE is the most important factor integrating other-wise independent groups of kinsmen: it provides a link between them by providing them with a common interest. Thus marriage serves not only the ends of ordered procreation but it has also emotional, domestic, economic and political functions. The integrative role of marriage is of great political importance, because the Tonga political system is basically a system of over-lapping networks of kin groups and kin interests. And it is the wife's virilocal residence which greatly contributes to the wide spread of kinship interests. With regard to some marriages (for example, intra-village marriages) the political aspect is explicitly stated: they are contracted for the specific purpose of attracting or retaining dependants in village or hamlet.

In this chapter I will argue that many of the interests which are bound up with a marriage are 'intangible': their infringement is, on practical or legal grounds, not always actionable in law. It is the payment or non-payment of bridewealth which gives a marriage its 'tangible' content: for bridewealth generally provides a basis for action if a party to the marriage feels wronged in regard to any of the other 'non-actionable' aspects of the marriage. In other words, the ties created by marriage are based upon and reinforced by material interests; the latter can be scrutinized (for example, by a court) in a way that other, more intangible interests cannot.

Marriages are usually not pre-arranged (except perhaps in intra-village marriages) nor are there many marriage prohibitions which exclude large categories of people from marrying one another. Likewise there is not much pressure towards enjoined or preferential marriage between persons of particular categories. Since on the whole people have no reason to move far away from their villages, the majority of the marriages are between people living within the same relatively limited area. For instance I noticed that most of the marriages of the men and women whom I found living in Greater Kamisa had been contracted with part-ners who live or lived in the string of villages between Nkata Bay and the Luweya River.[1] Similarly at Kawiya and again at Mzenga the majority of the marriages were contracted within a comparatively limited radius.

Formal Marriage: Go-between and Attorney

A man who wishes to marry a woman goes to her village and hands her directly, or through her grandmother or a female cousin, a *chikholi* or betrothal payment[2] which varies from five shillings to £1. It is not part of the bridewealth, is not returnable, does not establish any legal rights, and may be omitted altogether. The transactions which precede a formal marriage begin with the despatch of a go-between or *nthenga* (lit. a messenger) from the man.[3] He can be anybody and need not be related to either party, nor does he have to belong to a particular village. Nominally the go-between is sent by the headman of the village where the man resides, that is his 'father', if the bridegroom is a village son, or his maternal 'uncle', if he is a village owner; in fact however the go-between is usually asked to do the job by the bridegroom himself. In the woman's village the messenger speaks in the name of the village headman.[4] For instance John (Map. C 11) asked Nyali of Chinyafwa (Chin. F 4) to go for him as he considered Nyali a skilled negotiator who would be able to keep the price down.[5]

[1] Nkata Bay is six or seven miles (about three hours' walk) north of KAMISA, whilst the Luweya is about fifteen miles or a morning's walk to the south. Practically all the villages are contained between the lake on the east and the road on the west. This is the only road along the lakeshore within the District and runs up to the Luweya along the watershed between the lake and the Limpassa River. The Limpassa runs through a wide marshy valley which creates an uninhabited gap between the lakeshore villages and those in the hills.

[2] The root word *koli* (or *kole*) occurs also in the Tumbuka and Nyanja languages with the meaning of (*engagement*) *pledge* or *hostage*: cf. Scott (1892), p. 66, and Turner (1952), p. 51. However, English-speaking Tonga invariably translate *chikholi* as *hostage* when they are referring to the betrothal payment. This is the more remarkable since I have never heard the Tonga word used in the sense of hostage. I do not know the origin of the Tonga usage of the English term *hostage* for betrothal payment.

[3] The differences between formal and informal marriage are summarized on p. 120.

[4] In theory, the headman, as the leader of the dominant matrilineage, is the most senior kinsman in the village; it is as the bridegroom's kinsman and not as his headman that he is supposed to send the go-between.

[5] The Tonga word for bridewealth is *chilowola* which is adopted from the Ngoni *lowolo*. The Tonga also use *chuma* which means riches or wealth in gen-

PLATE 3. (*a*) A group of female relatives of the bride taking food, including baskets with cassava flour, pots with relish (*dendi*) and a young goat (led by the boys) to the bridegroom's village for the impending marriage

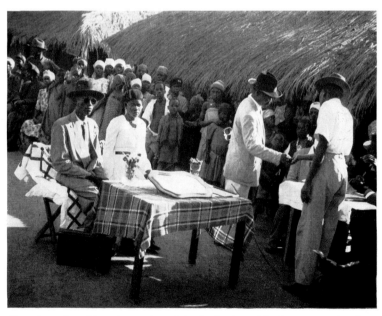

(*b*) A formal wedding (*zowara*). Whilst the bride and bridegroom sit by their own table, three or four men at the other table note down the gifts (mostly cash) which friends and relatives of either side hand to the *spikara* (the 'speaker' or master of ceremonies)

When he arrived at the woman's village, Nyali's opening gambit was: 'Bwana[1] Mussa (Map. A 1) has a cock and has heard that there is a hen in your village.' Of course Mussa, as the headman and John's most senior kinsman at Mapalassie, knew that Nyali was asked to negotiate John's marriage and Nyali afterwards reported to him; but it was John who asked Nyali to go in the first place.

The question of who is to send the go-between, i.e. in whose name he is to negotiate, can be a point of dispute in the struggle between the 'father' and the 'uncle' for the local allegiance of their 'children' or 'sister's children', as in Lovemore's case below (p. 93). The general rule is that the go-between comes from the village where the suitor is resident. Thus if he lives patrilocally it will be his patrilateral kin who officially send the go-between, while if he lives matrilocally with his maternal 'uncle' the go-between is likely to be their representative. It is also the go-between who hands the bridewealth to the bride's kin. The assumption is that the bridewealth is partly or entirely provided by the kinsman who sends the go-between, *viz.* by either the 'father' or the 'uncle', depending on where the suitor lives. Conversely, it is assumed that the bridegroom will set up his household with whomsoever paid or helped with the bridewealth. In other words, ideally the Tonga see a connection between the go-between's starting-point, the village which is the source of the bridewealth, and the place of residence of the married man. This ideal connection may correspond, at least partially, with the reality. But it is a fact that suitors often find their own cash for the bridewealth by earning or borrowing. Thus John found the whole of his bridewealth himself. Nevertheless the arrangements regarding the go-between and the bridewealth are often an issue in the competition

---

eral. Rather more colloquially and in reference to the actual negotiations *mtengo* (*viz.* price) is also used for bridewealth.

Nyali was also the go-between for Golo (Mul. C 11).

[1] Bwana is the term of reference and address for headmen (*mafumu*). In Greater Kamisa Mussa is in everyday life addressed and referred to as *ada* (father) like any other man. But on official occasions like this one, or in other official discussions or at funerals, the leading personages are addressed and referred to as *bwana* irrespective of whether they are people with hereditary titles. This is related to the all-pervading idea in Tonga society that every man—or at any rate, every freeman—is a potential *fumu*: see also p. 201. As in other parts of Africa European men are also addressed and referred to as *bwana*.

between paternal and maternal relatives for the residential allegiance of their kin. This is clear from the cases of Lovemore and Waison.[1]

The go-between is a crucial witness in a formal marriage: in fact the existence of a go-between can in itself be evidence of a formal marriage. If there is a dispute as to whether a case of cohabitation is a formal or informal marriage, the first and often decisive question is: 'Who was the go-between and who received him?'[2] Once the go-between is dead or has gone away, there is no one who can speak in his name. This is not the case with the person who sent him and the bridewealth, i.e. the *nkhoswe* or attorney.

The position of the *nkhoswe* or attorney[3] is not a personal one like that of the go-between. The individuals who act as attorney in relation to a particular person may vary according to the situation. An attorney is not merely a surety who is responsible for the principal's payments: a sister may act as attorney in court for her brother in his absence when the latter's wife has committed a wrong against her absent husband. Death, which may deprive a man of his go-between, cannot deprive a man or a woman of his/ her attorney: it is only slaves who do not have attorneys.[4] The position of attorney *vis-à-vis* a particular person is a function of the kin group which claims the 'ward' as a member. Consequently an attorney is not chosen or elected: he acts as a kinsman whose position of attorneyship is inherent in his position in the kin group to which he and his ward belong. Nor is the role of attorneys restricted to the marriage of their kin; everyone (except a slave) has an attorney from birth because all freemen are born into a kin group. This is generally a matrilineal kin group; but as I will show presently a woman's father can also act as her attorney at her marriage and receive and keep her bridewealth. A father's right to the attorneyship of his daughter, however, is generally more particularly related to his right to receive her bridewealth, and the corresponding liability for its repayment at his daughter's divorce.

---

[1] See pp. 93 and 102.

[2] This was Nyali's question regarding his sister's marriage in which, as he alleges, no bridewealth was paid: see Case 1, p. 48.

[3] I have adopted the term 'attorney' which expresses more adequately the duties and the position of the *nkhoswe* among the Tonga than 'surety' as used by Mitchell for the Yao situation: cf. Mitchell (1956), p. 149.

[4] See p. 254.

But whilst the father is his daughter's *nkhoswe* in the more re-stricted sense of being liable for the repayment of the bridewealth in the event of divorce, the daughter's matrikin are at the same time also her *nkhoswe* by virtue of the matrilineal relationship; a free woman (or for that matter, any freeman) has her (his) attorneys from birth, *viz.* her (his) matrikin who are concerned about her (his) protection and welfare throughout her (his) life.

Matrilineal descent has greater significance than patrilateral kinship. Nevertheless, paternity also has social, economic, poli-tical and emotional value of some significance. These two op-posed principles—paternal and maternal control of offspring—constitute one of the major conflicts inherent in Tonga society. The importance of paternity is given recognition in the marriage negotiations and the distribution of the bridewealth. When the father has paid bridewealth for his daughter's mother, he may even act as his daughter's *nkhoswe* (attorney) in marriage. How-ever, the father's attorneyship is more restricted in scope than the attorneyship which is a function of the matrilineal group into which every free Tonga is born. Attorneyship is not exclusively associated with any one individual. It is the manifestation of the control of the matrilineage over its members and its concern for their security and welfare. But this concern must be represented by an individual; it cannot express itself *in abstracto*.

Attorneyship is ill-defined both regarding the rights and duties involved and as to the persons responsible for their performance. This lack of definition is a general feature of Tonga institutions, as I will show when I come to deal with headmanship, land-rights, the matrilineage and, indeed, with marriage itself. For instance, the question of attorneyship is one of the principal points of dispute in 'Meya's Death'. Just as marriage and the rela-tionships it creates often become foci for political claims and disputes, so, too, attorneyship often entails more than responsi-bility for a person's social security or for certain economic re-lationships: it may acquire a political aspect. This may happen when the question of the attorneyship becomes involved in a question about the headmanship, as in the case of Banda and LUWOMBA.[1] All one can do is to present the broad outlines of the rules of attorneyship as a framework within which the struggles for social, economic and political control take place.

[1] See Case 18, p. 240.

H

The question of who is to be the attorney of the man depends to a certain extent on whether the parents of the man were formally married or not: this is illustrated in Cases 4 and 6. In fact, I have heard few disputes over the attorneyship of a man. This is probably because anyone who claims to sponsor a man's marriage can reasonably be expected to produce the necessary cash for his bridewealth.

The counterpart of the attorneyship of the man's marriage (*viz.* the responsibility for sending the go-between and contributing to the bridewealth) is the attorneyship of the woman's marriage, which is vested in the relative who receives the go-between with the bridewealth. Here a great deal is at stake. Firstly it is now not a question of producing cash, but of receiving cash. More important, the control of the matrilineage to which the bride belongs is at stake; and, if the woman bears children, the control of the potential ancestress of a new matrilineage. The struggle for control over offspring, and particularly their residential allegiance, is one of the central themes of Tonga life, and therefore of this study. On the one hand, there are the father and his kinsmen who want to keep the children in the father's village or at least keep the father-child bond as strong as possible. I have dealt with this competition in the previous chapter and it is one of the main issues in 'Meya's Death' and other cases. On the other hand, there are the children's matrilineal kin who always consider the children's patrikin a threat to the unity and authority of the matrilineage, particularly when the children are living patrilocally. The control of bridewealth is one of the foci of this struggle for dependants and, on the part of the matrilineage, the struggle for control of its members. The situation is often complicated by the fact that this is not always a straightforward conflict between matrikin and patrikin; either or both camps may be divided amongst themselves on the issue of control over offspring.[1]

The decisive factor determining whether the bride's attorney shall be a matrilateral or a patrilateral kinsman is not where she lives, but rather whether she herself is the product of a formal or an informal marriage. Ideally, if the bride's father paid bridewealth for her mother then he will be able to act as his daughter's attorney at her marriage: he will receive the go-between, control the

---

[1] 'Meya's Death' illustrates such an internal conflict among patrikin: see p. 149.

negotiations,[1] fix and receive the bridewealth for his daughter. Strictly speaking, in these circumstances the father can keep the entire bridewealth for himself and spend it, or 'eat' it as the Tonga say.

The negotiations are initiated by the bridegroom's go-between in the village of the bride. Soon after he has stated the purpose of his visit, the go-between puts down £1 or £2 as a sign that he means business. This payment is called 'the money to open your [i.e. the woman's attorney's] mouth' or by some other metaphor, and is intended as an inducement for the attorney to 'give his price'. The bride's people may want a larger 'mouth-opener' as an indication of the bridegroom's—and his sponsors'—good faith. After some bargaining and appealing to old friendship, kinship ties or other reasons for leniency, the go-between will give in and put another ten shillings or a pound down. He has prepared for this: he has a separate note all ready in a separate pocket so that he will not have to get all his money out to get at this note, because if the other party sees how much (or how little) he has on him, they might put their price up (or cancel the negotiations altogether). When the go-between has 'opened their mouths' the woman's attorneys will state their price. The go-between, who has his instructions as to the maximum the bridegroom's party is prepared to pay, then begins another round of bargaining. Agreement is rarely reached at the first meeting and the go-between has to return to the bridegroom's village for new instructions. Agreement is generally reached on the second visit.

The amount of the bridewealth varies from £5 to £15 including the initial payment 'to open the mouth'. But the bridewealth is practically never paid in full: the two parties agree on what part shall be paid in cash; for the remainder (generally about half of the total bridewealth including the 'mouth-opener') the bridegroom gives a promissory note (*kalata*) or just a verbal promise. Some people nowadays obtain from the courts a marriage certificate which records the total amount of the agreed

[1] In fact the father or whoever is the real attorney never actually conducts the marriage discussions; he is always invisible and the person who does the talking has no authority to make any decisions: he is merely a mouthpiece or go-between although he is not officially known as *nthenga* (go-between) like the bridegroom's emissary. In order to avoid complications I will not introduce this 'mouthpiece' in my description of the negotiations—after all they are entirely controlled by the bride's kin, that is, her attorney(s).

bridewealth and the amount actually paid by the bridegroom or his attorneys. Not only is the bridewealth not paid in full at the beginning of the marriage: in many cases (probably in most cases, but I have no quantitative data) it is never paid off at all, even if the marriage does not end in divorce.

The mere existence of a go-between and the payment and acceptance of the 'mouth-opening' money are proof of public marriage negotiations and they establish a formal marital relationship. Hence the go-between's initial payment is also often called 'the money to visit the village' (i.e. the village of the woman).[1] If the woman now sleeps with another man, the suitor can sue her. After the handing over of the cash and the *kalata* there are sometimes still various other minor payments and discussions, for instance about whether there is to be a big white wedding (*zowara*) or a plain one (*mtimba*),[2] but often there is no question of a wedding and the new wife enters her husband's village without any ceremony. Strictly speaking a formal marriage contract is not concluded until the cash and the *kalata* have been handed over, and if the suitor takes the woman into his house before this he is said to have abducted her (*kusompo:* to snatch, abduct). In fact, however, it frequently happens that men take their brides to their house after paying the first instalment ('to visit the village'). But since the formal and public negotiations have been initiated and a formal marital relationship with a marital debt has been established, they cannot be sued by the woman's attorney as in cases of real abduction[3] which have not been preceded by any public opening of marriage negotiations.

The bridewealth received by the woman's attorney can generally be 'eaten' by him; the mere fact that he controlled the negotiations and received the bridewealth is supposed to show that he has *nthazi* (strength, power, authority) over the woman, or at any

---

[1] The difference between these two phrases for the same payment is one of context: when talking about the actual discussions of the go-between with the woman's attorney, the importance of this payment lies in its purpose of getting the discussions going and of inducing the woman's people to name their price. But in the context of the marital relationship the importance of that payment lies in the fact that henceforth the man is 'known', that is, legally and publicly, in the woman's village as her suitor. Consequently, this payment is generally referred to, in the courts and elsewhere, as 'the money to visit the village' (*ndrama za kuchiziya pamuzi*).

[2] See p. 56, n. 4.   [3] See Case 4, p. 93.

rate over her marriage. The attorney who has received the go-between is under a moral obligation, however, not to act too autocratically[1] and independently. He should communicate with the woman's other kin (i.e. either her matrikin or her patrikin, depending on to which group the attorney in the marriage himself belongs) and perhaps let them share in the bridewealth.

This is brought out by Nyali's (Chin. F 4) account of an argument he had with his 'father-in-law' Malalanje (Mul. B 19) about the bridewealth of Nyali's daughters Sala and Maliya (Chin. G 6 and G 7) who were both living with their father at the time of their marriage. A couple of years after Maliya's marriage (she married after her elder sister Sala) when Maliya's baby was already a year old, Malalanje came to Nyali and asked him for his share of Maliya's bridewealth because he is the 'father' of Maliya's mother Nyamwale (Map. C 10 and Chin. F 5). Malalanje is the younger brother of Nyamwale's father Golo (Mul. B 15) who died some years ago.[2] Nyali told Malalanje that he was too late, because at the time of the marriage discussions he, Nyali, had sent the go-between, who had come from Maliya's suitor to his own house, on to Malalanje as the *chirumi* (patrikin) of Nyamwale. But Malalanje had refused the honour, saying that Nyali had married Nyamwale with bridewealth and that therefore his daughters were 'in his hands'. Nyali had also sent the go-between to the *chikazi* (matrikin) of Nyamwale, *viz.* to Nyamwale's 'sisters' Nyankhamoza (Map. C 7) and Nyadalo (Map. C 9) and to Nyamwale's 'daughters' Foster (Map. D 5) and Nyabanda (Map. D 6). They too told Nyali to go ahead with the discussions by himself, which meant that they agreed that he had full authority in this marriage because he had given bridewealth for Nyamwale. For these reasons Nyali denied that Malalanje had any claim by right when he

---

[1] This is a significant feature of this fiercely egalitarian society: one should never make one's superior status or claims too blatantly clear. Independence of action in kin relationships is easily condemned as pride, 'uppityness' or 'self-love, (*kujanja*: the reflexive form of *kwanja*, to love) which is a term of opprobrium, of abuse almost. The basis of this attitude is that a freeman 'has a father as well as a mother', *viz.* has kinsmen on both sides, and neither side should try to exclude the other. Cf. Fany's remark to this effect in 'Meya's Death' (para. 20); indeed, one of the issues in this dispute was the authoritarian attitude of Mussa and Ziba.

[2] See Genealogy IV, facing p. 149, or the Genealogies of Mapalassie and Chinyafwa villages.

made the demand two years later. But he added that he might still give Malalanje a part of Maliya's bridewealth. Nyali was annoyed, however, that Malalanje came to ask for his share as if it were his due.

I do not know whether this story is true, nor do I know why Nyali's offers (if he ever made them) should have been declined; it all happened long before I ever came to the village. But I relate his story because it illustrates something which happens in many marriage discussions. Although Nyali gave his wife's matrikin and patrikin first option to conduct the discussions, they could not by right claim either a part or the whole of Maliya's bridewealth, because Nyali, the girl's father, had paid them already for his wife Nyamwale. All the same he made a decent gesture and showed them that he knew his duty. It was his moral obligation to inform the wife's relatives of what was happening to Nyamwale's progeny. Nyamwale's matrilineal kin (and thus her daughter's) especially would expect to be kept informed of what happened to a member of their matrilineage since, after all, Nyali's children do not really belong to his village but to their matrilocal village Mapalassie. He, Nyali, had 'only produced them' at Chinyafwa.

As for Nyamwale's bridewealth, I was told that in her own marriage discussions the go-between from Nyali came to Donald at Mapalassie (Map. B 13) who is her maternal uncle; Donald apparently also received her bridewealth.[1] This was really meant for Malalanje who is Nyamwale's father's brother, but he was abroad at the time. Donald died before Malalanje's return from abroad, and Donald's financial responsibility in respect of Nyamwale's marriage was inherited by Ziba (Map. C 3) who is Donald's classificatory sister's son. When Malalanje returned from abroad Ziba handed Nyamwale's bridewealth to him, so the financial responsibility in that marriage now lies with Malalanje. This means that if this marriage ends in divorce and Nyali is entitled to the return of the bridewealth he gave for Nyamwale, it will be Malalanje who will have to return the money to Nyali. Thus in that respect Malalanje is the *nkhoswe* of Nyamwale. But Ziba who is Nyamwale's 'brother' is also her *nkhoswe*, in all matters except for the financial liability.

In relation to his other 'sister', Nyadalo (who is Nyamwale's full-sister and who lives at Mapalassie), Ziba has full powers of

[1] See Genealogy IV, facing p. 149, and Genealogy IX for Mapalassie village.

attorney, also in respect of her bridewealth. For I was told that in Nyadalo's first marriage the go-between was received by Donald who also kept ('ate') the bridewealth; after Donald's death Ziba became financially responsible for her marriage.[1] Thus the marriages of Nyamwale and Nyadalo are examples of how the financial responsibility for the marriages of two full-sisters can be 'in the hands' (*mu manja*) respectively of the patrikin and the matrikin. But this does not derogate from the matrikin the general power of attorney (*unkhoswe*) in relation to these two women, where it concerns the general well-being and security of members of the matrilineage.

This is clear in the case of the marriages of another set of sisters at Mapalassie: the daughters of Mordecai (Map. B 11) and Nyalongwe (Map. B 12) whose matrilocality is near Bandawe, about a day's walk south of Mapalassie. Whilst in the case of Nyamwale and Nyadalo the people at Mapalassie are their matrikin, as regards Mordecai's daughters the Mapalassie people are their patrikin. About the marriages of Mordecai's two eldest daughters, Hope and Nelly, the Mapalassie people say that 'we kept these marriages in our own hands', because Mordecai had paid bridewealth for his wife Nyalongwe. This means that the marriage negotiations were conducted and controlled, and the bridewealth kept ('eaten') at Mapalassie. In the case of Hope this meant that in all her three marriages the bridewealth was received and kept at Mapalassie;[2] on the divorce of the first two marriages the bridewealth was returned by Mordecai's matrilineage, including Nyamwale. But the marriages of Mordecai's younger daughters, Fany and Lizzy, were 'put in the hands' of their matrikin at Bandawe—

---

[1] When Nyadalo divorced her husband on account of his long absence abroad, the husband was not entitled to have his bridewealth returned. Her second marriage was to the widower of one of her sisters; as the man had already paid bridewealth for the sister he did not have to pay again when he married Nyadalo as his late wife's substitute. Nyadalo has now also divorced this husband, or at least she is separated from him. As far as I can make out no bridewealth has (yet) been returned. Nyadalo is barren: see also Case 9 (para. 5). Barrenness does not constitute a ground for divorce and therefore does not entitle the husband to the return of the bridewealth. If in a divorce of a fruitful marriage the husband is entitled to the return of his bridewealth, he will generally forgo the whole or part of it 'for the benefit of the children' (see p. 107). But in a childless marriage the husband will accept what is due to him.

[2] But not in all cases by Mordecai himself since he died some time ago.

and it was they (and not Mordecai) who later, on Fany's divorce and on the death of Lizzy's husband, had to return the bridewealth.[1]

However, the fact that Nelly's and Hope's marriages are 'in the hands' of their patrikin at Mapalassie does not deprive the matrikin at Bandawe of their attorneyship (*unkhoswe*). Indeed, the major issue in the dispute following Meya's death is the claim of the Bandawe matrikin that Mordecai's wife, Nyalongwe, and her offspring are after all still members of their matrilineage at Bandawe. And the matrikin came to Mapalassie with the specific purpose of asserting their rights. Similarly, the Bandawe matrikin of Adi (Map. D 9) gave the people at Mapalassie a very clear warning that they should not presume that they can say anything they want either to or about Hope's daughter Adi (who does not live at Mapalassie) because they, the matrikin, would see to it that Adi's interests and welfare were protected. At the same time the matrikin from Bandawe, whilst making sure that Nelly, as a wife and a mother, should receive proper treatment at the hands of her husband and her patrikin in general, did not make any claims as regards Nelly's bridewealth; they hinted at the subject but did not make it a direct issue,[2] because they have no legal right to the bridewealth.

It is now clear why the position of the go-between is not hereditary, unlike the attorneyship. The go-between is merely a mouthpiece and witness—the one who carries the bridewealth; he is not in any way responsible for the bridewealth or the marriage. The attorneyship (*unkhoswe*), however, has two aspects, both of them closely linked with the marriage. One aspect is the liability for the financial arrangements, i.e. the marital debts on which the marital relationships are based. These marital relationships and the corresponding marital debts often outlast the marriage itself: they continue to be of importance even after divorce or the death of one or both spouses, especially when there are children of the marriage. Hence it is clear that there should always be agents to

---

[1] That Ziba does not seem to have given any bridewealth for his marriage to Nelly is irrelevant in this context. The point here is that Mordecai and Mussa exercised their right to arrange Nelly's marriage according to their own discretion, even if that meant that they would forgo bridewealth: cf. 'Meya's Death', paras. 1, 3, 20 *et passim*.

[2] See Case 9, paras. 26 and 27, and p. 174.

exercise control over the proper discharge of the financial liabilities which have been created by the marriage, whether formal
or informal. The other aspect of attorneyship is concern and
responsibility for the general well-being of the wards, that is, the
responsibility to see that the status of the ward is not abused. In
this respect, too, it is necessary that there should always be agents
available to exert the required vigilance.

Attorneyship in financial (bridewealth) matters may be in the
hands of the patrikin or the matrikin but ultimately it becomes the
function of a matrilineage. For when the father or the patrilateral
relative who originally sponsored the marriage dies, his rights and
duties are taken over by his matrilineage which is thus not the
matrilineage of the marriage partner concerned. When marriage is
financially 'in the hands' of the matrikin then it is the woman's
matrilineage which is involved.

As for the attorneyship's concern about the woman's status and
security, this is generally a duty of the matrilineage. This aspect of
attorneyship is, of course, not exclusively connected with marriage: as I mentioned before, every freeman is born into a kin
group and has *ankhoswe* or attorneys to protect his or her status.
Marriage is only one of the occasions on which attorneys come
into action—death is another occasion, as evidenced by 'Meya's
Death'. And although patrikin also often try to gain or retain
control over their seminal descendants, among the Tonga the
emphasis is on the whole on matrilateral relationship and membership of a matrilineal kin group.

Marital Debts: Tangible Basis of Relationships

The evidence I have shows that in general the bridewealth is
shared by the bride's patrikin and matrikin;[1] the pattern of this
sharing depends on the conditions of the marriage of the bride's
parents, e.g. whether it was a formal or informal marriage. If the
patrikin control the marriage negotiations and receive the bridewealth, the matrikin will expect a share of it, either as a legal right
or as a moral obligation. The same applies, *mutatis mutandis*, if the
matrikin receive the bridewealth. Consequently, there is generally an element of potential or actual debt in the relationship

---

[1] Similarly, if there is a wedding party, the guests are invited to make contributions towards the expenses of the feast and these contributions are divided
between the *akuchikazi* (matrikin) and the *akuchirumi* (patrikin) of the bride.

between the bride's[1] matrikin and patrikin, irrespective of whether her parents' marriage was formal or informal.[2]

In a formal marriage, where the bridegroom has duly paid bridewealth to his wife's attorney, there is still a debt involved in his relationship with his wife's people. As previously stated, it rarely happens that he pays the whole bridewealth at once: he gives a *kalata* (promissory note) for about half, which he will pay 'another day when he has found the money'. But generally the debt is not mentioned again until the death of one of the two spouses. If the husband predeceases his wife the *kalata* may be mentioned at his death and later again at the wife's death. This outstanding debt in no way interferes with the husband's marital rights, one of which is his right to 'eat' his daughter's bridewealth —a right qualified by his moral obligation to share with his in-laws some of the bridewealth received for his daughters.

One of the criteria of a formal marriage is the existence of a go-between: this implies the formal establishment in public of a debt relationship between the two contracting kin groups. The legal consideration of the contract is the bridewealth or at least part of it, however small that part may be.[3] The essential difference between formal and informal marriage is that the latter is not based upon a formal and public agreement in which a definite sum has been fixed as the bridewealth; and that no consideration has been given as proof of the agreement. As there has been no go-between and no discussion, 'no mouth has been opened' and thus no bridewealth has been mentioned, let alone fixed. The amount of the debt underlying an informal marital relationship is therefore uncertain. This fact may be exploited when the woman dies: the informal husband may then be charged with a much larger debt than he would normally have paid as her bridewealth.[4]

It frequently happens that a man takes a wife in an informal

[1] I use 'bride' in general, for the woman who is in the process of becoming a wife or who has just become a wife. Thus here it can refer to the woman who has entered into an adulterous union, or as I call it, an informal marriage.

[2] For a summary of the similarities and differences between formal and informal marriages, see p. 120.

[3] We saw that even if only the first small payment has been made by the go-between 'to open the mouth' the bridegroom is sufficiently 'known' to be able to 'visit the village' and take the girl to his village without being considered an adulterer: see p. 86.

[4] Cf. p. 118.

marriage and thus, strictly speaking, commits adultery,[1] without being sued for damages or made to return his (informal) wife to her home. Informal marriages of long standing are very common.

Several of the points discussed so far are illustrated in the following case.

CASE 4: LOVEMORE'S ABDUCTED WIFE

Lovemore used to live with his mother Lidasi in the village of her 'father' Mphoza. Although Mphoza[2] is genealogically a cross-cousin of Lidasi, he calls her his 'daughter' since he has taken the place of his maternal uncle, who was Lidasi's father. Mphoza lives near Chizi which is less than two hours' walk north of KAMISA. Lidasi went to live in Mphoza's village (and died there) after she had left her husband Salima; Lovemore went with her. Salima (of Mulombwa) did not pay bridewealth for Lidasi. Some time ago Lovemore abducted Nyankhoma, whose home is in the hills, and 'put her in his house'. After that Mphoza sent a go-between with £3 (which was Lovemore's own money) to Nyankhoma's people.[3] Nyankhoma's *nkhoswe* (attorney) in her village in the hills said that £3 was inadequate and that the go-between should come back with at least £6, then they could begin to think of opening the marriage negotiations and of disclosing their price, because after all the man had taken the girl into his house already. (The £6 was meant to be damages for the abduction and adultery and would not be part of the bridewealth—the usual procedure in abduction cases.) The girl's attorney kept £1 and sent the go-between back with the other £2. (The £1 which the girl's people kept was a token that they were prepared to discuss the marriage and acknowledged that there was in fact a marriage already—but they wanted a higher opening bid. If in the meanwhile another man had

---

[1] The term adultery should only denote extra-marital intercourse when either or both parties are married. Considering the flexibility of Tonga marriage arrangements it is not always easy to decide whether a case of illegitimate sexual intercourse is a matter of adultery or seduction. There is little point in distinguishing the two, since the Tonga do not. They have only one term, *chigororo*, which I translate as adultery.

[2] See Genealogy I and also VIII and XI for Mulombwa and Chinyafwa respectively.

[3] Mphoza was entitled to send a go-between since Lovemore was living with him. I do not know whether Mphoza consulted Lovemore's father Salima about this matter, as he should have done.

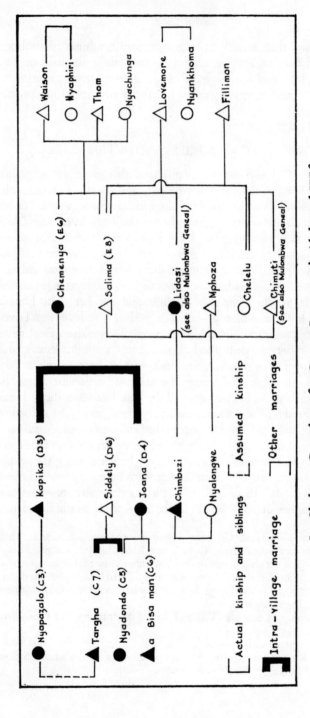

I.—Skeleton Genealogy for Case 4: Lovemore's Abducted Wife

Letters and numbers in brackets refer to Genealogy XIII for Chinyafwa Village. See also Genealogy X for Mulombwa Village

seduced Nyankhoma, Lovemore would have been able to sue him for adultery.[1]) As soon as Salima heard about the negotiations he went to Mphoza and asked him why he, Mphoza, had assumed the role of Lovemore's attorney; he insisted that the go-between should come from him, Salima. Apparently Mphoza told Salima that he, Salima, could send a go-between if he wanted to. Salima also tried to persuade Lovemore to come and settle with him again. Lovemore refused because he said that Salima did not get on with his children[2] and that he preferred to stay with his 'grandfather' Mphoza.

I was told that Salima did send his own go-between with the £2 which were left from Lovemore's original £3 but I was unable to find out whether and how the negotiations ended. One of the houses in Salima's hamlet at Mulombwa is said to be Lovemore's—it used to be the house of Waison,[3] another son of Salima—before he went abroad. It appears that Lovemore never really lived with Salima for any length of time after he had left with his mother Lidasi, but that he just stayed there for a short while after the affair of the trousers (to be described shortly) and before he fled to Rhodesia. It is also possible that Salima is just saying that the house is Lovemore's, as part of his campaign to get Lovemore and his wife to live with him.[4]

Shortly after the abduction, Lovemore went to visit his 'wife' Nyankhoma's sister's husband; and there he took a pair of trousers which belonged to a certain John and which were drying in the sun in the village. Soon afterwards he went to a wedding in these trousers. There he met a relative of John; this relative informed the owner that he had seen his trousers on Lovemore. Lovemore when asked said that he had only borrowed them. The owner said that he had been looking for his trousers for some time and that Lovemore had never informed him that he had them and that Lovemore had therefore stolen them. Soon afterwards Lovemore evaded the possible repercussions by going to Rhodesia. This was in September 1954.

Lovemore left his wife Nyankhoma with Mphoza when he went abroad. After he had gone Salima went to see the girl, not in public but in secret, and tried to persuade her to come and live in his hamlet.

---

[1] This initial payment does not confer uxorial rights on the prospective husband; he has no *right* to sexual intercourse nor is he entitled to 'put her in his house'.

[2] A reference to Waison's quarrel with Salima: see Case 6, p. 102.

[3] See Case 6, p. 102.

[4] See p. 64 for a parallel situation concerning GURU and his nephew.

She is said to have refused, saying that Lovemore had left her behind at Mphoza's and that was where she was going to stay. And that is where she still is.

In May 1955 during a smallpox scare a Government vaccinator passed through the lakeshore villages with instructions to vaccinate everybody. A great many people evaded him, and those whose names he could trace were prosecuted in the Native Authority courts. Among those prosecuted were three women of Mphoza's village who were fined five shillings each. Mphoza immediately came forward to pay for two of them—the one for whom he did not pay[1] was Nyankhoma, Lovemore's abducted wife. The Native Authority MANKHAMBIRA asked Mphoza: 'Don't you want to "redeem" your daughter-in-law?' Mphoza answered: 'No, her *mweneko* [lit. the owner, i.e. the one who is responsible for her] is present', meaning Salima. Salima, sitting among the public, grunted that it had nothing to do with him. Mphoza had a whispered conference with Salima whilst Nyankhoma, sobbing, was led out of the court by a court messenger and put in a hut, more or less like a prisoner. The public showed surprise and sympathy expressed in remarks like: 'They really must hate her.' After a while Mphoza came back into the court and explained that the girl was indeed his daughter-in-law but . . . and then he gave the history of the marriage and the quarrel over who was to send the go-between. He concluded by saying that as Salima was so keen to act as Lovemore's attorney he should therefore now face his duties and 'redeem' the girl. He asked the court to allow him until the next day whilst he would send a messenger to Salima's village. The court agreed and set the girl free.

The next day Mphoza reported to the court that Salima still refused to pay, that he had sent a messenger to Salima's brother Chimuti who also refused[2] and that he himself was still not prepared to pay. The court persuaded him that he would do a good deed if he did redeem the girl; he could after all always keep a claim of 5s. against Salima. The girl was called into the court and asked whether she was keeping all right in Mphoza's village and whether she got on with her 'father-in-law' Mphoza. She said she had no complaints at all. At last Mphoza relented and agreed to pay for her but insisted that he should get a

[1] In this situation the phrase *kuwombo*, to redeem from slavery, was used.

[2] It is very unlikely that Chimuti would have assisted Salima in this matter because the brothers have not been on good terms since Salima made off with Chimuti's wife Chelelu whilst Chimuti was abroad.

receipt (*kalata*) so that he would always be able to show that it was he who had 'redeemed' her.

Lovemore entered into a *de facto* marriage (he put Nyankhoma 'into his house') without any of the formal and public preliminaries. The girl was not pregnant. Although in this situation the man is said to have abducted (*kusompo*) the woman, what in fact often happens is that the woman installs herself in the village of the man who seduced her with promises of marriage but who seems to be forgetting about them. After the man has paid damages to the woman's people, and if he wants or is forced to marry the woman, the procedure is the same as in a formal marriage and the status of the marriage is also the same. Without this subsequent procedure of marriage negotiations through a go-between and so forth, the abduction becomes an informal marriage if the woman stays with the man.

An impatient lover may not always want to wait until the end of the marriage negotiations (which can be protracted) and will 'put a woman in his house' soon after the go-between has handed over the first instalment of the bridewealth on his first visit, i.e. 'the money to open their mouths'. In this case the man is also said to have abducted the woman. But he is not liable for damages because the existence of a go-between and his visit to the woman's village have put the relationship on a formal level.

Adultery and Informal Marriage

When an unmarried woman finds she is pregnant, her attorney will be informed of the fact. He will go and see the relatives of the man whom the woman has named as the father,[1] to 'present him with his wife'. The man may and often does deny any responsibility. If the case is taken to court the alleged lover does not stand much chance, as in Tonga law legal presumptions on this point are weighted heavily against the man. Outside the court the woman's attorney has no means of enforcing damages. If the man accepts responsibility the woman may go and live with him as his wife, or she may stay in her own village, in which case the man will still be expected to accept the normal economic and other

---

[1] If the woman has had affairs with different men the one she names is of course not necessarily the father. But she or a family council may pick on the man whom they consider to be the most suitable husband and son-in-law.

duties of a father and husband. Indeed in many respects the man
living with an informal wife has the same rights and duties as the
husband in a formal marriage—he can even sue for adultery.

The Tonga concept of marriage (*nthengwa*) is essentially empirical: as soon as a man and a woman have offspring and/or
live together they are considered married. The chief difference
from the situation as it was before this union is that, apart from
possible children of the union, relationships have altered. There is
now a marital debt relationship where there was none before.
This applies to both formal and informal unions: whether a
marriage is formal or informal can often only be ascertained
during crises, such as death (either of a spouse or of a child), marriage of one of the children of the marriage, quarrels, and so forth.[1]

An informal wife living with her husband hoes the man's
garden, cooks his food, and may bear him children who will
always be his children with most of the rights and duties involved.
But since the marital relationship is not based upon a formal
marriage contract the man is not entitled to all the economic
rights accruing from a formal marriage. He can sue for adultery
anybody who usurps his sexual rights in his wife, but he can in
turn be sued by his wife's attorney for the amount of the damages
he received from the adulterer as the following case from Mzenga
shows.

CASE 5: RETALIATORY ADULTERIES[2]

Some time before 1940 Milward (Mz. E 8) committed adultery
with Nkhunguru's (Mz. D 12) wife Wanjapo. Nkhunguru did not
take the matter to court but it was discussed in the village. He divorced
Wanjapo and received his bridewealth back but he did not claim any
damages from Milward. In 1943 Nkhunguru committed adultery with
Gutamo (Mz. D 14), the informal wife of Milward's 'younger brother'
Chisani (Mz. E 10). Chisani's father Simon took the case to court
where Nkhunguru was ordered to pay £3 damages to Simon who
kept the money and 'ate' it. Subsequently Gutamo's people sued Simon
for the damages he had received from Nkhunguru because neither
Simon nor his son Chisani had ever paid any bridewealth or opened
marriage negotiations for Gutamo. Simon was ordered by the court

---

[1] For the main features of formal and informal marriage see p. 120.
[2] See Genealogy II.

to pay £3 damages to Gutamo's people. Gutamo continued to live with Chisani for the time being.

About a year later, however, Nkhunguru put Gutamo in his own house in Kamoti's (Mz. D 8) hamlet where she still was when I left the area. Nkhunguru then went abroad. He did not pay any bridewealth for Gutamo, who now has children by him.

Kamoti's comment on this affair to me was that he felt that if now anybody else came along and committed adultery with Gutamo, he would not feel inclined to sue the adulterer. He said that if Simon had had any sense at the time of Nkhunguru's original adultery with Gutamo, he would not only have given Gutamo's people the damages which he had received from Nkhunguru, but he would also have opened marriage negotiations, thus formalizing the marital relationship of Chisani and Gutamo. As for Gutamo's people 'they just "ate" their £3 and allowed Gutamo to stay with Chisani without either suing him [*viz.* for his own adultery with Gutamo[1]] or demanding bridewealth'. Later again Gutamo was taken by Nkhunguru and put in his house and again her people did not press for bridewealth. And if somebody else now commits adultery with Gutamo, her people cannot sue the adulterer: they will have to wait until Kamoti or Nkhunguru sues him and then Gutamo's people can recover their damages from them. 'But', added Kamoti, 'I would not bother to sue an adulterer because I would only be working for Gutamo's people. And if I were to judge a case like this I would not allow any damages because it looks as if Gutamo's people are only using their daughter to obtain money in damages. I would tell them: "You have failed on several occasions to ask for bridewealth. You only want your daughter for the damages. She is just like a dog: anybody can now take her and we will never allow your case in court again!"' Kamoti's words may not correctly sum up what a court in this case would say (one is very unlikely to hear such a harsh and abusive comparison with a dog in a Tonga court) but they do reflect what the court might think.

Interestingly enough, there was another set of what one might call retaliatory adulteries in this village. In the early 1940's, Samu (Mz. D 3) committed adultery with the wife of Nkhuni (Mz. D 24); Nkhuni was abroad at the time. This case was also discussed only within the village: the woman was divorced but Nkhuni's mother, Nyaulanda,

---

[1] Chisani was never sued by Gutamo's people and thus never paid damages for his adultery with her.

I

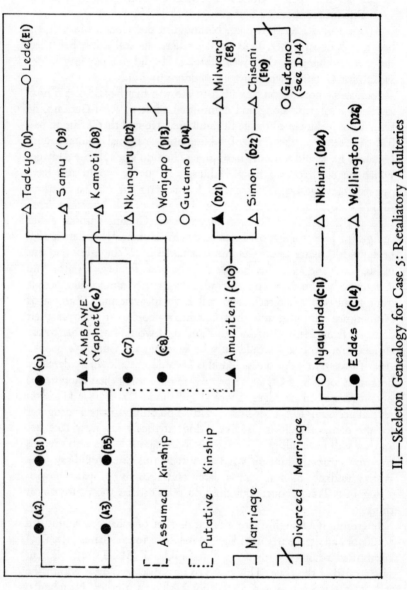

II.—Skeleton Genealogy for Case 5: Retaliatory Adulteries

Numbers in brackets refer to Genealogy XIV for Mzenga Village

did not claim damages. In 1954 Nkhuni's 'younger brother' Wellington (Mz. D 26) committed adultery with Samu's 'daughter' Lede
(Mz. E 1). But unlike the first case, this one was taken to court, which
irritated Wellington's mother Nyaulanda.[1]

Gutamo's case shows that in an informal marriage the wife's
people (*viz.* her *ankhoswe*) never lose their right to ask for bridewealth. And until marriage negotiations have put the marriage on
a formal basis the husband will forfeit his right to keep any damages
he may be awarded for adultery, and also the right to the bridewealth of at least his first daughter. Moreover, as there is often a
connection between a woman's residence and her attorney, a man
who has not paid any bridewealth for his wife may also jeopardize
his chances of getting his adult children to settle in his village. That
is why Tonga say of a man who belatedly pays bridewealth for his
children's mother: *apenja wana*, i.e. 'He is after (lit. seeks) children.'
  The bridewealth for a daughter of an informal marriage goes to
her matrilateral kin; in other words her attorney will be a matrilateral kinsman. The daughter's suitor will send the go-between
to her mother's village and if by any chance the go-between
should arrive at her father's village the latter should redirect him
to his wife's people. We saw that in a formal marriage the father is
fully entitled to keep the negotiations and the bridewealth for his
daughters' marriages entirely in his own hands. In fact, however,
he will generally show that he recognizes that the matrilateral kin
also have a claim on his children by informing them of an impending marriage and offering them a share in the bridewealth.
Similarly in an informal marriage the wife's kin may be entitled
to the bridewealth of her daughters, instead of the bridewealth
they never received for her, but normally they, too, will share the
bridewealth of the daughters with the father. In general, a share
in the bridewealth may consist of either the total bridewealth of
one or some of the daughters but not of the others, or a portion of
the bridewealth of some or all daughters.[2]
  The following case shows that claims for bridewealth, i.e.
marital debts, do not lapse. It also illustrates how, in the general
struggle for dependants, the matrikin consider that they have a
particularly strong claim to the residential allegiance of their

[1] See also p. 67 and Case 11, p. 195.
[2] Cf. the marital histories on pp. 87–8.

matrilineal descendants if the father was never formally married. I suspect that Waison has a particularly urgent reason for formalizing his marriage so that he can claim to be the pater of his wife's offspring even if he is not the genitor.

CASE 6: THE FATHER WHO ATE THE BRIDEWEALTH[1]

Salima married Chemenya (Chin. E 6) many years ago but never handed over any bridewealth to anybody at Chinyafwa, Chemenya's home. In spite of this debt to his wife's people, when his daughter Nyachunga married a few years ago Salima received the bridewealth and did not pass on anything to Chinyafwa. Moreover he kept both the other children of the marriage, Thom and Waison, with him although they should really have been living at Chinyafwa.[2] When Waison went abroad some years ago he left his wife Nyaphiri, for whom he never paid any bridewealth, behind with his father Salima. Then, in about 1952, Waison's 'brother' Fillimon apparently 'entered' Waison's house[3] and the result was that Nyaphiri, who in the meantime had returned to her home village, had a baby. Waison, still abroad, heard about the affair, and wrote an angry letter to his father Salima accusing him of just sitting by and watching Fillimon 'entering' his, Waison's, house. He also wrote a letter to Siddely at Chinyafwa enclosing £13. He said that he no longer wanted to live with his father Salima but wished to return to his mother's village, Chinyafwa. In this letter he also accused Salima of allowing Fillimon to take his wife and said that he, Salima, had probably 'sent'[4] Fillimon to his wife: 'How can my father allow this? Am I dead that my brother enters my house?'[5] To prove that his intentions of shifting from his father's village to his matrilocal village were serious, he sent Siddely the £13 out of which he had to pay for Nyaphiri's bridewealth and

[1] See Genealogies I, VII and XI.

[2] It is very likely that one reason why they are not living at Chinyafwa is that up to a few years ago Siddely, their maternal uncle, was abroad: after his return there was no peace at Chinyafwa: see Case 3, p. 68.

[3] The expression 'to enter' a man's house means that the one who enters does so either as a lover of the man's wife, or as the one who has inherited the man's widow.

[4] This is the usual phrase in this sort of situation. It implies that the sender is 'in' on a scheme to have the wife of a sterile husband impregnated.

[5] I did not see the letter myself but this is how my informant Nyali, of Chinyafwa, quoted it to me.

perhaps damages—thus choosing Siddely as his *nkhoswe* (attorney). He also wrote that he did not want to take a case against his 'brother' Fillimon: he merely wanted to move away from Salima. From the fact that Waison still wanted to keep his wife in spite of her adultery with Fillimon it looks as if Waison was sterile and not displeased that his wife had this child. Waison might even have had foreknowledge of Fillimon's intentions: even if he had, he would still have had to pretend some surprise and anger so as to avoid a charge of collusion, in which case legal action would have lain with Nyaphiri's people. But considered as a case of straightforward adultery, action lay with Waison. Waison hoped to give his marriage a more solid basis by formalizing it through bridewealth so that Nyaphiri would come to live with him again with the child. By rearing the child he might try to become its pater. Waison may succeed in this since the genitor was his 'brother'— it would be much more difficult if the genitor had been a stranger. This is the only hope for sterile men to have children.[1] When I left the village Siddely had not yet done anything about the bridewealth and it was therefore still uncertain whether Nyaphiri's people were prepared to accept Waison and his bridewealth.

Waison's message to Siddely about moving his residence gave Siddely a chance to bring home to Salima how wrong he had been in respect of his own marriage to Chemenya and his children's marriages. He went to see Salima and told him about Waison's intentions. Salima became very angry and accused Siddely of being a thief in wheedling away his son. Siddely, he said, had always been very 'jealous'[2] and had shown his spite by using sorcery against Nyachunga who was now barren. He said that he did not believe that Waison had written this to Siddely. They took the matter to Nyachenga (Mul. C 5) but Salima was too unco-operative to accept any advice.[3] For instance, Nyachenga suggested that Siddely and Salima should each write a separate letter to Waison to ask him to let Nyachenga or someone else know what his intentions were.

Siddely considered that Salima was adding insult to injury since he, Siddely, was the wronged party and could never be accused of 'theft'

---

[1] I have come across similar cases—e.g. Fany (Map. C 15) once had a sterile husband. It is a public secret that 'his child' was really begotten by another man, but the husband claims the child as his. He lavishes every care on this, his only child. His unstinted material support of the child is also—at least partly—in support of his claim to the child.

[2] See p. 67, n. 2.   [3] See also p. 207.

for the following reasons: (*a*) Salima first took Chemenya without any bridewealth; (*b*) when she died he did not pay anything either; (*c*) when the daughter of this marriage, Nyachunga, married he 'ate' the bridewealth; (*d*) Salima kept all the children with him although they should have gone to their mother's village, Chinyafwa.

Siddely wanted to sue Salima in court on these four grounds; but when I left, Nyali was still successful in preventing him from doing so. Nyali argued, that: (*a*) it would be better to see first what would happen—whether at last Siddely would get his due; (*b*) Salima had no money so that he would never be able to pay damages in any case; and (*c*) as Salima would never pay anything and the court would be unable to make Salima fulfil his non-monetary obligations, a court case would only create bad blood and that would do nobody any good since after all they had to live together.[1] Moreover Nyali is confident that it will only be a matter of time before Chemenya's three children change their domicile at Salima's death from Salima's village to Chinyafwa without an awkward court case.

So far I have discussed the case of the man who does not deny his responsibility for the woman's pregnancy. But there are many cases of men who do deny it even after a court has found against them and they have paid damages. In these circumstances the woman will stay in her own village. But after some time (perhaps some years) most genitors will go to the woman's village and claim their progeny because 'what man would be mad enough to throw away any children?' As the sole economic responsibility for bringing up the child, for example the expense of feeding and clothing it, and perhaps the cost of medicines, has so far fallen entirely on the mother and her family, the man is asked to pay his share which is called *ndrama za kulela*, i.e. 'the money for the upbringing'. This 'money for the upbringing'[2] is not part of the bridewealth which the genitor may belatedly pay for his child's mother in order to formalize the marriage. After the payment for the upbringing, the father will be allowed to take the child to his

---

[1] There is much intercourse between Salima's village Mulombwa and Chinyafwa—they use the same net-shelter. Siddely is an old, frustrated and rather quarrelsome man (see Case 3). Salima is also old and inclined to be short-tempered and often in trouble, e.g. he took his brother Chimuti's wife—see also Lovemore's case (p. 93).

[2] Cf. also the case of John and Jenetti, pp. 62–3.

village for short periods at a time. The relationship between the man and the child's mother then becomes that of an informal marriage, whether or not the woman takes up residence in her husband's village. If she does not go to the husband's village the situation resembles that of a divorce in an informal marriage but, as I will point out later, a divorce need not affect the status of the child at all.

Location of the Marriage

Although the married man usually resides where he lived before his marriage, we saw in the cases of 'Lovemore's abducted Wife' and 'The Father who ate the Bridewealth' that both patrikin and matrikin always try to persuade their male kinsmen to set up home with them. Implicit in this endeavour is the recognition that the village where a person has grown up and where he knows the local inhabitants and surroundings may have a greater attraction than a place where he has only kinship ties.[1] Hence the importance of getting a marrying kinsman, or at any rate a kinsman with a young family, into the village, so that the children will grow up there. The bonds thus created between the children and the village will reinforce the children's matrilateral ties (if brought up matrilocally) and alternatively strengthen their patrilateral ties (if brought up patrilocally).

Virilocal Marriage: A Focus of Inter-village Relationships

Tonga wives almost invariably live virilocally. Reference to a man living uxorilocally provokes a remark like: 'Just like the Yao! But then the Yao are like chickens anyway—they sleep together and have children and don't pay any bridewealth.' Among the Tonga uxorilocality is very rare and never occurs in formal marriages. Uxorilocal marriage conflicts with a man's desire for his children to grow up and stay in his village—children who grow up with their father in their mother's village are much less likely to settle in their father's village. Moreover a Tonga father has a political, economic and emotional role of some importance *vis-à-vis* his children which would conflict with his subordinate position as a son-in-law living in his wife's village.[2] Finally, uxorilocal marriage would also conflict with the dominant role of the husband in the home. The words *mkumwana*

[1] See also pp. 63, 77 and 245.   [2] See also p. 141.

(daughter-in-law) and *mkosano* (son-in-law) have very clearly the same implications as *mlanda* (orphan) and *kaporo* (slave),[1] *viz.* being without power in the village. A phrase like: 'Oh, she is only a daughter-in-law here', puts the woman thus indicated in a position of powerlessness in the village.

Because the status of a wife in her husband's village is one of subordination and isolation she relies for moral and legal support on her own village. This prevents her husband and his kin from abusing her weak position in the village. And this dependence of a wife on her own village for her emotional and legal security creates a most important link between the two villages.[2] A wife keeps in close contact with 'home'. Crises in her life are frequently weathered in her own village: for instance childbirth (wives are almost invariably confined in their home village), her own or her children's illnesses, or quarrels with the husband or other villagers. Whilst the wife is staying with her husband her own kin keep themselves informed as to how she is treated by her husband, lest he should treat her as a person without family protection, that is, like a slave.[3] And her own kin generally include both her paternal and her maternal kin who normally[4] live in different villages. Conversely, when a wife is staying in her own village, be it her paternal or her maternal village, her husband keeps an eye on her actions and movements. These various interests, on the part of at least three different kin groups, which centre on the married woman, also extend to her children. Thus a woman and her children create a common focus and hence ties between at least three kin groups. Since divorce or death do not alter the relationship between these groups and the children, the ties between them are permanent. Indeed if the woman remarries elsewhere (and especially if she takes her children with her to her new husband) the new marital village is also drawn into the network of the ties which she created in her previous marriage. For if at divorce the children follow their mother to her new husband's

[1] See also p. 262.

[2] This is the fundamental difference between a free wife's status and that of a slave wife and slaves in general or even 'orphans'. A slave's only status is his subordinate one in the village of his residence. He has no status in a wider network which would neutralize his subordination in his village. See Chapter V, p. 254.

[3] See also p. 49, and Case 9, p. 149.

[4] One of the exceptions is a cross-cousin marriage: see pp. 128 *seq.*

village, their father will keep an eye on his children lest his paternal rights are infringed.

Divorce: Perpetuation of Marital Links and Debts

Either party can initiate divorce proceedings and it depends on the circumstances of the case which party will forfeit the bridewealth—if it was paid at all. But the possible loss of the bridewealth is not the only or even the only important consequence of a divorce; in many marriages no bridewealth has been paid at all. Even in formal marriages, if the husband is entitled to have his bridewealth returned to him, he generally waives his right to part or the whole of the bridewealth when there are children. Divorce does not alter the respective rights of the parties to the marriage with regard to the children and their bridewealth. This applies to both informal and formal marriages provided that, in the latter case, the husband has not broken his relationship to the children by accepting the return of the entire[1] bridewealth.[2]

Another consequence of divorce is that the wife who used to live with her husband returns to her own village or, on re-marriage, goes to her new husband's village. On these moves she generally takes the children with her, especially if they are still young. It is this fact that is on the whole a greater disadvantage for the husband than the possible loss of bridewealth which he does not get refunded by his wife's people, if he is the guilty party in the divorce. Although the ex-husband will always remain the father of the children and retains the rights and responsibilities which go with this, in the struggle between the children's matrilateral and patrilateral relatives for the children's residential allegiance (i.e. residence in the village) the father who is separated from his children is always at a disadvantage. In spite of this separation, the fathers are still expected to take an active interest in their children and most of them do. A father will continue to visit his children and will make financial contributions, for instance towards school fees, cost of medical treatment, clothes and so on.[3] Often he may also take his child with him to stay in his

---

[1] By 'entire' bridewealth I mean that part he actually paid.

[2] On p. 104 we saw the obverse—a man who originally repudiated his offspring can later establish his relationship with them by paying the *ndrama za kulela.*

[3] Cf. the interest of Jenetti's patrilateral kin in her illness, pp. 62–3.

own village for a while so that it may get acquainted with its patrilateral relatives and the village itself. We thus note continuous efforts on the part of the father to try and keep (or attract) his children as local dependants against the odds that they will settle with their matrilateral kin.[1] To this end, familiarity with the father's village is considered important.

Death of Husband: Position of Widows

Death does not fundamentally alter the debt relationship between kin groups which were linked by formal or informal marriage. A debt is the tangible basis of relationships created by formal and informal marriage: but these relationships do not affect only the spouses or their immediate kin but also large groups of people which are interlinked by marriage (and not by a political hierarchy). Relationships and debts are therefore not allowed to lapse with the death of one or both spouses. The debts involved in the relationships are the liability of the respective matrilineages[2] and are inherited within them.[3]

On the death of the husband, as on divorce (if the husband is not the guilty party), he or his kin are legally entitled to the return of the entire sum he paid towards the bridewealth. But to accept this money would further weaken the (late) husband's and his kin's relationship with and claims on the husband's children, whose ties with their patrikin are already weaker than those with their matrikin. This weakening of the relationship comes out in the fact that after acceptance of the return of the bridewealth the patrikin cannot claim as a legal right the bridewealth of a marrying daughter. They are thus in the same position as the father or patrikin of children of an informal marriage. Therefore, when there are children, the general rule is, on divorce as well as on the husband's death, that the husband or his kin waive their right to the return of the whole or part of the bridewealth, lest they should lose the children and the widow.

These matters, concerning the future of the widow(s) and the

---

[1] Cf. pp. 62–3 and 105.

[2] Note how in Case 18 Abeni tried in vain to evade his inherited liability for the return of bridewealth (p. 240).

[3] I do not know what will happen about Malalanje's liability for Nyamwale's bridewealth (see p. 88) when he dies: his mother was a Chewa and all his matrikin are in Chewa country.

PLATE 4. (*a*) Two widows are being shaved. The other two women sitting together nearby are close kinswomen of the dead man and are waiting their turn

(*b*) A new hamlet in a recent clearance in the forest in the hills. One house is still under construction. Note the patch of cassava in front of the houses

children, are discussed not on the day of the burial itself but on the subsequent 'day of the shaving' (*zuwa la kumeta*); and the discussions of that day are referred to as 'the discussions of the shaving' (*makani ngha kumeta*).[1] The 'shaving' is a reference to the fact that as a token of the conclusion of the discussions about the problems caused by the death, certain of the dead person's nearest kin have their heads completely or partly shaven. Until the shaving ceremony the people due to be shaved are handicapped by certain avoidances, such as the prohibition to cook, to touch salt, or to have sexual intercourse. And fellow villagers of the dead person are also supposed to be restrained in their economic activities: they are not supposed to do any hoeing of gardens, or fishing. In fact this rule is not always followed, especially if the interval between death and shaving is prolonged.

The mortuary proceedings for both men and women fall into two parts: the burial, which is generally the day after the death, and the shaving, which may be anything from a few days to some weeks or longer after the burial, for the shaving may be delayed if some kinsmen whose presence at the shaving discussions is of crucial importance are temporarily out of reach. On the other hand, the shaving may take place on the same day as the burial if the dead person has the status of a slave, or if for some other reason his (her) status and affairs are not considered to be the concern of his (her) kinsmen (i.e. attorneys) outside the village.[2] At a freeman's death both his matrilateral and his patrilateral kin must be informed. If he is not a freeman on both sides, at least the relatives on his free side have to be informed: the same applies to a freeborn woman. If possible these relatives should be present at the interment, but if they live too far or if for some other reason the funeral cannot wait until their arrival the physical remains can be disposed of without them. The various activities associated with the funeral, such as the washing of the corpse, the lyke-wake, the carrying of the corpse, and the digging of the grave, are mostly performed by the locals—at any rate these tasks are not apportioned to specific kinsmen.[3]

---

[1] I will adopt the term 'shaving discussions'. For the important differences between the proceedings of burial and shaving see Case 9, p. 149.

[2] See Case 9, paras. 13–17 *et passim*, where this is one of the central issues.

[3] The people who perform these funeral tasks are called *azukuru* (sing. *mzukuru*). The Tonga term for grandchild is *mzuku* (pl. *azuku*). It is interesting

The affairs of the dead man are the subject of discussion on the day of the shaving. Unlike the funeral, this shaving discussion cannot proceed without the presence of those kinsmen who are entitled to attend. If there have been any serious sorcery accusations at the death, or in other words, if some latent conflict has come into the open at the time of the death and because of it, this is not investigated during the funeral but is left for the shaving discussion. This has therefore something of the character of an inquest. Such an enquiry into the causes of death, and, possibly, into sorcery accusations, is bound to lead to a review of the dead man's position in the village and his relationship to the other inhabitants and to his kin outside the village. This enquiry is closely related, too, with the other aspect of the shaving discussion: the measures which are to be taken to fill the social, political and economic gap which the death has created. The dead man may leave behind widows, children, a 'name' and other property. That is why both his matrilateral and his patrilateral kin have to be present.

Since the shaving-day discussion will also decide the future of the widow(s), her (their) relatives must also be present unless, again, a widow has the status of a slave. Death is therefore an event which mobilises a variety of kin groups and brings them together in a common discussion, albeit with conflicting interests. The conclusion of the discussion—that is, the solution (which may be temporary only) of the problems created by the death—is

---

that the Tumbuka word *mzukuru* (pl. *azukuru*) means both grandchild and a person who performs funeral duties. There is no doubt that the Tonga *mzuku* (grandchild) and the Tumbuka *mzukuru* are the same word; elision of the final *-ru* is characteristic of the Tonga language. Mitchell (1956, p. 37) and Marwick (quoted by Mitchell, *loc. cit.*) report that among the Nyanja and Chewa peoples those performing funeral tasks do not do so because they are the dead person's grandchildren or other relatives but that they are given quasi-kinship status *because* they have performed these tasks. Tew (1951) suggests that in this area (which includes the Tonga) 'there might be some connection between funeral friends and the grandchildren of the deceased' (p. 124). This is not the case now among the Tonga nor apparently some sixty years ago: see MacAlpine (1906), p. 188. A Tonga told me there is a special relationship between the *azukuru* and the parents or other close kin of the deceased in that the former could take or demand property from the latter; I never found an actual example of this custom which may have been valid in the past. Thus at present the only connection among the Tonga between the *azukuru* and grandchildren (*azuku*) appears to be linguistic.

marked by the shaving of some of the relatives of the dead man, e.g. his widow, his sister and his children.

In law a man's property should go to his sister's son, but it appears that in practice sons also get a share, for reasons I will deal with later when discussing succession to office.[1]

When a man dies, the attorney of the widow or other relatives from her own village will try to get her back, with the children, to her own village. Whether they succeed depends on several factors. One is the length of the marriage—an old woman who has been married to the dead husband for a long time without too many open conflicts with the other villagers is more likely to stay in her husband's village. Moreover, in such a marriage the adult children also influence their mother's decision. Tonga say that children who are abroad on the whole like their mothers to stay in the village where they left them until their own return. But even adult children who are still in the village may prefer to stay in their father's village[2] and thus persuade their mother to stay too. On the other hand, a widow with young children is much more likely to go back to her own village taking the children with her.

Widows who do not leave their late husband's village are 'inherited' (*kuhara choko*, to inherit the widow). This does not necessarily mean that the kinsman who is said to have inherited the widow lives with her as his wife. It refers principally to the fact that he is now supposed to care for her as a husband would do. The kinsman is particularly unlikely to live sexually with the inherited widow if she is old or if they stand to one another in a genealogical relationship which would make a sexual union resulting in offspring a social impossibility. Sisters' sons who inherit their maternal uncle's title and office are also said to inherit their widows.[3] In fact, however, a sister's son never 'puts his late uncle's widow in his house', that is, he never lives with her as a wife, but only inherits the responsibility for her welfare—if she stays in her late husband's village at all. For instance, at Mapalassie

[1] I did not attend many shaving discussions of propertied men, and when I did, I generally found it impossible to get detailed genealogical information, since I was a stranger in the village.

[2] I will discuss some of these preferences when I consider the position of a son in his father's village: see pp. 228 *seq.*

[3] The Tonga term for 'maternal uncle' is *asibweni* and his wife is called *apongozi* (the singular *msibweni* and *mpongozi* are hardly ever used); these terms also mean: father-in-law and mother-in-law: see also pp. 128 and 148.

Ziba (Map. C 3) has inherited Tepambana (Map. B 14) and Nyalongwe (Map. B 12) who are the widows of his late maternal uncles, Donald (Map. B 13) and Mordecai (Map. B 11). Apart from the fact that these two women are a good deal older than Ziba, sexual relations with them would conflict with their respective genealogical and social roles in the village. Unless a particular man actually marries the widow who stays behind in her late husband's village, she is not really 'inherited' by one particular person but by the whole of her husband's kin group. It is the whole group which is responsible for the widow's welfare and in this sense it is possible for women to inherit widows: for example Nyamwale (Map. C 10) and Nyadalo (Map. C 9) both say that they inherited Tepambana and Nyalongwe. If Nyalongwe's matrikin think that she is not fairly treated at Mapalassie, they will hold Mussa[1] responsible because outside Mapalassie Mussa (or Ziba) represents the kin group into which Nyalongwe married.[2]

If the kinsmen of the husband were to accept or even demand the return of the entire bridewealth, as they are legally entitled to, it would be inconceivable for the widow to stay in her husband's village. But as far as I am aware, this is merely a hypothetical question, when it concerns a fruitful marriage. As stated before, both at divorce and at a man's death, the father or his kin will waive their right to the return of the bridewealth or at least part of it. To accept the return of the entire bridewealth from the widow's people would be tantamount to 'dissolving the marriage' (*kupata nthengwa*).[3] The general practice is that if the widow stays in her marital village no part of the bridewealth is returned. If she wishes to return to her own village, and if she has children of this particular marriage, her kinsmen will return part of the bridewealth; but even in this case it often happens that no bridewealth at all is returned particularly when she is an old woman who has been married a long time to her late husband.

Thus when a widow returns to her home village this is not necessarily a sign that the bridewealth has been returned. In any case, waiver of the bridewealth is not primarily aimed at retention of the widow for her own sake, but rather for the sake of retaining the children of the marriage in their father's village. If their

---

[1] Or Ziba who as Mussa's heir presumptive now generally acts for Mussa who is an old man.

[2] Cf. Case 9, p. 149.   [3] The same phrase is used for a divorce *inter vivos*.

mother stays in the village, her children are also more likely to stay. Hence the Tonga say: '*ako choko, ako wana*',[1] i.e. retain the widow and you retain the children. This is an aphorism rather than a legal rule. For the Tonga also say '*wana banangwa*', i.e. children are free, that is, to live where they want. When there are no children, widows are almost certain to return to their own village and the bridewealth is returned to the late husband's kin. An example of this is Lizzy (Map. C 16)[2] who had only been married for a few years when her husband died and who never had any children. She returned to her own hamlet (i.e. to her mother, Nyalongwe's [Map. B 12] house), and Msorowa's kin received the entire bridewealth back. But in this respect, too, advanced age of the widow and the length of her marriage tend in practice to make a difference, because such a widow frequently stays on virilocally even if she has no children in the village.

As I previously pointed out[3] the majority of widows, whether they have children or not, return to their own village after their husband's death. In my five sample villages I found twenty widows. Of these seven had been married to members of the villages where they were still living at the time of my enquiries; in other words they were still living virilocally. The other thirteen

TABLE VI

Residence of Widows

Widows who still live virilocally	7
Widows who have returned home[1]	13
Total	20

[1] Including those who have returned from their marital hamlet to their own hamlet within the same village

widows were all living in their own villages, *viz.* with the exception of two (see below) they had returned 'home' from their late husbands' villages. However, these figures do not reflect accurately the widows' *choice* as regards returning to their home village in widowhood. For of the seven widows who have remained in their late husbands' village three do not appear to have another choice; they are slaves, unlikely to know where they originally came from and having thus nowhere to go. This means that out of the total of twenty widows there are only four of them still living virilocally, who have any alternative. On the other

[1] See pp. 39, 70.   [2] See also p. 62.   [3] See pp. 61 *seq.*

hand, among the thirteen widows who are living in their home villages there are two women who, as far as I am aware, never married away but were married to men who belonged to the same village either as freemen or as slaves. Thus in the case of these two women (most probably of slave origin) their home village was also their marital village. The difference between these two widows and the three virilocal slave widows is that the latter were not born in the village or among the kin group where they live now, but were brought there as slaves, whilst the two 'uxorilocal' widows were both born as slaves in the village. The marriages of these five women of slave origin have in common that they resemble intra-village marriages of cross-cousins, or at least they have the same effect as is ideally expected from intra-village cross-cousin marriages. In such marriages a widow is more firmly attached to her husband's village than in inter-village marriages and the children are therefore less likely to leave their patrilocality.[1]

In another respect, too, the figures do not adequately represent the tendency of widows to leave their late husbands' villages. For instance Foness (Map. C 2) has been widowed twice and twice she returned to Mapalassie although in Table VI she is only entered once. My data regarding the marital histories of some of the other widows are not sufficiently reliable for me to break down the figures of this table into the total number of widowed marriages experienced by the twenty widows.

The tendency of widows to move back to their own homes can also be observed within the village where it becomes a move from one hamlet to another. For instance, apart from Lizzy's case at Mapalassie, which I mentioned previously, there is also the case of Nyaphiri (Mul. C 10) who returned from Ngai's hamlet, where she was married to Samweri (Mtomba B 3), to her own hamlet.

Wife's Death: Review of Marital Debt

We saw that at least three different kin groups are brought together at the death of a man.[2] What is at stake is the future of the man's widows, children, property and, possibly, his 'name'. All these interests are not always present but some at least will be and they are the focus of the many ties which are centred on

[1] For cross-cousin marriage see pp. 128 *et passim*, and slave status see pp. 267 *et passim*.   [2] Provided he was a free man.

the man. The death of a free woman mobilizes three similar groups: her patrikin, her matrikin, and her husband and his kinsmen. In this case the inter-relationships between the three kin groups are focussed on the dead woman's bridewealth.

Often when a woman feels ill, she will go to her own village; so women often die in their home village and are buried there. If she dies in her husband's village she is most likely to be buried locally. The inquest, i.e. the shaving discussions, generally takes place in the village where she died and/or was buried.[1] The grave of a woman may have some significance in the future settlement of the children. A person may base his claim to cultivate and settle on certain land on the fact that his mother or another matrilateral kinsman is buried there.[2] The underlying assumption is that the person in the grave must have had gardens on that land otherwise the grave would not be there and these gardens may be claimed by a descendant.[3] For instance, some twenty years or so ago the then inhabitants of Chinyafwa settled just across their own boundaries on KAMISA's land. When one of their number died [*viz.* Nyakaunda (Chin. D 12) the mother of Adamu (Chin. E 12)[4]] KAMISA very reluctantly allowed them to start a graveyard by their village, i.e. on KAMISA's land.[5] But when later another woman of a Chinyafwa matrilineage died, namely Nyakaunda's sister's daughter Valini, who was also survived by adult children, KAMISA did not want her to be buried on his land next to Nyakaunda's grave,[6] and she was buried in the graveyard of

[1] If a dead woman's marital village is near her home village and she (or her child) dies in her husband's village, her home village may want the body for burial.

[2] There is no ritual associated with graves—they do not become shrines.

[3] Cf. the Mapalassie people who seem to have started their own graveyard fairly soon after their arrival in KAMISA's village. The possession of a separate, independent graveyard has probably speeded up the independence of the Mapalassie people as a political unit: see p. 286.   [4] See p. 68.

[5] I have no reliable information about this period, e.g. why they moved at all as the Chinyafwa area is quite extensive, or why they did not bury Nyakaunda in the Chinyafwa graveyard which is only about ten minutes' walk from the place where they were living at the time. My principal informants at Chinyafwa, Nyali and Siddely, were abroad for most of that time.

[6] KAMISA was probably afraid to allow too many women who had adult children, to be buried on his land, lest there should be a group of people claiming the graveyard and the land by it as ancestral land: cf. the Mapalassie graveyard, p. 286.

K

a neighbouring village. There are nevertheless six other graves of Chinyafwa people—besides Nyakaunda's grave—on KAMISA's land. It is significant, however, that none of these six graves contain adults. In other words, none of the people in them died at an age at which they could have possessed any gardens or other rights which could be claimed by present or future kinsmen and which might have given the heirs a foothold on KAMISA's land. This may explain why KAMISA objected to having Valini's grave on his land but allowed the graves of these six young people.

Something similar to KAMISA's refusal happened at Mtemeni, a piece of land which is now under Nyali's control.[1] He had given some people of a neighbouring village permission to cultivate a few gardens just within the boundaries of his land. But after a while, so he told me, he noticed that they were extending their gardens farther inwards and had built a couple of huts by their gardens. Nyali told them that they could continue to hoe their gardens along the fringes of his land but not those farther inside it, and that they would have to remove their huts to their own village which is only ten minutes or so from their gardens. He explained to me that he did not want them there because one day one of them would die, and then they might want to start a graveyard on his land. Later one of the descendants would come along and claim the land as his on the basis of his ancestor's old gardens, pointing to the grave to corroborate his claim.[2]

There are very few cases in which the death of a woman does not give rise to a discussion about bridewealth.[3] The exceptions generally concern women who never married and have no children, and slave women. Even in a formal marriage the bride

---

[1] See Case 13, p. 211.

[2] The grave may be that of an ancestor and not an ancestress; after all, the original 'owner' of certain land is always a man. The present dominant matrilineage at Chinyafwa has a man, MAKALAMBA, as a 'founder', *viz.* he is the ultimate link (through his sister, not his wife) between the matrilineage and the land on which they are settled: see pp. 32, 211.

[3] I heard several accounts of discussions about the bridewealth of dead women being held before the funeral whilst the dead woman's people refused to give their permission for the disposal of the body, thus backing their demands with the threat of a decomposing body. I never witnessed such situations and very much doubt if they would occur at present; if they did occur it was probably a long time ago, cf. MacAlpine, 1906, p. 189. I was never told of similar occurrences at the funeral of a man.

wealth is never paid in full—the unpaid portion generally remains unpaid until the death of the wife.[1] Bridewealth is never returned to the husband or his kin group on the death of his wife. The Tonga say: '*Chuma chiwe cha pa nyifwa kweni pa umoyo pe*', i.e. bridewealth never goes back at death (*viz.* of a woman) but only during her lifetime (*viz.* at divorce). This applies equally to wives who have not borne children. Barrenness is not a ground for divorce; if a husband wants to divorce his wife in fact for barrenness but ostensibly on other grounds, he is not awarded the return of the bridewealth he paid.

Even in formal marriages, negotiated through go-betweens, the payment and the amount of the bridewealth are not necessarily undisputed. For instance marriages which started off with adultery and/or abduction may give rise at the shaving discussions to a dispute between the respective parties as to whether the initial payment handed over by the go-between was damages for the adultery or abduction, or the first instalment of the bridewealth. From this point a further difference may arise: whether the husband of the dead woman was right in 'eating' the bridewealth of his daughters. The death of a widow or a divorced woman also calls for a discussion of her own bridewealth and consequently that of her daughters. It is not uncommon for a husband (or his kin) to deny the wife's family's allegation that the woman's bridewealth has been returned to him (them), for example, on

---

[1] The Tonga say that in the old days a husband always had 'a big case' when his wife died, whether the union was formal or informal. The payment he had to make to his wife's people was called *chisoka* and even recently I have heard the balance of the bridewealth paid at the woman's death referred to as *chisoka* money. The modern meaning of *soka* is something like 'bad luck'. The old *chisoka* payment is said to have consisted of hoes (and probably guns and beads and slaves), but also land, as in the case of MAKALAMBA's 'sister' (cf. p. 32). There are names of localities derived from the word *nyifwa*, death. It may be that the present practice of splitting the bridewealth is a compromise between the old *chisoka* payment and the introduction of the bridewealth (by the Ngoni?). It seems there was a time when the Tonga did not pay bridewealth, like their southern neighbours the Chewa, who still do not pay bridewealth: see Marwick (1952), p. 132. MacAlpine (1906, p. 189) reports that when the relatives of the dead person arrived in the village where their kinsman or kinswoman had died, they expected a present. The value of this present was sometimes considerable 'especially at the death of a woman'. When the relatives had been satisfied they would give permission to bury the body, or else discussions would go on and the body might not be buried for some days.

divorce, and that he (they) therefore has (have) no say in the marriages of his daughters.

The most frequent comment from the Tonga when discussing an adulterous or informal marriage is: 'It is all very well to live with a woman without giving bridewealth but the difficulties come if she dies in your home [*viz*. whilst still your wife], especially if she dies during pregnancy or in childbirth. Then you have a big case and her people can claim any amount of damages. In the old days they would make you a slave if you could not compensate them with land or hoes.' Here again, the bridewealth (or in this case its non-payment) is the tangible and reinforcing link between the parties concerned. Dolnard's case illustrates some of the issues at stake.

CASE 7: DEATH OF INFORMAL WIFE

Dolnard had abducted Nyasaka and lived with her in his matrilocal village at Muroli. Nyasaka had been with Dolnard for about one year (without conceiving) when she became ill, whereupon she went to her matrilocal village, Dirika, where her mother Nyamuhoni still lives. Dolnard, a young man of about twenty-five, was present at Dirika when Nyasaka died. The next day Nyasaka's matrilateral kin and the other inhabitants of Dirika and nearby villages assembled. Later that day Nyasaka's patrilateral kin, living some distance away, also arrived. Nyasaka's husband Dolnard was present at this meeting but not his kinsmen, although they had been informed. Among Nyasaka's patrikin was Milton Saka[1] who is the son of a younger brother of Chigwenembe, Nyasaka's father, who died some years ago. Chigwenembe had not paid bridewealth for Nyasaka's mother Nyamuhoni who had returned to her own village on her husband's death. Milton and Nyasaka's other 'fathers' sat together and they tried to convince the Dirika people that they, the patrikin, should also have a say in the discussions about what to do with Dolnard. Their claims were ignored and Milton and a few others went off in a huff; but other patrikin stayed, though without saying a word. In the meanwhile a small group of the leading personalities at Dirika were having hushed—not public—consultations amongst themselves for most of the morning, until one of them gave instructions for the body to be washed and prepared for burial.

[1] See also p. 223 *et passim* and Genealogy VII.

The burial took place in a graveyard a mile or so from Dirika in what is now uninhabited forest. On their return from the graveyard the Dirika people discussed (this time audibly) what to do with 'son-in-law'. They never referred to Dolnard by his name but only by the term *mkosano* (son-in-law), denoting his status in Dirika village and thus emphasizing his subordinate position.[1] Indeed the way they treated him gave very much the impression that they considered him to be in their power. The Dirika men debated whether to keep their son-in-law at Dirika until his relatives should come and redeem him, or whether to send him to his own village. One of them suggested: 'It is now Monday. We ought to keep son-in-law here until Wednesday and then send him home with a big escort to announce a meeting here for Thursday. If his father and maternal uncle (*asibweni*) refuse to come and discuss the matter with us, the escort can take a statement from them and we can then take the case to court on the Friday.[2] In the meanwhile it is no good asking son-in-law too many questions—we had better wait until his people come.' [3] In the event they sent him home the next day accompanied by two Dirika men, and the meeting between the Dirika people and Dolnard's people took place on the following Wednesday.

Those present at this second meeting were Nyasaka's matrilateral kin of Dirika village, Dolnard's father from near Bandawe and his mother from Muroli;[4] none of Nyasaka's 'fathers' were there. Dolnard's father and mother were told, jointly, that they would have to pay bridewealth of £15 and until they had paid it the people of Dirika would not shave Dolnard. At another stage of the discussions the Dirika people also threatened that they would keep all three of them, *viz.* Dolnard, his father and mother, at Dirika until they had paid up. Later they said that they would keep Dolnard and his mother so that his father could go back and look for money. In the end Dolnard's people produced £1 which the other party accepted not as an adequate first instalment, but as a token that Dolnard's people agreed that they 'had a case'.[5] Dolnard and his parents went away and

[1] Cf. pp. 106 and 262.

[2] The court sits on Tuesdays and Fridays.

[3] The implication is that this matter does not just concern the individual, Dolnard, but also his matrilateral and patrilateral kin groups.

[4] Muroli is some ten miles or four hours' walk from Bandawe; both are by the lakeshore.

[5] *Nde ndi mlandu*, lit. 'I have a case', i.e. 'I have a case to answer' or 'I am in trouble'.

returned the next week with another instalment of £3, in return for which his in-laws reduced their price (not at once but after long bargaining) from £15 to £10. For the remaining £6 Dolnard's father gave a promissory note (*kalata*) which was signed in the names of Dolnard, his father and his mother, although the latter was not present at the second meeting. After that Dolnard was shaved and so were Nyasaka's mother and the latter's sister.

Milton Saka, one of Nyasaka's 'fathers', later told me that he was very annoyed at not having been consulted about Nyasaka's bridewealth as he was after all her 'father'. But he could wait, he said. He would see how much Nyasaka's matrikin were going to receive from Dolnard and then he would go and ask for *his* share. And, he added, as for this business of Nyasaka's people saying that her father had never paid any bridewealth for her mother, the obviousness of this lie would be patent, later, to any one who would be present at the shaving discussion when Nyasaka's mother, Nyamuhoni, died.

We see that there are two debts (claims) involved in this case: the actual debt of Dolnard, that is, the posthumous bridewealth which he owes his late wife's matrikin, and the disputed debt which Nyasaka's matrikin owe her patrikin, i.e. part of the bridewealth. This latter, disputed, claim in turn arises from the dispute between Nyasaka's patrikin and matrikin about whether or not bridewealth was paid for Nyasaka's mother Nyamuhoni.

Dolnard thus paid bridewealth without obtaining the corresponding claim on a daughter's bridewealth. In other words, in his case money did not make money, nor did money create potential dependants. It is to prevent situations like this that one finds that a man who has impregnated some woman will begin by denying his paternity even if the court finds against him and he has paid damages. If the woman were to die during pregnancy or in childbirth the self-confessed husband and father would have 'a big case'. By denying any responsibility he tries to avoid this risk and can still claim the child later through the payment of 'the money for the upbringing'.[1]

Differences between Formal and Informal Marriages

In this discussion of marriage I have concentrated, as the Tonga themselves do in practice, on the common features of all hetero-

[1] See p. 104.

sexual unions and not on the different ways in which these unions come about. One of the similarities is the fact that the production of offspring gives these unions lasting effect, because, among the Tonga, the biological parents should also be the social parents. Another important similarity is the fact that all such unions, which I have called 'marriages', create obligations and relationships with a material basis: my 'marital debt relationships'. That these marital debts spring in some cases from a formal contract whilst in others from a quasi-contract does not alter the fact that the Tonga call all heterosexual unions which have produced or are likely to produce children 'marriages' (*nthengwa*). And in such unions the man is a 'husband' (*mlumu*, pl. *alumu*) and the woman is a 'wife' (*mwolu*, pl. *awolu*).

Where I had the necessary information for particular marriages I have distinguished, in my analysis, between 'formal' and 'informal' marriages. The formality or informality of marriages is, however, only relative and generally not apparent in daily life, but only at the inception of the marriage and at such critical points as disputes, death, marriage of the offspring and also (though not invariably) at divorce. Indeed the existence of a marriage itself is by no means always observable, for instance when the husband is abroad or when the spouses live separately without any divorce proceedings. And it may happen that a woman goes from one informal marriage to another, or, to put it differently, lives successively with and has children by two different men without any intervening public ceremonies or discussions. Verbal information on informants' own or other marriages cannot always be accepted without some corroborating evidence of these public acts. The most fruitful sources of information on particular marriages are disputes—not merely disputes directly connected with marriage but disputes in general (for example political disputes), because marital issues are frequently used to air other grievances.

For this and other reasons, such as the general lack of ritual or other ceremonial associated with marital life, it is difficult to make large-scale enquiries and to collect quantitative data related to marriage: incidence of formal and informal marriage; distribution and circulation of bridewealth;[1] rate of divorce, and so forth.

[1] Bridewealth and other marriage payments are nowadays invariably paid in cash which is not as easily traced as goods.

I have, therefore, based much of my analysis of Tonga marriage on qualitative data which accrue from intensive observation of marital matters in a few villages.

The criterion of a formal marriage is that the marital debt is the result of a formal and public contract. But in spite of its formality and publicity, and the use of a go-between, even in this kind of marriage disputes may arise about the debts involved and, in general, about whether a marriage is formal or not. An informal marriage is a union which creates marital debts as the result of a quasi-contract. I do not want to call this kind of quasi-marital union 'adulterous marriage' because that would smack too much of the exceptional, and informal marriages are too common to be considered so. Moreover the Tonga do not normally use different terms to distinguish such unions from formal marriages. And if they do it is generally only in courts or in disputes in general that they use the term *chigororo* (adultery) or such descriptive phrases as: *nthengwa ya dondo* (a marriage of the bush) and *nthengwa ya ubwezi* (a marriage of friendship).[1] During the hearing of a matrimonial dispute in court one frequently hears one of the members of the court ask: 'And how did this marriage begin—with a go-between or in the bush?', when he wants to find out whether it is a formal or informal marriage.

The two principal parties concerned in any union are always the woman's kin and those of the man. Indeed, every apparent sexual union must have two *known* partners. For instance, it sometimes happens that a woman is accused of adultery and that she refuses to name her lover and says that she does not know him. When there is a child to prove a sexual union the court will tell her: 'There is no child without a father.' Thus a child is not allowed to be entirely absorbed within its matrilineage: it must also have known patrilateral relationships—in other words a child should always be a link between two kin groups.

The difference between formal and informal marriage is not a question of different groups of kinsmen being involved: the distinction is rather a matter of different debts which fall due and can be claimed at different points in the course of the marriage. I will briefly summarize from the previous analysis and cases the

---

[1] Cf. also Nelly's outcry about being 'bought for fish' in Case 9 (paras. 1 and 14). As fish never constitutes part of the bridewealth, the clear implication of her remark is that no bridewealth was paid on her marriage.

main points of difference between marital debts in formal and informal marriages.

In a formal marriage, during the life of the wife and the duration of the marriage, a man legally owes his wife's people the unpaid part of the agreed bridewealth. Morally he owes them part of the bridewealth he receives for his daughter(s). If his wife commits adultery, the husband has an action for damages against both his wife and her lover, because they have 'spoilt his house' (*kunanga nyumba*). The wife can take no action against her husband on the grounds of his adultery because Tonga men may marry more than one wife. But a wife or her people can sue her husband if he conspires with another man to impregnate because he is sterile. On divorce, if his wife has been proved the guilty party, he is legally entitled to a refund of the entire sum he paid on marriage, but out of this sum he has a moral obligation to give his wife's people about half 'to help the children'.[1] At the wife's death he is under a legal obligation to pay the remainder of the agreed bridewealth. But the wife's people are under a moral obligation not to press too hard for the payment of the whole of this debt, and it frequently happens that even after the death of his wife the husband has not paid all the agreed bridewealth. This is particularly likely to happen when the marriage has been of long duration and without much friction between husband and wife and their respective kin. In such cases the husband will plead with the wife's people that he has always been a good husband and son-in-law and that the marriage has been 'without badness' (*kwambura uheni*). In these cases the widowed husband's remaining debt is often allowed to lapse; I have recorded no instances of claims of the wife's people for this remaining part of the debt, although it is possible that claims for such unpaid debts are exploited later in a different social or political context.

In an informal marriage the husband owes his wife's people damages[2] and an unspecified bridewealth; when the husband has

---

[1] The courts generally award the husband the refund of the bridewealth without making any order in respect of the part for the children; this is not a legal obligation of the husband and is left to the parties to settle between themselves.

[2] *Ndrama za chigororo*, i.e. 'the money for the adultery,' or *ndrama za pa mutu*, i.e. 'the money on the head', viz. of the seduced woman; both are used interchangeably.

paid damages his affines will 'mention their price' [1] so that the erstwhile unspecified marital debt becomes an agreed sum. From then on the marital debts are those of a formal marriage. If the marital relationship of the parents has not been formalized before the daughters of an informal marriage marry, the negotiations for the marriage of the first daughter at least should be put into the hands of the wife's people. When the wife's people receive the bridewealth for the daughters of an informal marriage, as they are legally entitled to, they are under a moral obligation to share some of it with the daughters' father. The Tonga say that the first bridewealth received by the wife's kin for her daughters is set off against the marital debt of the informal husband and counts as if it were his bridewealth for his wife. Informants told me that from then on the marriage is considered formal and the husband can 'eat' the bridewealth of his other daughters. But I was not able to record whether bridewealth received by the wife's people for her daughter(s) cancels out the 'big case', that is, the exemplary damages which, theoretically, are demanded from the informal husband at his wife's death.[2]

Even in an informal marriage the husband has an action against the lover of his wife, but not against the wife herself.[3] This is explained by the rules that a child's genitor should also be its pater, and that a woman's child is considered her husband's unless proved otherwise. But the damages awarded to an informal husband can be claimed by his wife's people.

The Tonga generally assert that at the death of his wife, the husband in an informal marriage is faced by a demand by his wife's people for the payment of a sum which is larger than he would have paid as bridewealth at the start of his marital union: this is the 'big case'. This does happen. But I have also recorded cases in which the sum demanded was what the husband would probably have paid as bridewealth. Case 7 is an example; the £15, later reduced to £10, is the average amount of bridewealth.

[1] *Kupaska mtengo*, i.e. literally, 'to give the price'. This expression is equivalent to the phrase: 'to open their mouth' (see p. 85) which I mentioned in my description of the formal marriage negotiations. These two phrases are not exclusive terms with a restricted usage, they are, rather, metaphors which are frequently (but not exclusively) and interchangeably used in this context.

[2] See p. 118 and Case 7.

[3] See Case 5, p. 118. A wife's adultery and the husband's action against her lover does not necessarily end the marriage.

It also illustrates another feature which is common in such cases: Dolnard's party were let off with a cash payment of £4 and a *kalata* (promissory note) for the remaining £6. It is most unlikely that the creditor party (in this case Dolnard's dead wife's people) will ever receive this £6 or indeed any of it, unless the two groups concerned have entered or will enter into other relationships for which this debt may become the tangible basis. At the time of my acquaintance with Dirika village (Dolnard's wife's village) there were no signs that the relationship between Dolnard's and Nyasaka's respective kin groups would be perpetuated, because there were no children of the marriage or any other focus of common interest. And thus Nyasaka's people's legal, specific and easily definable claim for £6 may not be mentioned again unless it becomes the vehicle for another less exact and less easily definable claim which may arise from possible future relationships.

A debt such as Dolnard still owes his dead wife's kinsmen is only one of the great variety and countless number of debt relationships between individuals and small groups. These debts do not arise only from marital relationships but also from other interactions, such as borrowing money, particularly loans to pay for men's journeys to the towns.[1] The network of such debt relationships is as complex as the network of social relationships in general. The existence, the source and the course of these debts are difficult to trace, within the relatively short span of time available to the anthropologist, because most of these claims are dormant, sometimes for long periods of fifteen years or more.[2]

Marital Debts as a Basis for Political Disputes

In the context of my analysis I have only been able to summarize certain aspects of the variations and implications of marital bonds among the Tonga. And in this context the salient features of Tonga marriage are: Firstly the bonds created by a heterosexual union are rarely broken, either by death[3] or divorce,

---

[1] Such loans are frequently a stage in the circulation of bridewealth money which is often invested in them; loans which are taken outside the country have to be repaid with 100 per cent interest irrespective of the period.

[2] Cf. Case 18, p. 240.

[3] I am concerned with the continuity of bonds between groups—kin groups, villages, etc.

especially when there are children. Secondly, even if patrilateral relationships are, on the whole, less important than matrilateral relationships, they still play an important role in the interlinking of individuals and groups.

Marriage creates in the course of time many relationships of multiplex character: they may serve or be exploited by a variety of interests, for example, political, economic, or emotional. These interests are not always explicit and may not be susceptible to precise definition: but the bridewealth which is the basis of marital relationships also provides a material basis for the other, more elusive, aspects of these relationships. Arguments over the authority over children, and their residence; the wife's people's control over the husband's treatment of her; the rank and the seniority of lineages or succession to office, can be (and often are) based on and developed from disputes over bridewealth. This is illustrated in, amongst other cases, the case of 'A Cross-cousin Marriage without Bridewealth' (p. 133).

Marriage, whether formal or informal, is always reinforced by a debt relationship, if not with regard to bridewealth for the wife herself then with regard to the bridewealth of children. The debt is perpetual and is rarely dissolved, at least during the lifetime of husband and wife. Even after the death of either or both spouses a marital debt relationship persists between the affinal kin groups. The fulfilment of one obligation creates another: if a man has paid bridewealth to his wife's kin, he still owes them a portion which he is expected to pay at his wife's death. In the meanwhile a man owes his wife's people at least part of his daughter's bridewealth. If a man has not paid any bridewealth he owes his wife's people not only his wife's bridewealth and damages, but also at least part of what he may receive himself for his own daughters, or if his wife's people handle the negotiations for his daughters' marriages, they owe him part of the bridewealth received.

Tonga marital relationships can commence and continue in many ways: through a go-between; as abduction with damages; as an informal union of partners living together or separated; or as a divorced or widowed marriage. This makes it difficult to decide (not only for an anthropologist but also for the parties concerned) what exactly the position is. Even the mediation of a go-between who publicly hands over the bridewealth is no guarantee of certainty. It frequently happens that money handed over is considered by the husband as a part of the redeemable bridewealth, while the wife's people maintain that the money represented irredeemable damages which did not formalize the sexual union but was a payment once and for all. The reverse also happens: the wife's people may pay a sum of money to the husband which they later maintain was part of the bridewealth they returned to him. The husband or his kin group may say that this money was not part of the bridewealth but damages due to him on account of his wife's adultery. The significance of such damages ends at the moment of payment without creating any further obligations as bridewealth does.

But this very vagueness regarding the legal basis of so many marriages gives those marriages additional importance as the basis for the political cohesion of the Tonga. The controversial legal foundations of these marriages give rise to a great many disputes in or out of court. Thus the less easily definable relationships springing from marriage are often corroborated and kept alive by relationships based upon concrete claims and counter-claims which are discussed in public. Moreover this constant source of claims and counter-claims which are capable of exact formulation (i.e. as sums of money), can provide a convenient and readily available legal basis for political claims which are not so easily defined or which a person may not *want* to define too clearly.

The corollary of the perpetual debt relationship between husband and wife and/or their respective kin groups is that a man's relationship to his children remains the same for life and need not be affected by divorce or death.[1] A man is not ousted from his position as father by his children's mother's subsequent husband. As a rule therefore the genitor is always the pater. This explains why among the Tonga substitution of a friend or even a brother for a sterile husband is not allowed, as in many other tribes. The same applies to a woman's intercourse with her husband's brother or other close kinsman—this is actionable as adultery. Although secret substitution does occur, the wife or her people, if they want to, can sue the husband if it is discovered. A child born in wedlock is presumed to be the husband's unless the opposite is proved.

All these factors help to ensure that the genitor is the pater, and

---

[1] See for a different situation the position of the father among the Yao: Mitchell (1956a), p. 185.

to strengthen his position. Although the position of the father is thus safeguarded, in the struggle with his children's matrilineal kin for the loyalty and the guardianship of the children the father is still in a weaker position. Yet patrilateral relationships contribute to the ultimate integration of individuals and small groups into the larger social unit which is recognizable and recognized as the Tonga people, who are as such distinct from surrounding peoples.

The Tonga depend for their political and social cohesion not on common allegiance to specific centres of authority within a political hierarchy[1] but on widely dispersed ties interlinking a variety of groups and individuals. It is clear that the importance accorded to the principle of paternity greatly increases a person's effective ties with other persons and villages. These relationships, which are based upon paternity, are permanent, and because of the high rate of divorce the majority of men and women are involved in relationships arising from more than one marriage. This results in very considerable complexity and overlapping of ties, and consequently an increase in their cohesive value.

Cross-cousin Marriage

I often discussed with Tonga a father's problem: he has a weaker claim on the residential allegiance of his children than the mother has, and often sees his children leave his village to go to their mother's village. Tonga remark that a man can forestall this loss of children by marrying his cross-cousin (*msiwani*, plur. *asiwani*). Cross-cousin marriage is considered the ideal form of marriage. Indeed, the terms for father-in-law and mother-in-law are those appropriate for a cross-cousin marriage: *asibweni* means both maternal uncle and father-in-law, and *apongozi* stands for both maternal uncle's wife and mother-in-law. The assumption here is that a man marries his maternal cross-cousin, i.e. his mother's brother's daughter (MBD) and not his paternal cross-cousin, i.e. his father's sister's daughter (FZD). Ideally a cross-cousin marriage is supposed to keep the children of this union in their father's (i.e. the male cross-cousin's) village, since that is also the village of their mother. Tonga also state that cross-cousin mar-

---

[1] The aim of the British Administration has been to establish an apical system of graded centres of authority. I will later discuss the interaction of this Administrative hierarchy and the forces operating within the traditional political framework of the Tonga.

riage is the sort of union which village headmen eagerly desire for their daughters as a means of strengthening the internal bonds of the village. Finally, another advantage which the Tonga claim for this sort of marriage is the fact that a man willingly accepts his nephew as his daughter's husband without bridewealth because of the advantages I have just mentioned, and also because his nephew is, in any case, his potential heir.

Thus, from a discussion with Tonga about cross-cousin marriage in general these four ideal functions and characteristics emerge: it prevents the children from leaving their natal,[1] that is, their father's village; it reinforces the political cohesion within the village; it requires no bridewealth; the implicit assumption is that a man marries his maternal and not his paternal cousin.

When one compares the observed facts with the Tonga theory of cross-cousin marriage, it appears that there are two different categories of cross-cousin marriages. Firstly there are the cross-cousin marriages in which the spouses come from different villages, and secondly those in which the spouses are of the same village. We will see that marriages of the former type work out differently from those of the second type. Whilst cross-cousin marriages between people of different villages are in practice the same as any other marriages, marriages between people of the same village come much nearer to the ideal of cross-cousin marriage.

Every Tonga has a large category of persons whom he may call his relatives (*abali*, sing. *mbali*)[2] and among these are many whom he may refer to as his cross-cousins (*asiwani*). But the phrase 'cross-cousin marriage' (*nthengwa pa usiwani*) often covers marriages between distantly related kinspeople, so that cross-cousinship (*usiwani*) becomes practically synonymous with *ubali*, i.e. kinship or friendship. At any rate it is clear that, whether the marriage is between distant or close relatives, as long as the spouses come from different villages the children are still liable to leave their father's village, as in any other marriage. Nor is this kind of marriage likely to reinforce internal cohesion in a village. I mentioned that ideally in cross-cousin marriages a man should

[1] It is their natal village in the sense that it is the village where they are brought up. It has been pointed out before (p. 106) that women are generally confined in their home village and not their husband's village.

[2] *Abali* can also mean friends.

marry his MBD. In practice, however, one finds in inter-village cross-cousin marriages both patterns: a man may marry either his MBD or his FZD.[1] Finally there is the question of the dispensation of the bridewealth which, ideally, is a characteristic feature of cross-cousin marriage. As shown above, a woman's marriage and her bridewealth are the concern not only of her patrilateral but also of her matrilateral kin. Even if her father were prepared to waive his claim for bridewealth for his daughter, members of the woman's matrilineage may not feel inclined to do the same. As far as I am aware, marital relationships in cross-cousin marriages between spouses of different villages are based on bridewealth (paid or unpaid), just the same as in ordinary marriages.

Cross-cousins and Bridewealth

I will now examine some aspects of intra-village marriages. We will see that the features which the Tonga ascribe to cross-cousin marriage are really only consistent with intra-village marriages. Indeed, the ideal cross-cousin marriage and its expected benefits can only be realized, if at all, between spouses of the same village. This applies especially to the desire on the part of a father to keep his children in his village. For instance, Ziba (Map. C 3) often said that the advantage of marrying his 'cross-cousin' Nelly (Map. C 14) was that this made it more likely that his children would stay at Mapalassie.[2] Since it is almost certain that Ziba will succeed to the leadership of this village at the death of Mussa, Ziba was here speaking not only as a father, but also as a headman, for whom children are potential villagers and a reliable source of support within the village.[3]

When discussing the probability of his children staying at Mapalassie, Ziba pointed out that because of this cross-cousin marriage (see Genealogy IV, p. 149) his children would be able to say that they were 'born twice' in this village, as both their father and their mother belonged to the same village. And he quoted Nelly's father Mordecai as expressing his satisfaction over this marriage by saying: '*Sono ndabara kachiwi*' (Now I have begotten

[1] See pp. 139 *seq.*
[2] That the pull of the matrikin is ever present will be clear from 'Meya's Death': see p. 174.
[3] Cf. GURU's plight on p. 64.

for the second time). On these grounds, Ziba continued, his children would have 'great power' (*nthazi yikuru*) at Mapalassie. He gave as an example the hypothetical case of his daughter Nyamusumba having a row with his sister Foness. In the heat of the argument Foness might chase Nyamusumba away, telling her to go to her own matrilocality, i.e. the village at Bandawe where Nelly's mother Nyalongwe comes from. If Nyamusumba were to take this case to court they would tell Foness that she could not possibly chase Nyamusumba away since Nyamusumba was 'born twice' at Mapalassie. Although this is only a hypothetical case it does illustrate the importance which Tonga attach to links between a kinship group and a specific locality. Therefore Ziba hopes that his children will stay at Mapalassie not only because it is the natal village of both their father and their mother, but also because they may be able to claim a higher status in the village where they are 'born twice', i.e. where they have a double link (especially if their father is the headman), than in their matrilocality where they may only have a single, albeit matrilineal, link.

In accordance with the assumption that a man marrying his cross-cousin is not asked for bridewealth Ziba also claimed that when he married Nelly, the matter of bridewealth was not even considered—after all was she not his cross-cousin, and in the same village too? Considering the Tonga rule that nephews succeed maternal uncles it would seem reasonable that a nephew need not pay bridewealth to his uncle whose property he may inherit in any case. However there are two complicating factors. In the first place, it is not only the uncle who has an interest in his daughter's bridewealth; the wife of the uncle, and through her the matrikin of her daughter, also have a vested interest in the uncle's daughter's bridewealth. In the second place, especially in intra-village marriages, the 'cross-cousins' concerned are generally classificatory 'cousins' belonging to different collateral lineages. Consequently the maternal uncle (*asibweni*) to whose position the nephew will succeed is usually not the same man as the maternal uncle whose daughter he has married.[1]

If a man wants to give his daughter in marriage without claiming any bridewealth, a prerequisite is that he himself should have paid bridewealth for his daughter's mother. But even then the

[1] See 'Meya's Death': Case 9; Ziba's father-in-law is Mordecai but he will succeed to the headmanship of Massa.

L

daughter's maternal kin still maintain a claim on her which makes it difficult for the father to assume the sole right to dispose of his daughters in marriage, ignoring the claims of his in-laws.[1] For, although I have not recorded any case establishing a legal right of a wife (or her kin) in a formal marriage to a share in her daughter's bridewealth, the strong matrilineal ties and the pull of the matrilocal village are always present. Widows in particular are under a strong pressure to return to their own village For these reasons a man will act warily lest he give the impression that he feels entitled to treat his wife and/or daughter as if they were his chattels, ignoring their status as members of another matrilineage. Membership of a matrilineage constitutes the difference between the status of a freeman and that of a slave. Mordecai (Map. B 11) had paid bridewealth for his wife Nyalongwe and he had sent the bridewealth for at least one daughter, Hope, to Nyalongwe's village. He was therefore in a strong position when he arranged the marriage between Nyalongwe's daughter, Nelly, and Ziba without demanding any bridewealth. But in the discussions which arose out of Meya's death, Nelly's matrikin nevertheless took the opportunity to remind Mordecai's kinsmen that no bridewealth had ever been paid for their 'daughter' Nelly. Mordecai's relatives on their part carefully avoided giving the impression that they felt legally in the right and did not expect any interference from Nyalongwe's kin. Ziba and his kin went out of their way to assure Nyalongwe's relatives that they in no way wanted to treat Nyalongwe and her daughters as if they were slaves at Mapalassie; that they recognized the claims of Nyalongwe's matrilineage on their own members; and that they had no claims on the children but were only the begetters of those children. Mordecai's kin at Mapalassie, i.e. Nelly's patrikin, had to prevent Nyalongwe's relatives from exerting too much pressure on Nyalongwe to return to her village instead of staying on at Mapalassie as Mordecai's widow. If Nyalongwe were to go back to her own village that would seriously weaken the cross-cousin marriage of Nelly and Ziba and thus defeat its purpose of tying the children firmly to their father's village. This indicates that an intra-village cross-cousin marriage may contribute to greater cohesion within the village, but that it is not necessarily successful in achieving this. Moreover, whether or not Ziba paid

[1] See pp. 87 *seq.*

bridewealth for his wife Nelly, and although his children are 'born twice' at Mapalassie, they and their offspring will never be members of the dominant lineage in their father's village but will always occupy the subordinate status of children of the village at Mapalassie. Only at their matrilocality could they possibly have claims to positions of political authority. This factor might eventually make them leave Mapalassie in spite of their double roots there.

The cross-cousin marriage of Marita (Chin. F 7) and Nyali (Chin. F 4) within Chinyafwa is another example of an attempt to realize the Tonga ideal of a cross-cousin marriage without bridewealth. This case, too, shows that whilst there are always two parties with rights in a woman's bridewealth, it is invariably only one of the parties who has a vested interest in bringing about an intra-village marriage and who is therefore prepared to forgo the bridewealth. The dispute over the bridewealth for Marita, which I will now discuss, supports my suggestion that bride-wealth provides an easily definable and legal basis for claims which otherwise are not so easily defined. Behind this bridewealth argument is Siddely's desire to re-assert, whenever he can, his position in the village: this desire springs from his insecure status as a slave descendant in this village, as we saw in Case 3.

CASE 8: A CROSS-COUSIN MARRIAGE WITHOUT BRIDEWEALTH

The descendants of Nyapazalo form the dominant lineage at Chinyafwa; in Tonga idiom they are the owners of the village at Chinyafwa. Siddely's father, Targha (Chin. C 7), as a member of this matrilineage, was also an owner but Siddely (Chin. D 6) is only a village son at Chinyafwa. Moreover he has one other serious disability: his mother, Nyadondo (Chin. C 5), was a slave. This makes it possible for somebody like Adamu (Chin. E 12) to call Siddely himself a slave, too, although strictly speaking the status of Siddely's mother is irrelevant at Chinyafwa with which he is linked through his father. Nevertheless the fact that his mother was a slave, so that Siddely 'has nowhere else to go',[1] reflects on Siddely's own position in the village. As I got to know

[1] Siddely has nowhere else to go in Tongaland—i.e. he has no alternative village where he has status. He has freeman status in Usiska, again through his father, but this is irrelevant in a Tonga situation.

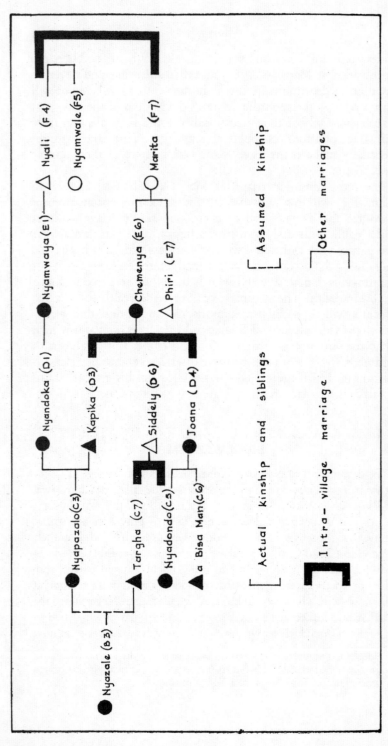

III.—Skeleton Genealogy for Case 8: A Cross-cousin Marriage without Bridewealth

Letters and numbers in brackets refer to Genealogy XIII for Chinyafwa Village

the village I sensed that Nyali treated Siddely with some condescension although Nyali is years younger. I suspected that in one way or another Siddely might be of slave descent; but since slave-hood (*ukaporo*) is a very delicate subject I could not ask any direct questions about it. It was not until shortly before I left the area that someone in the village told me very confidentially that Siddely was 'only a slave'.[1] The secrecy shows the humiliation inherent in the position of a slave; obviously Siddely knows that that is how people consider him. He himself would consider the status of his mother unimportant at Chinyafwa because she is not his link with this village. He would emphasize the freeman status at Chinyafwa of his father; he wants to be considered as the son of a freeman father who was a member of the matrilineage at Chinyafwa and not as the son of a slave mother.

According to Nyamwale, Joana (Chin. D. 4) was Siddely's half-sister by his mother and not his full-sister as Siddely himself told me. Apparently when Nyadondo was taken by Targha as his wife she had a 'small child on her back', which was the offspring of a previous union in her own country which is said to have been Bisa country. This child was Joana who was thus Siddely's half-sister.

Nyali (Chin. F 4) started an affair with Marita (Chin. F 7) without any previous formal discussions or payments. He says that he had a perfect right to do so, without consulting or asking permission from anybody, provided Marita (Chin. F 7) agree. After all, so he argues, she is his 'granddaughter' and she 'comes from Chinyafwa twice'; her mother belongs to Chinyafwa and so does the father of her mother: 'Therefore the power of attorney [*unkhoswe*] in Marita's marriage lies in our own hands. Even if her father Phiri paid bridewealth for her mother, he only begat her.' Nyali has indeed a strong case and normally nobody would object to this argument. But as I mentioned before in relation to the cross-cousin marriage of Nelly (Map. C 14) and Ziba (Map. C 3) at Mapalassie, any apparently autocratic decision regarding a woman's (or for that matter, any person's) status may give the impression that one considers the woman as a slave. It so happens that Marita has in fact the status of a slave at Chinyafwa, through Joana and Nyadondo. In any case Siddely seems to have taken exception to Nyali's independent behaviour, which would be interpreted as that of a headman *vis-à-vis* a slave of the village. This would obviously also reflect on Siddely's status in the village, since he belongs to the same matrilineage as Marita.

[1] Note that it was not a kinsman, like Nyali, who gave this secret away but a virilocally living wife, who is of course an outsider at Chinyafwa.

Moreover, because Marita belongs to his matrilineage, Siddely reckons that he has a stronger claim to be considered Marita's attorney (*nkhoswe*) than Nyali. Siddely considers himself to be·the head of a matrilineage of which his mother Nyadondo is the founder. From that point of view he would be in charge of lineage matters affecting the matrilineal descendants of Nyadondo, including Marita, and Kapika would merely be a husband who 'only produced' (*wabara waka*) Marita's mother.

But Nyali takes the more comprehensive view by going back to Targha's mother Nyazale from whom all parties concerned are descended within the Chinyafwa context.[1] All those living at Chinyafwa do so because in one way or another they trace their descent from a common ancestress.[2] From Nyali's point of view Targha's descendants come under his authority because Targha was a member of the dominant matrilineage of which Nyali is now the leader. Consequently Nyadondo does not count, because as a slave she is a person without any status within Chinyafwa village. Of course, if Siddely had moved somewhere else and had his own village and position of leadership, and if Marita were living there with him, then he could claim undisputed authority in matters concerning matrilineal descendants of Nyadondo. In those circumstances Nyadondo's descendants would form an independent matrilineage on their own land, and Nyadondo's status as slave would be of no importance: she was only a slave in relation to Chinyafwa village.

The relationship between Nyali and Siddely is that between a leading member of the dominant matrilineage and a village son. This relationship, which always tends to be somewhat uneasy, is here complicated because Siddely's already subordinate position as a village son is further weakened by his slave ancestry on his mother's side. Whilst I never noticed Nyali emphasizing his own superior status in relation to Siddely, the latter would rarely miss an opportunity, either in general conversation or in action, for asserting his right to live in this village, and for emphasizing the importance of his father Targha. He often added that nobody could possibly order him, Siddely, about. The marriage of Marita (who was pregnant by Nyali when I left Chinyafwa) was one of these opportunities. Nyali quietly presumed that

[1] For a similar genealogical argument in which either view may be correct, depending on the context, see Case 16, p. 233.
[2] In this context I use the terms 'descent' and 'descendant' not in the restricted sense of lineal descent as the socially recognized mode of tracing kinship but in the wider sense of tracing any cognatic relationship.

his marriage to Marita was entirely an intra-village affair, and, since he is the leading member of the village, entirely a matter for his own discretion. Siddely took exception to this independent behaviour and interpreted it as an attempt on the part of Nyali to bring home to Siddely the latter's subordinate position. Siddely reported the affair to Marita's father, Phiri (Chin. E 7), who lives a few miles away, and, according to Nyali, tried to persuade Phiri to sue Nyali for adultery. Phiri is reported to have taken the stand that 'he had no power in this case since both Marita and Nyali came from Chinyafwa and Marita came from there "two times" whilst he had only produced her'. Phiri therefore told Siddely that he himself could take the matter to court if he wanted to. Siddely did and he was awarded damages which he handed to Phiri.[1] In this way Siddely tried to create the impression that he had sued his kinsman and fellow-villager, Nyali, on behalf of an outsider, Phiri, and not on his own account. In fact, however, Siddely had really sued Nyali on his own behalf. He had done this not for the sake of the adultery or the damages; rather the adultery complaint was the means whereby Siddely wanted to bring his political—status— conflict with Nyali into the open in an attempt to obtain, indirectly, a public pronouncement on it.

There is little doubt that without this political aspect Nyali's affair with Marita would not have caused the ill-feeling it did and would not have been taken to court. The court's finding against Nyali implies of course a legal vindication of Siddely's point of view regarding his status *vis-à-vis* Nyali. Whether it affects the realities of the political relationship between Siddely (and his matrilineage) and Nyali (and his dominant matrilineage) at Chinyafwa is another matter.[2]

As Marita's matrilineal kinsman Siddely claimed the right to act as her *nkhoswe* and in that capacity he complained about what he considered Nyali's illegitimate association with Marita. Since Marita's father, Phiri (Chin. E 7), had paid bridewealth for her mother, Siddely did not want to act independently of Phiri and therefore consulted him. It is significant that Phiri apparently did not want to take the matter up himself. He was probably moti-vated by the consideration that given the genealogical position of the two lovers—who are moreover members of the same village —it is somewhat unusual to treat the affair as a case of adultery.

[1] The party which sues for damages is not always entitled to keep them: cf. Case 5, p. 98.   [2] Cf. the many similarities with Case 11, p. 195.

Phiri was probably also aware of the political aspect of this case and did not want to get mixed up in Chinyafwa politics.

I have argued that contrary to the stated ideal, in practice bride-wealth is not necessarily waived in intra-village marriage of cross-cousins. And if bridewealth has not been paid in such a marriage, the claim is only dormant and can be resuscitated (as in any other type of marriage) on any suitable occasion. This point comes out clearly in 'Meya's Death'. In that case we will see how the poten-tial debt resulting from an intra-village cross-cousin marriage be-comes an important aspect, if not the legal basis, of the struggle for leadership within Mapalassie.

Strictly speaking the legal issue in the Siddely-Nyali case was adultery not the non-payment of bridewealth. However, Siddely's legal argument was an essential preliminary before he could establish his own or Marita's father's or for that matter anybody else's right to claim bridewealth for Marita from Nyali. Recognition of this right is implicit in the court's judgment.

As I indicated before, another aspect of Siddely's legal argu-ment is that he considers that he and Marita belong to a *separate*, independent kin group (a localized matrilineage in fact) which is merely patrilaterally linked, through Kapika (Chin. D 3), to Nyali's matrilineage. The implication of this argument is that only Siddely or another member of his matrilineage has the right to act as Marita's *nkhoswe* (attorney); Siddely denies this right to Nyali or any other member of Nyali's matrilineage. Siddely's insistence on the recognition of the separate identity of his matrilineage explains why he wanted to treat Nyali's affair with Marita as illicit and why, to put it in more general terms, he would want to see a marriage between members of these two matrilineages based on bridewealth.

Nyali's view of the matter is that he, Siddely and Marita do not belong to two separate kin groups but to one, and that he, Nyali, is responsible (i.e. can act as *nkhoswe*) for them all. Nyali reckons that in this affair he is only answerable to himself or as he put it 'the power of attorney in Marita's marriage lies in our hands'. From this point of view there can be no question of adultery or bridewealth: Nyali as Marita's husband would only be paying to Nyali as Marita's attorney. (The same argument underlies the controversy between the two kin groups at Mapalassie as recorded in Case 9.) The controversy at Chinyafwa turns on the protagonists' different views of Nyadondo's (Siddely's mother's) genealogical and political position at Chinyafwa. For Siddely she is just like any other free woman producing descendants genealogically and politically recognized as her own. But from Nyali's point of view, genealogically and politically Nyadondo does not count at Chinyafwa because her position was that of a slave and she did not produce for her own line but for her husband and the village.

In conclusion I want to emphasize the dual role of bridewealth. On the one hand, it draws together and links two kin groups, or sets of kin groups, of husband and wife respectively. The payment or non-payment of the bridewealth (that is, the marital debt relationships) is a focus of common interest for both groups. This linking aspect of bridewealth is prominent particularly in marriages between members of different villages. On the other hand, the actual or expected passage of bridewealth from one group to another presupposes at least some degree of genealogical and social differentiation or separation of the groups receiving and paying bridewealth. Thus the other role of bridewealth is to maintain, accentuate or even establish (as in the Nyali-Marita affair) a degree of separate identity. This divisive aspect of bridewealth can be most easily observed in marriages between members of the same village and more especially between members of sub-units of a kin group. As is clear from the Nyali-Siddely controversy, the conflict is then between the dominant matrilineage's vested political interest in maintaining the corporate identity (*viz.* as regards bridewealth and attorneyship) of the more inclusive group, and on the other hand the political aspirations of the sub-group which seeks separation by establishing its own, independent, corporate identity. As a result, for the former there is no question of bridewealth whilst the latter insist on it. This point also emerges clearly from the conflict recorded in the case of 'Meya's Death'.

This last case requires a fuller understanding of the different implications of paternal (FZD) and maternal (MBD) cross-cousin marriage within the village. This will be discussed next.

Ranking among Cross-cousins

As pointed out before, the term *asibweni* applies to both maternal uncle and father-in-law. This implies the norm that a man should marry his MBD. And when in a discussion about cross-cousin marriage in general a Tonga wants to give an example he will invariably say: 'If I were to marry the daughter of my maternal uncle, etc. . . .' but he will never give as an example his marriage to his FZD (father's sister's daughter).[1] I have rarely heard a Tonga explicitly disapprove of a cross-cousin marriage of the FZD type. And sometimes when I asked whether a man could marry either cross-cousin, *viz.* either MBD or FZD, the answer would be in the affirmative. But when I asked John (Map. C 11) whether he could marry Nyamwale (Map. C 10) if she were not so much older and married already, he emphatically said he could not. The explanation of this apparent contradiction lies in the status distribution within the village, which involves the villagers' relationship to and control over specific areas of land and the offices which go with them.

Outside the village FZD marriages do occur but for all practical purposes they are like any other marriage. Marriages within the village are as a rule of the MBD type.

Every village contains a dominant matrilineage to which the headman belongs. Next in the scale of political status come other matrilineal groups which often challenge the dominant lineage for the leadership of the village. These matrilineal groups are linked to one another and to the village through actual or assumed matrilineal ties. They are the *owners of the village*. A second category of villagers consists of groups or individuals who claim a patrilateral link with the dominant lineage and thus with the village. This category has the status of *sons of the village*. Lowest in rank and status are those groups or individuals who are of slave descent or other resident strangers, including the virilocally residing wives. Some of them may have a putative link, either matrilateral or patrilateral, with the village. Although they may also be referred to by their fellow-villagers as village sons, their status is fundamentally different from the real village sons who claim actual or assumed patrilateral links.[2]

[1] The Tonga make a terminological distinction between these two categories of cross-cousins. A person's father's sister's son or daughter is his (or, her) *mphwao wa ada*, i.e. the nephew (niece) of my father, but a person's mother's brother's son or daughter is his (her) *mwana wa asibweni*, i.e. the child (son or daughter) of my maternal uncle.

[2] The differences between these three categories will be more fully discussed in Chapter V.

Succession to leadership in lineage or village is ideally restricted to matrilineal descendants. That is why those villagers who are matrilineally linked to the village are called owners of the village (*weneko wa muzi*). Although villagers in the other categories may occupy positions of respect and great personal influence and may even *act* as headmen, ultimately their status is inferior to that of those who potentially have access to hereditary political office.

If, among freemen, a man were to marry his FZD in the same village, that would in effect mean that he as a village son would marry a woman who is an owner of the village and who is therefore of superior status in the village. For instance at Mapalassie, whilst the headman Mussa (Map. A 1) is alive the matrilineal descendants of Lena and Mzake (Genealogy IV) are owner lineages which will provide Mussa's successor. John (Map. C 11) has the respected status of village son in this village but his status is inferior to that of, say, Nyamwale (Map. C 10) who is matrilineally related to the headman and the village. If John married Nyamwale and stayed in this village he would, in the political framework of the village, occupy a position inferior to that of his wife and this would be in conflict with the superior status of the husband in marriage. He would virtually live in his wife's village; and this would be in sharp conflict with the role of the Tonga husband for whom the thought of living uxorilocally is anathema. Moreover this kind of quasi-uxorilocal residence of the husband would also conflict with the customary role of the husband as a father. In virilocal marriage, where the children live with their father, the children owe their position and their gardens in the village to their father. At the same time they owe their status in a matrilineage in another village to their mother. However in an uxorilocal marriage or quasi-uxorilocal intra-village marriage the children would owe both their economic assets (gardens) and their political status (membership of a matrilineage) to their mother only. This would reduce the father to a mere begetter, with whom the children would have emotional ties but not much else. And in these circumstances the children would have more power and authority in the village than the father with whom they are living.

This explains John's (Map. C 11) denial when I asked him whether he could marry his cross-cousin Nyamwale (Map. C 10).

Apparently some time ago John was informally married to the elder daughter of Elinara (Map. B 14) to whom he stands in the same genealogical relationship as to Nyamwale: both are father's sisters' daughters. This marriage did not last long because many of his 'mothers', including Nyamwale and Nyadalo (Map. C 9), were against it. The marriage of Ziba (Map. C 3) and Nelly (Map. C 14), however, does not militate against the customary position of the husband and father. Ziba is a member of the dominant lineage at Mapalassie[1] and in fact he is already acting for Mussa (Map. A 1) who is an old man whom Ziba will probably succeed. Nelly is only a daughter of the village at Mapalassie and her 'own' village (that is, her mother's village) is somewhere near Bandawe. Whilst the children of this marriage are living with their father at Mapalassie they depend for their gardens on their father, or at least on their father's matrilineage. Their status in the village is also determined patrilaterally, and they do not derive any benefit at Mapalassie from the fact that they are Nelly's children or from their membership of Nelly's matrilineage.

The different status which village sons and village owners occupy within the village—and in relation to one another—is expressed in the kinship terminology. Cross-cousins in general are *asiwani* but among *asiwani* there is a status differentiation, not limited to relationships within the village, according to whether one is descended from a male or a female sibling of the group of siblings from whom the cross-cousinship (*usiwani*) is ultimately derived. I say 'ultimately' because this group of siblings need not be in the first ascending generation; it may be several generations back. Moreover, since the same people may be cross-cousins in more than one way, the point of reference in the genealogy for the cross-cousinship may be different from one situation to another (cf. 'The Theoretical Kinship Argument', p. 233). Those cross-cousins who claim descent from a female sibling occupy a status superior to those who are descended from a male sibling. The subordinate status which John occupies *vis-à-vis* Nyamwale is expressed in the terminology of the parent-child relationship.

[1] Whilst Mussa is alive, he himself and the matrilineal descendants of his two 'sisters', Lena and Mzake, are all considered members of the dominant lineage at Mapalassie. If after Mussa's death the leadership passes to Ziba, then this lineage will fall apart into several smaller lineages and the dominant lineage will then consist of Lena's (or perhaps only Alinda's) descendants: cf. Case 9.

Consequently John (Map. C 11) and all his male and female siblings call Nyamwale (Map. C 10) and all her male and female siblings, born of John's father's sister, *ada* (father) and *ama*[1] (mother) with the reciprocal term of reference *mwana* (child— either son or daughter). Thus John and his siblings and their descendants will always be in the subordinate position of village sons or village daughters at Mapalassie, because they will always be cross-cousins with the status of 'children' in relation to the members of the matrilineage descending from Mzake (Map. A 3). Hence John is a cross-cousin to Nyamwale, Aweze (Map. C 3), Albert (Map. D 4) and Foster (Map. D 5), with the status of a 'son'. Similarly, in relation to Nyamwale etc. James and his daughter Jenetti are also cross-cousins with the status of 'child' in relation to Nyamwale etc. Thus cross-cousinship and the relative status persists, through the generations, between the original cross-cousins and their descendants whether matrilineal or otherwise.

Although cross-cousins may stand to one another in a relationship of 'parent' and 'child', this terminology only refers to their actual or potential political relationship. It does not interfere with the normal behaviour between cross-cousins which is free and easy to the point of sexual horseplay. The attitude of respect and avoidance is limited to actual or classificatory 'parents'; and here, too, there are gradations depending on genealogical distance, age, and other factors.

I have no record of an intra-village marriage between freemen in which the wife is of higher status, within the political framework of the village, than the husband. When one finds an intra-village marriage in which the husband's status within the village is subordinate to that of his wife it is practically certain that the

---

[1] *Ada* and *ama* are also the terms of address between people in general. Cross-cousins can address one another in a variety of ways: by their surnames; by the general terms *ada* or *ama*; or by the kinship terms appropriate to their relative genealogical status. *Msiwani* (i.e. cross-cousin) is a term of reference only and not a mode of address. A person can address a female cross-cousin of the 'parent' category as *ama* (i.e. mother) or *mbuya* (i.e. grandparent) and a male of this category as *ada* (i.e. father); the reciprocal term of address is *ada* or *ama* and not *mwana* which is only a term of reference. Male maternal relatives are also sometimes addressed as *ama* (i.e. mother). In short there are no strict and precise rules about modes of address; and one cannot, from the mode of address, deduce the relative genealogical position of the speakers.

husband is of slave descent or a stranger.[1] A case in point is the marriage of Lizzy[2] (Map. C 16) and Msorowa (Map. C 23). Another instance is the marriage of Ros (Mz. D 20) and Lenox (Mz. E 9) at Mzenga. Ros belongs to the matrilineage which up to the death of KAMBAWE (Yaphet) (Mz. C 6) was the dominant lineage containing the headman; now there is a struggle for the succession between this lineage and the children of Lede (Mz. C 1). This leads one to think that Lenox and his other seminal kin (i.e. the seminal descendants of Amuzini: see p. 61) had the status of slaves at Mzenga. Even if they were not slaves the owners of the village at Mzenga are likely to have considered them as slaves in the village because this is the sort of marriage which is generally consistent with the position of slaves in the village. It is possible that such an attitude on the part of the dominant lineage at Mzenga might have caused or deepened friction between the two groups which would have been a contributory reason for Duncan and the others to leave the village.

The restrictions on intra-village marriage are related to access to land and political office. These two factors, land and office, are operative mostly within the village. In general, a matrilineage only acquires significance as a corporate political and land-holding unit when it becomes localized; that is when lineage leadership acquires political importance. The Tonga village is in most respects the largest independent[3] political unit within the Tonga political structure; and the genealogical ranking (as expressed, for instance, in the parent-child terminology for cross-cousins) is largely relevant only within the political framework of the village. Nevertheless, the distinction among cross-cousins between des-

[1] People of slave descent and strangers have no constitutionally recognized political status in the village. This does not mean they are necessarily without any influence. A man may acquire influence by skilful intrigue and manipulation of the traditional powers in the village; or through the power structure of the Administration or of some religious organization. Husbands who live uxorilocally, even if they have political status in their own village, are considered of no account in their wives' villages.

[2] But note that Lizzy herself is not a matrilocal resident at Mapalassie even though she has higher status than Msorowa.

[3] I use the epithet 'independent' with some hesitation because it is difficult to separate the life and existence of one single village from the well-integrated complexity of individuals and villages which together constitute the Tonga 'nation'. I should therefore modify this 'independence' with important qualifications; see Chapter VI.

cendants of the male and those of the female sibling is also applied to cross-cousins outside the village. Individuals may settle in another village where erstwhile significant kinship ties become unimportant and *vice versa*.[1] Likewise, a nephew living elsewhere may be called to his maternal uncle's village to succeed to his office. On the other hand, the fact that the restrictions on certain types of cross-cousin marriages between people of the same village are of less importance outside the village may be taken as an indication of the greater political significance of the cross-cousin relationship within the localized kin group than outside it. It is, on the whole, only within the village, in relation to particular sources of economic and political power (for instance land and office), that kinship relationship can be most effectively and fruitfully manipulated. And it is mainly within the political framework of the village that the three 'estates' of village owners, village sons and slaves have significance. Within the village, therefore, kinship relationships acquire significance with reference to these three political[2] categories: the owners of the village try to exploit kinship in order to maintain their status and the existing political stratification, whilst village sons and slaves (or strangers) exploit kinship in order to raise their status and break through this stratification.

Outside the village, kinship acquires a different political significance. The effect of extra-village kinship is that it creates bonds between individuals or small groups in different villages. Thus, whilst within the village kinship relationships are manipulated in a way which highlights internal political divisions, outside the village the apparent effect of kinship relationships is that they tend

[1] Cf. the hypothetical case of Siddely moving out of Chinyafwa, p. 136, and the relationship between Ziba and Chimbaza in different villages, p. 233. See also Case 16, p. 233.

[2] The distinction between these categories is almost entirely political rather than economic, at least at present; it may have been different in the past. Now, in the subsistence economy of the village, lower political status does not as such necessarily entail economic disadvantages: village sons, slaves and strangers may have gardens of the same size or quality as the village owners, and their rights in their cultivated and old gardens are equally protected (see pp. 272 *seq.* on land-holding). Ambitious village sons, slaves or strangers may cultivate larger gardens (for cash crops) than owners of the village. Ndazakale, who feels unjustly treated in that respect, is not a slave but a village owner; in his case he is discriminated against *because* he is a village owner and therefore a potential rival of Ziba (see Case 10, p. 190).

to draw geographically separated individuals and groups together around a common focus of interest, which greatly contributes to the cohesion of the Tonga as a people.

Intra-village Marriage

What one might call the Tonga theory of cross-cousin marriage is on the whole relevant only within the framework of the village, *viz.* in relation to the control over land and the distribution of power within the village. The characteristics ascribed by the Tonga to cross-cousin marriage (including its function in the internal cohesion of the village) are in reality not so much the characteristics of a marriage between cross-cousins as the characteristics of a marriage between members of the same village. That is why intra-village marriages between slaves or between freemen and slaves really belong to the same category as cross-cousin marriages. In fact intra-village marriages involving slaves are often referred to as being *pa usiwani*, i.e. between cross-cousins.[1]

The village provides the main framework within which the kinship system comes to life as it assembles, and dissolves, into its component parts of small groups of people or individuals competing for power. Seen from another angle, the kinship system provides the framework for intrigues and manipulation of relationships between people. It is the sociologist's task to abstract these intrigues and relationships between individuals into a political or kinship system. We saw how kinship acquires different values within the village when compared with the values it acquires outside. Kinship and kinship status do not exist in a vacuum but in relation to a certain stake, for the acquisition of which one or another relationship can be exploited. In Chapter VI I will consider the role of kinship and its possibilities of exploitation in the wider political field outside the village. Inside the village, kinship should be considered in relation to the localized kinship groups and the political authority (or lack of it) that is associated with these various kinship groups. Outside the village the same people may exploit different relationships. For instance whilst they are at Mapalassie, it is Ziba who is the 'father' of Chimbaza (Map. B 1), indicating the latter's subordinate position. But working within a different genealogical context, in Chim-

---

[1] This is also a way of covering up the slave descent of one or both spouses.

baza's matrilocal village (where Ziba has patrilateral ties), their roles are reversed: Chimbaza becomes 'father' to Ziba (an identical situation will be discussed in Case 16 on p. 233). If one analyses kinship 'on the ground' it is clear that, on the whole, the significance of what the Tonga call cross-cousin marriage (*nthengwa pa usiwani*) is not that it is between cross-cousins or even kinsmen in general but that it is between residents of the same village. And when one of the spouses leaves the village the cross-cousin marriage loses its special political significance.

When one considers the intra-village marriages of the villages under discussion, it is noticeable that only two of them are between children of full- or half-siblings, i.e. between spouses with a common grandparent. All other intra-village marriages which I recorded have either partners from lineages with an assumed link or with a distant common ancestress, or partners of slave descent. The exceptions are the marriage of KAMBAWE (Mz. C 6) and Lucy (Mz. C 5) and the marriage of John (Map. C 11) and the elder daughter of Elinara (Map. B 14) which later ended in divorce. Since this union was strongly resisted, very probably it never was a marriage, but simply a period of cohabitation as part of the customary liberties allowed between cross-cousins. It might have become a marital union had there been any children. It took place before I visited the village. I do not know the circumstances of KAMBAWE's marriage; I was told about these two unions but there are no children to prove their one-time existence. KAMBAWE may only have inherited Lucy without entering into a sexual union. The marriage between Smart (Chin. E 10) and Elena was not an intra-village marriage because Smart at that time was resident at Chinyafwa and Elena (Chin. E 11) comes from the hamlet of Mtomba. Nyali's comment on this marriage was that he and others 'laughed at Smart and asked him whether he was perhaps going to marry his sister next'. Nyali did not entirely approve of the marriage.

When discussing this sort of marriage (*viz.* between children of half- or full-siblings) with Tonga I used to ask why it did not occur more often since close cross-cousins are after all allowed the same degree of robust freedom as classificatory cross-cousins. I never managed to elicit an explanation or rationalization. The clue lies probably in Nyali's remark about Smart next marrying his sister. The Tonga want to keep hereditary office, e.g. that

M

of headman, within the matricentric group of descendants if this is at all possible, and prevent it from going to collateral matrikin or matrilineages with an assumed matrilineal link. Thus we saw (p. 48) that Nyali at Chinyafwa made all possible efforts to get his sister's daughter Mary from Deep Bay to Chinyafwa although there is a collateral successor available in the person of Dorosia (Chin. G 5) who is the granddaughter of Nyali's mother's younger sister Nyamphato (Chin. E 3).

The successor to office also succeeds to his predecessor's genealogical position. Ideally, therefore, a man is succeeded by his sister's son and consequently the predecessor's children become the 'children' of the successor. A man marrying his mother's uterine brother's daughter might find himself at his uncle's death with a wife who is at the same time, together with her siblings, one of his 'children'. Moreover his uncle's wife, who is his mother-in-law, would become his 'wife' and a 'co-wife' to her own daughter.[1] Theoretically the same situation should arise among classificatory kin when the succession goes to some distantly related classificatory 'nephew' if he has married his predecessor's daughter. However things do not work out that way in daily life. For although ideally there is a particular pattern of behaviour associated with, for instance, the mother-son relationship, in practice there is a difference according to whether the mother is the genetrix or some distantly related classificatory 'mother', who lives in a different village.

Thus, whilst trying to keep political office and succession within the matricentric kin group, the Tonga avoid marriage inside this group in order to avoid the kind of complications just described. This practice might be taken to imply that *all* matricentric groups harbour some office, succession to which should not be allowed to complicate daily life in the village or hamlet. Obviously at any one time there is only a limited number of hereditary offices in comparison with the total number of matricentric kin groups. But, as will become apparent in the course of this analysis, one of the features of the strong individualism so noticeable in Tonga society is the hopeful expectation on the part of every Tonga that perhaps one day he will be the founder and leader of an independent dominant lineage with its own village.

[1] For a similar situation among the Luapula peoples, see Cunnison (1956), p. 37.

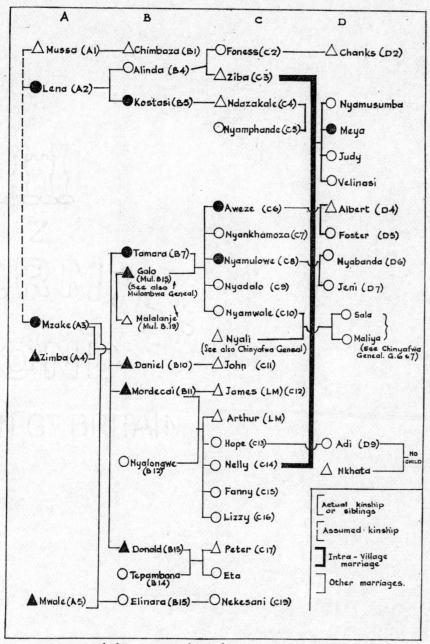

IV.—Skeleton Geneology for Case 9: Meya's Death

Letters and numbers in brackets refer to Genealogy IX for MAPALASSIE Village

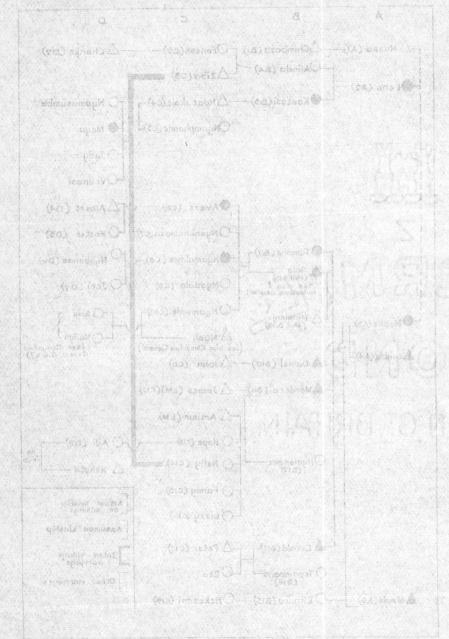

This practice of keeping the kin group, within which succession (or potential succession) should move, separate from the kin group within which cross-cousin marriages can be contracted, can thus be interpreted as an attempt to avoid a conflict between the ideal of cross-cousin marriage and the rules of succession. But this practice has also another effect: it widens the lineage span within which a cross-cousin marriage can fulfil its ideal function of strengthening the ties between lineages. Ziba at Mapalassie by marrying Nelly should reinforce the link between Lena's and Mzake's matrilineages. Mordecai and Mussa, who arranged this marriage, hoped to increase the chances of keeping the two lineages, and those patrilaterally linked to them, within one village.

Marital and Cross-cousin Relationships in Action

An analysis of some of the latent conflicts in the marriage of Ziba and Nelly (and at Mapalassie in general) which came into the open because of the death of their daughter Meya will show in operation several of the principles and ideals mentioned in this chapter.

CASE 9: MEYA'S DEATH

1. It was only through public discussion on this occasion that I learned how the marriage of Ziba and Nelly had come about. It appears that Mordecai and Mussa agreed that it would be a good thing if Ziba were to marry one of Mordecai's daughters. Mussa's attitude was probably that since Ziba was his likely successor, this marriage might reinforce the link between his lineage and Mzake's descendants. Mordecai, or rather his kinsmen, would benefit in that it might keep his widowed wife and thus her offspring, or at least Nelly's offspring, in the village after his death. Moreover since his own sons had gone abroad, Mordecai would at least have a son-in-law in the village who would support him in his old age, e.g. with fish. Nelly interpreted this arrangement in terms of being 'sold for fish'.[1] Ziba took Nelly into his house without sending a go-between or making any payment. Nyamwale told me that he paid £1 as damages for this 'adultery' (as, strictly

---

[1] See para. 14 of this case. For easier reference the paragraphs of this case are numbered.

speaking, his marriage to Nelly is) to her or at least to the Mzake group.[1] I do not know how true this is because as Mordecai himself was a party to this marriage one wonders why Ziba should have been asked to pay damages. If these damages were in fact paid, they may have been a token payment demanded not by Mordecai but by other members of the Mzake group who wanted to make it clear that Ziba had no inherent right to take Nelly as he belonged to another lineage. The Mzake group may have wanted to express in this way their separate identity from the Lena lineage so as to avoid being considered merely a part of the more comprehensive lineage descending from Mzake's and Lena's common ancestress. Ziba and the other members of Lena's lineage,[2] into which the leadership seems likely to pass, are of course more inclined to take the comprehensive view. (We saw that a similar divergence of opinion underlay the Siddely-Nyala controversy: see p. 138.) The significance of these different points of view will become clearer as this case develops.

2. Alinda is an old woman of about 70 and has no father, maternal uncles or brothers among the living members of the Lena lineage; they all died long ago and so did her husband. She has therefore no *ankhoswe* (attorneys) in her own lineage. This makes her in the eyes of the Mzake people an 'orphan' or *mlanda*, that is somebody who stands alone in this world and has to fend for herself (or himself). The word *mlanda* carries overtones of being almost in the same position as a slave.[3] But in a wider context, in which both kin groups claim descent from a common ancestress, Mussa is Alinda's *nkhoswe*, since he is her classificatory maternal 'uncle' (*asibweni*). Mzake's sons Daniel, Mordecai and Donald are also Alinda's *ankhoswe* because they are her classificatory 'brothers'; to Ziba they are his maternal 'uncles' or *asibweni*. In other words, Alinda depends for her moral and legal support to a great extent on the Mzake group who tended to adopt a somewhat patronizing attitude when discussing this situation. And when Alinda's husband died it was Mordecai who fetched her back from her husband's village because 'they [i.e. the husband's people] were not looking after her and the children very well'. Apparently the immediate reason for fetching her and the children back was that her

---

[1] For the negotiations and arrangements of the marriages of Nelly and Mordecai's daughters, see pp. 89 *seq.*

[2] For brevity's sake I will refer to Lena's descendants as the Lena lineage and to Mzake's descendants, who include seminal kinsmen, as Mzake's group.

[3] Cf. p. 262.

daughter Foness, then still a baby, fell in the fire and was badly burnt. Nyamwale told me how she and her sisters were enjoined by Donald and Mordecai to stand by Alinda and look after her and not grudge her *dendi*.[1]

3. Nyamwale told me how some years ago Nelly and Ziba had a quarrel. Nelly's own father was dead so it was her 'younger father' Donald who called his nieces and told them to 'fetch Nelly home'. They went to Ziba's hamlet (about one hundred yards from Donald's hamlet) and they upbraided Ziba for his bad treatment of his wife. To Nelly they said: 'Take your pots and come back with us—we do not want this marriage.' Ziba was told that he might as well call this marriage off: 'If you tell us how much you paid in bridewealth we will return it to you.' Nelly stayed 'at home', that is, in Donald's hamlet, for some weeks, until Ziba came to offer his apologies and took Nelly back to his house.[2]

4. The responsibilities of Donald and his brothers as the 'brothers' and maternal 'uncles' respectively of Alinda and Ziba of the Lena lineage devolved upon the Mzake group. Thus the role of the attorney-ship (*unkhoswe*) as regards Alinda and Ziba has become the responsibility of Donald's matrilineal kin, *viz*. Elinara, Nyankhamoza, Nyadalo and Nyamwale, Albert, Nyabanda and others.[3] But Elinara and the others are also of course the matrilineal core of the Mzake group, the attorneys (*ankhoswe*) of the interests of Donald, Mordecai and other members of this group including the patrilaterally linked members. That is why John, the son of Daniel, could say: 'We are all in their

---

[1] In a context like this 'helping with *dendi*' (i.e. relish) means 'helping your kinsmen with what you have got': cf. p. 14. This exhortation by Donald and Mordecai is also a specific reference to the fact that the Mzake group are the only people at Greater Kamisa's and several other neighbouring villages, who possess a large seine net (*mukwao wa passe*) for the purchase of which Daniel a long time ago sent the money from Cape Town: for another reference to this net see para. 20 of this case.

[2] This is normal practice in a marital crisis. The husband in an informal marriage (without go-between and bridewealth) is obviously in a weak position, even in an intra-village marriage, because the wife can run off to her own home with impunity.

[3] Albert is the only male member of Mzake's matrilineage at present living at Mapalassie. Being a school-teacher in another village he is away during the week and as he has only recently come across from Likoma he has not built a house yet at Mapalassie. His wife and children are still on Likoma. He is unlikely to play a leading role in Mapalassie affairs for some time as he is still a comparative stranger there.

hands', referring to Elinara (her daughter Nekesani is still too young) and Nyamwale and her sisters.

5. In the context of the present dispute when referring to Ziba and Nelly and their children, Nyamwale could say: 'I am the man and the woman.' [1] She and the other three women also frequently pointed out that: 'We stand in the middle.' [2] The literally central position of Elinara, Nyankhamoza, Nyadalo and Nyamwale was very clear in the discussions which followed Meya's death. Among these four Nyamwale played the leading role, not so much because she had any special genealogical status but rather because of fortuitous circumstances. Elinara is in much the same situation as Alinda in that she is an 'orphan' (*mlanda*) without living full- or half-brothers or maternal uncle. As she said herself, when in the course of the inquest she thought that the 'court' was trying to browbeat her: 'What am I? I am alone. I have nobody behind me [tapping her back]. That is why you think you can shut my mouth.' And unlike Alinda, Elinara has not even got a son. She lives alone in her own hamlet with her daughter Nekesani (other daughters having married out) and is always complaining that she is only a poor, lone 'orphan' for whom nobody cares and whom nobody remembers to help with money or fish. Nyankhamoza and Nyadalo are both barren; and childlessness is a serious handicap in Tonga society. Moreover Nyankhamoza is a rather quarrelsome woman and people generally avoid getting involved in an argument with her. Nyamwale is an intelligent woman with a forceful character who is listened to and commands respect. Although she married out, and lives with her husband, Nyali, at nearby Chinyafwa, she is a regular and frequent visitor at Mapalassie.

6. Ziba and Nelly have had five daughters, the first of which died as a baby. The eldest surviving child is Nyamusumba, about twelve years of age, and the youngest is Velinasi, about two years old. Meya was about eight years old when she died on Saturday, June 4th, 1955. She had been suffering from some very wasting intestinal disease. It

---

[1] *Ine nde munthukazi ndi munthurumi*, an elliptical way of saying: 'regarding this marriage I can represent both husband and wife'. See also p. 130.

[2] *Isi te pakatikati*. In this frequently used metaphor the speaker sees himself as a genealogical centre where many kinship ties converge, in contrast to a person who has, like a slave, only a few tenuous links with some kinship group, if any at all. This is an expression of the Tonga ideal of being associated with a certain locality by more than one link (see p. 130): if the network of kinship ties, of which the speaker sees himself as one of the centres, is localized in one village, this enhances the status of the speaker: see also Chapter V.

was obvious that there was something seriously wrong with her. Her parents felt rather helpless after they had unsuccessfully tried many herbal cures as well as European medicines. Ziba had taken her to a mission dispensary in the charge of a European nursing-sister at Nkata Bay where he had bought some pills which proved ineffective. The Government African hospital assistant at Chinteche could not cure her either although he had had her for treatment for at least a week. As Chinteche is about a morning's walk from Mapalassie, Meya was going to stay for the duration of the treatment with her 'sister' Adi, the daughter of Nelly's elder sister Hope, at Adi's husband's village which is only about one mile from the hospital. Adi came to collect Meya, but Ziba did not want her to go and stay at Chiwaza, the village of Adi's husband Nkhata. When Ziba went to his millet garden, Adi and Meya went off with the consent of Nelly. The reason Ziba gave for his objection was that Adi had given her this disease to begin with, after Meya had been taken by Adi to go and stay at Hope's husband's village which is only a few miles from Mapalassie. Nelly and Adi said that that was nonsense because Meya had been ill before she went to Adi's mother; the very reason for the visit had been that they hoped that Hope might know some efficacious medicinal herbs. Although Adi of course denied that she had made the child ill, she nevertheless felt very anxious to do anything which might effect a cure, not only out of affection for her sick 'sister' but probably also in order to make it quite obvious that she had no evil intentions towards Meya.

7. Meya came back from her stay with Adi and her husband and from her treatment at the hospital in a state worse than before she went. Ziba is reported to have said something like, 'I told you so'; he certainly adopted that attitude. This was so obvious that Adi's husband Nkhata one day came to Mapalassie to offer Ziba five shillings towards the cost of consulting a diviner (*nganga*).[1] Nkhata said that he had heard that all sorts of people were being accused of having brought this disease upon Meya and that it would therefore be better to consult a diviner and find out whose sorcery had made her ill. Unless Ziba did this everybody would accuse everybody else and that would be very bad for the unity (*chimango*)[2] of the village and it might also affect relationships with other kinsmen outside this village. Ziba did not follow up this suggestion.

8. In the morning of the day Meya died, when she was already

[1] The *nganga* performs the functions of diviner as well as that of herbalist.
[2] See p. 67, n. 2.

obviously getting very weak, Nyamwale came to Ziba's house to enquire after Meya. Although everyone knew about Meya's illness, Nyamwale adopted an attitude of what one might call 'judicial ignorance'. Ziba acted accordingly and told her the history of the illness. Nyamwale became rather angry with Ziba and asked him why he had not told her about it before. He should have told her about it officially, that is, he should gave gone to her house preferably in the company of somebody else (as a witness) and informed her of the illness and the measures he had taken. Later Nyadalo and Nyankhamoza came and also reprimanded Ziba for his incorrect behaviour.

9. Meya died at sunset. Immediately there was something of a pandemonium which seemed to be an expression of a state of nervous tension. The women of the hamlet concentrated around the house of Nyalongwe, the mother of Nelly, and began wailing. Nelly in her wailing cried: 'Ziba has killed my child.' Other women from other hamlets at Mapalassie and from Mulombwa village came running to Nyalongwe's house where they joined in the wailing. As far as I could make out from the words of the wailing women, the air was filled with accusations of sorcery and killing. Adi, who happened to be at Mapalassie at the time, had a fit of *maschawi*.[1] Mussa came from his house and walked through Ziba's hamlet shouting, without addressing anyone in particular, '*Magwira nchitu*' ('Now you have done it', lit. 'You have done a job'). John said, also without specifying to whom he referred: 'The child has died and *now* they are crying although they killed her themselves.' Ziba and his sister's son Chanks threatened the wailing women with sticks and told them to stop their wailing as they themselves had killed the child. This did not make any impression on the women. But shortly afterwards Nyamwale appeared on the scene and she managed to reduce the wailing considerably. Afterwards the sorcery accusations seemed to have disappeared from the wailing. And after about two hours the situation had returned to a more quiet mourning atmosphere.

10. Nyamwale told me later that she had forbidden the women to

[1] To a layman it seems a kind of nervous disorder similar to hysteria from which, seemingly, women are more likely to suffer than men. It is noteworthy that there is a fair percentage of barren women among the sufferers. Adi's marriage so far has been childless. The symptoms of *maschawi* generally only become apparent in crises like this and round about full moon when some *maschawi* patients dance to the accompaniment of drums. The connection between *maschawi* and the moon may be that the Tonga do not have any public activity at night except when there is moonlight.

wail and had said that if they did not stop she would go home and not return for the funeral or the inquest. She explained that uncontrolled wailing is a dangerous thing because people stricken with grief are too liable to bandy about all sorts of accusations, or other thoughts which are uppermost but which normally would not be expressed. This was bad because it could, later, give rise to further quarrels which would upset the peace in the village or relations between relatives. This is what in fact happened later.

11. During her illness Meya had been sleeping in Ziba's mother's, i.e. Alinda's, house and she had spent the days either there or by Ziba's house. At about four o'clock in the afternoon of that Saturday she was still lying in the sun by Ziba's house but apparently she was later carried to her grandmother Nyalongwe's, i.e. Nelly's mother's house, where she died. From then on all the women, before and after the funeral, concentrated by Nyalongwe's house. Nelly, too, spent the next week or so at her mother's house, together with her sisters. Nyalongwe's house is in Ziba's hamlet next to Alinda's house and not more than about ten yards or so from it. But betweeen the two houses there is always some long grass and also the ruins of a small hut, so that Nyalongwe's house gives the impression of being slightly set apart.

12. A big fire was lit outside Nyalongwe's house and people of Mapalassie and of surrounding villages, both men and women, arrived with mats for the lyke-wake. In the meantime Chimbaza, a son of Mussa, had joined Ziba on the verandah of the latter's house where Ziba spent the next few days in solitude. Chimbaza came to discuss with Ziba what they should say in their *maronji* (introductory speech) the next morning when people would assemble for the funeral.[1] Ziba told Chimbaza: 'Just tell them that she died of stomach trouble.' In the event, people were only told that Meya had been ill for some time and that she died. Later in private conversations some people commented on this unsatisfactory introduction; and an unsatisfactory introduction often gives rise to public suspicion.

13. Early the next morning, Sunday, Mussa came to the house of Ziba and he called for the four women[2] who had spent the night

---

[1] Every official gathering is always opened with the *maronji* giving a short résumé of the purpose of the gathering or the events occasioning the meeting. Subsequent arrivals are individually received by the speaker of the meeting giving them the *maronji*.

[2] To avoid lengthy repetitions of names I will refer to Elinara, Nyankhamoza, Nyadalo and Nyamwale as 'the four women': in the circumstances of this

partly sleeping and partly singing hymns with the others at the lyke-wake. Mussa wanted to discuss with them what line to take about the funeral and the subsequent shaving discussions or inquest, if any. He started by explaining to the four women how he and Mordecai arranged this marriage of Ziba and Nelly; Mordecai felt that he was getting old and wanted someone in the village who would help him with fish. The women said that they did not believe this story; they did not think that Mordecai could have made such an autocratic decision about the marriage of his daughter, thus completely ignoring the claims of his daughter's matrilineal kin. Mussa further said that this was a marriage of the village and all matters related to it (such as the death of Meya) were only a 'family affair' [1] of concern to the people of Mapalassie only. He therefore did not expect any lengthy or difficult discussion at the inquest. He added that if Nelly's and Nyalongwe's matrilineal kin from Bandawe wanted to be present at the inquest they would be welcome, but they could not, of course, claim any say in the matter—they could just listen. If it had been Nelly herself who had died, yes, indeed, that would have been different. The four women, however, maintained that the various difficulties surrounding Meya's death (such as the sorcery accusations) should be thrashed out in public —that might clear the air and dissipate suspicions. They did not want to discuss these matters just between themselves, *viz.* Mussa and the four women. Mussa was persuaded but insisted that the inquest, after the burial, [2] should be arranged amongst themselves. They finally discussed the form of the *maronji* (i.e. introductory speeches) for the burial later that day.

14. Apparently Nelly overheard or was told of Mussa's account of his arrangement with Mordecai. This produced another crisis and she began to wail loudly again—now on the theme 'I have been bought for fish'. Nyamwale soon silenced her again; but the harm had been done. The alleged arrangement had become public, and was to become a prominent feature of the inquest.

15. When the mourners from the surrounding villages arrived

---

case their interests ran, on the whole, together, and they seemed to act as a group. Where there seemed to be internal differences between these four women, I will refer to them by name.

[1] He used the phrase *weneko weneko pe*, i.e. literally: the owners only; *weneko* is the plural for *mweneko*: see p. 43, n. 1.

[2] Normally the burial can take place only with the consent of all parties concerned, *viz.* the dead person's matrikin and patrikin. See also p. 109.

Chimbaza (who is a village son at Mapalassie) was the spokesman; his introduction merely informed the public that Meya had been ill and that she had died the day before. At about midday the body was taken out and buried in the Mapalassie graveyard. As is usual, this was the sign for the women to vent their grief in renewed wailing and two women, including Adi, had another fit of *maschawi*. But again Nyamwale curbed the wailing with the threat of going home.

16. After about two hours the burial party rejoined those who had stayed behind at the house of death and they exchanged speeches (*maronji*).[1] It is customary that after this exchange, the kin group in whose hands the authority (i.e. the attorneyship or *unkhoswe*) and the leadership over the dead person lies,[2] announces when the day of shaving (*zuwa la kumeta*), that is, the inquest, will be. Between the burial and the inquest, the lyke-wake (*vimba*) is maintained. In spite of his previous concession to the four women, Mussa announced through his son Chimbaza that the 'shaving' was over and that there was therefore not going to be a further lyke-wake.[3] One of the mourners said that he had heard announcements like that before, 'And then one day, thinking that the shaving is over, we will be on our way to catch fish or hoe when somebody will stop us and ask: "Are you not going to the shaving?" "What shaving? Has somebody else died?" "No, the same death as the other day, for which the shaving will be to-day." "But they told us that day that the shaving was over and done?" This may happen in this case too.' Suddenly Mussa himself got up to go and with some annoyance said: 'I say that the shaving is over to-day. I do not want people to stay any longer for the lyke-wake.' He then went away. Gradually the other mourners drifted away, too. There was no sign of any hair being shaven, which is normally the sign that the inquest is over and that the parties concerned have come to an understanding.

17. Thus Mussa hoped to impose his contention that the death, and by implication the status of the children, and thus by further

---

[1] A grave is never prepared in advance; and in this case it took some time to dig since the ground is rather rocky at Mapalassie. The general procedure is that on the return of the burial party to the house of death, the two parties exchange *maronji*, respectively as to how they fared in the graveyard and as to what happened at the house of death during the absence of the burial party. Those who stay behind at the house of death while their time away in general conversation.

[2] One of the central themes of this case was the question who the attorney was and who should take the decision about the 'shaving'.

[3] 'Shaving' means not only the act of shaving hair but has also the pregnant meaning of 'inquest'. At this point no actual shaving took place: see para. 20.

implication the marriage of Nolis, were entirely an affair of Mapalassie, that is, of himself, the Lena lineage and the Mzake group. By overruling the wishes of the four women representing the Mzake group he wanted to assert his leadership at Mapalassie. This, however, was not made too easy for him. For later in the afternoon one of the four women, Elinara, came to him and in the usual indirect and polite manner questioned him on the matter of shaving. She had been sitting by Nyalongwe's house, which had become the rallying-point of the Mzake group, and of Nyalongwe and her daughters. Nyalongwe and her offspring as a nuclear matrilineal group are, as it were, an enclave at Mapalassie of outsiders whose matrilineal loyalties link them with their Bandawe village. Elinara asked Mussa what arrangements he had in mind for the shaving. He repeated to her his decision of that morning, after the burial. She answered that it was all very well for him to decide this on his own but he should realize that there were some people who had questions to ask about Meya's illness and death and matters connected with it. Why did he not want to give them a chance to speak and ask questions? Moreover by deciding so autocratically and ignoring the claims and status of the Bandawe people in this marriage he was treating them with contempt. They might think that he, Mussa, considered them as slaves whilst in fact they were *anangwa ukongwa* (i.e. fully freemen; *ukongwa* means literally: very).

18. In the meanwhile no message had been sent yet from Mapalassie to Nyalongwe's people at Bandawe. Nkhata, Adi's husband, wrote a letter which Chanks was asked by Mussa to take to Bandawe. But Chanks refused. He is a rather grumpy young man who is never very keen to oblige. This may have been the simple reason for his refusal. Or it may have been his expression of the general feeling in Lena's lineage that this whole affair lay within their own independent jurisdiction and that the presence of Nelly's matrikin was not really necessary. Nkhata himself was also asked to take the message. He was not very obliging either, after all the rumours and accusations that Meya had been bewitched in his village. However in the end the news reached Bandawe—though not through a direct message from Mapalassie—and on the Friday following the death a middle-aged man and woman arrived. They were 'children' to Nyalongwe and they came as her *ankhoswe* or attorneys.

19. Before these emissaries[1] from Nyalongwe's matrilocality arrived

---

[1] To reduce the confusion of names I shall refer to them simply as the emissaries or the Bandawe people.

there seemed to be a growing anxiety about what the emissaries would say. And despite his previous attitude of, 'This is the concern only of us here at Mapalassie', even Mussa began to worry, and said so to Nyamwale. She told him to relax because she was sure that the emissaries would return to Bandawe in complete agreement and without Nyalongwe and her daughters. Nyamwale told me later that this anxiety sprang from previous visits of Bandawe emissaries. When they came for the inquest on Mordecai's first child 'they forgave him because they found him a good son-in-law who treated their daughter [Nyalongwe] properly'. The same happened at the death of Nyalongwe's second child; but when the Bandawe people were called for the death of a third child they were angry. They were also rather angry at the death of the first child of Nelly and Ziba and accused the latter of having killed it. Moreover, then as now they had not been officially called by a message from Mapalassie but had just heard it 'from the birds'.

20. On the Wednesday evening after the death and before the arrival of the Bandawe emissaries, Ziba had a quarrel with Nyankhamoza, one of the four women, whom he saw settling down for the night at Nyalongwe's house. For in spite of the summary dismissal, before any real shaving had taken place, of the mourners taking part in the lyke-wake, the lyke-wake was still on as far as Nyalongwe, her daughters, and the four women were concerned. Ziba asked Nyankhamoza why she was still sleeping there contrary to Mussa's instructions. Nyankhamoza answered him: 'I am still sleeping here because I am worried about Nelly who is still upset and does not eat. If anything happens to her we will be blamed.[1] Moreover although it is said that the lyke-wake is over, this may apply to outsiders but we [i.e. the four women] are owners[2] of this child [i.e. Nelly] and how could you forbid us to sleep here?' Shortly afterwards Nelly's elder daughters, Nyamusumba and Judy, were quarrelling and refused to eat. Nelly said to them, 'Don't be as silly as your father and don't talk such nonsense as he does.' Ziba apparently heard this (and was probably meant to hear it); he came to Nyalongwe's house and took his two

[1] The usual explanation for the lyke-wake is firstly to prevent necrophagous sorcerers from snatching the corpse from the house and feasting on it; and secondly to prevent acts of despair (like suicide by hanging) on the part of the bereaved whose minds are confused.

[2] *Isi te weneko*, lit. we are the owners, i.e. those who are responsible for, closely associated with the child.

daughters away, saying to Nelly and in general to all the women assembled there, 'What are you all saying here? These are my children —I am the father. The same goes for all your talk about my having killed my other child [Meya]. Even if I had killed her, so what? She is my child. As for you, Nyankhamoza, if you sleep here again I will beat you.' [1] Nyankhamoza said: 'All right, beat me'; but then Nelly's sister Fany threw herself into the argument after she had taken her baby from her back. Fany is said to have attacked Ziba with the following blistering speech: 'What are you talking about, you *broody foor*?[2] What is your position here in this village? Have you forgotten your state of "slavery" at Bwerero?[3] We [identifying herself with her father Mordecai, Ziba's maternal "uncle"] rescued you from there. We brought you up here—fed you and clothed you and got you *dendi* (fish) with *our* net and *our* canoe. Now what have you got to show in return? You are not giving *dendi* to any of us [meaning herself, her sisters, her mother and other members of the Mzake's group which had "saved" him]. Where is your canoe and your net? And have you ever gone back to your village [i.e. Bwerero]? Now that our father, the one who saved you, is dead, now you suddenly behave as if the whole village were yours. As for your statement that the child is yours, just tell me how much bridewealth did you pay? And has a child only a father, or also a mother? Well, the mother of your child is *us*—Nelly is our womb. You say that Nyankhamoza should not sleep here because the shaving is over. Well, what is all that hair on your head? And look at Nelly's hair. There has been no shaving and we will wait until those of Bandawe come.' Nelly also contributed to the quarrel

[1] These incidents and arguments were reported to me by Nyamwale, one of the four women in the Mzake group. It is therefore possible that this account is somewhat biased from the Mzake point of view. Even if it is, it is nevertheless interesting as an expression of the conflicting claims for attorneyship which are the background of this case.

[2] *Broody foor* (i.e. bloody fool): this is now a standard term of invective in Tonga vocabulary.

[3] She is said to have used the word *ukaporo*, lit. slavery. Apart from indicating a state of slavery it is also often used in a loose sense for any kind of dependence. Thus a man may say: 'We men are only slaves of our wives—the children we produce by them are theirs.' In an argument a person may use it about his opponent when the latter is in any way under an obligation to the speaker. As far as I am aware Ziba's father, who is dead, did not have the status of slave at Bwerero where he belonged and therefore his son has not either. Why Fany thinks she can make out a case for Ziba's dependence on the Mzake's group is clear from her own speech. See also para. 2 of this case.

by telling Ziba that she did not want to go back to him. In fact, however, after about ten days she went back to his house as his wife. Nyamwale and Nyadalo were not present at this dispute because both slept at home—Nyamwale to deliver Mary's baby (Chin. G 7) and Nyadalo because she felt ill. But early next morning, Thursday, they both came to Nyalongwe's house where they were told what had happened. Nyamwale said that she told them: 'We here are only women—we don't sit in a court [*mphara*]—we cannot decide anything. But let us wait until those from Bandawe come, then we will find out how things stand and then we will settle everything.'

21. 'Those from Bandawe', whose claims and importance Mussa and Lena's lineage had tried to belittle but whose arrival had been eagerly awaited by the women at Nyalongwe's house, arrived at Mapalassie early on Friday. They had stayed the night in a village nearby[1] where they had collected some gossip regarding Meya's death and related matters. For instance they seemed to have heard the story of Mordecai's alleged deal with Mussa—the fish story. Soon after their arrival the public gathered around. Those present were: the people of Mapalassie except for one or two who were in paid employment; Nyamwale from Chinyafwa but not her husband Nyali who had stayed behind with Mary and her newly born baby at Chinyafwa; Hope, Nelly's sister, and Ziba's sisters, all of whom are married out; and most of the men from Mulombwa including acting KAMISA (Elton; Mul. D 3) but not the real (*mweneko*, owner) KAMISA (Nyachenga; Mul. C 5).[2]

22. The seating of the parties and individuals involved in the inquest reflected spatially the alignments and conflicts within the apparent unity of Mapalassie. People were sitting roughly in a circle, taking in Ziba's house, and, somewhat set back, Alinda's house. On the right of Ziba's house sat the four women, Nelly herself and other women of the Mzake group including Adi's mother Hope who married out. On the left was Tepambana, alone—her son Peter sat with the men whilst her daughter Eta had joined the Mzake group. In front of Alinda's house were assembled members of the Lena lineage including daughters of Kostasi and Alinda who married away, and Ndazakale's wife. Adi had obscured herself somewhere in the background, near Nyalongwe's house. Nyalongwe sat alone. It seems as if Nyalongwe and Tepambana (unlike their children) considered themselves still outsiders in this village and therefore did not join any of the kin groups

[1] They probably stayed with Nelly's sister Hope.
[2] For this distinction see p. 216.

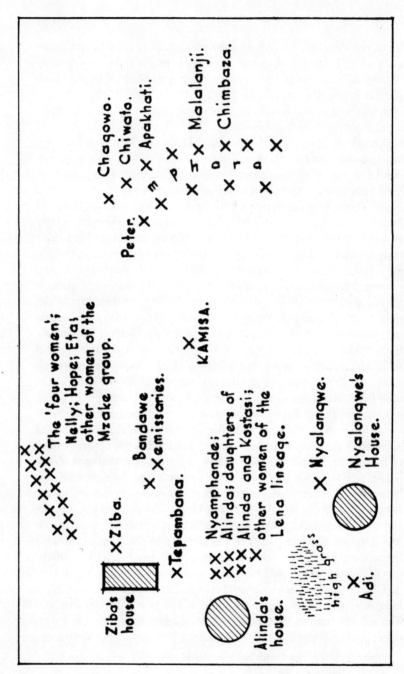

MAP III.—Seating Plan of the Parties at Meya's Inquest

related to Mapalassie. Facing Ziba's house sat the court (*mphara*)[1] consisting of all the men present except Ziba. Within this group of men there were no divisions except that Apakhati, Chagowo and Chiwato of Kamanga village sat next to one another. Just within the circle were the two main parties in the dispute:[2] Ziba in front of his house and the Bandawe emissaries a couple of yards away on his right. KAMISA sat alone near the centre of this circle.

23. Whereas at the funeral the spokesman had been Chimbaza, at the inquest the principal spokesmen were Chiwato (Kam. C 12) and Malalanje (Mul. B 19) who did most of the questioning, although the woman from Bandawe also did a fair amount.

24. The two main issues, as Chiwato remarked in a recapitulation halfway through the case, were: the death and the position of the woman (Nelly), that is, the marriage. As regards the circumstances surrounding the illness and the death the question was: who was responsible for Meya's death; or more bluntly: who killed her? As Ziba had always maintained that Meya had gone to Adi against his will and that she had come back very ill, the point to be decided was: was she ill or not when she left Mapalassie to go to Adi's house? The evidence clearly went against Ziba—the girl became ill whilst still at Mapalassie and she went to stay with Adi *because* she was ill. When questioning Adi at one point Chiwato asked her: 'Do you know that a war can kill us?' The implication of this question was: Do you realize that a bad quarrel may disrupt the village and, since sorcery accusations often lead to a bad quarrel, your answers will help us to determine whether there was any sorcery or not and thus to determine the fate of this village? In spite of this warning one had the impression that Chiwato and Malalanje in their questioning were on the side of Ziba in trying to establish the fact that Meya left the village in good health.

25. After the questioning about sorcery had continued for about two or three hours, KAMISA, i.e. acting KAMISA (who had remained

[1] For the meaning of this word see p. 34.

[2] Strictly speaking this was not a dispute but an inquest at which the dead girl's matrilineal kin expected to hear the cause of death, as they are entitled to. But just as an inquest in England may be a preliminary to or result in a case in court, so too with the Tonga an examination of the causes of death often assumes the character of a review or re-assertion of the respective legal, economic, political and/or other relationships between the individuals or groups concerned. I have argued before how these relationships are often based on a debt relationship created by the payment or non-payment of bridewealth: see pp. 125 *seq.*

N

silent), suddenly intervened.[1] He began by saying: 'You [i.e. the emissaries] have arrived in KAMISA's village—not at MANKHAMBIRA's or at MPEREKAWANGA's or any other headman's village, each of whom has his own village with his own "children" (*wana*). This is the country [*charu*, lit. land] of KAMISA.' He then pointed out that he had no bias and that he did not think that the people at Bandawe, i.e. the matrilineal kin of Nyalongwe and her daughters, were not entitled to take cognizance of the events now under discussion, because it was he who had, on the Sunday of the funeral, asked Mussa whether a message had been sent to Bandawe. The tone of his speech matched the conciliatory role in which he had obviously cast himself. On the point of sorcery the gist of his speech was: 'Forgive us. Do you want to go back to your village and tell them there that you found KAMISA and others saying that the child was killed at Chiwaza [Adi's marital village] and do you want to start a case in court and take it up to the High Court if necessary? No, don't! For we all know that of course the child became ill here, but at a death people are distressed and are liable to talk nonsense. That is why Ziba slandered [*kupalamula*] Adi. Please forgive us—we all know that that is nonsense.' The reply of the Bandawe emissaries was that they were prepared to forgive but how could they forget what the inquest had revealed, *viz.* that Ziba thought of Adi as capable of killing her own 'sister'; and that they feared that one day in a quarrel with his wife Ziba might say: 'Your child [Adi] killed my child [Meya].' By doing that he might bring death upon Adi. And if Adi suddenly died they would now know who had caused that death. And the Bandawe emissaries ended by saying: 'Be careful and never mention Adi's name again!' [2]

26. That finished the enquiry into the sorcery accusations, although they were mentioned parenthetically in the remaining part of the inquest, especially the warning about mentioning Adi's name. The

---

[1] Until then he had been sitting in the background almost unnoticed but now he moved into the middle of the gathering and became, at intervals, the central figure in the discussion.

[2] Although statements like this were made on behalf of both emissaries most of the talking and questioning was actually done by the woman—with the gravity of a public prosecutor. The apparently minor role of the man may have been due to the fact that he merely acted as escort for the woman whilst the latter was the person who really represented Nyalongwe's matrilineage at Bandawe. I was unable to check this. Although Tonga women may carry a good deal of authority, they rarely exercise it without a male 'front': see pp. 216 seq.

next point discussed was the status of the members of the Bandawe matrilineage at Mapalassie, i.e. the status of Nyalongwe and her daughters, including Nelly. Related to this question of status were the following points which were discussed severally: (*a*) The fact that Bandawe had not been officially informed—with the implication that it was not really their affair (paras. 13 and 18); (*b*) the announcement of the shaving without waiting for the emissaries (paras. 16 and 17)—with the same implication; (*c*) the emissaries' accusation that the people at Mapalassie had not shown proper care for the health of Meya and that they did not look after Nyalongwe very well either. The implication of this accusation was that Nyalongwe and her offspring did not receive the proper care and attention due to freemen but rather were treated with the neglect and lack of interest appropriate only for slaves, who have no kin group behind them to back them up against abuse, The points (*a*), (*b*) and (*c*) were discussed as if they were isolated facts. and their significance was implicit rather than explicit; but their importance in relation to the question of the status of Nyalongwe and her offspring was obvious to the public; (*d*) the emissaries addressed the following direct question to those of Mapalassie; did they think that they (i.e. Nyalongwe, her daughters and their kin at Bandawe) were slaves (*akaporo*)? 'Are we slaves where you found our child Nyalongwe?' Nyamwale emphatically denied this: 'No, you are real freemen and not slaves.' A bit later the emissaries returned to this point and phrased their question differently: 'Adi and the daughters of Nyalongwe, to whom do they belong?' Mussa and Elinara rather imprudently answered that they belonged to them (i.e. Mapalassie) but Nyamwale immediately contradicted this and said: 'They belong to Bandawe —we here have only begotten them.' This question as well as questions (*a*), (*b*) and (*c*) contained something like a threat: Well, if you treat our kin with such neglect and, worse still, think that they are your slaves, they had better go back to their own, their matrilocal village where at least their status of freemen will be recognized. Here again, this threat was never formulated by the emissaries but it was implicit and the public was aware of it. Whether Mussa and Elinara were so sure of their own case that they bluntly declared that Nyalongwe's offspring belonged to Mapalassie or whether they were just thoughtless, I do not know. But it was obvious that Nyamwale at least was acutely aware of the implications of the question, as was clear from her answer and from what she told me later.

27. Finally there was the question of the bridewealth in the

intra-village cross-cousin marriage of Nelly and Ziba. The bridewealth is crucial as the material, tangible basis for the relationships created by this marriage and it defines the authority of the respective parties *vis-à-vis* the progeny of the marriage. I mentioned two previous occasions on which Ziba's failure to pay bridewealth had also been an important issue and is said to have been explicitly stated (paras. 3 and 20). But during the inquest the bridewealth was not mentioned. And as for the alleged agreement between Mordecai and Ziba the Bandawe emissaries said that they had heard 'rumours in the way' about Nelly being 'traded for fish'. This was staunchly denied by all at Mapalassie. Although the feeling on the part of the Mzake group had been very strong about Ziba's not paying any bridewealth and although this fact had been introduced and exploited in previous quarrels, during the inquest the Mzake group seemed to be united in their support of Ziba, even if only in a negative way by not pressing the subject of the bride-wealth and the agreement.

28. KAMISA again intervened—this time on the question of the status of Nyalongwe's offspring at Mapalassie. He mentioned again that he had urged Mussa to send a messenger to Bandawe, thus making it clear to the emissaries that he, KAMISA, at least had recognized their claims. He continued by saying that neither he, KAMISA, nor the people at Mapalassie wanted to give the impression that they could do just as they liked with Nyalongwe or her offspring as if they were their slaves in the village. 'No,' KAMISA said, 'we have no authority [*nthazi*] over them—they are still in your hands.'

29. There was not much left then to discuss; and the people of Mapalassie expected the emissaries from Bandawe to settle matters there and then by announcing their satisfaction or dissatisfaction with the explanations given. However the emissaries did not want to appear too easy to convince; they apparently considered it better to keep the other party in suspense for a little longer. They said that they had heard the Mapalassie arguments and would now go home and report the matter to MLENGA MZOMA and CHIMBANO.[1] But KAMISA pleaded with them again and said: 'You *are* MLENGA MZOMA and you *are* CHIMBANO. Why should you have to go back first? It is better to con-clude the discussion now.' The emissaries let themselves be persuaded; and after they had re-iterated their warnings about mentioning Adi's name and not treating Nyalongwe and her progeny as if they were

[1] Two village headmen near Bandawe who are apparently related to Nya-longwe.

slaves without kin to protect them, the inquest was really over. The people of Mapalassie felt relieved that the Bandawe people had not said anything about taking Nyalongwe back with them to Bandawe. Chiwato then addressed the various parties on the virtues of living in peace. This point was given particular emphasis when he talked to Nelly and Ziba on the dangers of strife in the house: 'As long as there are quarrels in your house, death will not depart.' He warned Ziba not to let his sister interfere in the marriage and break it up.[1]

30. In the general relaxation which followed the official discussions the women of the Mzake group heckled the men of the court about their bias (as the women considered it) in favour of Ziba. Elinara said to the court: 'You know that I have nobody behind me and that is why you try all the time to silence me' (cf. para. 5). Nyamwale made the same complaint and added that if only Arthur and James had been there as their spokesmen (*viz.* of the Mzake group) in the court,[2] then the court would not have been able to browbeat them. There were a few arguments during the inquest between these women and the court when the women expressed their dissatisfaction with the court's high-handedness. In one of these arguments Tepambana called to her son Peter not to sit with the men in the court but to sit with the Mzake group. But Peter stayed where he was.

The discussion had lasted from about 9 a.m. until about 5 p.m. without a break. Nyalongwe and her daughters could now be shaven, which happened the next day without ceremony.

[1] The Tonga are keenly aware of a man's divided loyalty and attachment between his own children and his sister's children. One often hears stories of wives accusing their husbands of loving their sister's children more than their own and, *vice versa*, sisters accusing brothers of preferring their own children to those of the sisters. E.g. Jeni (Map. D 7) used to live with her mother's brother on Likoma Island but 'he loved his wife more than the child of his own sister' and that is why Nyamwale brought Jeni from Likoma to Mapalassie where she lives now. And, as Chiwato also remarked in this speech, there is the parallel conflict between a man and his sister's husband so that, as Chiwato expressed it: 'a brother may try to send his sister's husband away so that he will have her children to help him catching fish'. The implication is that a divorced woman generally goes back to her matrilocality, that is, to her brother, taking her children with her. I have treated this problem so far in terms of children's attachment to both their paternal and maternal kin; the choice of residence; the struggle for the control of the children as expressed in conflicts over the control of bridewealth; and the political significance of the multifarious intra-village and inter-village relationships.

[2] James and Arthur are working abroad.

Summarizing the main points we see, in the form of a legal argument about the causes of the death of a young girl, a triangular conflict between the Mzake group, the Lena lineage, and the Bandawe people representing the matrikin of some of the residents of Mapalassie. But the conflicts are not on the same level and we can group them into the conflicts between the Mzake group and the Lena lineage within Mapalassie, and the conflicts between Mapalassie village and the Bandawe people. Or one can see it as a conflict between the Lena lineage and the Bandawe people with the Mzake group in between, with a foot in each camp.

Although the marriage of Nelly and Ziba was an intra-village cross-cousin marriage, it is clear that, as I pointed out before (p. 130), the non-payment of bridewealth is not necessarily acceptable to one or both of the parties concerned, i.e. the woman's patrilateral and matrilateral kin. In the case of Nelly her matrikin, from Bandawe, are not legally entitled to a bridewealth payment—and they did not claim any, especially as they had already received the bridewealth for Nelly's sisters, Fany and Lizzy. But Nelly's patrilateral kin, that is, Mordecai's matrikin (i.e. the Mzake group), consider this marriage to be subject to the payment of bridewealth. They lost no opportunity of reminding Ziba not only that he had never paid any bridewealth, but also that authority over his children lies with the Mzake group (paras. 3, 20). And a short while before Meya's death, Nyadalo had told me, in a back-biting sort of way, that I ought not to think that these children were Ziba's; because Ziba had never paid anything the children were still in 'our hands' and would of course later 'build with us' (i.e. the Mzake group) and not with Ziba. Although this question of the bridewealth was mentioned in quarrels within Mapalassie it was not exploited by the Mzake people in the presence of the Bandawe people at the inquest.

As Nyamwale told me afterwards, she was careful to take up an intermediate position in the Bandawe-Ziba controversy because they (*viz.* the four women) were after all *pakatikati*, in the middle (paras. 2, 4, and 5). She did not want to embarrass Ziba too much in the presence of Bandawe because she wanted 'to preserve the peace between the two houses' (*viz.* the Lena lineage and the Mzake group). She did not want to let Ziba down by asking him awkward questions then; she might do that 'in the village without outsiders'. She argued that if the Bandawe people had received the impression that Ziba was too autocratic in his attitude towards his children and even Nyalongwe and her children, treating them as if they were slaves without relatives and thus ignoring, or even arrogating, the claims of the Bandawe people, then the latter might have been determined to get Nyalongwe back to her matrilocality at Bandawe. On the other hand she did not want to give the Bandawe people the impression that she stood behind Ziba through thick and thin, condoning these autocratic tendencies, because then the Bandawe people might have concluded that they, the four women, had failed in their role as *ankhoswe* (attorneys) for Mordecai's offspring. In this event, too, the Bandawe people would have decided that their matrilineal kin were not treated properly at Mapalassie and this would have given them an excuse for taking Nyalongwe back to her own village. That is why at the inquest Nyamwale had flatly denied that Mordecai had ever entered into an agreement with Mussa about Ziba's marriage to Nelly. And she had added the logical argument that 'Mordecai could not have done that' because he knew his obligations and would not have done such a thing without consulting his in-laws at Bandawe (*viz.* the matrikin of Nyalongwe and Nelly). Moreover why should they (Nyamwale and her sisters) have been sent to bring Nelly back and to threaten Ziba with divorce (para. 3)? And, she asked, why should Ziba have been made to pay £1 damages for adultery (*ndrama za pa mutu*: p. 123, n. 2) if this marriage had been arranged by Mordecai himself, as Mussa alleged (para. 1)? Finally, she had said that they all realized that Nyalongwe could still return to Bandawe and that this marriage was no guarantee against this possibility; whilst on the other hand Tepambana, the widow of Donald, was still in her marital village although all her daughters had married out.[1]

In order to understand why the Mzake group wanted to keep the dispute within the village we should first consider the power

---

[1] These were only logical, if not legalistic, arguments meant to demonstrate to the emissaries the rectitude and good faith of the Mzake group. As a matter of fact the analogy with Tepambana is unrealistic because it is unlikely that Tepambana is in the same position as Nyalongwe; as far as I am aware she has no other village to go to—her mother is also buried at Mapalassie. Tepambana came originally from Likoma and even assuming that she has her own village there it is not very likely that her children would want to settle there. Presently I will deal with Nyamwale's other two arguments—that this marriage is no guarantee against Nyalongwe's departure and the divorce threat.

structure at Mapalassie. The leadership rests with Mussa and it seems quite certain that Ziba will succeed him as headman. In terms of the kinship structure at Mapalassie, Mussa is the leader of the major lineage which is dominant at Mapalassie and which comprises the two minor lineages[1] (Lena's and Mzake's) of equal political status in the village. In other words, with Ziba's succession the Mzake lineage, from being a constituent lineage of the dominant lineage, will become a collateral lineage which will be politically subordinate to the then dominant Lena lineage, although genealogically these two lineages are of equal status. Mzake, Lena and Mussa have an assumed common ancestress and there is no evidence that either of the two 'sisters', Lena and Mzake, is senior although their respective descendants claim seniority one over the other. It should be remembered that neither Mzake nor Lena ever lived at Mapalassie but Mussa came from Likoma with the offspring of his 'sisters' Mzake and Lena; the latter both died on Likoma.

Since Mussa was the only man in his generation in this kin group who settled on KAMISA's land, he was the obvious leader. That Ziba is the heir presumptive (if not apparent) is also due to the fact that he is the only eligible man at present living at Mapalassie. As I mentioned on p. 71 and as is clear from, say, Nyamwale's role in this dispute, although women may wield a great deal of influence, the incumbents of positions of political power are generally men. Therefore a kin group with potentially equal (or, indeed, superior) political status but without men to act as spokesmen for, or executives of, the political authority is at a disadvantage *vis-à-vis* its political opponents if the latter have men to represent their interests. Until recently the Mzake group did not have any male member of the matrilineage in the village. That was the reason Albert gave for settling at Mapalassie (p. 72). But until Albert came (and even now he has not yet properly settled in the village) there was nobody in the Mzake matrilineage who could have succeeded Mussa. There are of course Peter and John who are patrilaterally linked to the Mzake lineage and who, as sometimes happens, might act as leaders.[2] But neither is particularly ambitious and both are planning to go abroad; John had been

---

[1] I am using 'major' and 'minor' relatively and not in the sense of lineage groups of specific depths.

[2] Cf. Chapter V on the role of sons.

in paid employment outside the village for some time before he began to work for me, which also took him away from the village. This weakness in the position of the Mzake group in relation to the Lena lineage was keenly felt by the four women, who accused the court of taking advantage of it (para. 30).

On the other hand the Lena lineage has always had a male member in the village in the person of Ziba.[1] It should be remembered that Chimbaza went out of his way to get Mussa back to the village and that Ziba was persuaded by his brothers to stay in the village and not to go abroad (pp. 70–2). As Ziba himself said, his brothers expect him to 'keep the village together'. And it may be assumed that they not only want the village to be kept together but also that they want it to be kept together by the Lena lineage: and therefore they require at least one male representative of this lineage in the village.

It was clear from the behaviour of Mussa and Ziba that they wanted to establish, in relation to Bandawe, their right of independent action in relation to the children of Nelly and to eliminate the influence of Bandawe, in order to bind Nelly's offspring more strongly to Mapalassie. Mussa and Ziba wanted to exclude the Bandawe kin from all the formalities connected with the death of Meya. For instance, Mussa did not send a message to Bandawe (paras. 13, 17, 26) and then wanted the formal shaving, which signifies the conclusion of the inquest, to take place without waiting for the Bandawe emissaries. But Mussa and Ziba not only wanted to keep the matter within the village: they also wanted to keep it within the Lena lineage. This was clear from the way Mussa ignored the wishes of the Mzake group about the shaving (paras. 13, 16, 17) and from Ziba's argument with Nyankhamoza over the lyke-wake (para. 20). The inherent, but normally hidden, conflict between the two lineages, had come to the surface on the occasion of Meya's death. The tension was very noticeable at this time in the general atmosphere and in many small incidents. But soon after the inquest the village returned to its previous superficial calm. After all, the Lena lineage is only trying to assert its

---

[1] It may be that there are also other, historical, factors which have influenced the choice of Ziba as the heir presumptive. If so I have not been able to detect them owing to a general reticence of the people about the past. I have to depend, therefore, largely upon my own observations and whatever past events were brought up in present quarrels.

dominance in preparation for the actual succession to the leadership now held by Mussa. But Mussa is still alive and the real struggle will, I expect, come when he has gone.

Whilst the Lena lineage is trying to establish its dominance in the political structure of the village over the Mzake group, the latter never loses an opportunity to assert its own independence and political equality. It is very unlikely that the Mzake group will be able, for the time being, to claim effectively the succession to the leadership at Mapalassie because Ziba's succession seems, as things stand at the moment, a foregone conclusion; and the Mzake group have no resident males whom they could put forward as alternative successors. Nevertheless, the Mzake group does not accept this course of events as unalterable and they hold on to the possibility that perhaps in the future the leadership in the village may come to their lineage or, alternatively, that they may have their own independent village. It was this possibility of an independent village which prompted Nyadalo to tell me that she expected Ziba's children to 'build with us' (the Mzake group) as Ziba had not paid any bridewealth. If these two kin groups are to continue to live in the same village, her remark would be meaningless, because in that case Ziba children would have their own hamlets. Since, within the same village, one hamlet cannot be said to have been 'built with', that is, to 'belong' to another hamlet, Nyadalo's remark clearly implied that the Mzake group expect, one day, to have their own village. The people of the Mzake group are confident that they will not always be in such a weak position without resident men. Already it seems certain that Albert, who belongs to the Mzake matrilineage, will settle at Mapalassie. Although Peter and John do not carry much weight in the village, Peter's older brothers and James are often spoken of as great potential assets as spokesmen for the Mzake group in village affairs. They have been abroad for a long time but, as with all labour migrants, as long as they are alive they are never considered finally lost even though they have no wives or children at Mapalassie.[1]

If ever the Mzake group should set up their own village, they,

[1] I understand that James (Map. C 12) and his seminal brother Arthur (see Genealogy for 'Meya's Death' and also para. 30 of that case) returned to Mapalassie for good in 1960. I do not know what effect their return has had on village affairs.

naturally, would want to muster as many kinsmen as possible. Amongst these kinsmen would be Nyalongwe and her off-spring, including Ziba's children by Nelly, so the Mzake people are careful not to lose their hold over this group of offspring. This explains the seemingly contradictory attitude of the then leaders of the Mzake lineage who are said to have demanded damages for adultery from Ziba in a marriage they themselves had arranged (para. 1), and who later threatened him with divorce (para. 3). The Mzake group wants this intra-village marriage and the children from it, but they do not want to allow Ziba too much authority over his children. Hence they do not forgo an opportunity of reminding him that he did not pay any bridewealth; his damages for adultery are evidence that there is no formal marriage[1] and that he therefore cannot claim the children.

Cutting across these divergent interests of the Lena lineage and the Mzake group is their common interest in producing offspring with a double link with the village, such as this intra-village marriage has produced. But whilst Ziba sees these offspring as members of *his* kin group at Mapalassie where his matrilineage is in power, the Mzake group sees them as potential members of a new village in which the Mzake lineage would be the dominant lineage—and this new independent village might very well be on the same land where the Mzake group lives now. Consequently both the Mzake group and the Lena lineage stand to lose if the Bandawe people are ever able to persuade Nyalongwe and her children to return to their matrilocality at Bandawe. Thus both kin groups consider the matter of Ziba's marriage and whatever conflicts may arise from it as an intra-village and an intra-lineage issue for Mapalassie. To that extent these two kin groups make a common front, and act as members of a single matrilineage against Ban-dawe, although, for tactical reasons, Nyamwale did not want to make this too obvious to the Bandawe emissaries at the inquest. That is why Nyamwale, in the presence of the Bandawe people, played down the alleged collusion between Mordecai and Mussa about Nelly's marriage to Ziba. It also explains why she did not want to let Ziba down too much: she was then acting as a member

---

[1] At least for the Mzake people it is evidence; Ziba might maintain, if it ever came to a test, that the money he paid was an instalment of the bridewealth: see also p. 117.

of the major lineage comprising both the Mzake and the Lena lineages.

However, cutting across the corporate interests of this major matrilineage is the common interest of the Mzake (minor) lineage and the Bandawe people: both are concerned lest Ziba and his matrikin arrogate full powers over Ziba's children and both, therefore, want to remind Ziba that he is not formally married as he did not send a go-between or pay bridewealth. This common interest of Bandawe and the Mzake people is clearly illustrated by the way the Mzake group pressed Mussa to recognize the rights of Bandawe (paras. 13, 17), and by Nyamwale's remark, pinning her hopes for a public discussion on the arrival of the Bandawe people (para. 20).

The internal differentiation within the major lineage, i.e. between the two component minor lineages of Mzake and Lena, was clearly marked 'on the ground': at the inquest the Mzake and Lena people sat widely separated. Moreover, Nyalongwe's house became the rallying-point not only of her own offspring but also of the Mzake group. It should also be remembered how, in the previous quarrel between Nelly and Ziba, Nelly had 'run away' to Donald's hamlet (para. 3), which shows that even in an intra-village marriage a wife can have a 'home' whither she goes for legal and moral support if she feels abused by her husband.[1]

It is noteworthy that Nyalongwe's matrikin at Bandawe still have a recognized interest in Nelly's children, the second generation uterine offspring of Nyalongwe, whose marriage was the original link between Mapalassie and Bandawe. Although Ziba tried to ignore the claims of Bandawe and wanted to eliminate their matrilineal interest in Mapalassie residents and affairs, Bandawe found support within Mapalassie from the Mzake group. And once the Bandawe emissaries had arrived, Ziba and others submitted to questioning about matters which Ziba and Mussa had been saying were purely lineage and village matters and no proper concern of Bandawe. The fact that Ziba did not pay any bridewealth underlay many of Bandawe's questions and complaints; but they never explicitly stated during the inquest that Ziba's marriage was not formal, and still less did they claim any bridewealth, because they are not entitled to it. After all, Mordecai

[1] This is the essential difference between a free-born and a slave woman who has 'nobody behind her' to protect her.

had already discharged his obligations towards his wife's kin at Bandawe when he put the marriages of Fany and Lizzy into their hands. The right to arrange and negotiate the marriages of Hope and Nelly had been retained at Mapalassie. But the Bandawe people made it quite clear (para. 25) that the Mapalassie people should not think that they could therefore say what they liked to Hope's daughter, Adi, and treat her arbitrarily. The Mapalassie people should realize that whatever happened in the matter of the bridewealth of Hope's marriage, they, the people of Bandawe, were still Hope's and Adi's matrikin—and therefore their *ankhoswe* (attorneys)—when it came to fair treatment and security.

The continuous pulls and influences from outside the marital village are a characteristic feature of Tonga marriage and family life: they tend to break up marital and filial bonds, but at the same time create relationships interlinking different villages. The marriage of Ziba suggests that these outside influences are not necessarily excluded in an intra-village marriage. Conversely, the role of marital bonds interlinking members of different villages which are characteristic of marriage between spouses of different villages, can also be observed in an intra-village marriage like Ziba's. The fact that they have a group of their matrikin living at Mapalassie gives the Bandawe people a particular interest in what happens at Mapalassie, and, what is more, Bandawe may be actively involved in some of those events. As in this case, situations may arise wherein the Bandawe people are united with some of their affines (in this case the Mzake group) by a common interest which cuts through lineage and village unity at Mapalassie. And in crises Nyalongwe and her offspring at Mapalassie look to their matrikin at Bandawe for protection and support.

The desire on the part of Tonga men to keep their children in their own village is in conflict with the ideal norm that children follow their mother. Ideally, the influence of matrikin, pulling children away from their father's village, should be eliminated in a cross-cousin marriage. When cross-cousin spouses come from different villages this is obviously not the case. But even in a marriage between cross-cousins of the same village (for example the marriage of Ziba and Nelly), this ideal is not realized. For in this latter type of marriage, too, there is still the basic conflict between patrilateral and matrilateral kin because, as stated before, in an intra-village marriage between freemen a man tends to marry his mother's brother's daughter; thus his wife and consequently his children are still subject to pressures from their matrikin who are outside the village.

Even if Ziba's children do not eventually leave Mapalassie for their matrilocality at Bandawe (with or without their mother Nelly and their maternal grandmother Nyalongwe), there is still the possibility that Ziba will lose them, as residents in his own village, to their mother's patrikin (the Mzake group), if the latter set themselves up independently from the Lena lineage to which Ziba belongs. Among the Tonga the political separation of a group from its parent village need not be accompanied by spatial separation. If, therefore, the Mzake group were ever to establish themselves as an independent political unit, and if by then Nelly's children by Ziba were still at Mapalassie, they will almost certainly ally themselves politically with the Mzake group. Thus the combined effect of the desire on the part of children to follow their mother (particularly when she is still alive), and of the possibility of a political shift without the necessity of a physical move, may eventually frustrate the aims of Mussa and Ziba. These aims are to tie Ziba's children more firmly to his village than would be possible in an extra-village marriage, and to re-link the two minor lineages of Mzake and Lena within the one major lineage and the one village.

Mapalassie itself is an example of a political shift without a geographical move.[1] Kamanga's village, too, seems to be in the process of separating itself politically.[2] Soon after the founders of what is now Mapalassie had arrived from Likoma Island at the beginning of this century, Tamara (Map. B 7) married Golo of KAMISA's village (Mul. B 15). Tamara (the mother of Nyankhamoza, Nyadalo and Nyamwale) and the others from Likoma had settled in KAMISA's village where they could claim matrilineal kinship with the KAMISA's dominant lineage. This marriage of Golo and Tamara was an intra-village marriage of cross-cousins. But in the course of time the Likoma arrivals increasingly disassociated themselves from KAMISA so that they now constitute a separate village. None of the children of the marriage of Tamara and Golo are now to be found in KAMISA's village; some (e.g. Nyadalo, Nyamwale and the granddaughter Jeni) consider

[1] See pp. 50–1. [2] See pp. 30 and 219.

Mapalassie to be their village,[1] and others are on Likoma. Thus this marriage did not reinforce the kinship bond between the two kin groups by linking them both into KAMISA's village, nor did it result in Golo keeping his offspring in his village. Similarly the marriage of Ros (Mz. D 20) and Lennox (Mz. E 9) did not prevent the seminal descendants of Amuziteni from leaving Mzenga village (p. 61).

The dispute between Siddely and Nyali at Chinyafwa about Marita's bridewealth (p. 133) should be seen in the same light. Siddely sees himself as the leader of a matrilineage and is concerned to establish its independence as a corporate group with full rights over the bridewealth of one of its female members, as a preliminary to possible political independence. But Siddely, because of his patrilateral link with the village, is in a weaker position at Chinyafwa than the Mapalassie ancestors were in the village of KAMISA, with whom they claimed a matrilineal link. Similarly, in his dispute with Salima[2] over the bridewealth for Chemenya and Nyachunga, Siddely was trying to assert his position as the leader of a matrilineage within the larger kin group of which Nyali is the leader. The disagreement between Nyali and Siddely about whether or not to sue Salima is another expression of the struggle for power at Chinyafwa. Nyali told me about quarrels and a general atmosphere of disunity and unrest at Chinyafwa whilst he himself was working in Southern Rhodesia (p. 68). He mentioned quarrels between Siddely and Adamu (Chin. E 12) who is matrilineally related to Chinyafwa and is therefore of superior political status to Siddely, who is a son in the village. Siddely is also said to have had rows with Yakobi, his uterine nephew. All these quarrels were the result of Siddely and others trying to establish their own leadership at Chinyafwa in the absence of Nyali, the leader of the dominant matrilineage.

The conflicts at Chinyafwa and Mapalassie show that intra-village marriages, while they are meant to attach a group of followers to the dominant lineage and the village, may at the same time weaken the political security of the dominant lineage. For the followers are at the same time potential political rivals who may want political independence in the same village area. The success of the rival kin group depends on such factors as the number and

[1] Tamara is buried in the Mapalassie graveyard.
[2] See p. 102 and Genealogy No. I

the quality of the personnel in either group. The group of Mussa and his kinsmen who migrated from Likoma and settled in KAMISA's village as KAMISA's matrilineal kin was large enough to become the nucleus of an independent village. The Mzake group at Mapalassie is also sufficiently large to become the core of a village, but it lacks a male leader. I do not know what following Siddely could command at the time of Nyali's absence (Chemenya's children by Salima were then only in their middle teens) but it could not have been much. At present his potential followers consist only of Sowamo (Chin. E9), Marita (Chin. F7), and possibly Chemenya's son Thom (Mul. C 17), if he were to leave his father Salima at Mulombwa and join Siddely at Chinyafwa.

There is one other feature of intra-village marriage which emerges from an analysis of Ziba's marriage. The struggle between the Mzake group and the Lena lineage is for the leadership in the major lineage and hence for political leadership in the village, and for the allegiance of the children of the Nelly-Ziba marriage. The competition for political power in the village existed before, and is independent of, the marriage between the two kin groups. We may therefore conclude that an intra-village marriage may not only fail to eliminate political conflict between the groups concerned and thus fail to promote political cohesion within the village, but it may even add another source of conflict. The struggle for the allegiance of the children is added to the struggle for political leadership: indeed, the question of Nelly's bridewealth and of the position of the children has become the focus of the primary political conflict. This same feature is also present in the dispute at Chinyafwa over Marita's bridewealth. This illustrates again how marriage and bridewealth provide a readily available and 'tangible' basis for a discussion of political issues which are less easily formulated in terms of legal rights and wrongs (pp. 125 seq.).

So far I have considered three intra-village marriages: The marriage of Tamara and Golo in KAMISA's village clearly failed to promote political cohesion; Ziba's marriage at Mapalassie also seems unlikely to succeed in neutralizing the inherent conflict between the Mzake group and the Lena lineage; Marita's marriage at Chinyafwa is still too recent to have had any effect, although it has exposed the structural opposition between Siddely and Nyali firstly as between village son and village owner, and secondly as between the leader of a shallow matrilineage and the leader of a larger kin group comprising the former. I briefly mentioned the marriage of Ros and Lennox at Mzenga which ceased to be an intra-village marriage when one of the kin groups involved left the village altogether, taking Ros with them. But there are or have been other intra-village marriages in the five villages under discussion. Marita herself is the descendant of an intra-village marriage at Chinyafwa (see Genealogy No. III). Kapika (Chin. D 3) married his MBD Joana (Chin. D 4) and they had three children: Yakobi lived and died at Chinyafwa; Chemenya of course spent her married life outside but eventually returned to Chinyafwa where she died; another son, Kristof, works abroad but a few years ago came to Chinyafwa for a holiday and Nyali is certain that he will eventually return to Chinyafwa. Marita is Chemenya's only child by her first marriage and she lives at Chinyafwa. Chemenya's three surviving children by Salima are at present all resident in their father's village Mulombwa. It is however fairly certain that they too will eventually return to their matrilocality at Chinyafwa.[1]

The intra-village cross-cousin marriage of Joana and Kapika appears therefore to have had the desired result of firmly linking the descendants to Chinyafwa. This is due not so much to the type of marriage but rather to the fact that the matrilineage to which Joana and Chemenya belong is firmly anchored at Chinyafwa: the ancestress of this matrilineage is Nyadondo who was a slave (of Bisa origin?) and thus had 'nowhere else to go' in Tongaland.[2]

The marriage of Evans and Morsay (Kam. C 3 and 4 and also Mul. C 19 and 14) may have been an intra-village marriage: it depends on when the marriage was contracted in relation to the process of the political separation of Kamanga's village from KAMISA's village. However, the question is largely theoretical because the facts are that at present this process is taking place and

[1] Cf. also Waison's case, p. 102. It is significant that the two children of Chemenya and Salima who died young are both buried at Chinyafwa and not in Salima's village.

[2] I was told that Siddely was born in Usiska. I am not certain when, or for how long, Nyadondo actually lived at Chinyafwa, or indeed whether she lived there at all. But in the kinship structure at Chinyafwa her position is that of the slave wife of Targha and whether she ever lived at Chinyafwa is immaterial when it comes to assessing the status of her descendants at Chinyafwa.

o

that Evans's and Morsay's respective kin groups now belong to two different political units.[1] Even if it had originally been an intra-village marriage it evidently failed to prevent the political separation of the two kin groups concerned.

Besides the marriage of Ros and Lennox, mentioned before, I recorded three other intra-village marriages at Mzenga. Of the marriage of KAMBAWE (Yaphet) (Mz. C 6) and his mother's brother's daughter Lucy (Mz. C 5) I have no details except that Lucy never had any children, or at least none reached adulthood (p. 147). Samu (Mz. D 3) who married Lonas (Mz. E 3), the granddaughter of Lucy's putative 'sister' Chindoko, is in Southern Rhodesia with his wife and children. Waison's (Mz. D 18) marriage to Etina (Mz. D 5) was dissolved before his death and Etina married elsewhere taking her daughter with her: the daughter has since married and is now abroad with her husband. Time alone will show whether Etina and her uterine descendants will return to Mzenga. As for the Samu-Lonas marriage, both lineages concerned are still domiciled at Mzenga even though several individuals are at present abroad. The future residence of these two lineage groups and their links with Mzenga will be influenced by the present struggle for the succession to the headmanship, which has been vacant since the death of the last KAMBAWE (Yaphet) in 1953 (see Case 11).

Summary

Before proceeding to the political relations between the various groups (hamlets, villages, etc.) within Tongaland as a whole, I summarize the salient features of the village kinship structure.

The village is composed of localized kin groups which are generally matrilineages with non-matrilineal kin attached. The constituent groups of the village are anxious to maintain their separate identity within the village even when they are closely related. The groups (and, indeed, individual villagers) are ranked according to their political status which in turn depends on whether their ultimate kinship link with the village is patrilateral (for village sons) or matrilateral (for owners of the village). There is one

[1] The marriage took place probably fifteen to twenty years ago and their only surviving child, a boy in his middle teens, has of course not yet settled anywhere: I saw him in both villages.

PLATE 5. A hamlet and part of another, both belonging to the same village. Note on the right the tall kapok trees, frequently found in the lake-shore area

matrilineage (the dominant lineage) which is supposed to provide the village headman. However, in reality the system is a good deal more flexible than the Tonga formal concept suggests. In fact, a conspicuous feature of intra-village relationships is a lively competition for political leadership *vis-à-vis* the dominant lineage within the existing political framework of the village. In addition, political ambition is expressed in the desire of the constituent groups (hamlets) to establish themselves as independent villages. Such political separation is facilitated by the fact that it does not necessarily involve spatial separation. I have already touched upon these aspects of village organization but I will discuss them in greater detail in the following chapters.

In my analysis of Case 8, 'A Cross-cousin Marriage without Bridewealth', I pointed out that bridewealth or, in general, marital debts do not only unite groups which in other respects are separate, but they are also a means of establishing or maintaining the separate identity of groups which in other respects are united. This aspect of the role of bridewealth is also clearly illustrated, for instance in Case 9, 'Meya's Death'. The Lena group—to which Ziba belongs—refused to admit their liability for bridewealth in Ziba's marriage to Nelly of the Mzake group, on the grounds that they were all one matrilineage. On the other hand, the Mzake group argued from the point of separate identity and therefore held Ziba liable for bridewealth.

A further fissiparous factor are the various pulls from outside the village on individuals and groups within the village. Consequently, it requires great skill on the part of the leaders (headmen) of village and hamlet to keep their followers together. These pulls are particularly noticeable in the conflicting demands of the matrilateral and patrilateral kin on the partners and children in a marriage. I have related this conflict to the inherent contradiction of virilocal marriage and matrilineal descent as the accepted principle of organization. The relative importance attached to patrilateral bonds should be interpreted as a compromise between these two conflicting norms. Furthermore, this very compromise sharpens the contradiction between the two norms because to some extent it accepts the natural corollary of virilocal marriage, *viz.* the creation and maintenance of socially recognized patrilateral links. Thus one norm—i.e. virilocal marriage—acquires additional significance at the expense of the other—i.e. matrilineal

descent. I have pointed out that the conflicting demands of patrilateral and matrilateral kinship make themselves felt not only
across village boundaries (*viz.* in inter-village marriages) but also
within the village in intra-village marriages. The fissiparous effect
of this conflict is observable in both categories of marriage
despite the integrating role which Tonga ascribe to cross-cousin
marriage.

Matrilineal descent, then, is the main principle of organization;
it is the norm in terms of which the Tonga prefer, if at all possible,
to explain and rationalize actions and situations even when the
facts appear to indicate the operation of other factors, for instance
patrilateral kinship. As in all organization there must be a permanent focus or a stake (as I have called it). Hence the continuous
attempts of matrilineages to localize themselves, *viz.* to focus
their organization on corporate control over land and to become
independent political units. Hence, too, the struggle for depen-
dents, *viz.* for residential allegiance and not merely the recognition
of the genealogical status of kinsmen. As a result the localized
matrilineage wants to retain the residential allegiance of, as well
as control over, its members, for example its women and their
children, by attracting them back from the husbands' villages. At
the same time, playing upon the recognized patrilateral bonds, the
localized matrilineage endeavours to retain the wives and the
children of its own male members.[1] The latter situation is one of
the main themes of 'Meya's Death'.

The Tonga are conscious of this problem and verbalize it when
they idealize cross-cousin marriage as a means of counteracting the
fissiparous tendencies in marriage and thus the village. I have
argued that this ideal is not necessarily realized and that in fact an
intra-village cross-cousin marriage may have the opposite effect.
Firstly, it adds to the political conflicts within the village another
source of dissension, *viz.* over the bridewealth and the children.
Secondly, the children of such a marriage constitute, together

---

[1] Richards (1950, p. 227) wonders whether there is 'a correlation between
divided authority, as between the father and mother's brother, and the existence of social differentiation and a hierarchical political system'. Assuming that
the situation among the Tonga as regards the relationships between children
and their parents and the respective kin groups of the latter, falls within
Richards' definition of 'divided authority', the Tonga data at least would suggest that there is no such correlation.

with their mother, a clearly identifiable and potentially secessionist group within the village. We saw in 'Meya's Death' how at Mapalassie the Mzake group in its structural opposition to the Lena group relied on the support of the group of Mordecai's (Map. B 11) wife Nyalongwe (from Bandawe) and her children. I have tried to bring out the essential quality of Tonga kinship: there is little point in considering it in the abstract, for genealogical relationships acquire significance and are manipulated in relation to particular interests or situations (see for instance Case 16). Thus we found that the results which the Tonga ideally associate with cross-cousin marriage can in fact only be realized if both partners belong to the same village. And even if such a marriage has the desired effect it is not so much because it is a marriage between cross-cousins but rather because it is a marriage between partners from the same village. Moreover the Tonga theory about the advantages of cross-cousin marriage does not distinguish between MBD and FZD marriages. Again the reality is less general: not only are the advantages of cross-cousin marriage limited to intra-village marriages, but there also appears to be a distinct preference, in practice, for those of the MBD type, at least among freemen. I have therefore suggested that the observable realities of cross-cousin or other preferential marriages should be clearly distinguished from the people's own ideals and theories. Moreover, these marriages should be described with reference to such factors as control over land and succession to office besides the often quoted factor of cohesion of the village or other groups.[1]

---

[1] This factor of cohesion is perhaps not always sufficiently critically analysed. E.g. Mitchell (1956, pp. 197 *seq.*) discusses the integrating role of cross-cousin marriage in the Yao village. He reports that: 'A person may marry either type of cross-cousin but in practice preference is given to a father's sister's daughter' (p. 197). The reason for this preference *in practice* is not stated but one may assume that it refers to commoners only. It may be significant that the uxorilocally marrying Yao prefer to marry their FZD in contrast to the virilocally marrying Tonga who prefer to marry their MBD in intra-village marriages. On the other hand, one may assume that Yao headmen, who tend to marry virilocally and who of course belong to the dominant matrilineage in the village, must marry a MBD if they want to marry a cross-cousin within the same village. Similarly, Richards (1950, p. 228) states that among the Bemba cross-cousin marriage in general (FZD and MBD) increases the stability of the extended family unit. The reason she gives is that the son-in-law moving into his wife's village is not a stranger and is 'closely identified by descent with the

So far I have concentrated on the multifarious links, expressed in terms of kinship, between individuals and small groups. I have also indicated the flexibility of and the scope for manipulation in this system of kinship links. In the following chapters I will examine the village as a corporate political unit and discuss the manipulation of the kinship system for political ends, *viz.* the political leadership within and among villages.

---

leading men of the group'. This is not very convincing and applies, one would have thought, only to the man marrying his MBD; the man marrying his FZD is not matrilineally related to his father-in-law. Indeed, Richards mentions that the MBD cross-cousin marriage is the more common. This would seem to indicate that the question of the stabilizing influence of cross-cousin marriage is more complicated than would appear from her statement. In any case, it may be true that a cross-cousin husband is not a 'stranger' in and is already 'closely identified' with his wife's village, but this does not exclude the possibility that he is even more closely identified with another village whose pull may eventually prevail. Reports from other areas also show that cross-cousin marriage has not received the critical attention it deserves. Furthermore, descriptions of cross-cousin marriage often seem to represent the people's own evaluation of this institution rather than the authors' analysis of observed situations.

CHAPTER V

STATUS WITHIN THE VILLAGE

I HAVE already discussed the three categories of inhabitants of Tonga villages: village owners, village sons or daughters and slaves.[1] I shall now describe the respective status of these three categories of persons and their roles in village politics. I shall deal with their formal, constitutional relationship to authority and to the centres of power in the village, and contrast with this the reality as it appears in actual relationships, showing how individuals, even if their constitutional status puts them outside the competition for leadership, can (within the constitutional framework) exploit their own capabilities and manipulate what personal loyalties they can command. In this chapter the emphasis will be on succession to office; the incidents of office will be examined in a subsequent chapter.

Village Owners

The owners of a village are those members who are matrilineally linked to the headman and thus to one another. This link may be actual or assumed but not putative. An assumed genealogical link is a link which is generally accepted for what it is said to be, but whose exact kinship content, if it ever existed, is now forgotten. A putative link is a link whereby an individual or a group is genealogically tied into the village kinship structure, although this link is generally known to be fictitious. It is generally slaves and foreigners who are thus linked to their village, partly to cover up their origin. What I call actual links are genealogically traceable.

The Tonga distinguish between these three categories of relationships: actual, assumed and putative. When necessary they make it clear that they are speaking about actual kinship links. For example, by giving the phrase 'of the same womb'[2] verbal stress they can indicate that they are not using 'womb' in the metaphorical sense of a matrilineage of unspecified depth, but are referring to the fact that the persons concerned have the same

[1] P. 140.　　　[2] For 'womb' and other kinship terms, see pp. 43 seq.

mother. Another way of indicating actual kinship is by giving the names of both parents of the persons concerned; this also excludes the possibility that the speaker is talking about an unspecified matrilineage. The assumed character of a kinship link can be expressed in such a phrase as: such-and-such are sisters, *pa be* (or *khamu* or *fuku*, etc.) *lao pe* (lit.: but only as regards their breast (or *khamu* or *fuku*)); the phrasing and the intonation clearly convey that they are sisters 'but only by kinship' with the implication of 'distant and unknown' kinship. This lack of specificity in some kinship relations can be expressed by the use of the word *ubali* which can mean friendship and also kinship in its widest sense. Similarly, when necessary, the information that a particular person is matrilaterally or patrilaterally related to the village may be qualified by the addition of: 'Well, when he [or a forbear] came to the village we just gave him a Tonga surname so that other people might think that he was one of our kinsmen.'

It is now generally impossible to discover whether or not an assumed link was originally putative; in any case it is unimportant in the context of this analysis. What matters here is whether the assumed relationship is now generally accepted or not. Conversely, if it is not accepted by all parties concerned, one wants to know who are the people who disagree and whether they have a political or other reason for their attitude.

In my genealogies I have represented this distinction between the three categories of links, despite the fact that there is rarely universal agreement among the villagers concerned about the exact nature of the genealogical ties of some of the villagers to the village. There is rarely disagreement about actual links. There is less scope for fiction in this category because it generally concerns kin groups of little span, often limited to the descendants of a common grandparent.

There is, however, clearly an element of chance in my classification of assumed and putative links. Firstly, I cannot be certain that I heard of all disagreements about the assumed or putative character of particular links. Secondly, an element of personal evaluation entered into my interpretation of those disputed links. I have, nevertheless, maintained the distinction between these two types of links in my genealogies because it represents more faithfully the social reality of Tonga society than the identification of these two types of kinship links would do. And to obscure this distinction would create inconsistencies. For instance, the fact that Amuziteni's (Mz. C 10) matrilateral link with Mzenga was only putative (indeed the very fact of his having a genealogical link with Mzenga at all is putative) explains the marriage of Ros (Mz. D 20) and Lennox (Mz. E 9) (p. 144) and perhaps also the departure of Amuziteni's seminal descendants from Mzenga (p. 61).

I define a matrilineage as a group of kinsmen who are descended. through traceable matrilineal links from a common ancestor[1] or ancestress. Every village contains a number of matrilineages which claim common matrilineal ancestry but cannot actually trace their descent from a specific ancestor or ancestress: they are therefore, on the basis of my definition, related through assumed matrilineal links.

I should perhaps emphasize again that neither the Tonga use of the term *nyumba* (house), *khamu*, and so forth, nor my use of these kinship terms or the term 'minor lineage'[2] are restricted to lineages of a specific depth. The span of these lineages is entirely relative. The Tonga use terms such as 'house' (*nyumba*) to distinguish not only between collateral lineages, but also between two entirely unrelated lineages. The Tonga do not have a single term which specifically denotes a lineage (or for that matter, a kin group in general) of a standard composition and depth; nor is any such group to be found as a regularly occurring unit with specific corporate activities.

In 'Meya's Death' we saw that all the owners (*weneko*, sing. *mweneko*[3]) of Mapalassie village tried to maintain a common front *vis-à-vis* the outsiders from Bandawe village. And in daily life it is difficult to observe any differences between categories of owners. Indeed village sons and, to a lesser extent, slaves, too, may refer

[1] Sometimes the person acclaimed as the founder of a matrilineage is a man. In that case the members of the matrilineage are descended from the ancestor's 'sister'. E.g. the people of Chinyafwa tend to refer to MAKALAMBA as the apical ancestor rather than to his 'sister' to whom they are matrilineally or patrilaterally related.   [2] See also p. 170, n. 1.

[3] *Mweneko* means owner in general; it is also a kinship term, see p. 43, n. 1. I translate *mweneko* in the political context also as owner. It does not indicate a specific category of people but is used relatively. In one context it can indicate the members of all matrilineages in a village, whilst in another it refers only to the dominant lineage, and in a third context it may refer to still another category.

to themselves or be referred to by others as owners,[1] particularly in contrast with outsiders. As I will explain below, the real owners generally refrain from unduly emphasizing their owner status in the village.

The Dominant Lineage

We also saw in 'Meya's Death' that in spite of the attempt to present a common front against the Bandawe people, the owners at Mapalassie are not internally undifferentiated: Ziba (Map. C 3), supported by Mussa (Map. A 1), considered his own Lena lineage as the dominant matrilineage. Although the Tonga do not have a specific term for the concept of a dominant matrilineage, they can phrase it in various ways. The Tonga criterion of a dominant matrilineage is primacy: the dominant lineage consists of the matrilineal descendants of the founder of the village, i.e. the person who first created the association between the village, as a political unit, and its present site. And one is told that succession to the office of headman should be confined to this lineage. But an examination of the vicissitudes of the office and title of KAMISA in Case 12 shows that the office can, and generally does, pass from one lineage to another. This is also clear from the incipient struggle for power at Mapalassie. I will therefore use the phrase 'dominant lineage' empirically: the dominant matrilineage is the lineage which at the time contains the holder of the title. This is in fact the way the Tonga reason, either explicitly or implicitly: those who consider themselves to be members of the dominant lineage do so *because* the present holder of the office belongs to it. The implication is that, according to the rules of succession, the office could not be in their lineage but for the fact that theirs is the dominant lineage. And *ex post facto* this situation is then explained by arguing that theirs is the lineage which is directly descended from the founder of the village.

Throughout this analysis I will use the term 'dominant lineage' relatively, indicating which lineage is in the ascendancy at any given time. For example, I will presently contrast Nyali's lineage ('house'), at Chinyafwa, with the lineage which consists of the descendants of his mother's uterine sister. In this context Nyali's

---

[1] Strictly speaking they are not; and I will reserve the term *owner* for those villagers who have actual or assumed matrilineal links with the headman and the village. This is also the general practice among the Tonga.

(Chin. F 4) lineage is dominant. But in a wider context both Nyali's 'house' and his mother's sister's descendants are minor lineages of the lineage which has Nyapazalo (Chin. C 3) as its ancestress. In this latter context both minor lineages are dominant with reference to the matrilineal descendants of Nyalombo (Chin. C 8) or the putative matrilineage to which Labeka (Chin. E 13) belongs. The ascendancy in the political structure at Chinyafwa may shift to, say, Smart (Chin. E 10), when the political alignment alters. This could happen if Smart, Adamu[1] (Chin. E 12) and other members of Nyalombo's lineage settle at Chinyafwa. For the dominant status of a lineage is not in *fact* hereditary, but rather a result of political manipulation and the alignments at a particular time. I have illustrated this with the struggle at Mapalassie.[2] Whilst Mussa (Map. A 1) is still alive both the Mzake and the Lena lineages are of equal status in relation to Mussa. But when Ziba (Map. C 3) has succeeded Mussa, the Lena lineage will be dominant and the Mzake lineage subordinate. I have already explained that Ziba's succession, and thus the ascendancy of his lineage, are not the result solely of inherent and hereditary right, but rather of political manœuvring.

The desire to attract followers can easily conflict with the desire on the part of the dominant lineage to maintain its authority and land intact. I mentioned on p. 115 that Nyali of Chinyafwa turned some people off his land and that the Chinyafwa people themselves had been told to leave KAMISA's land. Here the chances that the encroaching strangers might eventually usurp the land[3] on which they were living were too real for Nyali and KAMISA to ignore.

The following case points to a similar situation at Mapalassie. Ziba (Map. C 3) and Ndazakale (Map. C 4) are parallel-cousins (their mothers, respectively Alinda and Kostasi, are full-sisters) and genealogically they are of equal status at Mapalassie. Ndazakale is therefore Ziba's potential rival for the headmanship at Mapalassie; Ziba is confident that he will succeed Mussa as headman. In that event the matrilineal descendants of Alinda will be the dominant lineage in relation to the matrilineal descendants of Kostasi.

---

[1] He used to live at Chinyafwa: cf. Case 3, p. 68.
[2] See Case 9 and particularly p. 170.
[3] See also section on land-holding, p. 272.

CASE 10: THE NDAZAKALE-ZIBA STRIFE

Ndazakale used to live patrilocally at KATOTO's village, about two hours' walk south of Mapalassie village. Ndazakale's mother Kostasi (Map. B 5), like most of the original Mapalassie people, came over from Likoma Island. She never had her own garden at Mapalassie (see p. 77), and she lived all her post-Likoma life with her husband at KATOTO's village where she died in 1952. Consequently Ndazakale has no *masara* (*viz.* old gardens: see p. 273) from his own mother, which he could cultivate by right. Ndazakale's 'mother' at Mapalassie is Kostasi's elder sister, Alinda (Map. B 4), who is morally obliged to provide Ndaza-kale with a garden. Ndazakale alleges that, when he wanted to settle at Mapalassie in 1952, she offered him a very stony piece of land which he declined.[1] He was then allowed by Apakhati (Kam. C 1), of Kamanga village, to build a house on the latter's land and cultivate a garden there. Apakhati's land adjoins Mapalassie gardens. But after only about one year Apakhati told Ndazakale to move because he, Apakhati, needed the land himself. According to Ndazakale this is all part of a dark plot of Ziba's to get rid of him: first they offer him an inferior piece of land and then they urge Apakhati to chase him off altogether.

Ndazakale told me of other incidents which are an expression of his friction with Ziba. For instance some years ago Ndazakale apparently stayed at Mapalassie in Ziba's house (a large three-roomed house of sun-dried brick). Then they had a quarrel over Ndazakale's dog: he is very fond of dogs but Ziba and his wife Nelly objected to it. Ndazakale packed up and went to KATOTO's.

At the same time, however, there were situations demanding co-operation between these kinsmen within the kinship frame-work. In 1954 Ndazakale's younger full-brother Selby died in Durban. This death created complications because Selby, like so many other Tonga, had entered and lived in South Africa with false papers under another name. This was sorted out by the Boma at Nkata Bay, with the co-operation of Selby's relatives, both his matrilateral and patrilateral kin. When eventually Selby's estate (£60, or so Ndazakale told me) was handed over by the Boma, those who went to receive it were: Ndazakale;

[1] This is Ndazakale's own account; and even if it is biased it is still significant as an expression of friction between him and Ziba. The latter denies that there is any truth in this story.

his full-sister Anni; Ziba and his full-sister Nyamanda—all of them representing Selby's matrikin. Dick, as Selby's father's uterine brother, represented the patrikin. Until his departure to Durban Selby had been living patrilocally at KATOTO's village and it was therefore Dick who actually received the money as an attorney (*nkhoswe*) of Selby; the others were witnesses. Dick was also the one who was responsible for dividing the money.[1] A total of £6 went to Selby's matrilateral kin at Mapalassie; Mussa received £2; Alinda also £2; Ziba and his full-sister each £1.[2] Dick, or at any rate Selby's patrikin, kept the rest.

In this matter it is clear that the individuals and kin groups involved mutually recognized their kinship rights and status. This is in contrast to the difficulties raised when Ndazakale tried to settle at Mapalassie: Ziba manipulated local forces and personalities; he probably persuaded Alinda to deny Ndazakale a good garden, and urged Apakhati to request Ndazakale to move off his land.[3]

This case also shows that genealogical status alone does not give a person status in a village. The authority (*nthazi*) which the Tonga say goes with the status of sister's son, especially of a headman, is qualified by political and other factors within the village. Kinship status should be considered within the actual context of the village. It appears then that although genealogically Ndazakale occupies the same position as Ziba, in the Mapalassie context he is in a weaker position because of the historical accident that his mother never had a garden at Mapalassie. This situation is exploited by Ziba who does not want Ndazakale in the village for political reasons. But Ziba does not openly say so, because legally and theoretically Ndazakale has every right to settle at Mapalassie. But unfortunately, there are no fallow (*masara*) or current gardens at Mapalassie (e.g. his mother's) which he can

---

[1] As Ndazakale expressed it, he was 'the owner of the dividing' (*mweneko wa kugawiya*).

[2] Ziba's sister 'belongs' to Mapalassie although she lives virilocally elsewhere.

[3] There is no shortage of land. With others from Mapalassie, Ndazakale cut down some forest for a garden, a short distance across a small stream from where he lives and hoes now. I could not discover why Ndazakale did not want to build his house on this newly opened land. Perhaps he considers the site too isolated. Possibly the land is claimed by another kin group who would not want him to build on it. I could not determine the owners. One would have to wait for a legal suit or other public discussion to learn the validity of the various claims on it.

claim by right. Similarly the fact that the leadership of Mapalassie will go to the Lena lineage and not to the Mzake lineage seems largely due to the fortuitous absence of suitable spokesmen for the Mzake group at Mapalassie, and not to any inherent constitutional disability of the Mzake lineage.

This situation seems to contradict the cases I mentioned before[1] of GURU and KAMBAWE who were called from their patrilocal villages to succeed their maternal uncles as headmen. I did not witness these events; they happened about thirty years ago or more. Perhaps each of the dominant lineages in those villages at that time lacked suitable personnel and had to get a kinsman from elsewhere lest the leadership should fall to a different lineage (possibly a slave lineage) in the village. It may also have been an attempt to prevent the struggle for succession from developing into such fierce rivalry that disintegration might have ensued.[2] One also wonders how the rivals in the villages concerned reacted to the arrival of an outsider. On the other hand, it might be that the rivals were in too weak a position to oppose the assumption of the title by an outsider.

The only comparable instance on which I could collect detailed information is that of Nyali of Chinyafwa, who went to Deep Bay (see p. 48) to fetch his full-sister's daughter and son in order to ensure that the succession should fall to his own minor lineage or 'house', which consists of uterine descendants of Nyali's mother Nyamwaya (Chin. E 1). The only alternative successor available at Chinyafwa is Dorosia (Chin. G 5) who belongs to 'the other (junior) house' (*nyumba inyaki*) of the uterine descendants of Nyamwaya's sister Nyamphato (Chin. E 3). Nyamphato is Dorosia's grandmother and lives at Chinyafwa. Dorosia used to live there but is now living with her husband Samuel (Mul. D 6) at Mulombwa. Nyali himself conceded that if no successor were available in his own 'house' (i.e. among his mother's uterine descendants), then the 'ownership' of the headmanship at Chinyafwa should go to Dorosia.[3] But he added that he would prefer the 'name' to stay in his own senior 'house'. In any case Nyali has at

---

[1] See pp. 60 *seq.*

[2] Cf. the succession struggle at Mzenga (p. 195) which is leading to disintegration of the village.

[3] I am only considering the possibilities on the basis of the situation at Chinyafwa as I found it. There are many potential Chinyafwa residents at

present a comparatively free hand to make what arrangements he deems necessary in order to secure the succession for his own senior lineage. There are no serious rivals present at Chinyafwa and Dorosia has 'nobody behind her' to protect her interests in this matter. It is true that Nyali acts as her *asibweni* (maternal uncle), and thus her *nkhoswe* (attorney). But he is only her classificatory uncle, and if he had to choose between the interests of Dorosia and Mary (who is his real sister's daughter) he would no doubt favour Mary.[1]

Owners and Succession

Ideally succession should never give rise to difficulties because there is the clear rule that a title should be inherited by the previous holder's sister's son or sister's daughter's son. But there are always complicating factors; and none of the successions which I know of was quite so straightforward. In the background of 'Meya's Death' we saw signs of the political struggle for leadership at Mapalassie which may ensue when Mussa (Map. A 1) dies. If, as seems likely, Ziba (Map. C 3) succeeds, then his matrilineage (the Lena lineage) will be the dominant lineage at Mapalassie. I myself think that it is probable that either of two things may happen: the Mzake group may separate themselves politically and become an independent political unit; or if they stay at Mapalassie and if the succession to the leadership of Mapalassie comes into dispute again, the Mzake lineage would almost certainly claim the title on the grounds that it had always been theirs. In this event they might argue that previously it had fallen to the Lena lineage only because at that time the Mzake lineage had nobody available to succeed.

I heard such an argument in at least four cases of disputed successions. One of the cases was at Mzenga. The competition for the title of the late KAMBAWE clearly shows that the ascendancy of the dominant lineage is not so much a matter of constitutional rights; rather it is the result of control of the political forces at a particular time, as the next case shows.

---

present working abroad. If they return the political situation at Chinyafwa may be materially altered: cf. the situation at Mapalassie, p. 172.

[1] For a similar situation where an 'orphan' (*mlanda*), who has 'nobody behind her', feels in a weak position, see the cases of Elinara and Alinda, pp. 150, 152.

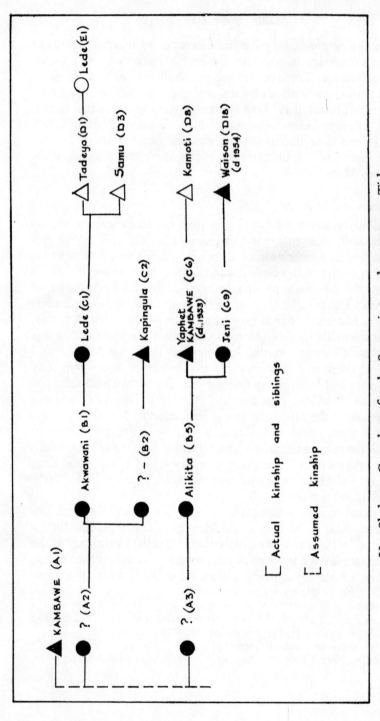

V.—Skeleton Genealogy for the Succession to the KAMBAWE Title

For the position of Akwawani (B 1) and Alikita (B 5) *vis-à-vis* KAMBAWE (A 1) on the Genealogy see note to Genealogy XIV for Mzenga Village. Letters and numbers in brackets refer to Genealogy XIV for KAMANGA Village

CASE 11: ADULTERY AND SUCCESSION
AT MZENGA[1]

I had heard that there was serious dissension at Mzenga about the succession to the office at KAMBAWE, but I did not observe it until the adultery of Lede (Mz. E 1) and Wellington (Mz. D 26) brought it into the open. The three competing parties were: Kamoti (Mz. D 8), a son of the late KAMBAWE; Waison (Mz. D 18), a uterine nephew of KAMBAWE; and Samu (Mz. D 3) and Tadeyo (Mz. D 1), KAMBAWE's nephews in a collateral lineage. The late KAMBAWE (Yaphet) also held the appointment of Administrative Headman. In addition he was a councillor in the court of the Native Authority KABUNDULI for which he received a monthly remuneration of £1 10. 0. Thus KAMBAWE, besides being a village headman, had the prestige of possessing a tax register or Book and of his councillorship. KAMBAWE was an important political figure in the area.

Before KAMBAWE (Yaphet) died in April 1953, his son Kamoti had for some time been acting for his father (or, as the Tonga say, he had been 'walking' for his father), because the latter was too old. When Kamoti was acting for his father KAMBAWE, it was as if he himself *were* KAMBAWE: he was addressed in court and elsewhere as KAMBAWE and he also signed documents in that name. After his father's death Kamoti continued acting as KAMBAWE and people continued to address him as KAMBAWE. Even now many people still address him and refer to him by his father's title. But soon his opponents in the village accused him of wanting to usurp the 'name' (*viz.* title) and Kamoti began to sign with his own name. Kamoti told me that he was not greatly interested in the KAMBAWE headmanship since the Book has been given to a neighbouring headman. He wanted however to stay in the village because he had economic interests and political influence which he had largely acquired on the strength of his father's position in the area. He also wanted to keep the job as councillor. N.A. KABUNDULI reassured Kamoti that he would keep his councillorship since it had nothing to do with the KAMBAWE title. Kamoti made doubly sure by securing Boma backing for it.

In about July 1953, N.A. KABUNDULI was selected by the Boma for a course in Local Government at the Jeanes Training Centre in Domasi (Southern Province). KABUNDULI was to be accompanied by a few

---

[1] See also pp. 60, 66, 98, 245 *et passim*.

other members of the N.A. bureaucracy. Kamoti was selected as one of them. There was, however, one difficulty. Kamoti was certain that he would never be chosen for succession to the KAMBAWE-ship and he was not sure whether the Boma considered the councillorship an appurtenance of the KAMBAWE title or whether they, like KABUNDULI, considered it a personal appointment.[1] He decided to sound the District Commissioner on this point. He explained to the D.C. that he would like to go to Domasi. But since he had no right to the name KAMBAWE, the people in the village would accuse him of usurping the name if he went as councillor KAMBAWE; and if another person in the village suc-ceeded to the KAMBAWE title later he, Kamoti, might lose his job as councillor. And if that happened, he was afraid that the Boma might be annoyed at having wasted money on his training as a councillor. Kamoti received an encouraging answer. The D.C. confirmed what KABUNDULI had told him before: that the councillorship had nothing to do with the name KAMBAWE; and if somebody else were chosen as KAMBAWE's successor in the village, Kamoti would still keep his posi-tion as councillor. So Kamoti went to Domasi.

Before his death old KAMBAWE had in his person combined the village headmanship, the Administrative Headmanship, and the coun-cillorship (and the eldership of the kirk); henceforth the name KAM-BAWE would be of significance within the village only, *viz.* a headman's title but deprived of the Book and the councillorship. This of course greatly reduced the political stature and financial attraction of the KAMBAWE title. This is why Kamoti, when he told me, in 1954, about the Mzenga troubles, could sit back and laugh at the other competitors. He said that he was no longer interested in the name KAMBAWE: 'Let the others fight, they will never get the councillorship and that is what they are after.' He added: 'Anyhow, who are they? They say they are my father's uterine nephews (*aphwao*, sing. *mphwao*), but where were they when my father was still alive? Who gave him this door for his house and who gave him this chair and always helped him with money? I did, and they were nowhere.'

The struggle for power at Mzenga was between two matrilineages and by the matrilineages against a village son. One of the nephews was Waison (Mz. D 18) who claimed that he was the obvious heir to the name KAMBAWE since he was the late KAMBAWE's (Mz. C 6) uterine

[1] Strictly speaking councillors are appointed by the N.A. or subordinate N.A. but they have to be approved by the D.C. who has, in general, an effec-tive say in such appointments.

sister's son. But the other claimants, Tadeyo and Samu (Mz. D 1 and 3), maintained that the name belonged by right to their matrilineage because the late KAMBAWE's predecessor (Mz. A 1) was their direct matrilineal ancestor. But at the time of his death there was no successor available among his own direct descendants as they were all away or too young and therefore Yaphet, from another matrilineage (*viz.* the one which Waison (Mz. D 18) now represents), had been chosen as a 'temporary successor'. Tadeyo and Samu argued that since there were now suitable candidates available again in the 'real owner lineage', *viz.* their own matrilineage, the title should come back to them. Kamoti disputed this view and maintained that his father's, i.e. Yaphet KAMBAWE's, 'house' had precedence over the 'house' which Samu and Tadeyo represented.

These were the arguments used between the two competing matrilineages. Their arguments against Kamoti's alleged usurpation were of course that he was a son and had no constitutional right whatever. They are reported to have asked Kamoti: 'What are you doing here, anyway? Have you not got a matrilocality and a "name" of your own? Why don't you go there?'[1] Although Kamoti had made several gestures, such as insisting on not being called KAMBAWE and signing documents in his own name and not as KAMBAWE, to prove that he had no aspirations to the title, his opponents still suspected him of secret aspirations. What really rankled was that Kamoti had managed to break the KAMBAWE-ship down into its component parts and had already secured for himself one of its more valuable parts, *viz.* the councillorship, whilst another status-conferring part, *viz.* the Book, had been lost altogether to a neighbouring headman into whose Book the Mzenga tax-payers had been incorporated. What was left of the late KAMBAWE's political status (which the rival heirs had hoped to inherit intact) was not particularly attractive. This may be one reason why there seemed to be no great urgency in settling the matter. Another factor may have been that the men of both matrilineages had been abroad for several years. At the time of the court case Waison and Samu had only just returned; soon afterwards Samu went back to Southern Rhodesia and Waison died. In the meanwhile the village seemed to be disintegrating. This was probably the cause of the census being transferred to a neighbouring village. We should, however, not exclude the possibility that at the same time neighbouring headmen had been exploiting the weakness of this leaderless village and had been

[1] See also p. 66.

manipulating political forces and factors in an attempt to have the census roll of Mzenga village added to their own.

As I mentioned before, the course of the adultery accusation through the village, to the court, and back to the village, made the political conflict overt. Usually if an intra-village adultery is complained about at all, it is taken to the headman and settled within the village. Kamoti had been effective headman for a long time not only because he was acting for his father but also because he was in the village whilst the other men of the village were abroad. Therefore, Wellington (Mz. D 26), the lover, and his 'mother' Nyaulanda (Mz. C 11) (actually his mother's sister) came to Kamoti to discuss the matter. Kamoti sent them away, saying that he was no longer the *fumu* (chief, headman) and had therefore no authority to settle it; they should go to the two nephews of his father. They obviously did not want to go to Samu (Mz. D 3) as he was the 'father' of the woman (Lede, Mz. E 1) in the case. Kamoti told me later with a broad grin: 'They went to Waison and so Waison was *fumu* [chief] for one day.' Not surprisingly the discussion led nowhere: the combination and interplay of forces, which alone make arbitration possible and support its decision,[1] were lacking in this disunited situation.

The same day that Wellington, the lover, and his 'mother' Nyaulanda had been to see Kamoti and Waison, Lede had taken out a summons at KABUNDULI's court, which in itself was a sign of a serious rupture in the village's unity. The hearing was delayed for some time because KABUNDULI himself was away. Normally Kamoti, as councillor, presides over the court in KABUNDULI's absence but this was now impossible since Kamoti was too much involved, and the political controversy at Mzenga, as much as the adultery, would be on trial. Indeed both before and during the hearing there appeared to be a certain reluctance to proceed with the case; nobody really wanted to get involved in this political quarrel. Several headmen, especially the neighbouring ones, who normally are quite ready to participate in legal arguments in the court, now kept quiet, or when pressed only made non-committal remarks.

Kamoti, quite properly, did not take part in the questioning or deliberations. At one stage, however, KABUNDULI said: 'Now we would like to hear what KAMBAWE has to say about this case of adultery in his village.' This caused some surprise and agitation in the court. Samu got up and said rather excitedly that as Kamoti had secretly

[1] Cf. 'Meya's Death', p. 149.

assumed the title KAMBAWE, although he denied it officially, he had better answer the call. KABUNDULI said: 'I am sorry. I forgot that the owner of the name died some time ago and that no new KAMBAWE has been chosen yet. But as there is no KAMBAWE, I would like Kamoti to tell us what he knows.' KABUNDULI told me later that he had not made a mistake at all (of course he knew the position at Mzenga as well as anybody else), but that he had deliberately called upon KAMBAWE to make a statement. He wanted to know who would respond to the name KAMBAWE. He had warned Kamoti beforehand that he would do so, as he wanted to know how far the two opposing matrilineages had progressed towards a solution of their conflict. Moreover, he, KABUNDULI, did not want to announce officially that he did not recognize Kamoti as the successor to the name. KABUNDULI had therefore told Kamoti to sit tight when he called upon KAMBAWE as this would be a clear indication in public that Kamoti did not aspire to the name. But he wanted to see which of the two nephews would answer the call for KAMBAWE. The point was that KABUNDULI could not, of course, officially voice his opinion about whether he favoured or recognized Kamoti as the successor or not. This was entirely outside KABUNDULI's authority, both as village headman and as N.A. All that KABUNDULI wanted to do here was to make it clear that he was not interfering with or putting pressure on village politics by continuing to recognize Kamoti as KAMBAWE. My impression was that KABUNDULI wanted to keep Kamoti as councillor but did not particularly care who would be the next KAMBAWE.

The court found Wellington guilty of adultery and he was ordered to pay damages to Lede. KABUNDULI in his judgment also expressed the hope that peace would now return. This was ostensibly meant for the parties in the adultery but could equally well have been intended for all the Mzenga people. When some weeks afterwards I asked Kamoti whether there were any signs of peace returning to Mzenga, he answered that things were still as they were before. And as evidence of the seriousness of the disunity he added that Lede's people had not even returned to Wellington the money he had paid to them in court as damages.[1]

Although I have set this court case against its background of a

[1] I have been told of other occasions on which damages were paid in court between parties of the same village or other closely associated parties, but subsequently repaid in the village. The parties had only wanted to obtain legal

struggle for power in a village, the court hearing itself was ostensibly concerned with adultery and provided an uninitiated outsider only with a faint hint that there might be something else behind it all. In other words, as in previously mentioned legal disputes, a political conflict was discussed in the terms, and within the framework, of a marital (or quasi-marital) dispute.

It should be added that none of the parties competing for the KAMBAWE title are either old or old-fashioned.[1] They are all middle-aged, have all spent a considerable period working in the industrial centres abroad, and speak and probably write English.

This struggle for the leadership at Mzenga started before the death of the late KAMBAWE (Yaphet). Apparently the tension began to rise before KAMBAWE died and, as mentioned (pp. 61 and 67), the departure of the Amuziteni group may well have been connected with this atmosphere of acute dissension. This competition was an aspect of the political and structural opposition between the kin groups within the village, and the rivalry became an open conflict when the political leadership became a critical issue. The parties to the conflict were the late headman's son, Kamoti, and two matrilineages. Waison (Mz. D 18) was a representative of the dominant matrilineage as he was the late KAMBAWE's uterine sister's son. Therefore Waison's own title, the 'name' (*zina*) he would inherit from his mother's brother (*asibweni*), was KAMBAWE. Samu is a representative of another matrilineage related to the dominant matrilineage of KAMBAWE through an assumed matrilineal link. The title which is said to be associated with this lineage is KAPIN-GULA and this is also the title which, according to Kamoti, Samu has adopted.[2]

I was frequently told of matrilineages which were not dominant

---

opinion on their controversy or to bring their dispute into the open without, however, wanting to aggravate the situation by inflicting financial losses. As I never managed to obtain any specific evidence for cases in which damages were actually returned, I do not know whether this is only an ideal, or in fact practised.

[1] In contrast with, for instance, the Ndembu where only the old-fashioned are said to care for the headmanship: see Turner (1957), pp. 133–6.

[2] Any freeman can adopt his maternal uncle's name as a title. However, Samu is still referred to and addressed by his surname (*chiwongo*), Chirwa. The accuracy and significance of this information can only be assessed situationally. I call these titles which are not offices, subsidiary titles: see also pp. 59, 211.

in their respective villages but which had their own particular, supposedly hereditary titles. In most cases I simply had to accept (or not accept) these claims to subsidiary titles since the situations in which their veracity and practical significance can be tested are few. Although subsidiary titles are said to be hereditary, in fact I often found little effective evidence of continuity because the holder of a subsidiary title (or for that matter, of a headman's title) was frequently only the second incumbent of that title, having inherited it from a maternal uncle whose *personal* name it was. For instance Samu (Mz. D 3) adopted the name KAPINGULA as a title from his maternal uncle who, apparently, had it as his proper name, in the same way that Samu is called Samu. This should be seen in the light of the fact that the criterion of a freeman is his having matrilineal kin, or in Tonga idiom: 'a freeman (*mnangwa*) knows who his mother is and where she comes from'. And this means that he 'knows' who his maternal uncle is.[1] The adoption of your maternal uncle's name is evidence of your 'knowing' your maternal uncle and thus your matrilineal origin which shows you are a freeman indeed.

There is another aspect to this desire to adopt an ancestor's name as a title or, in general, to the desire of individual matrilineages for a title of their own (that is, a subsidiary title) apart from the title of the village headman which they may inherit as well. Every freeborn Tonga is a potential headman if he can manage to gather around him sufficient followers who will support him in his struggle to establish an independent political unit. Hence the terms *zina* (in the sense of 'title'), *unangwa* (freeman status) and *ufumu* (headmanship) are practically synonymous and are often used interchangeably. If Waison (Mz. D 18) had managed to continue the leadership of Mzenga village under the title KAMBAWE and Samu had felt strong enough to establish his leadership over a group of followers, he might have seceded from KAMBAWE and would then undoubtedly have adopted the title KAPINGULA as the title for the headmanship of the new village. This is one of the situations in which the veracity and significance of a matrilineage's claim to its own title become observable.

[1] Cf. Nyali's desire to show the paternal kin of his niece Mary that she was not a slave but had an *asibweni* (maternal uncle), p. 48. See also Case 2, p. 60; Charles's question about KAMISA, p. 208; and the discussion on slaves, pp. 254 *seq.*

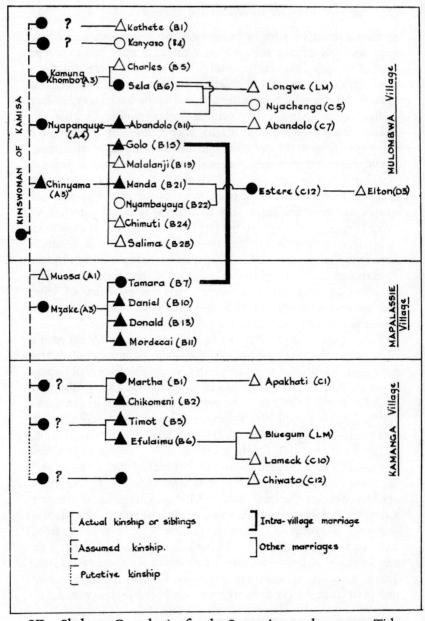

VI.—Skeleton Genealogies for the Succession to the KAMISA Title

Letters and numbers in brackets refer to Genealogies IX (for MAPALASSIE Village),
X (for MULOMBWA Village) and XII (for KAMANGA Village)

Sometimes the leader of a sub-group within a village is generally known and referred to by a particular title. In this way a historical relationship between two kin groups may be perpetuated. For instance, incorporated in NGOMBO's village is KAPEKENYA, who is said to be the headman's 'younger brother'. Another example is to be found in Chituka village, where the headman's title is MLENGA MZOMA. It is said that after the death of the previous MLENGA MZOMA there was competition for the succession between Alek and William. Eventually Alek succeeded. My informant concluded: 'After the installation of Alek as MLENGA MZOMA, William was given the name of a very important ancestor of the Kapunda Banda, called MUGOWAMONU.' [1]

The Chequered Histories of Titles

The recent history of the KAMISA title at Mulombwa shows conflicts similar to those at Mzenga and at Mapalassie, but the Mulombwa conflicts have progressed a few stages farther. The following summary of the history of KAMISA is typical of the chequered histories of Tonga titles.

CASE 12: *KAMISA* SUCCESSION

KAMISA[2] is said to have come from the country of the Nyaliwanga in the hills to the west and settled in his present habitat. KAMISA married a matrilineal relative (*mbumba*) of MAKALAMBA who lived nearby; and when his wife died KAMISA gave some land as compensation (the *chisoka* payment)[3] to MAKALAMBA—this is the present Chinyafwa.[4]

---

[1] Both stories are given here as I heard them from informants.

[2] I will, like my informants, merge the successive incumbents of this title in the single and perpetual identity of KAMISA. I do not have the data to distinguish the individual incumbents and to relate them chronologically. Apart from other possible factors responsible for their defective memories, the Tonga have little incentive to remember the detailed histories of their titles. They attach great prestige to a long, continuous association of a particular matrilineage with a specific village and a specific title (see also p. 46). Generally, however, titles have either a short history or the 'ownership' of most titles has been in several different matrilineages. For the Nyaliwanga, see also van Velsen (1959*a*), p. 6.

[3] Cf. p. 32, n. 2.

[4] This episode was almost certainly before the period of Ngoni invasions and the large stockaded villages (*linga*) where the Tonga concentrated.

There are several versions of how KAMISA lost his *nkhazu* (*viz.* a red or scarlet robe)[1] to CHIRIMBIRI. One story is that when KAMISA died his heir was too young and the *nkhazu* was safeguarded by KAMISA's 'sister' (*mbumba ya* KAMISA). She was called Nyanyi and was of great beauty. CHIRIMBIRI, who came from the west, married her and settled in her village. Nyanyi, moved by love, gave the *nkhazu* to CHIRIMBIRI. But when the young KAMISA grew up he wanted the *nkhazu* back. As CHIRIMBIRI would not agree, there was a great quarrel and in the end CHIRIMBIRI left the village and settled where KACHIPAPA lives now, just south of Mulombwa. In spite of KAMISA's attempts to get the *nkhazu* back by force of arms, he did not succeed. Eventually KAMISA received a new *nkhazu* from his brother, Mukhumpha, on Likoma Island: Mukhumpha was given this *nkhazu* by the Arabs on the eastern shores of the lake.

There have always been many contacts between this stretch of the western shore and Likoma Island: for instance, the Mapalassie people came over from the island in the beginning of the century and settled in KAMISA's village (p. 50). During the Ngoni raids, apparently, many people fled from the mainland to Likoma. And it seems likely that there was some traffic in slaves, possibly in both directions, and particularly between MANKHAMBIRA's village and Likoma Island. Arabs and their agents were active on the eastern shores of the lake.

According to tradition, CHIRIMBIRI was the founder of a 'house' which contains several headmen who now live between the villages of KAMISA and MANKHAMBIRA, including KACHIPAPA. KAMISA claims that he was the original 'owner of the land' (*mwerne charu*)[2] and that he gave land to some out of kindness and to others as *chisoka* payments in compensation for the death of the recipients' 'sisters' (*mbumba*) whom KAMISA had married, e.g. MAKALAMBA's sister.

The most likely interpretation of these legends seems to be that CHIRIMBIRI and his 'house' were immigrants from across the lake, as MANKHAMBIRA,[3] KANGOMA,[3] KACHIPAPA and others are said to have been. It is possible that these immigrants entered this area directly from the east, i.e. across the lake and via Likoma Island. Alternatively, they may have crossed the lake from the east at a point farther north, wandered southwards along the watershed farther inland and finally

---

[1] A symbol of office comparable to the scarlet headband of the Yao: see p. 304.

[2] See p. 272 on land-holding.   [3] See van Velsen (1959*a*), p. 5.

entered this area from the west; for CHIRIMBIRI is supposed to have come to KAMISA's village from the west.

These immigrant groups probably were or had been in contact with Arab traders or their agents and possessed guns.[1] Thanks to his guns, MANKHAMBIRA, with the support of his fellow invaders, soon established his ascendancy in the area; at least it was MANKHAMBIRA (and probably KANGOMA too) who during the subsequent Ngoni raids organized and commanded the stockade just north of the Luweya River. In this stockade the ancestors of many of the headmen who are now established between the Luweya River and Nkata Bay took refuge. And it was by this stockade that the Ngoni were decisively defeated towards the end of the third quarter of the nineteenth century. KAMISA and CHACHAMARA (Vuwa)[2] were also in this stockade together. When KAMISA died he was succeeded by his 'nephew' CHA-CHAMARA. The present acting KAMISA (Elton) (Mul. D 3) told me that KAMISA had five nephews, of whom CHACHAMARA was the most junior. When KAMISA died he was succeeded by each of the older nephews in turn, but all of them survived only for a short period and eventually the 'name' (i.e. the title) fell to CHACHAMARA. He dropped the 'name' KAMISA in favour of his own 'name' CHACHAMARA because 'he had seen that the name KAMISA had killed many people'.[3]

Local tradition has it that when the Ngoni raids were over, KAMISA (whether CHACHAMARA or his predecessor I do not know) went to Likoma Island to persuade his relatives who had fled there to return to his village which was now safe. As a result, Daniel (Map. B 10), the son of Mzake (Map. A 3), went from Likoma to the mainland to reconnoitre. He landed near Bandawe[4] where he found a kinsman who took him to CHACHAMARA's village. Daniel met his *asibweni* (maternal uncle) CHACHAMARA who persuaded him to go back to Likoma and bring his kinsfolk back to the mainland. This Daniel apparently did. It is said that CHACHAMARA wanted to give Daniel the title KAMISA

---

[1] *Ibid.*, pp. 1, 6, and also below, p. 297.

[2] Although CHACHAMARA is not now a headman's or a subsidiary title, it seems to have been one in the recent past; Vuwa is his personal name.

[3] Most informants told me the same version of the second half of the story about the substitution of the name CHACHAMARA for KAMISA, but not about the five nephews. *Ufumu ubaya wanthu*, i.e. chieftainship kills people, *viz.* the incumbents of the chieftainship or those who aspire to it. The implication is that a chief or headman is the object of much jealousy and is therefore a likely victim of sorcery, a circumstance often described for other parts of Africa.

[4] A long morning's walk south of Mapalassie.

and the *nkholi*[1] (i.e. the right to hold the girls' puberty ceremony) but that Daniel refused the offer and went to Cape Town instead, whence he never returned.[2]

CHACHAMARA is said to have died about 1920. Before he died his 'nephew' Charles (Mul. B 5) had already been acting for him, and in due course succeeded him. The Mapalassie people say that the succession was first offered to Daniel again, or rather, as he himself was absent, to his brothers Donald (Map. B 13) and Mordecai (Map. B 11). But they refused the offer and Charles succeeded. Charles, so they say, dropped the title CHACHAMARA and returned to the title KAMISA. He seems to have quarrelled with people, and accused them of wanting to kill him out of jealousy. His first wife died and his second wife fell ill too. He said that he himself was on the way to becoming insane as a result of sorcery; so he fled and settled in his wife's village. Now Chikomeni (Kam. B 2) succeeded to the title but he died after a year or so. After Chikomeni, Abandolo (Mul. C 7) acted as KAMISA.

It seems that Abandolo did not last long either, because after a short period he handed the Book back, saying that he had become a Jehovah's Witness (Watchtower). Abandolo's place was taken by Efulaimo (Kam. B 6) who, so they say, had been intriguing for it for some time, claiming that the Book should have come to him after Chikomeni's death as he was Chikomeni's 'brother'.

Another version puts Charles's period after Chikomeni. When Chikomeni died, Daniel (Map. B 10) was already dead and the headmanship was offered to Donald and Mordecai again—but again they refused. Charles then took it on, fell ill, and moved away leaving the Book behind with Abandolo. Efulaimo began his intriguing until Charles intervened. He is reported to have asked Efulaimo: 'Do you want the name? All right, here is the Book, you walk', and thus Efulaimo 'walked' but, as informants put it, 'Charles left the name behind with his sister's daughter, Nyachenga (Mul. C 5), who became the owner of the name'. Charles then knew that it was Efulaimo who had killed his first wife, and had made his second wife and himself ill.

The trouble started again in about 1953 when Efulaimo died. Charles

---

[1] The *nkholi* used to be an attribute of headmanship, or at least of some headmen, but there are no traces left of either the rite or the distribution of these rites in the past, cf. p. 302.

[2] He married a South African woman, the mother of John (Map. C 11). Daniel died when John was about twelve years old. James (Map. C 12) sent money for his fare and John was sent to Mapalassie: see p. 230.

had told Efulaimo only to 'walk', that is, to act[1] as KAMISA and keep
the Book, but he had made it clear that he did not give him the
'ownership of the name' because this was entrusted to Nyachenga
(Mul. C 5). However, at Efulaimo's death, Chiwato (Kam. C 12) and
the other Kamanga villagers wanted to wait until Apakhati's (Kam. C 1)
return from Johannesburg before they decided upon the successor.
Lameck (Kam. C 10) did not agree[2] and suggested that a meeting be
called which Nyachenga and Kathere (Mul. B 1) should attend.[3]
Chiwato (Kam. C 12) and his supporters were asked at the meeting
whether they did not remember that Charles (Mul. B 5) had only
given the Book to Efulaimo (Kam. B 6) and had left the title behind
with Nyachenga (Mul. C 5), and that, in any case, the title did not
belong to the Kamanga people. Nyachenga then asked Salima (Mul.
B 28) to act for her. When Salima went to visit a relative in Tanganyika the Book was entrusted to Elton (Mul. D 3) who continued to
act as KAMISA after Salima had come back to the village. Elton and other
informants agreed that the person who should really be KAMISA is
Nyachenga's uterine brother, Longwe (Mul. C 3), who is at present
working abroad. Elton is a young man in his late twenties who has not
been abroad yet. He often complained that the job was not worth the
trouble, especially since the people did not show him any respect. He
considered giving it up and going abroad instead to get money and
decent clothes.

I was told that early in 1955 Kanyaso (Mul. B 4) had a quarrel with
Elton in the course of which she asked him what he was doing in the
village as KAMISA, since he was only a slave. (Apparently this was not
the first time they had a row.) Later Charles came to the village and
discussed the matter with Kanyaso and others. He agreed that Elton
should give up acting in the name of KAMISA. The ostensible reason
Charles is said to have given for his decision was that he had heard that
Elton's father at KANGOMA's village (about one hour's walk south of
Mulombwa) had not been told about Elton's job and that he did not

---

[1] I use 'acting' to refer to the executive of a title. Thus Elton (Mul. D 3), who
is acting KAMISA, is the executive of the title. He acts as KAMISA or, as the Tonga
say, he 'walks' (*watenda*, from *kwenda*, to walk).

[2] I could not discover why he should have opposed the kinsmen of his own
village. He is a member of a sect, very similar to the Watchtower movement,
which is opposed to secular authority; this may explain his attitude.

[3] Kathete and Nyachenga are generally considered, both at Mulombwa and
outside, as the most senior of the members of the KAMISA lineage resident at
Mulombwa.

like it because 'a chief dies too soon'. At one stage in this discussion Charles is reported to have asked the rhetorical question: 'What is the name which Elton can claim?' [1] knowing full well that Elton's maternal grandmother Nyambayaya (Mul. B 22) has no 'name' because she is a slave or *mwana wa malundi*.[2]

Legitimists and Usurpers

So far I have analysed in some detail the succession to political leadership in three villages: Mapalassie, Mzenga and Mulombwa. In none was the succession settled as easily as the simple-sounding rule—that a headman is succeeded by his sister's son—would lead one to expect. The complicating features include the facts that matrilineages localized in villages are shallow and contain few people, and that many potential executives are living abroad.

I observed the political developments in the three villages at different stages. At Mzenga the two competing matrilineages were nowhere near a solution. The solution was made particularly difficult for two reasons. The first was a lack of personnel. Secondly Kamoti (Mz. D 8), who as a son could not compete for the traditional and hereditary attributes of the KAMBAWE-ship, had already secured for himself one of the modern, non-hereditary and more worthwhile attributes of the office, leaving a comparatively valueless title which made a solution less urgent. At Mapalassie, where Ziba's (Map. C 3) succession to the leadership is a foregone conclusion as things stand now, we saw what sort of forces may nevertheless be brought into play by either party. Finally, at Mulombwa we saw the result of a series of struggles for leadership, · and the changing fortunes of the various matrilineages involved.

These changing fortunes at Mulombwa are represented in the accounts of the informants in such phrases as: 'choosing the successor' and 'offering the title'. In the light of what happened at Mzenga and Mapalassie it seems unlikely that the emergence of a successor was the result of a 'choice' on the part of electors. It is much more likely to have been the result of political manœuvring and of partly fortuitous circumstances, such as the absence abroad of potential rivals. We saw that after Chikomeni's (Kam. B 2) death the KAMISA title left the Kamanga group; but it returned to

---

[1] Cf. also pp. 37 and 201.
[2] Lit. a child of the legs, referring to supplicating slaves holding their masters' legs: see also pp. 254 *seq.*

this group after an interval during which Efulaimo (Kam. B 6) had been complaining that he had been passed over although he was Chikomeni's brother. Efulaimo worked for a long period in South Africa. It is likely that he was abroad at the time of Chikomeni's death and that there was no suitable candidate present among the Kamanga people, so that someone in another lineage group seized his chance. Something similar is happening at Mapalassie (pp. 170–1).

I have mentioned on p. 71 the fact that the Tonga try to organize the trips of their menfolk to the industrial centres in such a way that at least one man stays in each hamlet to look after the hamlet's women and the other interests of its kin group. And those men who are abroad are still keenly interested in the village politics of the tribal area. The conditions of their life and employment abroad are such that they cannot afford to cut their ties with the village. Tonga men experience the economic pressure of having to earn wages abroad in order to attain a standard of living which is now generally accepted as normal in Tongaland. But on the other hand there is the pull of political ambition at home. One should not rule out the possibility that some men are more attracted by the prospects of satisfying their political ambition at home, than by the prospects of economic betterment abroad. This may be so particularly when a man has the prospect of succeeding to a headmanship of special economic and/or political importance.[1] Such headmanships are few; and my evidence is that the attraction of the great majority of Tonga headmanships is on the whole not strong enough to counteract the pull of the industrial centres abroad.[2] This is borne out, for instance, by those cases in which a claimant for a headmanship returns to his village from abroad, sues for and acquires the headmanship, and goes abroad again.[3] For this reason I consider that the presence or

---

[1] E.g. a headmanship which, at the time, holds the Administrative office of N.A. or Councillor; or one which controls an important source of income but is not associated with an Administrative office, as in the case of NGOMBO, see p. 296.

[2] A complicating factor here is that even in those comparatively rare cases of men who have never worked abroad (e.g. Ziba of Mapalassie and Milton of Thoro—see pp. 72, 245 *et passim*), it is difficult to establish whether it is ambition, *viz.* the prospect of succession to a headmanship, or other factors which have influenced their decision to stay at home.

[3] See also van Velsen (1960), p. 276.

absence of potential executives at the time the succession to a
headmanship is being decided, is largely a fortuitous circumstance.
Few men seem to stay at home with succession to headmanship
in view.

When informants say that the KAMISA title was 'offered' to
Daniel (Map. B 10) or to other people who now belong to Mapalassie, this should probably be interpreted as meaning that Daniel
and the others were also competing for the leadership at Mulombwa. And when Daniel 'declined the offer', in reality he
probably lost the political contest. Having failed to capture the
leadership of Mulombwa village, this kin group established itself
as an independent unit which is now Mapalassie village. It is noteworthy that the Kamanga people who, apparently, have also been
competing for the leadership of KAMISA's village, are now also
emerging as an independent political unit. Indeed, it looks as if
there was a fourth kin group involved in this struggle for political leadership. Although reconstruction is now difficult, it seems
clear that CHACHAMARA and KAMISA belonged to two different
groups. It is possible that CHACHAMARA was a subsidiary title
within KAMISA's village[1] which replaced the KAMISA title when
the leadership of the village had fallen to the CHACHAMARA
group.

We have noticed that *in fact* the KAMISA title, either in its
entirety (*viz.* the Book, the executive and the 'ownership' of the
title), or only some of its constituent parts, has gone from one
matrilineage to another. This fact, combined with the ideal rules
of matrilineal succession, creates a situation in which several
matrilineages can with more or less justification claim the KAMISA-
ship. This is because each matrilineage, once having had a part or
the whole of the KAMISA-ship, considers that henceforth the succession to the KAMISA title should be confined to that particular
matrilineage. This same conflict between actual succession and
the ideal rule, and the resulting conflict of claims, is found in
other villages also, for instance at Mzenga and in other struggles
for succession which I will analyse later. Consequently, as regards
succession to titles among the Tonga there are almost invariably
rival claimants (a situation not peculiar to the Tonga of course).
But in addition, the past 'wanderings' of most titles, or parts
of them, make it almost impossible to ascertain whether one

[1] Cf. KAPINGULA within Mzenga village, p. 200.

claimant has a stronger case than another, or, indeed, whether
there is only one legitimate claimant whilst all the others are
usurpers.

Subsidiary Titles

The problem of subsidiary titles can be further illuminated by
an analysis of the situation at Chinyafwa.

CASE 13: THE HISTORY OF *MAKALAMBA*[1]

The history of MAKALAMBA also shows up the vicissitudes of Tonga
titles. Nyali's (Chin. F 4) official title is MAKALAMBA and I have seen
letters from kinsmen abroad addressed to Nayali by this title. This
proves that it is not only Nyali himself who claims this title: his claim
is supported by some at least of his kinsmen. I cite this particular piece
of evidence as an illustration of the difficulty facing an outside observer
(whether D.C. or anthropologist) who wants to assess the validity of
a claim to a title. Since traditional office at present largely lacks content and attributes,[2] such an assessment is really possible only through
observing situations (particularly disputes) in which title-holders play
a role and in which rival claims by other matrilineages are expressed.
But I came across no situation in Chinyafwa in which Nyali had to
assert his leadership against rival claimants. This is to a certain extent
due to the composition of Chinyafwa, which contains only twelve
adults without any potential matrilineal rivals of influence or importance (cf. p. 192). The only disputes I recorded were with Siddely
(Chin. D 6) who as a son of the village could, in any case, not easily
challenge Nyali's authority.

Although Nyali, as MAKALAMBA, now lives at Chinyafwa, the original MAKALAMBA lived at Mtemeni.[3] Mtemeni lies a mile or two north-
west of Chinyafwa beyond a low ridge. From Chinyafwa it can be
reached only on foot, and the walk, of about half-an-hour, takes one
over this thickly wooded ridge and through an area which is at present

---

[1] Nyali of Chinyafwa was my main source of information for this 'history'.
Most of the past events are unverifiable except where they have left some marks
in the present. Cf. also pp. 32, 48 and 68.

[2] For fuller discussion of this point, see pp. 219 and 292.

[3] Nyali derives this name from the verb *kutema*, to cut or to carve out, *viz*.
a piece of land from the bush or perhaps from another person's land.

Q

practically uninhabited. Mtemeni does not have, therefore, such easy access to the lake as Chinyafwa, which is only a few hundred yards from the lake. Mtemeni is uninhabited except for two huts of people on the outskirts who really belong to an adjacent village and who were told by Nyali to move (p. 116). Another inhabitant in the centre of Mtemeni is a woman called Nyalongwe who lives alone in the middle of her gardens, which have recently been cut out of the forest. Nyali told me that she was cultivating a previous MAKALAMBA's *masara* (old gardens). A dense bit of forest nearby marked the site of MAKALAMBA's grave, the trees being originally the poles of the screen (perhaps a stockade) around his house. Nyali remarked that he could not 'chase' Nyalongwe away from this land: as a seminal descendant of MAKALAMBA she had every right to live and hoe there. Nyali did not know any details of her descent. She expected, he said, to be joined by her 'sister' and the latter's son who lived in a village near Chinyafwa. About this 'sister', too, Nyali knew only that she was patrilaterally related to MAKALAMBA or perhaps a 'brother' of MAKALAMBA, but he did not know any genealogical details.

While MAKALAMBA (Chin. A 1) was living at Mtemeni, KAMISA married MAKALAMBA's 'sister' (*mbumba*). On her death, KAMISA gave a piece of land, which is now called Chinyafwa, as compensation (*chisoka*). According to Nyali, MAKALAMBA put CHIPETAMAWO (Chin. C 9) in charge of Chinyafwa, where the latter died in the 1920's and where he was buried; his grave was pointed out to me by various people. The name CHIPETAMAWO is considered a title and has been adopted, according to Nyali, by Smart (Chin. E 10). Since Nyali is headman at Chinyafwa and in that capacity has the title MAKALAMBA, the title CHIPETAMAWO is therefore a subsidiary title at Chinyafwa, at least at present. But if the leadership at Chinyafwa after the political defeat or death of Nyali should come to Smart or his matrilineage, it is likely that the headman at Chinyafwa will be called CHIPETAMAWO. At present Smart, like so many other assumed inhabitants[1] of Chinyafwa, is abroad. He has worked for several years in Tanganyika. He still corresponds with Nyali; not long ago he asked Nyali to effect his divorce from Elena, and he sent Nyali the necessary money.

Nyali told me that the original CHIPETAMAWO called MAKALAMBA his *asibweni* (i.e. maternal uncle) but this does not tally with the genealogy

[1] Many people who used to live at Chinyafwa show in their letters from abroad that they still consider themselves Chinyafwa people. It is assumed at Chinyafwa that they will settle there again if they return to Tongaland.

he gave me. Perhaps his statement merely indicates that there was some matrilineal relationship between these two. Or it may be a rationalization in terms of kinship of the fact that Nyali—a matrilineal descendant of a previous MAKALAMBA who used to live at Mtemeni—is now ruling at Chinyafwa, although this used to be the land of CHIPETAMAWO.

Another puzzling feature of Nyali's genealogical information is that all the people of Chinyafwa, including himself and the old CHIPETAMAWO, are supposed to be descendants of one woman, Nyazale Nyawana (Chin. B 3), who is said to have been a sister's daughter of MAKALAMBA. This Nyazale is said to have had twelve children. All, including Siddely's father Targha[1] (Chin. C 7), lived and died in Siska, except for CHIPETAMAWO who lived and died at Chinyafwa.

Considering that it is a MAKALAMBA who now exercises authority over both Mtemeni and Chinyafwa, it seems very likely that a much more complex political and genealogical situation has been condensed into the genealogy as detailed by Nyali. This genealogy seems to rationalize the present political reality in terms of formal values. I am making this assumption in the light of general experience in other similar situations and on the basis of internal evidence. Of this, the most important facts are the following. Nyali is about fifty years old and Siddely about seventy: the latter told me that his first trip to work abroad was in 1906. Whilst they differ in age by only twenty years, according to Nyali's genealogy he is two generations junior to Siddely. This suggests that telescoping may have taken place.[2] Moreover there is the fact that one woman, Nyazale, is supposed to have had twelve children all reaching adulthood and producing offspring themselves; this seems most unlikely and I myself have not come across a single verified instance of such fertility combined with such a high rate of survival. Finally there is the odd coincidence that Nyazale herself and all her children lived and died in Usiska except CHIPETAMAWO who lived and died at Chinyafwa.

It is clear that something occurred to affect the political or genealogical relationship between MAKALAMBA and CHIPETAMAWO, but it is now very difficult to find out exactly what. Perhaps when CHIPETAMAWO died there was no suitable successor among his immediate kin and the MAKALAMBA people captured the leadership at Chinyafwa.

---

[1] Cf. pp. 48 and 68.
[2] This fact could also be explained as a result of classificatory kinship. However, in my view this explanation is the less likely of the two.

What is certain is that, for the time being at any rate, the title CHIPETAMAWO has been eclipsed from the political scene.

Acquisition of Leadership

We have now considered some aspects of the problem of the continuity of, and the succession to, political leadership and titles in the five villages of Greater Kamisa, and at Mzenga. In each village the situation shows different aspects of the struggle for, and the characteristics of, a title. These accounts refer to different villages and titles, yet on the basis of my experience regarding other Tonga titles and of the evidence presented in relation to the five villages,[1] I feel justified in treating these accounts, for theoretical purposes, as one progressive series, representing different stages of one title.

Titles of village headmanships disappear, or go from one lineage to another, or from one village to another. There is a general lack of continuity in the titles of political leaders. This is particularly noticeable when one finds a confusion of names in the history of a present-day title (as in KAMISA's or KAMBAWE's cases), or when one finds that recollection stops at the predecessor of the present holder. This may be 'structural amnesia' caused by the fact that the title came from another lineage. Or the title may be a relatively recent creation: the leadership at Mapalassie does not even have a title, for a name does not become a title until it has been inherited at least once.

There is another factor which affects the Tonga's memory of titles and which, also, makes it difficult to define the position of the headman. The Tonga headman is essentially *primus inter pares* and his status depends mainly upon a combination of his individual capacities for leadership, his personal authority, the alignment of political forces in the village and his skill in manipulating these forces, and upon other, sometimes fortuitous, factors operating at the time.[2] At present, office among the Tonga is on the whole not marked by clear attributes of constitutional

---

[1] I include Chinyafwa. Although I have not observed it, there is no reason to assume that the succession to titles at Chinyafwa or Mtemeni has come about without conflicts of the kind reported for other villages. At any rate it is clear that the 'name' CHIPETAMAWO has disappeared and that some geographical and genealogical shift of the title MAKALAMBA has taken place.

[2] I discuss this in greater detail on p. 287.

authority, ritual functions or other prerogatives which would make it clearly recognizable.[1] Since village headmanship has this nebulous quality within an equally ill-defined political unit, I found difficulty in observing headmanship in action, and especially at times of its transfer. The question, 'What authority over whom in what area was inherited by whom?' is almost invariably difficult to answer.

I deal presently with the essence of political leadership. Here I am concerned with the acquisition of leadership. The struggle for political leadership, as we have seen, is essentially a contest between personalities backed by the group of their own immediate kin in the village. The outcome of this struggle for power, i.e. the acquisition of the leadership, is greatly influenced by such circumstances as the presence or absence in the opposing faction of suitable candidates. In spite of the apparently haphazard nature of the factors determining political leadership, political competition is set in a formal framework: the arguments are expressed in terms of the ideals of a formal political system. The arguments used in the overt struggles for village headmanship reveal the following ideal norms: a headman should succeed matrilineally, according to seniority, within a dominant lineage, which is by definition the lineage descended from the founder of the village.[2] The concepts of 'succession' and 'titles' subsume a certain formal framework within which the acquisition and transfer of leadership are effected. This same formal picture also appears in *ex post facto* reasoning. The present incumbent of a title will argue that *because* he now possesses the title, he is *therefore* the senior matrilineal descendant of the founder of the village. Thus at Mulombwa, since CHACHAMARA at one stage held the headmanship, CHACHAMARA *must* have been a nephew of KAMISA. The irregularity of CHACHAMARA's 'succession' is reflected in the genealogical position he is given: as the most junior of five nephews he would, theoretically, have had very little chance to succeed had it not been for the 'fact' that all the senior nephews are said to have died in rapid succession. In this way past vicissitudes

[1] In the past some headmen (probably the more powerful) had such attributes as the right to hold female initiation ceremonies. These made at least those headmanships recognizable. See also p. 302.

[2] See e.g. the succession dispute at Mzenga, pp. 195 *seq.* For the ideal and practical aspects of the concept of the dominant lineage, see also pp. 188 *seq.*

of the headmanship at Mulombwa are fitted into the ideal norms of headmanship. We saw that Samu (Mz. D 3) at Mzenga employed another device to rationalize an alleged irregularity in the past. He maintained that he is a representative of the most senior, the dominant, lineage, and that therefore the KAMBAWE title should return to him and not go to Waison (Mz. D 18). Samu explains away the fact that the late KAMBAWE (Yaphet) (Mz. C 6) belonged to Waison's lineage by saying that at the time of Yaphet's succession to the KAMBAWE-ship, there was no suitable candidate present in Samu's lineage and that therefore Yaphet was 'chosen', but only to fill the vacancy temporarily. Such irregularities, however, are the rule in the histories of Tonga titles: the ideal norms are rarely realized.

Acting Headman: Divisible Character of Headmanship

So far I have been considering how 'irregularities' of the past are being rationalized or 'normalized' in the present. But present 'irregularities' can also be fitted into the formal political system. We saw (p. 206) how Efulaimo (Kam. B 6) and others *acted* in the name of KAMISA whilst Charles (Mul. B 5) and Nyachenga (Mul. C 5) retained the '*ownership*' of the title KAMISA. This is a very common phenomenon. In most villages I was told in confidence at some stage: 'Of course you think that So-and-so is the headman and indeed he behaves as if he were, but really he only walks [*watenda waka*] and I [or somebody else] am the real owner of the title.' The fact that the speaker, as the real 'owner', had not in fact assumed the title, he would explain by saying that he felt too old to carry the burdens of office or that he lacked ambition, and so allowed 'the other fellow' to claim the honour. Or, again, a woman, like Nyachenga at Mulombwa, would explain that going to the court was not really a woman's job; and so she let somebody else (e.g. Elton (Mul. D 3) at Mulombwa) do the 'walking'.

A 'walker' in this context is the person who represents the executive aspects of a title. If the title-holder also holds Boma appointments (like the late KAMBAWE did), the executive 'walker' represents the title-holder in the courts or to the Boma. From this point of view the executive *is* the headman. It is difficult to see the practical significance of being merely the 'real owner' of the title, particularly when one considers the nebulous nature of headmanship among the Tonga. This differentiation between the 'real owner' and the executive ('walker') of a title symbolizes the controversy which generally surrounds the headmanship and the succession, and the practical implications of this dichotomy emerge perhaps most clearly at the time of succession. At that point in the existence of a title there may be a situation in which the executive and the 'owner' of the title belong to different lineages, and separate claimants for succession may be produced for the two parts of the office. This seems to have happened, for instance, after the death of Efulaimo (Kam. B 6) who was acting KAMISA. The possibility of the division of a title between an executive and an 'owner' provides a ready opening for a usurper. But as I pointed out before, the distinction between legitimists and usurpers is generally not clear. And the existence of executives and 'owners' emphasizes as well as rationalizes the ill-defined attributes of headmanship and succession. For this reason Tonga headmanship is not on the whole characterized by constitutional status supported by specific privileges or sanctions: it is rather a position of leadership. Hence a man, even a village son or slave, who possesses qualities of leadership may capture the title of headmanship, or at least may control it.[1]

The division of a title and the distribution of the two component parts of a title between two different persons who may even belong to different lineages is to a certain extent exceptional by ideal norms. But in one sense this division of the title is quite 'normal'. As I mentioned before, political authority is generally represented by men:[2] lineages which have a claim to office but have no suitable men available are in a weak position *vis-à-vis* lineages which may have weaker legal claims but which have a male on the spot. But since ideally succession and descent are matrilineal, the title should ultimately pass through the headman's mother, sister or sister's daughter. In that sense, the 'ownership' of any title always rests with a woman; and in that respect any male headman is only acting for a 'real owner' who is a woman. Thus Nyali (Chin. F 4) at Chinyafwa, whose right to the headmanship is not disputed, at least not within his own lineage, considers himself an executive who merely acts in the place of his

---

[1] Cf. Milton and the MUWANGA title and his designs on the KABUNDULI-ship; Case 14, p. 223, and pp. 250 *seq.*

[2] See p. 70. I have met one or two female headmen who acted as such and visited the courts, but they were exceptions.

female uterine kin, who are the 'real owners'. The Tonga men express this by saying: 'We only walk, but it is our sisters who are the real owners.' The implication is that on the premise of the ideal norm of matrilineal succession, biological and genealogical continuation of the lineage, which holds the title, rests with the women and not with the men. Nyali, discussing the future of the leadership at Chinyafwa, mentioned his efforts to get his sister's daughter Mary (Chin. G 3) to his village.[1] He pointed at her and said: 'She and her daughter, if she has one [she was pregnant at the time], will be the real owners here at Chinyafwa.' He thus by-passed himself and Mary's brother Gorogo who should be Nyali's successor.

The division of a title into executive and 'owning' elements is another aspect of the lack of precise definition in Tonga head-manship. This ambiguity provides a legal framework and a con-stitutional justification for the political manœuvring of rival claimants to a title. In spite of various constitutional concepts such as succession, titles, dominant lineage, etc., the Tonga headman is only *primus inter pares* and his authority is predominantly that of personal leadership. And the *de facto* situation shows that while the struggle for power lies between individuals and personalities rather than between occupants of definite status positions, it can, by the elastic application of ideal norms, be accommodated in the formal political structure.

The splitting up of a title between the title-holder or 'owner' and its agent or executive, allows scope for intrigue and 'usurpa-tion'. On the other hand, it provides a dominant lineage with an acceptable method of retaining the headmanship even in the absence of male members. While Nyachenga (Mul. C 5) pre-serves the title for her lineage until the expected return of her uterine brother Longwe (Mul. C 3) from Southern Rhodesia, the executive duties are carried out by Elton (Mul. D 3) as the acting KAMISA. This leads again to the question of the practical implications of this arrangement. How far is Nyachenga's claim to the title as its 'owner' reflected in the realities of political life in the village? Could one not say with equal justification that Nya-chenga's claim is merely a fiction and that for all practical pur-poses Elton *is* KAMISA, and not simply *acting* as KAMISA? Since I never stayed at Mulombwa I was not well placed to observe all

[1] See Case I, p. 48, and p. 71, n. 1.

the nuances of political realities there. And the lack of external, observable attributes of office does not make it any easier to determine where the centre of authority lies at any given time. But it seems to be a fact that although Elton has the Book he still appears to be under the control of Nyachenga, or at least of the faction which she represents. And even if Elton should want to usurp the leadership at Mulombwa, he would find it difficult because, *ceteris paribus*, his slave descent puts him in a weak position (see p. 207). Thus if Elton had political ambitions in conflict with his personal status, he would find Nyachenga and other groups in the village against him. Elton's constitutionally weak position makes him the ideal executive for the KAMISA title because he is less likely to be able to usurp it than a member of a collateral matrilineage.

The position was different with the acting KAMISA in Kamanga village. Although past political history cannot be ascertained, the political separation of the Kamanga from the KAMISA people shows that there were two different groups. At least twice, with Chikomeni (Kam. B 2) and Efulaimo (Kam. B 6), the executive part of the KAMISA title was in the hands of the Kamanga people. And it appears that the Kamanga people tried to keep the KAMISA-ship in their hands after Efulaimo's death, although theoretically they were only the executives while the 'ownership' was still in the hands of Nyachenga. I do not know how the political alignments lay in Mulombwa at that time, nor whose support Nyachenga could command, but obviously she managed to assert her claim to the 'ownership' and brought the executive KAMISA-ship and its one clear attribute, the Book, back under her control. This was essential because the Book distinguishes the Administrative Headmanship of KAMISA from other headmanships, such as those of Chinyafwa and Mapalassie which are not recognized by the Administration. Indeed, for KAMISA and most headmanships the Book is at present the only attribute of their headmanship. Any privileges and sanctions past headmen may have had have now disappeared.

The Book as an Attribute of the Traditional Headman

By 'headmen' I mean all headmen in the traditional political structure, either with or without the Book; when I refer to Administrative Headmen I will make this clear. By 'traditional political system' I mean the Tonga political system as it would be without the interference or support of the Administration. This is obviously entirely hypothetical, since it is impossible to ignore the presence of the Administration. It is an abstraction which cannot be tested any longer; but the Tonga make this abstraction, too. For them the concept of 'traditional' or 'the old days' (*chihami* or *kale*) represents an important value that is often used as a contrast with what is modern (*sono*[1]) 'new fangled' or 'of the Boma'. Tonga talk about *dangu la chihami*, the old, traditional law or custom. This phrase is often used with the implication: before the interference of the Boma, for instance in the treatment of sorcerers (*afwiti*, sing. *mfwiti*) or adulterers, or before the Boma and the Europeans in general encouraged the people to ignore or even despise their headmen and chiefs (*mafumu*, sing. *fumu*). The headmen maintain that they are not accorded the respect which headmen used to receive in the old days. Boma and *chihami* are often used as antonyms. For example, at the installation ceremony of CHIWEYO, a common theme of the conversation and the speeches was: 'This is *our* title [*zina*] and headmanship [*ufumu*] of the old days [*wa chihami*] which we do not owe to the Boma, which has nothing to do with the Boma. Even although the D.C. is present [and the D.C. *was* present], he is welcome to watch the ceremony but it has nothing to do with him. Before the Boma came to Tongaland, CHIWEYO was already a powerful chief.' The man was installed not only as headman with a traditional title, but also as Administrative Headman and subordinate Native Authority, both of which are Administrative offices. As sub.-N.A. CHIWEYO has political power over headmen who are his equals in the traditional political structure. For instance CHIWEYO and MLENGA MZOMA, who are neighbouring headmen belonging to the same 'house', have for long been political rivals.[2] Whereas up to 1933 CHIWEYO was MLENGA MZOMA's subordinate in the Administrative system, now the roles are reversed. Needless to say, MLENGA MZOMA objects to being CHIWEYO's Administrative subordinate and the latter makes every effort, with the support of the

---

[1] The root *hami* refers to the past as in the noun *mahami*, old site of an abandoned house or houses, or of a village. *Chihami* is that which is old; *chihami* and *mahami* are the only nouns formed of this root. *Kale* means 'long ago', with the same relative sense as its English equivalent; *kale* can be one hour or one hundred years ago. *Sono* means 'now'.

[2] See also van Velsen (1959*b*), p. 11.

Administrative system, to subdue MLENGA MZOMA. And every time MLENGA MZOMA is called to account and/or fined for insubordination (for example for not attending CHIWEYO's court), CHIWEYO is clearly not acting in his traditional capacity, which was so much emphasized at his installation, but as an agent of the Administration.

Thus, the Tonga ideal of a 'traditional' political structure has in fact inseparably absorbed the values and support of the Administrative system. A typical example is also GURU, who up to 1933 was Principal Headman in the Administrative system. In that capacity he was in charge of an area which no previous GURU had ever ruled before. With a change of the Administrative structure his erstwhile subordinates became his equals again, as in pre-British days. The present GURU (the same man who held the title at the time of the change) still talks about the diminution of his Administrative power in 1933 as if it had been a diminution of traditional authority and the result of the arrival and interference of the Administration.[1]

As I will clarify later Administrative appointments tend to be regarded (particularly by those who hold them) as inherent and inalienable parts of their traditional titles. Such appointments are therefore considered hereditary and not as personal appointments of the individual incumbents of the titles. Unlike such Administrative appointments as councillor or N.A., which confer political power and economic benefits as well as prestige, Administrative Headmanships confer on the whole only prestige. But this appointment, symbolized by the Book, is also competed for among the traditional headmen, because even this relatively unimportant appointment may be a first step towards the more rewarding Administrative offices. Moreover, Administrative recognition, even if only on the level of Administrative Headman, is considered (certainly by those who have been thus recognized) not as merely a whim on the part of the Boma, or as a matter of chance, but rather as a sign of the true and proper discernment of the Boma as to which headmen were formerly, and therefore are now, the really important headmen among the Tonga.[2] In this way the Book has become a symbol and attribute of the office of headman, not only within the Administrative system but also in the 'traditional' political structure. The great majority of

[1] Cf. also pp. 307–8.   [2] See also Chapter VI.

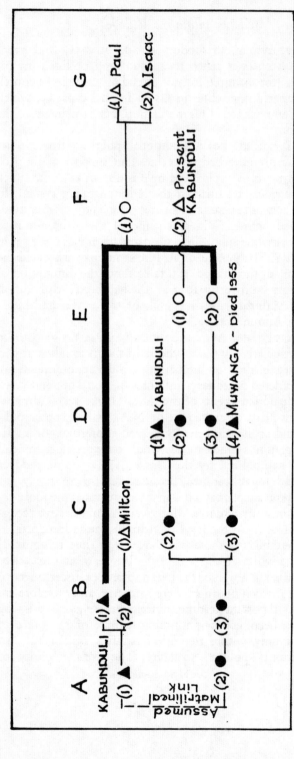

VII.—Skeleton Genealogy illustrating Milton's Quest for Power at Thoro

See p. 246. All people shown as still alive are at Thoro except for E1; F2 also lives elsewhere but he occasionally stays at Thoro. D4 used to live, and died, at Thoro and so did apparently B1, B2 and others, but not D1. This Genealogy does not show all those who are said to have been incumbents of the KABUNDULI title; there were apparently other KABUNDULIS between A1 and D1

headmen lack traditional attributes and sanctions which would distinguish headmen from others; nor do most of them have a tradition of historical prominence or of the possession of special privileges.[1] The Book, and the potential support and sanctions of the Boma, have therefore become, for the majority of traditional headmen, the only definable attributes of headmanship which are available to them. Thus it is of vital importance for those headmanships which hold Administrative appointments not to lose them; for their loss not only may rob the headmanships of their status, but also may jeopardize their very existence. At Mzenga the separation of the Administrative status from the KAMBAWE title has made the KAMBAWE-ship less desirable and less viable; the disunity in the village was aggravated and the KAMBAWE title may eventually disappear, at least temporarily.

Two or more villages often come under one Administrative Headman and all taxable men are on his census roll. For instance, Mapalassie, Kamanga and Chinyafwa villages are all on the census roll or Book of KAMISA of Mulombwa. One of the subordinate headmen may get the Administrative Headman's census roll in his hands through intrigue, or political manœuvring or even surreptitiously. When a rival goes to the Administration with the census roll actually in his hands and presents the Boma with a *fait accompli* together with a plausible account of why and how the Book has come to him, the Boma may accept the new situation and may transfer the Administrative Headmanship to him. I recorded one such incident at Thoro village which lies just south of the Luweya River in the Administrative area of KABUNDULI in his capacity of N.A. but in the country which the Kapunda Banda claim as their traditional habitat. According to the latter the country of the Phiri (including KABUNDULI) is traditionally farther inland, in the hills.

CASE 14: THE STRUGGLE FOR *CHASOLE'S* BOOK

CHASOLE's village adjoins Thoro village, whose headman was MUWANGA. Effective authority, however, lay in the hands of Milton though he is only a village son at Thoro. When MUWANGA died a short while ago, Milton adopted the title. Milton, when pressed, agrees that he is 'only a son' and can therefore not inherit any title, but can only

[1] See pp. 204, 206, n. 1, and Chapter VI.

act as its executive. He nevertheless dropped his name Milton and made it clear that he wanted to be addressed as *bwana* MUWANGA.

CHASOLE and MUWANGA did not claim membership of one family or 'house'. Until about the end of 1954 the Thoro people were included in CHASOLE's Book which was registered in CHASOLE's name. But twenty years or so ago MUWANGA had his own Book. I do not know how he lost it. CHASOLE died in 1952, and as no successor had been appointed since then, CHASOLE's Book had been kept by his 'elder brother' GURU who is also an Administrative Headman. GURU and CHASOLE claim close relationship in the same 'house' and they belong to that section of the Tonga known as the Kapunda Banda. Milton and the N.A. of the area, KABUNDULI, belong to the Phiri faction who are the rivals and opponents of the Kapunda Banda in Tonga political structure.[1] Indeed GURU has been for a long time one of the leading spirits among the Kapunda Banda in the anti-Phiri and particularly the anti-KABUNDULI movement. Milton, who has political ambitions, is ostensibly an ardent supporter of N.A. KABUNDULI since, at present at least, he needs KABUNDULI's support for his own ambitions.[2]

Some time in 1954, during GURU's temporary absence in Southern Rhodesia (p. 230), Milton somehow, in a rather surreptitious and 'clever' way, got hold of CHASOLE's Book.[3] I saw this tax register shortly afterwards and noticed that CHASOLE's typed name had been crossed out with ink and replaced by the name MUWANGA in Milton's (MUWANGA's) own handwriting. Although the final decision regarding appointments or changes of Administrative Headmen rests with the D.C., this episode took place long before the D.C. heard about it, or had made any decision regarding CHASOLE's Book. However, in the end the D.C. confirmed this change and thus accepted the *fait accompli*. In point of fact this new situation corresponds more closely with political reality because this Book contains more taxpayers from Thoro than from CHASOLE. Moreover, Milton is a very forceful personality whilst there is at present no CHASOLE at all.

Needless to say, GURU's resistance to KABUNDULI and the Phiri hardened. He feels that Milton, N.A. KABUNDULI and the Phiri in general have not only cheated him over CHASOLE's census, but have also scotched his ambition to reunite the two titles of GURU and

---

[1] See also p. 16 and Case 19, p. 247.
[2] See also pp. 244–5 and 250–1 on Milton's political relations with KABUNDULI.
[3] I use the terms Book, tax register, census and census roll interchangeably.

CHASOLE. It appears that under a previous GURU his 'brother' CHASOLE seceded from GURU's village and established himself as an independent headman. It is a fact that CHASOLE's official appointment as Administrative Headman took place well after GURU's official recognition. And it was obvious that the present GURU hoped to re-unite the two villages under his own leadership as a result of holding both census rolls, even though the two villages were not united geographically.[1]

As far as I am aware an Administrative village always comprises more than one traditional village. Although a Book is really a badge of office in the Administrative system, it also enhances the status of headman in the traditional system. There is keen competition for the Book among those headmen included in it.

Formally the Administrative Headmanship derives from the D.C. who is at the apex of the Administrative system in a District. But, as we saw in the case of CHASOLE's census, changes in the Administrative system may be initiated and even be effected at the traditional level and from there carried over into the Administrative system. The D.C.'s appointment of MUWANGA as an Administrative Headman merely sanctioned what was already an accomplished fact. In this way the Administrative system reflected the shifts of power and influence and the changes in the relationships between the headmen. There are several causes for these changes: (1) Milton arrived in about 1949 at Thoro from the hills, since when, I understand, the village has increased appreciably; (2) KABUNDULI (whose traditional home is in the hills) was appointed as Native Authority over this area; (3) KABUNDULI became closely associated with Thoro village, and this resulted in KABUNDULI's settling there early in 1955; and (4) Milton gained increasing influence over KABUNDULI. (Milton is a 'son' to KABUNDULI in any context, both at Thoro and outside it, because he is patrilaterally related to the KABUNDULI matrilineage.)

[1] GURU is less than a mile from Thoro with a few villages intervening. CHASOLE had his village next to Thoro but at some time he built another village next to GURU. GURU and CHASOLE are neighbours because CHASOLE's second village adjoins GURU's in the south, but between them flows the big Kawiya River. CHASOLE (and later GURU) continued to claim the headmanship over both villages: CHASOLE's original one and his second one. It is more likely, however, that in the traditional political structure they were two independent villages even if they remained (together with Thoro) on the same roll and thus continued to be one Administrative village.

Whilst the competition for CHASOLE's census was between unrelated headmen, in the case of WANCHA and MTEPERERA it was between two 'brothers'.

CASE 15: THE *WANCHA-MTEPERERA* RIVALRY

WANCHA and MTEPERERA are two headmen near Chinteche in N.A. KABUNDULI's area. They are members of the same 'house', and 'brothers'. They belong to the Kapunda Banda faction which opposed the appointment of KABUNDULI, a Phiri, as N.A. over this area which the Kapunda Banda consider their own traditional home. At the time of KABUNDULI's appointment as N.A., WANCHA had a Book including MTEPERERA's village. This situation was a source of friction between these two headmen. WANCHA as a Kapunda Banda has always taken the Kapunda Banda line and showed his disapproval of KABUNDULI as an N.A. whenever he could, for instance by not attending his court. MTEPERERA, although also a Kapunda Banda, has always been a supporter of KABUNDULI since the latter's N.A. appointment in this area and has regularly attended court. His support of KABUNDULI and his campaigning for a census of his own bore fruit in 1954 when KABUNDULI took WANCHA's census away and gave it to MTEPERERA—a decision which was later confirmed by the D.C. Now it is WANCHA who is included in MTEPERERA's census.

The CHASOLE-Milton and WANCHA-MTEPERERA rivalries exemplify the struggle for power (in which the Book is a much valued symbol) between neighbouring and sometimes related headmen. The fates of WANCHA and CHASOLE, as Administrative Headmen holding the Book, indicate the possible dangers which faced Nyachenga (Mul. C 5) and her supporters at Mulombwa when the Kamanga people tried to hold on to the KAMISA Book.[1] If the Kamanga people had managed to regain for one of their members the executive functions of the KAMISA-ship reinforced by the possession of the Book, they might have tried to establish themselves as the rightful successors to the Administrative Headmanship. So far this Headmanship has been in the name of KAMISA. But if the Book were securely in their hands the Kamanga group might adopt another title and get the Book away from the KAMISA people. This would not have been the first time, since at one stage

[1] See Case 12, p. 203, and pp. 218–19.

the title KAMISA is said to have been dropped and the title CHA-CHAMARA to have appeared. The Kamanga people with their new title and possession of the Book might have been able to establish (perhaps through N.A. MANKHAMBIRA) in the eyes of the Administration, their claim to be in the same 'house', and to be the rightful successors to KAMISA (albeit with a different title) and his Book. The Administrative Headmanship and the Book would then have been registered in the name of this new title.

Although KAMISA might have continued to exist, as a traditional headman, this development would have effectively established Kamanga as a separate village and undermined the status of KAMISA. The KAMISA supporters would have continued to agitate for their own Administrative appointment and within the Administrative village there would have been two rivals for the Administrative Headmanship. Both headmen might have wanted their own Book; or KAMISA might have striven to get his Book back. This sort of competition for Administrative recognition between old-established headmen, or between an old-established headman and a new one, puts a constant demand on the Administration for more and more independent Administrative Headmanships. Conversely, it also makes it easier for the Boma, if it is dissatisfied with one Administrative Headman, to find another man without having to resort to the creation of quasi-headmen with no place in the traditional structure. For there are always several traditional headmen competing for a limited number of Administrative appointments. There is always a traditional headman without a Book ready to slip into the place of an Administrative Headman and receive his Book. Moreover, every title, whether of traditional or Administrative headman, almost invariably has an incumbent who by the other matrilineages of the village is considered a usurper. This means that there is always a ready supply of substitutes available for the Administration to choose from if it is dissatisfied with a particular holder of an Administrative appointment. And the 'indirect rule' policy of the Administration in the area has always been to employ and manipulate as much as possible the local holders of power and draft these political forces, from underneath, into the Administrative structure covering the whole District and linking it, with other Districts, into the Protectorate Administration.

R

Sons of the Village

Those members of a village who have an actual, assumed, or putative patrilateral link with the village, I have called village sons.[1] In this I follow Tonga idiom which calls patrilocal residents *wana* (sing. *mwana*), *viz.* children, both male and female.[2] Although matrilocal residence is more common,[3] every village has its patrilaterally linked members who are also welcome and honoured citizens. None the less sons of the village are in a disadvantageous position constitutionally in the struggle for succession to headmanship, though personal qualities may make them serious rivals for effective leadership in the village.

In our discussion of Tonga marriage we noticed the enduring social, genealogical and political importance of fatherhood,[4] regardless of the status of the union which produced the children. When Tonga discuss their own (or another person's) parentage, they frequently distinguish between classificatory parents and biological parents.[5] Similarly when discussing siblings they often add whether they are siblings of 'the same father and the same mother', or 'the same father but different mother' or otherwise. And when a person has a well-known father, for instance if his (or her) father is a village headman, he will not fail to mention the fact. KABUNDULI belongs matrilineally to the Phiri but his father is a Kapunda Banda. In the many political controversies between the Phiri and the Kapunda Banda, KABUNDULI often

---

[1] See p. 36. I distinguish between sons and 'village sons'. The latter indicates an essentially political classification of the inhabitants of a particular village into those who are matrilineally linked to the village (*viz.* the 'owners') and those who are not (*viz.* the village sons or daughters). 'Sons', however, refers to classificatory sons. Thus 'sons' indicates an essentially genealogical classification of people which is not necessarily valid within one particular village only. Village son refers to a political relationship of a person to a locality whereas 'son' indicates a genealogical relationship to another person. A village son may at the same time be a classificatory 'son' in the same village but this is not necessarily so.

[2] Since *mwana* covers both father's child and mother's child, it may thus refer to matrilocal as well as patrilocal residents. It is generally clear from the context whether this term refers to children as opposed to adults; to children in the sense of a couple's offspring; or to patrilocal residents of the village.

[3] See Table II.

[4] Cf. p. 76

[5] E.g. *ada wakundibara*, *viz.* my 'father, the one who produced me'; and the same for mothers.

draws attention to his paternal links: 'Why do you, Kapunda Banda, think that I hate you? Do you not know that my own father is a Kapunda Banda?'

Reasons for Patrilocal Residence

Tonga may live patrilocally even after the death of both parents,[1] and this is a particularly suitable arrangement for those who find it difficult to live matrilocally. A person may have made himself unpopular in his mother's village and been forced to leave. I am not aware of an instance of this in my five sample villages, but I have met with one or two cases in other villages.

One category of patrilocal residents in Tongaland are those without a matrilocal alternative there: people with a foreign or slave mother. For example, Siddely's mother (Chin. D 6) at Chinyafwa[2] was a slave of Bisa origin. But not all foreigners among the Tonga are slaves, although in practice their position has similar disabilities. In the villages nowadays one can find children of Tonga fathers and of non-Tonga mothers who have never lived in Tongaland; these are the children of Tonga men who begat children at work abroad. Most of these Tonga working abroad are labour migrants, who maintain ties with their home village where they may eventually retire.[3] They often spend the greater part of their young and middle-aged adulthood abroad before they return to and retire in Tongaland. In the Tonga scale of values a man or woman is in an unenviable position if he or she has no offspring who are part of the Tonga tribe.[4] The Tonga man who is married to a Rhodesian or South African woman may find himself in this position on his return to Tongaland if his wife has divorced him or for some other reason has taken her children to her own village out of reach of her husband. The husband, or, if he is dead, his kin, will do everything they can to get effective custody over his children. When death or some other cause terminates the union between a Tonga husband and a wife who belongs to the area of his employment, disagreement often

---

[1] This is in contrast with, for instance, the Ndembu where only a negligible percentage of children live with their father after their mother's death. And after their father's death the children must leave his village: see Turner (1957).

[2] Cf. Case 3, p. 68, and Case 8, p. 133.

[3] See van Velsen (1960).

[4] Cf. Siddely's plight at Chinyafwa, p. 69.

arises over the status of the union. This generally turns on the question whether bridewealth has been paid or not, and involves the custody of the children, who according to the general rule of the South African and Rhodesian peoples are not 'free' as they are among the Tonga.[1] For instance GURU[2] went to Southern Rhodesia in 1955 in order to sue—unsuccessfully—the widow of the late GURU's son (i.e. the present GURU's mother's brother's son) for the custody of his cousin's children; the widow was living in Southern Rhodesia at the time. GURU, who is the successor to his dead cousin's father, feels responsible for his uncle's children.

Therefore a Tonga man working abroad and married to a local woman often takes at least one child of this union 'to show to the family at home', *viz.* in Tongaland, and leaves it there out of reach of his wife. A striking example of this was a man who had travelled for at least a fortnight from South Africa to Tongaland with a baby of about two years old. He had been married to a South African woman and had several children by her. At divorce he was 'allowed to keep this one to take back to the village'. Of course, Tonga couples living in the towns may also leave some of their children in Tongaland in view of urban conditions. Something similar happened in the case of John (Map. C 11) of Mapalassic. His father Daniel went to South Africa, married a local woman, and died there without ever returning to Tongaland. On Daniel's death a Tonga friend of his in Cape Town wrote to Mapalassie that he had managed 'to save' one of the two children, John, but that Daniel's South African affines had 'snatched' the other child; and that if they did not get John away quickly he might be lost too.[3] James (Map. C 12) provided the money for John's journey from Cape Town to Mapalassie. John was then about twelve years old, had been brought up in urban surroundings and spoke little Tonga. He now speaks the language as well as any other Tonga and is fully accepted as a Tonga himself. He would like to go back to South Africa to

[1] Cf. p. 35.   [2] Cf. also p. 64.

[3] This story was related to me by John's 'mothers' Nyamwale (Map. C 10) and Nyadalo (Map. C 9). Their phrasing of this story neatly reflected the struggle for the children which, according to many Tonga accounts, goes on in intertribal marriages abroad. For the relationship between John and Nyamwale, see pp. 140 *seq.*

work, but his 'mothers' and other relatives do not want him to go because they think that he might then remain with his maternal kin and be lost for ever. One of Alinda's (Map. B 4) sons also married a South African wife. A few years ago he brought home an eight-year-old daughter and left her with Alinda on his return to South Africa. Similarly a brother of Chimbaza (Map. B 1) left a boy of about the same age in Chimbaza's care. Thus there are at least two children of foreign mothers left in the care of their paternal kin at Mapalassie. Their only residence in Tongaland is patrilocal, *viz.* with their father's matrikin or patrikin. Such residence among the Tonga entails no great disabilities in everyday life. Thus Tonga society is well suited to absorb these results of the system of migrant labour. This feature of patrilocal residence may itself result from the way in which the Tonga originated as a tribe by absorbing offshoots of the various surrounding tribes and invaders.

TABLE VII*

Classification of Patrilocal Residents

D	Sons of headmen	5
E	Foreign mother	1
F	Slave mother	1
G	Parents 'Unknown'	
	No alternative village	5
H	No apparent reason	3
	Total	15

* This Table indicates the possible reasons for patrilocal residence for the people of category C of Table IV, i.e. patrilocal residents without living parental tie in the village. Thus, for instance, a patrilocal resident whose slave mother is still alive and resident in her husband's village is therefore not included in this Table.

In Table VII, I have tried to list the apparent reasons for patrilocal residence. The operative word here is 'apparent', because adequate proof is lacking: the Tonga themselves rarely formulate their reasons for patrilocal residence, and my sample is not large enough to be conclusive. Nevertheless these figures confirm an impression I received in other villages. This table refers only to people who have neither parent living any longer in the village. My reasons for making this the basis of this table are that a person is likely to stay in his father's village whilst the latter is still alive, and particularly if his mother is also still living there, but is liable to move to his mother's village on the latter's death and, especially, on the death of his father. As for the categories of this table, a certain amount of overlapping is unavoidable. I have mentioned already that a foreign mother may at the same time also be a slave mother.[1] And since in the old days headmen in particular were likely to have slave wives, especially if they were engaged in trade,[2] category D (sons of headmen) may well partly overlap with category E (foreign slave mothers). At least one person whom I included in category D had a foreign (Chewa) mother who may also have been a slave. Category G includes those persons who occupy slave status in the village because their father was a slave while their mother is also 'unknown'.[3] For instance I was told that Chimango's (Mul. B 33) mother was 'unknown' and that his father's father was also 'unknown'. Chimango, like the others in this category, does not seem to have an alternative village in Tongaland. Finally, this table tries to measure the incidence of slave descent among patrilocal residents only, and not among matrilocal residents. Thus Elton (Mul. D 3) is considered a slave at Mulombwa because his maternal grandmother Nyambayaya (Mul. B 22) is generally said to have been a slave. Although Elton's mother Estere (Mul. C 12) was a patrilocal resident with a slave mother, Elton himself is a matrilocal resident and he is therefore not included in this table.[4] These figures refer exclusively to adults, which explains why they show only one patrilocal resident with a foreign mother; all other similar cases concern young children.

Village Owners and Village Sons

When I discussed the political importance of cross-cousin marriage within the village (p. 144), I pointed out that in general such a marriage has special significance only within the political context of the village. The same applies to the relationship be-

[1] I am referring here to foreign women who came to the village as slaves in the old days and not to foreign women who have come more recently as wives of Tonga who have worked abroad.

[2] See p. 268.

[3] To say of a person that one or both parents are 'unknown' even if they are still alive is a way of saying that the parent(s) is (are) slave(s). Cf. pp. 259 *seq.*

[4] For Elton see also p. 36.

tween village owners and village sons. Thus the political significance of this relationship emerges only within the political
structure of one particular village and is not determined solely by
the genealogical position of the people concerned. I have already
given as an example of this the relative status of Ziba (Map. C 3)
and Chimbaza (Map. B 1). At Mapalassie Ziba is a member of the
dominant matrilineage, i.e. a village owner, whilst Chimbaza is
a village son and therefore in a subordinate position *vis-à-vis* Ziba.
But, by a different genealogical reckoning, at Bwerero village,
which is Chimbaza's matrilocality, the roles are reversed because
it is Ziba's patrilocality (see p. 146).[1] This point is clearly illustrated by the following recorded conversation.

CASE 16: THE THEORETICAL KINSHIP ARGUMENT[2]

This genealogical argument between Ziba (Map. C 3) and Nyamphande (Map. C 5) shows how pointless it is to discuss a genealogical
problem outside the context of political power. One evening in a
friendly discussion in which no interests were at stake, Ziba and
Nyamphande were arguing about their status *vis-à-vis* one another.
Nyamphande maintained that Ziba and his siblings were 'children' to
her in a cross-cousin relationship. Her point of departure was Alunguya and his siblings: since she was a descendant of a female sibling
Nyamphande claimed a genealogically superior position to Ziba, who
is a descendant of a male sibling.[3] Ziba refuted this line of argument by
saying that Nyamphande started at the wrong point in the genealogy
because: 'You [*viz*. Nyamphande, her mother and her maternal
grandmother] were our children first, before we were your children.
For although you start from Alunguya, I start from Alimbiya who produced Alunguya so that at the point where you start you were already
our children.' In this argument Ziba identifies himself with his maternal
uncle Mussa who in turn is identified with his maternal uncle Alimbiya,
so that Alimbiya's children become Mussa's 'children' and so become
Ziba's 'children'. Alunguya, who is the crucial figure in Nyamphande's
argument, belongs to Likoma Island whence Nyamphande also came

---

[1] I have no reliable data on their respective genealogical position at Bwerero
as distinct from their positions at Mapalassie. I accept the general statement
about their political relationship at Bwerero because it is based on information
from the two men concerned, as well as from others who have no axe to grind.

[2] See Genealogy VIII.   [3] Cf. pp. 142 and 146.

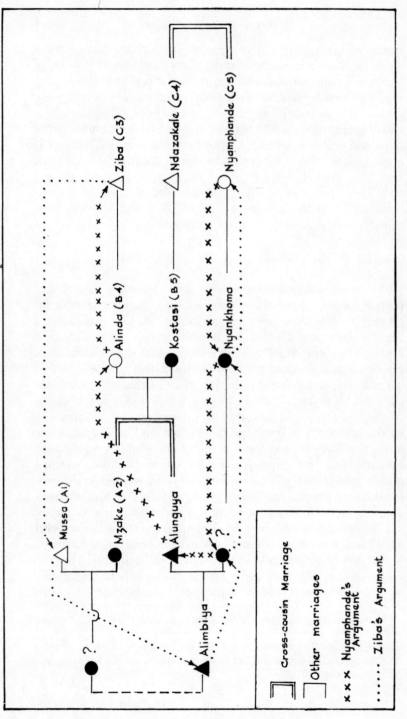

VIII.—Skeleton Genealogy for Case 16: The Theoretical Kinship Argument

Letters and numbers in brackets refer to Genealogy IX for MAPALASSE Village

a year or so ago; he never had any political significance at Mapalassie.[1] If this argument had taken place on Likoma in Alunguya's village, Nyamphande might well have been right, and Ziba and his siblings would have been genealogically and politically subordinate to Nyamphande. But since the argument took place within the political setting of Mapalassie, there was no doubt that Nyamphande occupied the status of 'child' in relation to Ziba.[2] Genealogical status is of practical significance only in relation to a particular village or, in general, to a particular stake.

The Position and Role of Village Sons

Land in a Tonga village is not under the legal control of the headman. Instead, the rights in land are held by various kin groups or individuals who have received the gardens from kinsmen or inherited them as *masara* (viz. old gardens which may have been lying fallow long enough to revert to bush: p. 273). I mentioned already (p. 54) that a married woman who lives virilocally often continues to cultivate a garden in her home village, besides the gardens in her husband's village. She can thus ensure that if her children want to live matrilocally they will find gardens or *masara* in their matrilocality.[3] Similarly a father who wants to keep his children in his village can provide them with gardens of his own and does not have to rely on the co-operation of the headman. This gives village sons a relatively secure and independent position in the village.

For instance Nyali (Chin. F 4), who claims authority over Mtemeni, once ordered some squatters to move. But he told me that though Nyalongwe had begun to cultivate her paternal *masara* without asking his permission, he could not order her to leave Mtemeni (p. 212); he did not consider her a squatter like the others. Similarly Siddely (Chin. D 6) at Chinyafwa is cultivating gardens which both he and Nyali say are part of Siddely's paternal *masara*. Nyali said that although he is the leader at

---

[1] It should be remembered that Mussa and several other inhabitants of Mapalassie came over from Likoma.

[2] For the sake of argument they ignored the fact that Nyamphande became Ziba's sister-in-law in 1954 when she married his 'younger brother' Ndazakale (Map. C 4).

[3] Cf. Ndazakale's difficulty at Mapalassie where he has no *masara* from his mother, p. 190.

Chinyafwa he could not possibly interfere with Siddely's gardens and *masara* (for instance, by hoeing them himself or by allowing others to do so without Siddely's consent). He added that if he tried to interfere with Siddely's gardens or *masara*, Siddely would ask him: 'Are you chasing me from the village?' I was told the same about Chimbaza (Map. B 1) at Mapalassie: unless Ziba wanted to get rid of Chimbaza, he would not interfere with Chimbaza's gardens.[1] To do so would exceed his authority as headman.

There are other reasons which assure for village sons a relatively secure position in their patrilocal village. At several points in my analysis we have seen that the attraction and retention of followers is an important aspect of aspiring political leadership. Patrilocal residents are a substantial minority in a village's basic population.[2] Thus neither the headman of the village nor his matrilineal kinsmen (i.e. the owners of the village) will antagonize the sons of the village unnecessarily[3] and risk their departure.[4] I heard of only one case of a patrilocal resident being chased from the village. The man in question used to live at Mulombwa and now he is said to live matrilocally. Such a fate, however, can also befall matrilocal residents who may then settle patrilocally.

It has already been noted that patrilocal residence is also an important factor in the general pattern of relationships between individuals and villages and contributes to the cohesion of the Tonga as a people (p. 74). These two aspects of the importance of

---

[1] At present Ziba could hardly do this, for although Ziba will probably take Mussa's (Map. A 1) place, Mussa, the father of Chimbaza, is still alive.

[2] I refer to those village members with some sort of 'birthright' to live in the village permanently, in so far as any Tonga's residence is likely to be permanent. Excluding virilocal wives or persons living in a village solely because of their job, e.g. a court clerk or forest guard, we saw that in our five sample villages 40 per cent of the basic residents live patrilocally and that 39·3 per cent of the hamlets are patrilaterally linked to the village. Even if we exclude those patrilocal residents who live with their mother, we still find 27·2 per cent villagers living patrilocally. See pp. 38 *seq.*

[3] Even among rivals for the leadership in a village one is most unlikely to find one party trying to drive away their opponent's patrilocal supporters. This would merely weaken the village as a whole. We saw in 'Meya's Death' how the two factions at Mapalassie made common front in the face of the outsiders' threat to take their kinsfolk away from Mapalassie; see pp. 168 *seq.*

[4] Cf. Amuziteni's seminal descendants who left Mzenga a few years ago. I am not certain about the immediate cause of this move; see p. 61.

patrilocal residents are of a different order: whilst the Tonga are explicit about the importance of patrilocal residents in a headman's following, they are not conscious of the significance of patri-locality as a cohesive factor in the wider system.

The Successor and his Predecessor's Children

Most village sons have a matrilocality in Tongaland. This gives them a lever to exact fair treatment from the owners of the village, including the headman. Hence Kamoti's (Mz. D 8) remark at Mzenga that if Waison (Mz. D 18), an owner, continued to treat him 'as if he were just anybody' he, Kamoti, would go to his other village, and this would 'reduce Waison's village to nothing' (p. 66). I witnessed a similar argument in GURU's village. A village son, the leader of a large hamlet comprising a substantial proportion of the village's population, complained to the headman that the headman and other villagers had repeatedly accused him of sorcery. He threatened that if the headman did nothing to stop this he would leave the village. To treat village sons in such a way that they want to leave the village is called *kudikizgha wana*, viz. to chase the children.[1] This phrase suggests astonishment at such an act of folly.

The charge of 'chasing his children' is often heard in discussions about succession. If a nephew succeeds his maternal uncle as headman, there are likely to be difficulties in the nephew's relationship to his uncle's offspring. The succeeding nephew's main problem is to prevent the disintegration of the village through the departure of the late headman's offspring, who may now want to move to their mother's village. Children who have been living in their father's village often leave at their father's death, especially if their widowed mother goes back to her own village. An additional factor is the latent hostility between a man's children, who have no legal right to his property and his title, and his uterine nephews, who claim his goods and his office. Kamoti expressed this hostility when he said of his cross-cousins that they, the nephews, neglected his father when he was alive but were ready enough with their claims when he was dead (p. 196). On the other hand the matrilineal kinsmen (i.e. the nephews) of a headman often suspect that the headman's children want to usurp their

---

[1] *Wana*, children, is here used in the sense that all the members of a village are the headman's 'children'.

father's title and other offices. This aspect of the latent hostility and rivalry between village sons and village owners in the political structure of the village is illustrated by the succession dispute at Mzenga (p. 195). In this affair it is not a matter of nephews 'chasing' the late headman's children but rather a matter of a son who is too firmly entrenched in his political position in the village for the nephews to dislodge him.

I have not witnessed a case in one of my five villages where a succeeding nephew antagonized his predecessor's offspring, but I recorded a case at KABUNDULI's court in which this was, or rather became, the central problem.[1]

CASE 17: A HEADMAN AND HIS PREDECESSOR'S CHILDREN

Rabban sued Chirwa for a debt of £2. Rabban was the son of the late headman MUSINJA. The latter supplied Chirwa some years ago with medicine for which Chirwa never paid the agreed price of £2. The late MUSINJA had promised the £2, if he got it, to his son Rabban who needed the money to pay off a pressing debt of his own. When his father died Rabban went to his father's successor and asked him for the money. The present MUSINJA said that he had not yet received the money from Chirwa and that he therefore could not help Rabban, whom the present MUSINJA calls 'son'. The emphasis of the case shifted from Chirwa's debt to the new MUSINJA's moral duty to help the son of his predecessor. Moreover the court found that Chirwa and MUSINJA were in collusion conspiring against Rabban, and that MUSINJA had received at least part of the £2. The court was shocked by MUSINJA's disregard of his moral duty to the extent even of preferring an outsider to his 'son'. 'Don't we all know,' the court wondered, 'that riches and children are not two different things?' In the course of the examination the court asked MUSINJA:

Q: 'Are you the nephew [*mphwao*, i.e. sister's son] of the late MUSINJA?'
A: 'Yes.'
Q: 'So Rabban is your son?'
A: 'Yes.'

[1] I did not know either the litigants or their village, but the village was near Mapalassie and the litigants and their background were well known to most people of Greater Kamisa with whom I later discussed this case.

Q: 'Who was the one who inherited the money, the medical craft, the *ufumu* [headmanship or title], the children, etc.?'
A: 'I did.'

The court then said that everybody knows that a nephew must not only look after his late uncle's goods but also his uncle's children, or else he will find himself without people. 'And a chief without people is no chief.' MUSINJA was unrepentant; but the court ordered him to pay £1 to Rabban and lectured him: 'You must realize that it is you who are looking for children—the children are not looking for a father. Therefore, because you want children, even if a child is wrong you still pay for him. If you have no children you will not be MUSINJA: you will just be alone.' The court meant that it is easy enough for a person to find someone to attach himself to, but that it is the headman who has to make strenuous efforts to attract dependants.

GURU behaved in a different way. He went especially to Southern Rhodesia to try to get the children of his 'son' (*viz*. his predecessor's real son) back to his village (p. 230). GURU showed by this action that his 'children' were really wanted in their patrilocality. Siddely's trip to South Africa to get his grandchildren back is a comparable case (p. 69).

Some headmen try to attach village sons more firmly to the village by giving them an official role in the political structure of the village,[1] for instance by allowing village sons to deputize for them and act as executives of the title. This is particularly the case when the headman is old or inactive; we saw instances of this at Mzenga and Mulombwa where village sons or other people outside the dominant lineage did the 'walking'. This may create political confusion in which it is no longer clear where authority lies, until a crisis arises which apparently has nothing at all to do with the question of political authority. But the crisis forces the question into the open, brings the facts under public scrutiny, calls for the opinion and additional evidence of outsiders who normally would not have been heard, and thus helps to clarify the political structure of the village and the relative status of the parties. This happened at Mzenga through the adultery dispute (p. 195). But since I witnessed no such situation at Mulombwa or Kamanga I found it difficult to assess the political realities within and between these villages.

[1] Or whatever larger unit the headman may control, e.g. an N.A. area.

But the following bridewealth case from another village illustrates this point and in addition shows that a court does not recognize a village son as the legal successor to his father's title.

CASE 18: FATHER, SON AND HEADMAN

The political question which was raised in this case was, ostensibly, only incidental to a bridewealth case in which Nyirenda had taken out a summons against Kaunda whose name was therefore on the summons form issued by the court clerk. Nyirenda was suing Kaunda for the return of the bridewealth which Nyirenda's 'younger brother' had paid for Kaunda's 'sister' Genera. Both Kaunda and Genera belong to LIFUPA's village where Kaunda is a 'son' of LIFUPA. Kaunda denied all legal knowledge of both Nyirenda himself and the bridewealth question. Nyirenda asked Kaunda with some surprise: 'But you were present at the discussions, were you not?' Kaunda answered: 'Yes, I was, but it has nothing to do with me. I cannot really speak in this case because I am a son. I cannot stand above my father and let him sit down when he is present. [He meant that it is the right and duty of his 'father' (*viz.* the rightful headman) to argue this case; for him, Kaunda, to do so whilst his 'father' is present would be presumptuous and would show that he did not know his place.] I have to be down and he must be above me. Indeed I am called LIFUPA but I am not the owner. If there were no owner present, ah, yes, then I could speak all right.' By 'owner' Kaunda meant: 'the owner of this marriage', i.e. the one who acted as the attorney (*viz.* LIFUPA) or his successor. The court then called out for Kaunda's *nkhoswe* (attorney), that is, the person who would be able to speak for LIFUPA. There was no answer. One of the members of the public pointed at Abeni and said: 'Why are you hiding?' Abeni stepped into the open space of the court, which was held under a large tree. He explained that he was not the *nkhoswe*: his mother was, but she was too old to come to the court and his elder brother was away in Durban.[1] The court questioned Abeni relentlessly until he agreed that he was Kaunda's attorney. The point here was that LIFUPA was the attorney in the marriage concerned and Kaunda as the 'son' of LIFUPA denied therefore that he had any responsibility. The LIFUPA who was a party to the original marital transactions had since died. Hence the court wanted to find out who

[1] As his mother was too old his elder brother was her next lineal representative.

the legal successor was to this attorneyship. They, like everyone else, knew that it was Abeni and that he was present in court. The court asked Abeni: 'Why did you hide and run away from this case?' Abeni: 'I am not LIFUPA—we gave the name of the late LIFUPA to Kaunda: The name is no longer in our hands.'

In a discussion afterwards I was told: 'The sons and the owners in that village [of LIFUPA] were living in peace. And to show Kaunda that they were pleased with him and to give him honour the owners gave the title of the late LIFUPA to his son Kaunda because they wanted him to stay with them as he was a good man.' After Abeni's remark about the name no longer being in the hands of the 'owners', the court asked him: '*Katundu wa asibweni winu waja ndi yani?*' [i.e. in whose hands is your maternal uncle's luggage?[1]]. Abeni: 'In my hands.' Whereupon the court triumphantly pounced upon him: 'Ah, right, then you *are* the *nkhoswe!*' Someone later explained to me: 'Of course, after the court's question about the *katundu* Abeni could avoid the issue no longer. If he had said he did not know in whose hands the *katundu* was or if he had denied that it was in his hands, the villagers would have been surprised and angry. They would have said: "He repudiates us. He chases his children away [*adikizgha wana*]." ' Abeni, obviously, did not want to run the risk of estranging his people for the sake of avoiding a responsibility which is pre-eminently the responsibility of a headman. Such an act of blatant repudiation might have gravely disturbed the peace in the village.[2]

When it came to facing LIFUPA's liabilities, Kaunda, who had been acting as LIFUPA, contracted out of the legal responsibilities which the late LIFUPA had had and which devolved upon LIFUPA's successor. Legally Kaunda was entitled to contract out of those responsibilities. Indeed the court judged that it is the uterine nephew who is the legal successor to a title and not a 'son'. The court had to establish the external corporate liability of the LIFUPA people *vis-à-vis* the other

---

[1] *Katundu* is literally goods, possessions, and particularly possessions which one carries, or luggage. This metaphor is frequently used with reference to a deceased headman's authority over his followers. And among the late LIFUPA's *katundu* were of course his 'son' Kaunda and also Genera. Cf. KABUNDULI's court's question to MUSINJA, p. 239.

[2] I recorded this case in N.A. MANKHAMBIRA's court at Kanyoli. I did not know the litigants or their village. The fact that this internal political question was brought into the open in the court and not worked out and settled within the village beforehand, suggests that there might have been an open conflict in the village already.

litigant, Nyirenda, who was an outsider. And the court ruled that Abeni was the legal successor (the *nkhoswe*) to the LIFUPA-ship and that he was therefore responsible for the liabilities of the LIFUPA-ship. At the same time it was recognized that there might be divisions within the LIFUPA group; but these internal divisions were not the concern of the court or of the outsider litigant Nyirenda. For, when the court had pinned Abeni down as the proper respondent to Nyirenda's claims, Abeni made a last effort to escape his responsibilities in a question which was directed partly to the court and partly to the public: 'If it is true that I am the owner of the case, can you tell me whether my name appears on the summons?' A member of the court replied: 'You and Kaunda are all the same.' And members of the public muttered things to the same effect. How the LIFUPA people apportioned the liabilities of this case amongst themselves was of little interest to the court, which only wanted to see their legal representative.

An interesting aspect of this case is that, as it appeared in the hearing, Nyirenda had allowed his claim to lie dormant for about fifteen years. When the court questioned him about this, Nyirenda had an unconvincing excuse, but this did not invalidate his case, which he won. From information which I gathered during the hearing and afterwards it was clear that Nyirenda's bridewealth claim really served as a basis for a political claim regarding the seniority of his matrilineage *vis-à-vis* some related matrilineages, in other words, a political issue entirely unconnected with LIFUPA. Indeed, within a few minutes of his opening statement it became clear that for Nyirenda the political issue was the crucial point of his formal complaint about the bridewealth and not the actual bridewealth money itself. It is the duty of the court clerk to prepare, for a possible inspection by the D.C., a neat record of the case, clearly exposing argument and counter-argument. At one stage he interrupted Nyirenda and asked: 'Now, what are you after—the bridewealth or what? You cannot come here to have your dispute discussed in general—you must bring a specific point.'[1] Nyirenda opted for the bridewealth controversy since his other complaints were not sufficiently concrete to stand up to discussion on their own (cf. p. 125). In the end, however, in

---

[1] Nyirenda's opponent in the bridewealth issue, Kaunda, was not a kinsman; the opponents in the political issue were only indirectly concerned with the bridewealth.

spite of the court clerk's formal attitude, Nyirenda received, besides his bridewealth, also an official, public pronouncement on his lineage seniority.

Sons as Acting Headmen

Kaunda is a village son in LIFUPA's village, but, as an informant put it, the owners of the village liked him and wanted him to stay so they gave him LIFUPA's job. Since LIFUPA is an Administrative Headman, Kaunda's tasks probably consisted of keeping the Book, representing the village in the court[1] or to the D.C. and other members of the Administration, and performing the other duties of headman both in intra-village and extra-village contexts. In this and similar situations a village son may be given quasi-headman status so as to attach him more firmly to his patrilocality. When owners of the village give village sons a position of authority in the political structure, they probably reckon themselves safe from usurpation on the part of these sons because of the sons' constitutional disabilities.[2] On the other hand, village sons among the Tonga have some scope to manipulate the political structure of the village, and they cannot be trusted to the same extent as apparently Yao sons were trusted.

Whatever the reasons may be, village sons are frequently given positions of authority. Tonga say that village sons are in some respects in an awkward position in the village because they have no voice in village politics; they have to sit 'quiet'.[3] They contrast this situation with that of the owners of a village 'who are the only ones who have any power (*nthazi*) in the village'. Yet a son might prefer to stay with his father if the latter has a position from which a son might expect to benefit. Table VII (p. 231) also suggests that there might be some connection between the incidence of patrilocality and the numbers of fathers who occupy positions of influence. One-third of the patrilocal residents on this

---

[1] Although it is not a written rule, Administrative Headmen are expected to attend the court of their N.A. regularly as a kind of honorary councillors.

[2] I never heard this explicitly discussed in these terms among the Tonga. It was a deliberate policy among the Yao who have a somewhat more clearly defined status structure. Cf. Mitchell (1956), p. 69.

[3] Lit.: silent, *cheti*. This phrase is often used to mean the silence of the person who 'knows his place', i.e. his place of subordination (e.g. slaves, strangers and in-laws) or with reference to an argument: the silence of the person who knows that he is wrong, who has been worsted in an argument.

s

Table are sons of headmen. If we take the patrilocal residents, that is, both those who have no parent in the village and those who have, we find that seven are sons of headmen out of a total of twenty-eight patrilocal residents (see Table II). But as I pointed out before (p. 232), the classification is necessarily somewhat arbitrary because of the overlapping of categories: sons of headmen often are also sons of foreign or slave mothers, in which case they have no alternative residence in Tongaland.

Although sons have a right to live in their fathers' village, ideally and theoretically they are supposed to be 'quiet' because they lack the *nthazi* (authority) which the owners have. However, this very lack of constitutional authority gives the sons of a village power in other ways, as it provides them with opportunities for playing important and influential roles in the village. As we saw, the very fact that sons may feel second-class citizens in their patrilocal village is often a reason for the owners to give them executive functions, thus dissuading them from moving to their matrilocal villages. Since sons of the village cannot legally succeed to a title they are particularly well suited to act for the headman in his absence or in his old age. Sons of the village also frequently act as the official spokesmen at meetings.[1] In a way they are strangers: by Tonga values their matrilocality and not their patrilocality is their *own* village. Since a spokesman at a meeting or dispute is merely a neutral intermediary who 'takes the words' from one party to the other, one often sees village sons in this role.

Since village sons lack authority (*nthazi*), when a village son appears to have some executive function in the political structure, he is said to be 'only walking', whilst the 'real owner' is somebody else. In reality, however, village sons are not always 'quiet' or powerless. We saw (p. 63) how Kamoti (Mz. D 8) at Mzenga, where he is a village son, reached a position of influence and held an official appointment in the modern Administrative system of the district. It was Kamoti's father KAMBAWE who, as a headman in the traditional political structure, had acquired official positions in the Administrative system. And Kamoti in his turn reached his position whilst acting for his father. Milton, too, although he is

---

[1] Cf. Chimbaza, the spokesman at Mapalassie at Meya's funeral, p. 157. A spokesman at a meeting, who gives the *maronji* (introduction), is generally called the *spikara*, *viz*. speaker or spokesman.

only a village son at Thoro,[1] attained a position of great political influence. Indeed, his influence on KABUNDULI is so important that Milton is something of a 'kingmaker'. It appears therefore that village sons in the traditional constitution may be unable to succeed to traditional political position but they are not power-less when it comes to achieving influence, and through this in-fluence they obtain official political status in the modern Admini-strative system. A village son's constitutional disabilities may thus be minimized (if not overcome) by his being a son of an important headman, by his own personality, or by other factors.

For example I am certain that the fact that Milton, who is 45 years of age, has never been away from Tongaland, has been an important factor in his political success. He struck me as a man who seemed to know practically everybody in the area and knew *about* them too: their genealogical relationships, their position in their villages, their quarrels, disputes and court cases, and other items of information which are necessary for successful political intriguing and manipulation in any political system. His political ambitions may be partly conditioned by a desire to show that he is not a mere nobody, because matrilaterally he has no status. The years that most other men spend working abroad, Milton spent and is still spending in going around the area, keeping abreast of everything that is happening.

On the road to power both Kamoti of Mzenga and Milton of Thoro did some 'walking'. As far as I am aware there was no open rivalry at Thoro between MUWANGA, the headman, and Milton who acted or 'walked' for him. Similarly at Mzenga, the late KAMBAWE did not in his old age try to prevent his son Kamoti from taking over the execution of KAMBAWE's offices of tradi-tional headman, Administrative Headman and court councillor. He encouraged Kamoti to do so. At Mzenga the rivalry was not between Kamoti and KAMBAWE but between Kamoti and KAM-BAWE's nephews, i.e. not between son and father but between the son and his cousins.

---

[1] See p. 223. Milton's mother was either foreign or else came from the ex-treme southern parts of Tongaland which border on Chewa country, and there are indications that she might have been a slave. This means that not only are Milton's links with his village patrilateral, but also his links with Tonga society (at least in the part where he lives). Furthermore his links with the KABUNDULI title and the political structure surrounding it are also patrilateral.

At Thoro there is at present no open rivalry between Milton and the late MUWANGA's nephews, Paul and Isaac, who also live at Thoro, although they are in the line of succession to the title and are in fact the most likely candidates now available at Thoro.[1] But they are also entertaining ambitions for the KABUNDULI title—to which they are matrilineally related—and the Native Authority post which has gone with this title ever since the creation of this Administrative post. For this political manœuvre, which was probably initiated by Milton, they are relying on political influence and support from Milton, alias MUWANGA, whom they call their mother's father's brother's son. Milton clearly favours this idea of the KABUNDULI title coming to his village since this would offer the opportunity to become a power behind the throne, again. For, until a few years ago, Milton used to live in another village where he was a close neighbour to the then ruling KABUNDULI. He acquired a reputation for alternately intriguing against him or wanting to dominate him. Eventually, however, KABUNDULI with the backing of the Boma forced Milton to leave the village whereupon Milton settled at Thoro. He has tried, so far unsuccessfully, to persuade the present KABUNDULI to join him at Thoro. KABUNDULI does stay at Thoro for longer or shorter periods but he has never said anything definite yet about his plans for the future.

Milton is playing a double game: at present he still needs the support of KABUNDULI as an N.A. But at the same time, and with KABUNDULI's support, Milton is strengthening his own political position[2] and appears to be preparing the stage for replacing the present KABUNDULI with his own protégé.

Hereditary Titles and Administrative Offices

There are now new avenues to power, e.g. through the Administrative system and church organizations. Kamoti reached his present political position as councillor through traditional channels, *viz.* through his father's headmanship,[3] but he no longer

---

[1] See Genealogy VII on p. 222.

[2] For which the acquisition of his own Book was one condition: see p. 223. See also pp. 250-1 for further details of Milton's political influence.

[3] I do not know to what extent the late KAMBAWE achieved his position as church elder through his political status as headman and councillor or whether Kamoti attained his own church eldership through his father's influence or through his own position as acting KAMBAWE.

needs the prop of the KAMBAWE-ship. He is prepared to let the headmanship go because the financial rewards of an Administrative Headmanship are negligible and the political significance of the KAMBAWE title is small in the present diminished village of Mzenga. Kamoti has left the struggle for the KAMBAWE title to his father's matrilateral nephews. As a son he could not inherit the traditional office but he did take over the non-traditional office of councillor. From the Administrative point of view Kamoti did not 'inherit' the post of councillor. This may be the legal position; but in the eyes of the Tonga he did inherit the councillorship. Here we see a divergence of opinion: Kamoti supported by KABUNDULI and the Boma divided the political status of the late KAMBAWE up into its constituent parts. Each of the three parties had its own reason for taking this stand. Kamoti knew he would not be able to succeed to the title but he did not want to lose the post of councillor with the title. The Boma did not want to establish a precedent by making the post of councillor go automatically with an hereditary title. I am not certain what made KABUNDULI support Kamoti as a councillor. On the other hand the late KAMBAWE's nephews consider their maternal uncle's political *persona* as one integrated whole. They see his Administrative appointments and his headmanship at Mzenga all as part of the KAMBAWE title to which they are entitled to succeed. The late KAMBAWE in fact held his two Administrative appointments (Administrative Headman and councillor) as KAMBAWE. As far as I am aware, these two posts are always held by traditional headmen.

This conflict over the content of a title does not occur only between village sons and owners. I recorded a similar controversy between two owners in a succession dispute in CHISAMBI's village.[1]

CASE 19: COUNCILLOR AND HEADMAN

The old CHISAMBI, who died in 1953, had been fairly immobile for some years and his 'nephew' (*mphwao*, i.e. sister's son) Muhoni had

[1] This village lies just south of the Luweya River and just north of Thoro village. I heard about the succession dispute and I attended public meetings on this dispute in the village, but as I never lived there my knowledge of the past and present background of this case is limited.

been acting in his place. This meant that Muhoni had been representing CHISAMBI as an Administrative Headman and as the councillor in the court of MALANDA, the sub-Native Authority of the area. When CHISAMBI died, Muhoni considered himself the successor of CHISAMBI in all his capacities: of village headman, Administrative Headman and councillor. Muhoni had the support of a group of villagers, the sub-N.A. and KABUNDULI who is the N.A. of the area. The rival claimant, CHIKASSA, who was also a 'nephew' of the late CHISAMBI, was supported by another group of villagers[1] and also by a group of Kapunda Banda headmen, most of whom lived outside CHISAMBI's Administrative village area. Of his supporters, only KAJILA lived in this area.

The three protagonists in this struggle for power were Muhoni who belongs to the late CHISAMBI's matrilineage; CHIKASSA who belongs to another matrilineage in the village; and KAJILA of a third matrilineage, who claims to be the 'maternal uncle' (*asibweni*), that is, genealogically the most senior of these three matrilineages.[2] The KAJILA-CHIKASSA faction claimed that before the late CHISAMBI the title in the village was CHIKASSA. Several CHIKASSAS died in quick succession, until in that one matrilineage there were no more men available; the succession went to CHIKASSA's 'younger brother' who dropped the title CHIKASSA and called himself CHISAMBI. When this CHISAMBI died in 1953, the name should have returned to the original CHIKASSA matrilineage, to which the present CHIKASSA belongs. The title should not, therefore, be inherited by a kinsman of CHISAMBI's lineage. This was the wish of CHIKASSA himself. It was also the wish of KAJILA, who as the most senior kinsman claimed to be the 'real owner' of the title and thus claimed the right to appoint the successor; and he supported CHIKASSA.

This succession dispute became involved in the Kapunda Banda campaign against the appointment of KABUNDULI (a Phiri) as N.A. over the lakeshore area which the Kapunda Banda claim as their home area.[3] KAJILA, CHIKASSA, and according to most people, CHISAMBI, are Kapunda Banda. Most Kapunda Banda show their disapproval of KABUNDULI's appointment over 'their' area by not attending the courts.

---

[1] Several informants told me that he had the larger following among the villagers. In this situation the relative size of the factions is largely a theoretical point when the issue is not decided by arms or vote. The quality of the followers and their political influence is more important.

[2] These three headmen, each with his own title, lived within CHISAMBI's (Administrative) village—not his traditional village.

[3] See also pp. 223 *seq.*

But some do attend for political reasons. CHISAMBI had always supported KABUNDULI and his sub-N.A. MALANDA within whose jurisdiction CHISAMBI's village lies. It is very likely that there was some connection between CHISAMBI's support of KABUNDULI and MALANDA, and his appointment as councillor in MALANDA's court. Other Kapunda Banda hold this against CHISAMBI and his 'walker' Muhoni.

A further complicating factor is that KAJILA claims attorneyship over a girl called Clara whom KABUNDULI wanted to marry. As part of the anti-KABUNDULI campaign, KAJILA, supported by many other Kapunda Banda headmen, resisted this marriage. This undoubtedly had some influence on KABUNDULI in his support of Muhoni.

As at Mzenga (cf. Case 11), the struggle between Muhoni and CHIKASSA was not only for the inheritance of the title in the village, but, more important, for the attributes which went with the title when CHISAMBI held it, i.e. the Book and the councillorship. These perquisites exacerbated the struggle for power. When after some months the people of the village had still not been able to settle this succession question, they called a meeting and asked KABUNDULI and MALANDA to attend it. They undoubtedly expected to find out the attitude of KABUNDULI and MALANDA to the above two Administrative offices: whether they would allow Muhoni to retain them even if he did not succeed to the title. The meeting did not produce a successor nor did the two N.A.'s make their views known. KABUNDULI simply told the people to make their minds up quickly and to present the successor at MALANDA's court.

Eventually CHIKASSA was taken to MALANDA's court and there presented as the rightful successor to the title and headmanship. CHIKASSA and his Kapunda Banda supporters expected that he would also be given the Book and the councillorship,[1] in spite of CHIKASSA's (and KAJILA's) past antagonism towards KABUNDULI and MALANDA and his court. This, however, did not happen. He was told: 'All right, you are now the headman in your village—that is your traditional right[2] but that has nothing to do with the work of the Boma:[3] Muhoni will keep the Book [i.e. the Administrative Headmanship] and his councillorship.' And Muhoni continued to sit in court as councillor. CHIKASSA considered this a great injustice because his party held that

[1] The post carries a monthly salary of about £2.
[2] *Dangu la chihami*: lit. the traditional law, or: the law of the old days: see also p. 220.
[3] *Nchitu ya boma*, i.e. work or job given by the Boma: cf. p. 220.

the Boma perquisites were an integral part of the title. But the decision was later confirmed by the Boma.

This case illustrates again the essentially vague character of Tonga headmanship. The norms of succession are, in theory, clear enough. In fact, however, there is wide scope for the manipulation of these norms. Thus there are always conflicting claims to any title. The lack of definition and the divisible character of a traditional title is further increased when Administrative appointments are associated with it: the more component parts to the one title, the more rival successors there may be. I have mentioned before (p. 208) that there is no clear distinction between legitimists and usurpers. This is also clear from this struggle for succession to CHISAMBI's title. Each of the two parties received a part of the political offices which the late CHISAMBI combined in his person, and each called the other a usurper.

Like Kamoti at Mzenga, Muhoni in CHISAMBI's village reached political office in the Administrative system as acting title-holder. His principal died; Muhoni established his position in the Administrative system in his own right, and was no longer dependent for political power on the traditional title which he lost. But Muhoni, with the prestige and power of his Administrative position, will probably attract followers and become a village headman in his own right.

In Chapter VI we will see that N.A. KABUNDULI is in a comparable situation. KABUNDULI is one of the oldest titles among the Tonga. The KABUNDULIS used to be headmen in the hills and for about the last 40 years they have also held Administrative appointments. The present KABUNDULI is a somewhat irresponsible young man, and although at one stage he had his own village, his people have drifted away. By the middle of 1954 the only people left in his village were his two wives, his mother, his mother's younger sister, his own sister and a 'son'. He has since sent his wives away, and following a quarrel, his mother and her sister departed and his village has virtually disintegrated. Thus without a village, KABUNDULI has now little status in the traditional political system. This would normally mean that the title would disappear or go to another kinsman, for according to traditional values he is now no longer a *fumu* (chief or headman) since 'a *fumu* without people is no *fumu*'. But he still holds the

Boma appointment of N.A. and having lost one traditional prop he is now anxious to get backing and status from another village. In other words KABUNDULI is at present a *fumu* in search of a village. And that is one of the reasons why he stays more frequently than he used to at Thoro, where he has matrilineal links and, what is more important, where he can count on Milton's political support. And Milton is ready, at least for the present, to give KABUNDULI this support; for Milton in turn needs KABUNDULI's support for his own ambitions.[1]

Hereditability of Administrative Offices

It appears then that village sons may be handicapped in attaining hereditary office in the traditional political system but they are not excluded from power or non-hereditary executive position. And through an influential position in the traditional structure village sons (and for that matter other categories of villagers, too) may attain a position in the Administrative system.

The Administrative positions I have discussed so far are those of N.A., sub-N.A., councillor and Administrative Headman. There are other positions in the Administrative bureaucracy, such as tax clerk, court clerk, sanitary foreman, and messenger. This latter group of officials have on the whole special duties of comparatively little political significance. There is no tendency to associate these offices with traditional titles nor are they considered hereditary; they are accepted as personal appointments. They resemble in many respects the salaried officers of local government in Britain. But the Administrative posts of N.A. and the like are more strictly political offices;[2] and the Tonga definitely tend to

---

[1] I have since heard that KABUNDULI has now definitely moved his N.A. H.Q. from the hills to a place about 1 mile inland from Chinteche Boma so as to facilitate contact with the Administration. For other references to the political relationship between KABUNDULI and Milton, see pp. 223–5 and 245–6.

[2] This applies also to a councillor although in theory he is only a member of the court of the N.A. or sub-N.A. of the area who is the judge. In practice, he is generally considered in his own and surrounding villages as the (sub-) N.A.'s lieutenant whom people may consult. I have also been told that people sometimes take their cases, which should go to the court, to him, which is illegal; I have recorded a few instances of this. The councillor also acts as judge in the court in the absence of the N.A. I use the form N.A. for both N.A. and sub-N.A. (except where the distinction is important) because in practice the sub-N.A.'s position differs little from that of an N.A.

associate these offices with traditional titles. Indeed, in practice the Boma generally gives them to people whom it considers to be traditional headmen with hereditary titles ·and allows these Administrative offices to be taken over by the person it accepts as successor to a traditional headmanship. Although the Boma accepts in practice the connection of Tonga title and Administrative office, it does not go so far as to recognize the office as inalienably tied to the title. The Boma appointment is a personal appointment. It is not necessarily a life appointment, for if the Boma is not satisfied with the incumbent, it gives the office to another headman or abolishes the office altogether. This happens frequently with the office of Administrative Headman.

The hereditability of Administrative offices is subject both to Boma decisions and to struggles in the traditional political structure. I recorded several cases where deceased Administrative Headmen were succeeded by kinsmen who inherited the Administrative office along with the traditional title. On the other hand, there is the case of the KAMBAWE title and the Administrative offices associated with it (p. 195). One appointment, the Administrative Headmanship, was removed from the village altogether, whilst the councillorship, which was explicitly stated not to be hereditary, went to KAMBAWE's son Kamoti. Similarly, after CHISAMBI's death neither the Book (symbol of Administrative Headmanship) nor the councillorship went to the heir who was officially presented .as the successor to CHISAMBI's traditional headmanship.

In the succession disputes at Mzenga and at CHISAMBI's village, Kamoti and Muhoni respectively failed to gain recognition as the rightful successors to the title; and it was they who insisted on the divisible nature of their principals' political status. On the other hand, their opponents (those who claimed to be the rightful successors to the title) insisted on the unitary character and the indivisibility of their predecessor's political status. Similarly in villages where the successors to the title inherited the Administrative office along with it, the new incumbents took it for granted that this should be so. As I stated above, this is the general attitude; the Administrative office should go with the title and is not a personal appointment. This is of course particularly the attitude of those headmen who have got a Boma office, for two reasons. Firstly, if the Administrative office is an inseparable and hereditary part of their traditional title, an appointment once made would no longer be subject to the discretion of the Boma and consequently its tenure would be more secure. Secondly, headmen who hold Administrative appointments consider these not as personal appointments, but rather as proper recognition on the part of the Boma of the historical political status of their traditional titles.

We saw that the Tonga distinguish between political authority which goes back to the old days (*chihami*) and that which is ultimately derived from the Boma. I have made the same distinction between traditional title, traditional political position, etc., and Administrative office, the Administrative structure, etc. But I have tried to make it clear in my descriptions of actual political situations that it would be entirely unrealistic to attempt to treat these two systems, the traditional and the Administrative, as if they were separate from and independent of one another. Even though one can discern the rough outlines of both, the two systems are interdependent, and together they constitute the political system of Tongaland. In some political situations Tonga may try to distinguish between the two parts of the political system, as it operates in Tongaland at present, but in other situations they will emphasize its essential wholeness. Status in the traditional political system is desired because, among other things, it increases the chance of acquiring a position in the Administrative system which often offers monetary rewards as well as power. Conversely, an Administrative position emphasizes and enhances status in the traditional system and it may make the possession of a title more secure. In fact, an Administrative appointment may give status in the traditional system. Thus KABUNDULI has largely lost his status as traditional headman, but since he has retained his position as N.A. he can still try to become headman of a village again, using his prestige as an N.A. Even in the instance I gave (on p. 220) where Tonga united in emphasizing the essentially traditional claim to authority of the headman they were installing, the headman was at the same time also a sub-N.A., from which position he derived his authority outside his own village.

The various churches and sects in the area offer additional avenues to power. However, I intend to treat this subject separately elsewhere.

Slaves

The question of slave status is still a very live issue for the Tonga, and it influences their actions a good deal. It is mentioned in practically every discussion on any subject. They see slave status as a condition which is the direct contradiction of all the ideals of Tonga life and of the prerequisites which make that life possible. For them the word *akaporo* (slaves) epitomizes what they consider is the absolute antithesis of the values which they accept as basic in their society in which, by implication, freeman status is the norm. It was partly through this antithesis that I myself became aware of the guiding principles in Tonga society. For instance, I have tried in preceding pages to bring out the extent of a person's dependence on support from kinsmen which alone enables him (her) to enjoy what one might call 'a full life' in Tonga society. This question is crucial for an understanding of a case like 'Meya's Death'. And conversely, 'Meya's Death' highlights this question and helps one to discover and understand it.

I should make it clear that the status of slave legally does no longer exist. When I refer to 'slaves' I am merely dealing with people who are of slave descent, that is, people who have inherited some social disabilities.

After the owners and the sons of the village come, in order of importance, the slaves (*akaporo*, sing. *mkaporo*) whose status and role in the village I have already mentioned incidentally at several points in this study.[1] The importance of slaves lay in their role as followers, warriors, and possibly merchandise, and also as breeders who were tied to the village. What the women who married between villages contributed to tribal cohesion, the slaves who married within a village contributed towards village cohesion. People of slave descent still have this significance, albeit to a lesser extent, because of their greater freedom nowadays.

---

[1] A fourth category of villagers are the virilocal wives. I will not treat them separately because my previous discussion of marriage and the kinship ties between villages was essentially an analysis of the status and role of married women. Husbands living uxorilocally are so rare that they do not merit separate discussion. Much of what I said about the status of virilocal wives, and the ties they create between villages, applies *mutatis mutandis* to uxorilocally living husbands.

Characteristics of Slave Status

Slaves were acquired through capture, trade and as compensation.[1] I mentioned Siddely's (Chin. D 6) mother who is said to have been a slave of Bisa origin.[2] I also met other people whom I have reason to believe are slaves or at least of slave descent and who seem to have originated on Likoma Island or further eastwards, or in Tumbuka country or further westwards. They may have been captured or bought. It is almost certain that there was some trade involving slaves through Likoma and also through the north end of the lake. I was told that a few people were slaves of Tonga origin who had been captured (or whose parents had been captured) some distance away from their present village. I never heard of slaves captured in villages near to the captor's village (within a day's walk or so). It seems that slaves always came from areas some distance away, probably so that they would be more effectively cut off from their homes and more effectively tied to their master's village.[3]

The British Administration prohibited by law the institution of slavery. This may have brought the slave trade to a speedy end but it could not by itself abolish the status of slaves. The status of slaves has never been so much the result of law, theory or decree, but rather a consequence of people being cut off in space and time (if they were second generation slaves) from their kith and kin and therefore at the mercy of the strangers among whom they lived. This situation could not therefore be remedied simply by a law or even the physical act of setting slaves free.[4] Fifty or more years ago communications were still poor and travelling hazardous, so that it must have been difficult for ex-slaves to rejoin their villages. But even at present if a legally free slave does not know

---

[1] Cf. Case 7, p. 118; and the note on *chisoka* payments, p. 117, n. 1.

[2] See Case 3. It is not very likely that she was captured directly from the Bisa by a Tonga raiding party. She was probably acquired in some way by the Tonga from the Ngoni.

[3] Perhaps I only met or heard of foreign slaves or of slaves from distant parts because they would not have been able to return to their homes, whilst slaves from villages nearer by (if any) are more likely to have found their way back, especially after the establishment of British Administration.

[4] Several early mission stations experienced this when they found that fugitive and freed slaves became the mission's liability: see e.g. references in Hanna (1956), pp. 27, 35, 49 *et passim*; also Johnson, pp. 35, 76.

his place of origin[1] or has not the means to return there, he still has the position of a slave in practice. A slave in this position, who can no longer be sold, was (and is) therefore a bondman not so much by will of a master as by force of circumstances. I do not know whether the Tonga acquired their commercial slaves and domestic slaves (or bondmen) from different sources, but this seems unlikely. In any case both categories are known in Tonga as *akaporo*.

The Administration in Tongaland was established in 1897 so it is only about sixty years since slavery was abolished in law. Considering the small Government establishment in those early days, it is possible that the slave trade continued, illegally, for some time after that. There are still quite a number of first-generation (original) and second-generation slaves to be found. I met several men and women who, I am fairly certain, are slaves and who are at least seventy years old.

Slave status carries with it some stigma and it is rare, except perhaps in a quarrel, to hear somebody being called a slave in public. Even in strict privacy, with only myself and an informant present, the latter would not easily admit to other people's slave status, let alone his own. They were afraid that I might later, incautiously (or worse still, purposely for my own ulterior motives), publicize this knowledge and its source. Indeed, this secrecy about people's status hampered me considerably in the collection of genealogies.[2] On the other hand those who were prepared to discuss with me in private their own and others' genealogies and the subject of slaves would sometimes give the impression that practically everyone in the village, except the speaker, was a slave, including the headman. This applied particularly to opponents in legal dispute, political rivalry, or other conflicts. One might hear: 'Who is he to do this to me? Has he

---

[1] E.g. I was told that Siddely's sister Joana (Chin. D 4) of Chinyafwa was still a babe-in-arms when she was captured together with her mother Nyadondo: see also p. 135.

[2] Slave origin is bound to come out in discussion of genealogies. Partly to avoid this embarrassing situation most Tonga were reluctant to give genealogical information. This may simply have been an excuse for the general suspicion about my ulterior motives, but it is still significant that the fear of revealing people's slave origin was generally chosen as the vehicle for this suspicion.

forgotten that I gave him a place [*maru*[1]] when he had nowhere to go and that I did this out of kindness?[2] I am the owner and he is only a slave.' In such situations the term slave is likely to be used as a term of abuse rather than as a reference to a person's descent.

It is of course impossible to collect any conclusive evidence about a person's alleged or suspected slave origin, particularly since this embarrassing fact is superficially hidden in the kinship system.[3] One can nevertheless make deductions by considering allegations of certain persons' slave status in relation to their treatment by other villagers and their own behaviour. This was clearly illustrated in a divorce case which I heard in KABUNDULI's court.

CASE 20: THE SLAVE HUSBAND

A woman, Telida, was suing her husband, Kamanga, for divorce. Her attorney (*nkhoswe*) was village headman KAMBUZI. At one stage during the proceedings KAMBUZI said to the court that nobody could end the marriage as both parties were his 'children'. He explained that Telida was his daughter and that her husband Kamanga was also his 'son' in the village. What KAMBUZI meant by this statement became

---

[1] *Kuphempa maru*, viz. to beg for a place, puts the supplicant in a position of subordination to the owner. A freeman who has a birthright to be in the village, either as a village son or as an owner, has his own *masara* (see p. 273) and 'will not beg anything from anybody'.

[2] I heard this argument used several times between rival headmen competing for a census or another Administrative post. Each tried to prove his own superiority and seniority in the traditional structure through the antiquity of his title. For instance KABUNDULI maintains that his title is older in the lakeshore area south of the Luweya River than the title of any of the Kapunda Banda, and that he is therefore the only one qualified for the post of N.A. in that area: which the Boma very properly (as KABUNDULI sees it) gave him. One of his arguments is that when the Kapunda Banda arrived in the area they found KABUNDULI there already and they 'begged him for a place' (cf. van Velsen (1959a), p. 4). The Kapunda Banda hotly deny this story. In this sort of context the word 'slave' is lifted from the level of personal genealogical reality and becomes a term of political abuse.

[3] The Tonga say that in the old days a master became *mbuya* (grandparent) to his slave. They add that if a person is cajolingly or superfluously addressed with *mbuya*, the person so addressed may ask the speaker: 'What is all this *mbuya* for? Are you my slave?' The owner of a dog is still called *mbuya*.

clearer later when he said: '*Aonani uyu munthu . . .*'[1] This was followed by a few remarks implying: who is he and what does he want here in court instead of coming back to my village where the case belongs: am I not the *nkhoswe* [attorney] for both husband and wife in this marriage? (Kamanga on his return from Rhodesia had not gone back to KAMBUZI's but to another village.) Whilst saying '*Aonani uyu munthu*' KAMBUZI rubbed both his knees with his hands to the obvious amusement of the public. This gesture signifies that the person to whom it refers is a slave.[2] I was later told that KAMBUZI had thus shown that Kamanga was not only his 'son' but his slave (his 'man') as well. This explained to me the almost imperceptible bias which the court seemed to show in favour of KAMBUZI and the woman. Probably KAMBUZI had been successful in suggesting to the court that this was really a village affair and that it would have been settled by him if it had not been for the presumption of this slave Kamanga who took the case out of the village to the court.

There are various other ways of indicating indirectly that some-one is a slave. For instance, sometimes when I enquired about the bridewealth a man had given for his wife, the answer would be something like: 'What? Bridewealth? Of course he did not pay anything: he just married her. Do you think he would have paid anything for *her*?' Even if my informant did not add that she was a slave, the implication was clear enough.[3]

---

[1] Lit: look at that man. *Munthu* is a genderless noun meaning 'human being'; more usual is *munthu rumi* (man), *munthu kazi* (woman), or the plural *wanthu* (people). The use of the genderless singular noun in this context carries over-tones of contempt.

[2] Often, when I was told that someone was a slave, the speaker would rub or just gently tap his knee and say: 'He is of this [*wa umu*]' which is an elliptic way of saying: he is a slave. This gesture can also be made quickly and unob-trusively in public as a secret communication, as we slyly tap our forehead when we want to indicate that someone is rather eccentric or a fool. Consider-ing the importance of the slave concept in the Tonga values, but also the humili-ation attached to slave status, this is a very useful gesture for passing on vital information in a way which is least likely to attract the attention (and the anger) of the person concerned. The origin of the Tonga gesture is that a supplicating slave used to express his submission by holding his master's leg. Hence the phrase '*wana wa malundi*', lit. children of the legs, i.e. slaves.

[3] It is not exceptional for a man to have a wife for whom no bridewealth has been paid yet (see p. 97). But normally when it concerns a woman for whom bridewealth should be paid and who has kinsmen to see to it that the husband

Other oblique references to a person's slave status or slave descent often implied slave status of the mother or, as the Tonga see it, the lack of a mother and thus the lack of maternal kin. This in turn implies the lack of a source of political status and authority, and the lack of legal support. When a man wanted to point out to me that his brother's wife was a slave, he said: 'When his wife died we just buried her and did the shaving without waiting for anybody. Her mother and her brother had also come to live in the village; when they died the same thing happened.' [1] And KABUNDULI once said about Milton: 'Who is Milton? Has he got a mother? Well, if he has one, I at least have never heard it.' [2] I mentioned how Charles (Mul. B 5) at Mulombwa asked what Elton's (Mul. D 3) 'name' was (p. 208). And conversely Kamoti in a quarrel at Mzenga pointed out to his opponent that he, Kamoti, should not be treated as a mere nobody or he would just go to his matrilocal village where, after all, he had his own 'name' (p. 66). Similarly, in the story of Yaphet KAMBAWE's succession, as told by Kamoti, we noticed this emphasis on having not only a matrilocality of one's own but also a patrilocality (p. 60). To be 'a freeman on all sides' (*munangwa kose kose*) is to be 'a freeman indeed' (*munangwa ukongwa*).

For a Tonga to be able to show that he is a freeman patrilaterally as well as matrilaterally carries additional status. The clearest proof of patrilateral freeborn status is a father with a title, like Yaphet KAMBAWE's father NGOMBO. But 'to have a mother', i.e. to be freeborn on the mother's side, is of prime importance. And here, too, to be able to claim a 'name' is considered conclusive evidence of free matrilineal descent. This 'name' is often, I suspect, nothing more than the proper name of a maternal uncle (*asibweni*), either real or classificatory, which is adopted as a title-'name' by the nephew. For to have an *asibweni* is to be free. Hence Nyali's remark that he went to Deep Bay to show his

---

does not get away with it, the husband is more likely to pretend that he did pay it. The connection between not paying bridewealth and the slave status of the wife is clearly seen in the arguments surrounding 'Meya's Death': see e.g. paras. 26–8.

[1] Burying and shaving without waiting for the maternal relatives was also one of the causes of the disputes after Meya's death: see particularly paras. 17, 26, 28.

[2] Cf. p. 245, n. 1.

T

sister's husband's people that his sister had a brother and that her children had a maternal uncle who would see to it that neither the mother nor the children were treated as if they were slaves (p. 49). This was also the purpose of the visit of the Bandawe people to Mapalassie after Meya's death: to show that the Mapalassie people could not take any liberties with Bandawe's matrikin, for instance by accusing Adi of sorcery (Case 9, para. 26).

The restricted freedom of a slave was (and to a certain extent, still is) due not so much to the fact that he was held captive, but rather to the fact that he could not move easily. If a slave felt dissatisfied with his master and his village, he had no alternative village where he would be received as a relative and where he could rely on the support of kinsmen. It seems likely that if a slave ran away from his master's village surrounding villages would be chary of helping him lest they found themselves in conflict (perhaps armed) with the master's village.[1] Moreover other headmen presumably would not want to create precedents by receiving runaway slaves, thus undermining their mastery over their own slaves.[2]

The peculiarity and weakness, therefore, of a slave was that he could not depend on the support of kinsmen because he had no kin, at least not within reach. He was alone. This is still his position to-day: a person of slave descent may still suffer social (not legal) disabilities, except that nowadays he has greater opportunities to escape his lot. He can move to a town where he can make himself independent. Even in his village he may now create for himself some support based on economic rather than on kinship ties. The modern cash economy offers relatively greater opportunities for individuals to achieve economic and social independence than they had in the old days, when trade and wealth were (probably exclusively) associated with and supported by political power. A slave now has a relatively stronger position thanks to the fact that Tongaland is more firmly integrated into larger political and economic units, namely Nyasaland, the two Rhodesias, Southern Africa and so forth. Within these units a slave has greater freedom to move than in pre-European days when the lives of the Tonga and particularly of slaves were more

[1] Mission stations experienced this, too: cf. Mitchell (1956), pp. 27–8.
[2] A similar consideration may have influenced the court's attitude to Kamanga: see p. 258.

narrowly confined to Tongaland. Tongaland was, of course, never entirely insulated and the Tonga were never cut off from contact with non-Tonga, least of all from the surrounding peoples: the Tonga carried on some external trade, they experienced the Ngoni invasions, and they also saw the immigration of other tribal groups. This is not the place to enlarge upon this point. Here I only want to indicate that the Tonga horizon has widened as compared with the period when the Tonga were still an independent tribe, that is, before they were fitted into a comprehensive system of administration including distant tribes with whom they had had no previous contact. But in spite of widened horizons, so long as a slave lives in a Tonga village his life is to a great extent still governed by traditional Tonga norms.

Social Isolation of Slaves

The Tonga village and the tribe never had a system of impersonal authority to guarantee to the individual full enjoyment of his legal rights. This guarantee had to come from a person's kinsmen who would support him and help him to manipulate political and social forces to obtain his rights. This is to a large extent still the case although the Tonga are now ultimately ruled by the Administration of the Protectorate Government. For, as I will explain more fully later, the Administration operates largely through persons and institutions of the traditional political structure, and the everyday life of a Tonga is still largely lived within this structure.

Although theoretically foreigners are not slaves, in practice they are in a very similar position. Their position is different only in that, if they want to leave the village and Tongaland, they know an alternative home where they can return either independently or with the help of the Administration.[1] Foreigners who (for various reasons) do not return home, often complain about life among the Tonga. I once heard a woman from Southern Rhodesia say to her Tonga husband in a quarrel: 'You Tonga always treat me unfairly because you know that I am alone and have nobody to help me. Oh mother, oh mother! I wish I could go back to my mother.' I recorded no cases of brutal or grossly unfair

---

[1] This is the converse of Tonga stranded abroad who may be fetched back by relatives or with the help of the Administration: cf. p. 230.

treatment; but when it comes to the test foreigners are less protected than, for instance, the matrikin of Bandawe at Mapalassie (cf. the case of 'Meya's Death', p. 149). And at her husband's death a foreign widow may have to fight hard to retain her share of the goods in the face of the demands of the husband's kin, although in the end she may well receive her due. Her ultimate sanction is that she may return (with the assistance of the Administration) to her homeland, taking her children with her. Foreigners have a sense of insecurity which is often expressed in their behaviour or in such a remark as I have just quoted. Few Tonga who marry foreign wives abroad bring them back to Tongaland, although they may bring some of the children. Their explanation is generally that their wives did not want to come.

Orphans (*alanda*, sing. *mlanda*) are in some respects similarly placed. The Tonga word *mlanda* has a wider connotation than its English equivalent; it is used for people of all ages who have lost their biological parents and who have no other close kin to protect or promote their interests and have to rely on classificatory kin who may put their own close kin first. Elinara (Map. B 15) expressed the insecurity which orphans are liable to feel when she complained that the court had tried to muzzle her because she was only a lone woman.[1]

I do not want to suggest that all three categories (slaves, foreigners and orphans) occupy the same status in the village and are treated alike. There is a difference between the position of an orphan and a slave. But one gets a strong impression that people of these three categories share a similar sense of insecurity. This illustrates the great importance which Tonga attach to the support of kinsmen[2] who will ensure that a person's interests are respected. And mention of 'orphans' and 'foreigners' suggests people who are handicapped socially and politically, who are like slaves, i.e. people with whom one can more easily take liberties.[3] The words *mkosano* (son-in-law) and *mkumwana* (daughter-in-

---

[1] See 'Meya's Death', para. 30; cf. also paras. 2 and 5.

[2] Elinara pointed at her back when she said that she was alone and said: '*Ndirivi akumusana*', *viz.* 'I do not have people at my back' (see p. 152). This gesture often accompanies mention of those who are considered to be alone, e.g. orphans.

[3] The implied equation of the position of orphans with that of slaves was so strong that for a long time I thought that *mlanda* meant 'slave'.

law) carry the same overtones; they too are 'alone' in their marital
village and are at the mercy of their in-laws if they have no kinsmen at home who watch their interests.[1]

In the course of this analysis of political life in the village we
have already come across several situations which indicate the
disadvantageous position of the 'lone ones' and which may
contribute to the sense of insecurity which they so often express.
It was not only Elinara who felt 'alone': her complaint against
the men of the court was in the name of, and supported by, the
other three women of the Mzake group (see 'Meya's Death',
para. 30). For in that situation where the Mzake women stood
against the Lena lineage at Mapalassie, the former were without
the support of their own male kinsmen who could have led their
faction, and stood up for its interests. Although the Mzake group
has male kinsmen with authority, these are at present working
abroad. In cases like these such absent kinsmen may try to influence matters in the village by writing letters or sending messages
with returning friends, and when they themselves return to the
village later they may try to redress whatever injustices they consider to have been committed in their absence. The fact remains,
however, that whilst these kinsmen were absent the Mzake
women felt alone and considered that they were unfairly treated
because they were alone.[2]

Much of the controversy which ensued from Meya's death
centred on the authoritarian attitude of the leaders at Mapalassie,
Mussa and Ziba, who treated Nyalongwe and her offspring 'as if
they were slaves'. This indicates what might have been the position of Nyalongwe and her offspring if their kinsmen at Bandawe
had not stood up for them, and had not been likely to persuade
Nyalongwe and the others to 'go home', i.e. to Bandawe. This
would have reduced Mussa's following.

A similar incident occurred in GURU's village. Mtiti had tried
to seduce Dolas whilst she was asleep in her hut at night. The way
he went about it made Dolas and others say that he had acted

---

[1] The case of Dolnard illustrates the position of the son-in-law among his
affines. At that time he was in their hands although he did not live there: see
also p. 106.

[2] If it had not been for the support the Mzake case received from the Bandawe people, possibly the Lena lineage would have been in an even stronger
position: see 'Meya's Death'.

like a sorcerer. Dolas however had repelled him and he had fled with only a shirt and a hat on. The case was settled by GURU in the village in the presence of Dolas's father and mother, but not Dolas's mother's brother, who lives only ten minutes away. Half-an-hour after the case was over the maternal uncle, Pamali, came to GURU. He was very annoyed and asked GURU why he had not called him: were Dolas and her mother GURU's slaves that GURU could settle an adultery case concerning Dolas without calling him? Pamali threatened to take the case to the court of the sub-N.A. Nothing came of it, partly at least because Dolas had no evidence which would be acceptable in an outside court. But in the village Dolas's evidence was sufficient. For as GURU said, 'We are all one and we must settle this amicably for the sake of peace: otherwise we cannot live together', and there was, therefore, more give and take than there would be in the sub-Native Authority court with its stricter rules of evidence. However, Pamali had made his point, and established his right: he had not allowed the case to become a precedent for reducing Dolas to the position of a 'slave'.

The adultery case of Lede (Mz. E 1) at Mzenga[1] was a clear illustration of the weak position of a 'lone one', whether slave or foreigner, whose rights are more open to abuse. Lede's husband, Kaunda (Mz. E 2), is a foreigner, a Chewa,[2] who is now in Southern Rhodesia. Normally, in the case of adultery of a married woman, the lover is sued by the husband or his family. In this case it was Lede herself, with the support of her father, who sued Wellington (Mz. D 26); normally this is the procedure in cases of spinsters' fornication (*chigororo*: see p. 93, n. 1) Initially the court said that they could not hear this case: 'How can we follow the procedure appropriate for an adultery case involving an unmarried woman whilst in fact Lede is married; moreover, what shall we do about damages for the husband?' However in the end the court did hear the case 'as if she were unmarried', but they made Lede's father responsible for this fiction by making him sign in the record of the case a statement to the effect that he had agreed to this procedure. The court said nothing about damages for the

---

[1] See pp. 67 and 195.
[2] Although Kamoti and others talked about him as if he were a slave, I was unable to prove his slave descent. As he could not have been older than thirty he was certainly not a first generation slave.

husband but warned Lede's father that he might be sued for them later.[1] What the court could (and perhaps should) have done was to refuse to hear the case unless Lede's people had a letter from her husband indicating that he knew about the adultery and the course Lede's people intended to take, and perhaps authorizing them to take the case to court in his name. Otherwise they could have suspended the hearing until the court had written to the husband, as courts often do. In brief, all parties concerned seemed to disregard Kaunda's rights as a husband. When I commented upon this to Kamoti, KABUNDULI and others, they agreed and said that Kaunda's position was really like that of a slave.

Kamanga's case was similar although he was present in person (see p. 257). His wife, Telida, had had an adulterous child in his absence but although he was KAMBUZI's 'son' nobody had sued the lover. The court knew about this adultery and they were aware that Telida had had several other casual affairs. It was she who sued the husband for divorce, and courts tend to be more severe as regards court fine and/or damages and/or return of bridewealth particularly, when the divorcing spouse has an adulterous reputation. But despite all this the court seemed to show a certain bias in favour of Telida who was ordered to return half the bridewealth and pay £1 court fine. Kamanga lost half the bridewealth[2] and paid £2 fine. From my experience of similar divorce cases in this and other courts I would say that it is likely that, without some bias on the part of the court, the woman would have been ordered to return the whole bridewealth and to pay damages as well to her husband for her adultery[3] whilst the husband might not have had to pay any fine at all.

---

[1] This seems very unlikely because such damages are payable by the lover. Kaunda is not likely to recover any damages from Lede's father instead of the damages from the lover, because her father only received £1 10s. from Wellington, the lover. The normal adultery damages from the lover to the woman's husband are £4 10s. The damages awarded in this case to Lede's father (£1 10s.) were below even those normally awarded to the father or the kin of an unmarried woman, *viz.* £3. As for Wellington, his liability was extinguished; he cannot be sued again.

[2] In fact Kamanga lost the whole £3 bridewealth he had originally paid because he refused the half which Telida had been ordered to return to him; he wanted his wife to keep it 'for the children': cf. p. 107.

[3] Her adultery was mentioned during the hearings but the point was not pursued by the court.

As political and economic horizons have widened for the Tonga, individuals have acquired, in certain respects, greater independence. On the other hand, labour migrants who leave behind marital, economic, political and other interests are now more dependent on kinsmen in Tongaland. A labour migrant has to rely on the co-operation of his kinsmen to see that his interests and rights are not abused in his absence, or if they are, that action is taken. But there were obviously no kinsmen who could or would take up the cases of Kaunda and Kamanga when their wives Lede and Telida committed adultery in their husbands' absence abroad.

Thus the slave is on the whole in a weaker position than the person of free descent, who has kinsmen prepared to defend his interests and who probably has an alternative village to reside in. This does not mean that slaves are necessarily defenceless or even that they are always in a weak position in all situations. This is for instance not true in situations where slaves have their own kin group in the village, which may be more common now, after one or two generations, than it was in pre-British days.[1] For instance when Samu (Mz. D 3) committed adultery with Nkhuni's (Mz. D 24) wife at Mzenga, it was Nkhuni's mother who dealt with the matter in the absence of Nkhuni himself (see case of 'Retaliatory Adulteries', p. 98). Indeed, this kin group at Mzenga descended from Matumba and Helena (Mz. B 6 & 7) (whom I have good reason to believe were slaves) shows that slaves may be numerically important in a village and thus find security in numbers. The descendants of Amuziteni (Mz. C 10), who was probably also a slave, were able to move off to another village altogether. The fact remains, however, that in my experience slaves, foreigners (and to some extent orphans, too) seem to occupy a special position in a village—a position which is often characterized by a certain humility and feeling of insecurity. I could sense it after I had been closely associated with the daily life

---

[1] Not only have slave descendants been multiplying for two or more generations since the capture or purchase of the original slaves but I presume that, particularly in this century, this multiplication has been unchecked. It seems likely that in the period of slave trade and payment of human compensation the ranks of the slaves and their descendants (and probably the orphans) were liable to be reduced in numbers from time to time when payments for compensation or merchandise had to be made.

of a village for some months. It is particularly noticeable in the case of slave and/or foreign widows who are still in their late husband's village where they remain outsiders, unable to return to any village which they can consider their 'own' village. And one fact which generally prompted me to enquire whether a person was perhaps a slave was the realization that that person was treated slightly arrogantly or himself behaved somewhat obsequiously—as very few other Tonga allow themselves to be treated, or behave.

Role of Slaves in the Village

I mentioned before that a Tonga man's ideal is to arrange his marriage in such a way that the children will stay with him. This ideal is said by the Tonga to be best realized in a cross-cousin marriage. But we found that this ideal can only be realized, if at all, in an *intra-village* cross-cousin marriage in which the crucial factor is that the spouses are domiciled in the same village and not that they are cross-cousins. But even in an intra-village marriage of cross-cousins the wife generally belongs matrilineally to another village, so that the children of such a union still feel the pull of a matrilocal village, away from the father's village.[1] This pull can only be eliminated if the father's village is also the mother's village to which she is firmly tied without an alternative home village.

A slave was (and to a certain extent still is) comparatively immobile—he generally lacked an alternative village. And he also lacked the backing of kinsmen in his quest for the enjoyment of his rights as a Tonga. The combination of these two factors, immobility and social isolation, made him[2] eminently manipulable in the hands of leaders of groups (whether village headmen or leaders of lineages within a village) who wanted to increase their following. The slave was not merely merchandise: he also played a part in the reproduction within a village and its cohesion.

To produce the desired result, an intra-village marriage involving a slave had to be arranged so that the free spouse was the one who would be likely to stay in the village in any case, i.e. who was a village owner who lived matrilocally. Thus a headman

---

[1] Cf. Nyalongwe and her offspring at Mapalassie who matrilineally belong to the Bandawe village: see 'Meya's Death' and p. 175.

[2] I am using 'him' to cover 'him' and 'her'.

used to have several slave wives to produce dependants who had to stay in their father's village as their mother was 'unknown'; they would not know their matrilocal home. These headman-slave marriages are still traceable, especially in villages whose headmen have old, established titles and are known to have been of some prominence (e.g. in war or trade) in the latter part of the last century.[1] The Tonga idiom of the 'unknown mother' aptly expresses the fact that socially the genetrix (a slave) is insignificant and therefore disappears after having fulfilled her biological function. In this way a headman (or for that matter any man who wanted to build up a following) could gratify a social and political ambition which was biologically impossible: he could produce children without a mater.

A headman or any other man with political ambitions not only wanted his own children in his village but also needed uterine nephews and nieces, i.e. the children of his sisters. But, as Tonga put it: 'Nobody can marry his sister.' By giving her a slave husband, the headman (or brother) could strengthen his matrilineage without seeing his sister leave the village and rear her children elsewhere.

It is difficult to measure accurately now the number of slave marriages in the past, either those between two slave spouses or those between a slave and a free spouse. One can only surmise who the slaves were: definite proof is lacking in most cases. And the incidence of unions between slave men and free women in the past is now almost impossible to gauge except in a few obvious cases. For the offspring of a free mother and a slave father would live in their mother's village, which by Tonga values would be their 'own village' in any case, whether their father were a free-man or not. And by now such a patrilateral slave kinsman is most likely to have disappeared from the genealogy: he is forgotten, or replaced by somebody whose origin is vaguely indicated as 'somewhere' in another part of Tongaland. None of these genea-logical phenomena are at all unusual among a people where patrilateral ancestors tend to disappear from genealogical memory. This is also likely to happen in unions between two slaves in the same village. The man is likely to have disappeared or to have

[1] Those headmen who used to be of some substance, particularly, are likely to have maintained their political significance through some generations. See p. 292.

been transformed genealogically whilst the woman may have become some assumed or putative matrilineal relative in the village.[1]

It is easier to trace unions between free men and slave wives.[2] The offspring of these marriages can often still be found in their free father's village where they may form a significant proportion of the patrilocal residents. In Table VIII I have tabulated

TABLE VIII

Patrilocal Residents who are apparently immobilized in the Village

A	Patrilocal residents with an apparently immobilizing matrilateral link to the village	13	46·5%
B	Patrilocal residents apparently without such a link	15	53·5%
	Total	28	100%

those patrilocal residents of my five sample villages who, as far as my evidence goes, seem to live patrilocally because they are, within Tongaland,[3] tied to that village, and cannot claim the right to settle in another Tonga village. It appears that just under half, or 46·5 per cent, of all the patrilocal residents in these five villages are apparently immobilized because their mothers (some of whom are still alive) are either foreign or slave or both.[4] These thirteen, apparently immobilized, patrilocal residents include John of Mapalassie (Map. C 11) whose mother is South African. He is a product of the present economic and social

[1] This genealogical reconstruction is based partly upon my general experience of the various ways in which genealogies are manipulated and 'reconstructed' by the Tonga themselves, and partly upon a few cases of people whose presence and position in the village I have reason to believe could be explained in this way.

[2] See also p. 104.

[3] If their mother is foreign and they knew her village (e.g. John at Mapalassie, see p. 230) they could settle there but they would then cease to be Tonga and become members of their mother's tribe. Similarly, Siddely of Chinyafwa could settle among the Siska but he would do so as a Siska and not as a Tonga; see p. 69.

[4] To be of foreign matrilateral descent tends in practice to have a similar effect as being of slave descent matrilaterally (see p. 260). Slaves often were foreign whilst a person with a foreign mother may be unable to settle matri-locally, or may not want to do so.

conditions of Tongaland. The other twelve may be of matrilateral slave descent but they are not the only villagers who are considered to be slaves. For this table refers only to patrilocal residents. Those whom I classified as matrilocal residents of these five villages also include people who are considered slaves, for example Elton of Mulombwa (Mul. D 3).[1] Although Elton's maternal grandfather Manda (Mul. B 21) was a son of headman CHACHAMARA, his maternal grandmother Nyambaya (Mul. B 22), who still lives with Elton at Mulombwa, is a slave so that matrilaterally Elton is of slave descent. Nyambaya is of course not included in Table VIII since she is a widow who lives virilocally.

Villagers who are still found in their patrilocal village give a rough indication of the success of the freeman-slave marriage in achieving its purpose of tying the children to their patrilocality. It appears then that of the 70 basic[2] inhabitants of the five villages, there are at least twelve[3] or 17 per cent who are patrilaterally tied to their village as a result[4] of what one might call with the Tonga, marriages of 'unknown' women. And the widows of these marriages are among the widows whom I found still living virilocally.[5]

---

[1] See also p. 37.

[2] See Table II. For the meaning of 'basic' see p. 236, n. 2.

[3] I.e. the thirteen people of Table VIII, A, less John of Mapalassie whose mother is South African and has never lived in Tongaland.

[4] Before one can describe patrilocal residents as 'immobilized' as a 'result' of a certain marriage (in this case a freeman-slave woman marriage) one has to find out whether *all* the offspring of the marriage are 'immobilized'. Several factors make this difficult: (i) The high proportion of labour migrants among the Tonga makes it often impossible to assess at any one time the domicile of about two-thirds of the male population. (ii) As women marry away the absence of the daughters may be due to marriage; they may still be alive or may have died virilocally. It is generally difficult to obtain reliable and observable evidence on this point. (iii) A person who is 'immobilized' may try to avoid the enquirer's conclusion that he is a slave, by claiming to be a child of one of his father's other wives who was not a slave.

[5] See pp. 113 *seq.*

CHAPTER VI

VILLAGE AND HEADMAN

IN appearance Tongaland is characterized by hamlets rather than villages; and these hamlets are on the whole small, discrete clusters of huts. The combination of hamlets into villages is in general less apparent. This is particularly the case along the more densely populated lakeshore; farther inland villages tend to be more clearly separated. This indefiniteness which is typical of the village as a residential unit also typifies it as a political unit. The Tonga use the word *muzi* for both hamlet and village.

The Hamlet

There is no regularity in the composition of the kin groups which inhabit the hamlets. A hamlet's inhabitants may form an elementary family or they may be related, patrilaterally or matrilaterally, to a common grandparent who may or may not live (or have lived) in the hamlet. Whilst the members of the hamlets are related to one another in a variety of ways, they are as a general rule close kin with actual kinship links.[1] The hamlet has no name and the hamlet leader as such is not an incumbent of a hereditary title.[2] There is no notion of permanency about hamlets in the way that villages are, ideally, considered enduring social and political units. Indeed the hamlet is an unstable unit whose composition and locality change frequently. Children grow up and daughters marry away or sons start their own hamlet; or individuals move from one hamlet to another in the same village. Hamlets also periodically break up socially and physically and some (or all) of its members may resettle a short distance away in the same village area with the same or different genealogical composition. In short there is little social or physical continuity in the life of a hamlet. For instance the older Mapalassie people have

---

[1] See p. 35. This is true of the hamlets I examined. It is possible that the composition of the hamlet used to be different and has been affected by the exodus of male labour migrants.

[2] He may, however, personally claim what I have called a subsidiary title: see pp. 201 *seq.*

lived on at least four different plots, each time with different people in the hamlet; but the hamlets have all been in the Mapalassie village area, only fifty or a hundred yards from their previous sites. The hamlet is not an economic unit: food production, storage,[1] preparation and consumption are by individual households. These and other activities like work-parties may be carried out collectively by the residents of one hamlet, but this is not a general rule.

Although the hamlet lacks an obvious corporate character, it is still a significant unit within the village. This significance is illustrated by the fact that the Tonga try to organize their labour migration on the basis of hamlets rather than villages. Furthermore, a hamlet is a potential nucleus of a new, independent village. Every Tonga is a potential headman: and the first step towards political independence and status is to establish one's own hamlet, even though residence in the hamlet of a senior kinsman does not necessarily mean less independence. But by starting his own hamlet on his own land a man is in a better position to attract followers and keep the leadership in his own hands.

The hamlet, lacking as it does corporate identity and continuity, does not own any land nor is it associated with a particular area of land. Thus the hamlet leader does not administer land on behalf of its members, for rights in land are held by individuals. In practice, however, members of a hamlet tend to receive their rights in land from their senior kinsman, the hamlet leader, unless they have created those rights themselves through first occupancy. This means that even if the hamlet does not have corporate interests in the land occupied and cultivated by its members, the inhabitants of a hamlet have some vague, common interests which are reinforced by the fact that the hamlet is generally a group of localized close kin. But land is still held individually and if a hamlet breaks up or if some members move off to another hamlet or start their own hamlet, they retain the rights in their land.

Land-holding

The Tonga pattern of land-holding shows the same features which characterize other aspects of their life, such as succession to

---

[1] The Tonga do not store cassava but many people grow small subsidiary crops such as rice, ground nuts, beans, maize, millet and so forth which are stored.

office, headmanship, kinship status and so forth. The control of land is vague and diffuse; in spite of formal and theoretical claims of ownership over large areas, control of land is not concentrated in persons of political prominence like headmen. The Tonga system of land-holding must be considered in the light of the fact that there is an adequate supply of land. The Tonga themselves are aware of this; and they often say how fortunate they are compared with other peoples in the District (like the Siska or the people of the Islands of Likoma and Chizumulu) or elsewhere. And it is symptomatic that neither in the courts nor in the villages did I record a single dispute over land as distinct from the fruits of land crops, trees or fish. The Ndazakale-Ziba dispute (p. 190), too, was not really about the possession of land. Even if we assume that Ndazakale's story is true, it was only one incident in the political rivalry between these two men.

All villages have a particular area of land associated with them—at least they claim this area as belonging to the village. Often, however, the boundaries are vague, particularly on the sides which border on uninhabited land like bush or forest. Generally the village area contains cultivated cassava gardens (*chikweta*, pl. *vikweta*); fallow land that has ceased to be cultivated only comparatively recently (*masara*);[1] and land covered with bush or forest (*dondo*).[2] A direct question about the rights in a particular stretch of *dondo* may produce two or sometimes three different answers, depending on the status of the person addressed. One person may claim that it is just virgin land belonging to the village and thus open to any resident in the village. Another answer may be that it is *masara* reverted to bush and thus open to descendants of the last cultivator—who is generally a kinsman of the speaker. Finally, one may be told that this land does not belong to the village at all but to the 'Owner of the land' (*mwene charu* or *mweneko wa charu*) who may live in the village next door or some miles away.[3]

[1] All land once cultivated, however long ago, is *masara*. In practice, rights in *masara* cease to be effective after a lapse of time; see p. 280.

[2] All wild growth is *dondo* and thus *masara* overgrown with bush, grass or forest is also *dondo*.

[3] The Tonga were on the whole just as chary about giving inside information about land as about genealogical matters, and there were very few occasions on which this information could be gained through observation, e.g. in disputes. For the same reason doubtful information could rarely be verified.

'*Owners of the Land*'

The office and function of the 'Owners of the land' are rather nebulous and have few practical implications.[1] In theory there is no land without an owner. 'Owners of the land' are not neces-sarily village headmen and they may live some distance away from the land over which they claim overlordship. Similarly the head-man of a village is not necessarily the 'Owner of the land' on which his village lies, but he may 'own' the land of another village. When I received GURU's permission to settle in his village he gave me an old garden of his own in which to build a tem-porary house. Immediately GURU himself, the D.C. and others were questioned by people from KAJULA's village nearby (about a mile or so to the north): they asked how GURU could possibly have given me permission to build there since it was not GURU's land; all the land was KAJULA's. And after a few weeks a man who works on the Copperbelt as a hospital assistant and who claims the KAJULA-ship wrote letters to the same effect to various Admini-strative authorities, e.g. the Boma at Nkata Bay and the Secre-tariat at Zomba. KAJULA claims that he is the 'Owner of the land' in an area which includes the whole of GURU's village. According to KAJULA, after the end of the Ngoni raids, when the people began to leave the large stockaded villages, GURU[2] (not the pres-ent one) came to KAJULA and begged (*kuphempa*) him for a small piece of land for himself and his old mother who was too old to go back to her pre-Ngoni village. KAJULA, moved by pity, gave GURU a site. But very soon GURU assembled a great number of relatives all of whom he settled around him and now GURU has forgotten KAJULA's act of kindness and claims the land as his own. Needless to say, GURU denies owing any land to KAJULA. There is reason to believe that there is some truth in KAJULA's story and that the land where GURU's village is now used to be KAJULA's land. But whatever may have happened in the past, for all practi-

[1] In Administrative reports, etc., a *mweneko wa charu* is often referred to as a 'landowner'. This is a very confusing, though literal, translation: its implied comparison with the English concept of landowner has given rise to mis-understanding and exaggeration of the significance and authority of a Tonga 'Owner of the land'.

[2] It is said that before the Ngoni raids GURU used to live farther inland. From there he joined CHINYENTHA's stockade and thence he moved to his present site. CHINYENTHA still lives by the mouth of the Luweya River, about three miles north of GURU: see van Velsen (1959a), p. 9.

cal purposes the land now belongs to GURU's village. Apart from KAJULA's protests after my arrival I did not record any acts which recalled this historical relationship.

Likewise, KAMBAWE at Mzenga is said to live on PASSO's land, whilst KAMBAWE himself 'owns' land some distance away from his present village. But in this case, too, I do not know of any practical implications of these claims. The land of Mapalassie village is also still known as KAMISA's land; this is clear from KAMISA's remark in 'Meya's Death' (para. 25).

One of the rare instances I recorded in which 'ownership' of land still has direct implications for the present is the case of PASSO's fishdam. Some time before the 1939 war KABUNDULI, as N.A. of the area, was given permission by the Boma to have a fishdam in the higher reaches of the Luweya River,[1] a privilege that he still maintains. This dam is built every year by PASSO but one bank (or both) of the Luweya on the site of the dam seem to 'belong' to KABILA. That is why in any one week KABILA is said to receive one day's catch, whilst KABUNDULI has another day, and PASSO has five days. The tribute to KABILA is disputed by THULA who claims that he is the real 'Owner of the land' because it was he (that is, some ancestral THULA) who 'helped' KABILA with some land.

It is also said that 'Owners of the land' can still demand a tribute from a person who cuts a large tree for making a canoe on his land. But on the other hand it is also said that 'Owners of the land' often do not get this tribute because a man who cuts a tree for a canoe must pay a timber royalty to the Boma and he reckons that that cancels out his tribute to the 'Owner of the land': Why should a man have to pay tribute twice for the same tree? Here again, I never recorded an actual case.

There are indications that some at least of these old, and on the whole inconsequential, claims to 'own the land' may have an indirect bearing on the present in so far as they influence political alignments. Or it may be that present political conflict is expressed in terms of 'owning the land'. These are, however, merely indications, and I lack sufficient evidence to argue this point in greater detail.

In the early 1930's many claims of 'Owners of the land' became

[1] To conserve the fish in this river, it is a Boma rule that no person shall build a fishdam without its permission. As far as I am aware PASSO's is the only legitimate dam in the Luweya.

U

the subject of legal disputes in the courts. This was a result of the new Administrative policy of Indirect Rule which came into force in 1933 although it had been announced previously. The Tonga understood that this meant that those who could prove, to the satisfaction of the Boma, their claims to traditional headmanships, would receive official recognition and a place in the new Administrative system as chiefs.[1] This seems to have been the last time that these archaic claims assumed any public, legal significance.[2]

A basic theme in the histories of all Tonga headmen is the attempt to answer the question: Who was where first and thus 'owned' the land, and who received or begged what land from whom? We saw that the answer to this question has at present little significance in the day-to-day life of the Tonga but it resumed some of its original importance *vis-à-vis* the Administration when it came to establishing the antiquity and seniority of titles in order to qualify for a position in the Administrative system. Traditional seniority and 'Owner of the land' histories received a boost from Indirect Rule, even though the Administration does not in fact use traditional seniority as the sole criterion in selecting a relatively small number of Administrative Headmen from among the many village headmen.[3]

Land Rights of Individuals and Villages

According to Tonga histories one way of acquiring land was as compensation or *chisoka* payment from the husband of one's *mbumba* (uterine kinswoman) at her death. We saw that MAKA-LAMBA is supposed to have received Chinyafwa as *chisoka* land from KAMISA.[4] Another method of acquisition was, according to these stories, 'begging for land' (*kuphempa maru*); naturally 'begging' stories are always told by the donating group, as in the case of KAJULA and GURU. Similarly KABUNDULI says that he was in the area first with his followers, and that the Kapunda Banda people came later and 'begged' him and his kinsmen for land. The ver-

[1] Historical seniority and status have continued significance for Tonga headmen since they believe that the Boma makes its appointments on those grounds: p. 307. See also van Velsen (1961).

[2] Many of these cases reached the Magistrate on appeal and were recorded. Although these records would obviously be of great historical and political interest, I have not been able to trace them and it seems that they have disappeared.   [3] Cf. pp. 301 *seq.*   [4] See p. 32.

sion most frequently told by the Kapunda Banda is, however, that they arrived in the area, did not find anybody by the lakeshore, and settled there; KABUNDULI and his people were living in the hills.

We saw an example of this process of what the one party may call 'begging for a place' and the other party may call 'just settling' within Greater Kamisa. There is no doubt that the people who now form the core of Mapalassie village came originally from Likoma Island at the beginning of this century. Initially they settled by the lake, near where the Kamanga people now live, but they soon moved a few hundred yards inland, to a site near a mango grove and just above the present site of KAMISA's village, which was apparently on roughly the same site then. This new site near the mango grove seems to have been uncultivated, like the bush and forest some hundred yards inland from Ziba's hamlet now. Although KAMISA still calls all the land of Greater Kamisa, including the hamlet sites and gardens of the Mapalassie people, KAMISA's land, he never says of the latter that they came 'begging', because KAMISA himself invited his Likoma kinsmen to join him: kinsmen do not beg, they are usually welcomed.[1] But whatever the formal, legal position may be, the land which the Mapalassie people used to cultivate and the land which they are cultivating now is to all intents and purposes Mapalassie land. None of KAMISA's people would build or hoe on this land without previous consent of the relevant person or persons at Mapalassie. There is no clear demarcation between Mapalassie land and KAMISA land. For instance Nyamwale (Map. C 10), who now lives virilocally at Chinyafwa with her husband Nyali (Chin. F 4) but whose home is at Mapalassie, has *masara* (fallow gardens) at Mapalassie which she can cultivate but she also cultivates a garden in KAMISA's village, which is her patrilocality. In addition she also has gardens of course in her husband's village. Similarly John (Map. C 11) says that he has a garden which he will cultivate as soon as he lives permanently at Mapalassie again and has a wife there;[2] this garden belonged originally to his father's mother Tamara (Map. B 7) and lies in KAMISA's area. I also saw other Mapalassie women working in gardens in KAMISA's area. They

[1] This is not necessarily true in all circumstances as is illustrated by the friction between Ziba and Ndazakale.

[2] He was then working with me and moving about a good deal. His wife was living in her own village.

claimed that those gardens were theirs. It is possible that in fact they had them on loan. Although it was often difficult to observe who controlled what, one thing was clear: I did not hear of a single dispute directly or indirectly concerned with land in KAMISA's village. The only apparent exception is Ndazakale being forced off Apakhati's land, but as I pointed out, this was in effect a political dispute.[1]

The basic principle then is that a person who has once cultivated a garden retains rights in that garden unless he cultivated it under a loan agreement. These rights include the right to give or lend the garden to another person. The owner of a garden can exercise these rights independently of the headman of his village or the village where the garden is situated. In other words possession of a garden in a particular village is not subject to residence in that village or allegiance to its headman. Finally, rights in land are not held corporately but individually; membership of a particular kin group does not automatically confer rights in land (as we saw in Ndazakale's case), although normally a kinsman (or for that matter any other person) who settles in a village is welcome and is given land, by one of the villagers, for a garden and a house, or he carves it out from the bush. And conversely, once a person has a garden in a village he retains rights in it even after he has left the village.

This can be seen from the evolution of Mapalassie as an independent village. When the Mapalassie people first settled in KAMISA's village they were not given a clearly demarcated block of land but received a general permission to build houses and cultivate gardens. They formed a group within the village through their common origin from Likoma; they built together and their gardens also tended to lie together. Eventually they also started their own graveyard where on one occasion they did not even want to bury one of KAMISA's villagers, although they later gave in. And now we see that the Mapalassie people form an independent village, in so far as Tonga villages can be said to be independent. One might say that the Mapalassie people seceded politically and took the land with them. I do not know whether this process took place without attempts on the part of KAMISA to stop this shift of allegiance and control over land. But in any case there is little he could have done to retain either the allegiance of

[1] See pp. 189–90 and 273.

the Mapalassie people or control over the land which they occupied and which originally was part of the village area of KAMISA. The constitutional authority of a headman is so tenuous and vague that the shift of allegiance could take place gradually and almost imperceptibly without any particular act indicating a definite break of the old political relationships. As for the land which the Mapalassie people took with them, it was the collection of individual rights in particular gardens rather than a corporate right in a certain stretch of land.

In such a situation in the old days, if KAMISA and his followers had wanted to retain control over the land occupied by the Mapalassie people, they could presumably have used force of arms if they felt strong enough. KAMISA might thus have retained control over the land but probably not over the people, who could have moved off elsewhere. It seems unlikely that he would have taken that course: even though the Mapalassie people had withdrawn their allegiance there might still have been an alliance between the two villages, with Mapalassie manpower still available to KAMISA for purposes of war or trade. Likewise in the present situation, the Mapalassie people still recognize KAMISA as a senior kinsman, which is illustrated by the fact that it was KAMISA who acted as the outside impartial arbitrator in the Mapalassie-Bandawe dispute after Meya's death. And, in a sense, KAMISA has even now not lost the manpower of Mapalassie; they are still on his Book. The composition of KAMISA's Administrative village follows closely the traditional political and social alignment: his census contains the people of Mapalassie and Kamanga, both offshoots from KAMISA, and Chinyafwa's people who also have a link with KAMISA who long ago married MAKALAMBA's *mbumba* (uterine kinswoman).[1]

I mentioned that Nyali of Chinyafwa told a few squatters to move off his land in order to avoid just such a situation as I have

[1] Administrative villages do not always follow so neatly traditional alignments—for example CHASOLE who is included in MUWANGA's census (p. 224)—but often they do. There are even cases of break-away villages which have moved off to another locality but whose members stay on the census roll of the parent village instead of enrolling with the nearest Administrative village. It so happens that my best data on village splits concern villages which have broken away politically but not geographically. I have also recorded cases in which political separation involved geographical separation (like the move of Amuziteni's descendants at Mzenga—see p. 61).

described for Mapalassie. It should be noted that Nyali was dealing with only two houses, whilst the Mapalassie people arrived from Likoma and settled in KAMISA's village with probably at least six families and soon afterwards numbered about a dozen families. Moreover the two groups were soon linked through the marriage of Tamara and Golo (see p. 176). There were, however, no such links between the squatters and the Chinyafwa people.

The ultimate sanction on which people who want to remove somebody from their land or out of the village can rely, is fear of sorcery. This is a powerful sanction whose efficacy is not restricted to particular categories of people; for instance it does not only operate among, say, certain categories of kinsmen or, conversely, only outside those categories. But it is considered to operate only against individuals or very small groups, and not against large groups. Thus it would have had no effect upon a group as large as the Mapalassie people, assuming that KAMISA had wanted to get rid of them.

Definition of Rights in Land

Rights in land are clearest when they concern land which is under cultivation. A person has the exclusive use of his land for either building or cultivating purposes; in the latter case he has exclusive rights in the crops. The owner of fallow gardens (*masara*) still retains the exclusive rights of building and cultivating, though he can also maintain his rights in the grass (for thatching) and trees which grow on them; whether he wants to maintain his rights seems to depend on the general availability of these natural products in the area. In any case these rights do not seem a ready source of conflict, at least I never recorded any disputes on this point. Theoretically rights in *masara* are vested in the owner and his heir in perpetuity. But in practice such land often seems to re-enter after some time the category of virgin land whose natural products and potentialities as a building site or garden land are available to any resident of the village within whose area it lies, or perhaps even to all comers.[1]

[1] There are no definite rules as to the period after which rights in *masara* lapse. My impression is that in practice it is unlikely to be less than a generation. Rights in *masara* are not invalidated if the holder moves to another village.

My information on the general rules governing rights in land is largely based on general statements from Tonga which I elicited through direct questioning and on stories of particular events which I did not witness, such as Nyali's story

PLATE 6. A seine net is being hauled ashore. Everybody on the beach has joined in to hold the bottom of the net down to prevent fish from escaping

I have pointed out already that rights regarding uncultivated land are rather nebulous except, of course, when they concern fallow land (*masara*) whose owner's rights are still effective. The practice seems to be that uncultivated land can be used by anybody or, if the land lies within a village area, by any resident of the village. He or she then, as the first occupier, acquires the normal rights of ownership which I have just outlined. Wild produce on uncultivated land which is not clearly *masara* can be gathered by anybody: firewood, poles for house building, bark for ropes, grass, mushrooms and so forth. Game can be caught anywhere by anybody, even on cultivated land.

Some villages, or rather, individuals in some villages, which are situated by or near a stream have *madimba* (riverside gardens). The rights in these and other kinds of gardens (e.g. millet and rice gardens) are the same as the rights in the ubiquitous cassava garden which I described above.

Riverbanks do not form a separate category: they are merely part of cultivated or uncultivated land in general. The same applies to the lakeshore; this is part of the area with which one village or another is associated. Theoretically only the residents of the particular village have a right to fish on their stretch of the lakeshore whilst members of other villages must ask the headman's permission first and should give a tribute of fish in return. In practice the procedure is different although the effect is the same. I have witnessed occasions on which persons of another village came to fish with their seine net without first asking the local headman's permission. The strangers generally come with one or two canoes manned by about six men who bring their own seine net. But the operation of this net requires at least two dozen men to drag it ashore. Their numbers are made up by local men, from several villages, who are always available because they naturally expect some fish as a reward; and fish is never so abundant that people would not welcome such an opportunity. The strangers never let the locals down in that respect, although the latter generally complain that the strangers are not generous enough. If the strangers were to depart without leaving any part

---

about the squatters on his land. Since rights in land (particularly in uncultivated land) were very rarely the subject of argument, in court or village, I did not have much opportunity either to discover the details (if any) of these rules or to test their validity or practical significance.

of their catch behind, the locals could do little, for it would be too late: their labour would already have been given. But the strangers are not likely to do this because that would spoil their chances for the future; if they were to come back to the same place they would not find any volunteers or, if they brought their own complete crew, the locals would make it impossible for them to fish, for the seine net (*mukwao wa passe*) can only be operated from the shore. Strangers do not always give the headman fish if he has not actually helped in the operation as an individual; he, too, cannot force them to give him tribute. And unless his grievance against the strangers is shared by his villagers so that they can make a common front against the strangers if and when they come back, the headman cannot prevent his people from co-operating with the same strangers in the future. After all, the villagers benefit from the strangers' net.

An analysis of the rules and practice of land-holding in Tonga society emphasizes what I have tried to show in other aspects of Tonga society: the individualistic character of this society and the diffusion of power.

The Village: its Identity

I will first describe the respects in which a village can be said to be a corporate unit. I will then examine intra-village and inter-village relationships and activities in order to see how strong the corporate identity of a village is in relation to other similar units and to the Tonga tribe at large.

In contrast to hamlets, a village has a name and a title for the headmanship. These names persist through time: the name of the village may persist even after it has been moved to another site where generally another name is adopted. In any case the village is often not referred to by its own name but by the headman's title, or by the name of an area containing several other villages. The title of a headman is treated as persisting through time, even if the time is not very long. But there are also villages whose founder-headman is still alive and whose name has not yet become a title, as in the case of Mussa of Mapalassie.

Theoretically the members of a village are matrilaterally or patrilaterally related to each other and to the village,[1] and the headman is supposed to be the senior member of the most senior

[1] See also pp. 185 *seq*.

matrilineage in the village. Hence marriage discussions, which are ostensibly a kinship and not a village matter, are conducted in the name of the headman (see p. 180). We noticed in 'Meya's Death' that Nyalongwe's matrikin from Bandawe came as emissaries from MLENGA MZOMA and CHIMBANO, two headmen near Bandawe ('Meya's Death', para 29). From the same case it was also clear that, in spite of internal factions, the people of Mapalassie put up a united front *vis-à-vis* the outsiders from Bandawe. We found that rival claimants for a headmanship may agree about its title but disagree about the incumbent's right to assume that title. Thus if Mussa had been the established title for the headman at Mapalassie, the Mzake group would not necessarily have contested the validity of the title but only Ziba's right to succeed to it. On the other hand, we also noted (e.g. p. 210) that a succession dispute may be about the incumbency of the headmanship as well as about the title itself.

The corporate identity of the Mapalassie people (at least *vis-à-vis* the Bandawe emissaries) was also emphasized by the fact that the dispute was arbitrated by KAMISA, an outsider. The explanation of this apparent paradox is that just because the Mapalassie people, including the headman, acted corporately against Nyalongwe's matrikin from Bandawe, Mussa himself was too much involved to be expected to arbitrate with even a semblance of impartiality. In situations like this it is often an outside headman who arbitrates.

Another fact which points to the corporate identity of a local group of people as against other similar groups is the possession of a separate graveyard. Indeed this was my ultimate criterion in deciding whether the Mapalassie and Kamanga people form separate villages within the wider grouping of Greater Kamisa, or whether, perhaps, the whole of Greater Kamisa should be considered as one village, *viz.* KAMISA's village.

The Village as a Loose Confederation of Hamlets

Despite these factors pointing to the corporate identity of the village, other aspects of village life often make it difficult to perceive any corporate unity. For instance, a village is not distinguished by corporate economic interests. We saw that land is not corporately controlled: rights in cultivated or regenerating fields are vested in individuals and their heirs. And as for unoccupied land, it is more correct to say that a village is associated with a particular area rather than that it corporately owns or controls that land; for one thing, the rights in unoccupied land are too nebulous to provide firm control over it.

Hoeing, fishing and other work parties are not necessarily restricted to members of one village; indeed economic co-operation is rarely so restricted and usually includes kinsmen from other villages. Thus, in general, participation in activities in a village is not restricted to members of the village concerned but involves members of other villages. I mentioned the case of Ndazakale's younger brother's death in Durban and the division of his estate, which involved people from three villages: the dead man's relatives in his father's village; his married sister who lives virilocally elsewhere; and his matrikin at Mapalassie (p. 190). The same applies to funerals and subsequent discussions: the lyke-wake, washing and burying the corpse and the 'shaving' are neither of purely local nor of purely kinship concern.[1] This is clear from 'Meya's Death'.

It is possible that in the old days a village used to be held responsible for the acts of one of its members. But this is not so today. A person who has to find money for the payment of damages or court fines is just as likely to ask for financial help from a kinsman outside the village or abroad as from a fellow villager. Indeed, in the preceding chapters I have tried to show the importance of both local and kinship ties and the cross-cutting tendencies of these two sets of relationships. If there is any predominance at all of one set over the other, it might be argued that kinship ties are more important than local ties.

Whereas hamlets are physical units which are generally clearly demarcated on the ground, villages are social and political units which are on the whole not clearly delimited as spatial units. A village is a loose confederation of hamlets—so loose that it is not immediately clear which hamlets form a village. For instance, when I first arrived at Mapalassie it was quite evident that the hamlets of Greater Kamisa formed at least *one* village. But after some months it became clear that in a vague sort of way there were social and political subdivisions within this large collection of hamlets, and that the cohesion within these subdivisions was greater than the cohesion between the subdivisions.

[1] Cf. pp. 56, 109.

I will consider some of the factors which unite and divide the villages within Greater Kamisa and which tend to blur the political and social alignments. The villages of Greater Kamisa (i.e. Mapalassie, KAMISA proper at Mulombwa and the people of Kamanga) all acknowledge their ultimate genealogical relationship with KAMISA. This superficial unity is seemingly confirmed by the fact that they are one Administrative village with KAMISA as Administrative Headman. On the other hand, the Chinyafwa men are also on KAMISA's Book but they are clearly not part of KAMISA's village. Another fact which seems to suggest that Mapalassie and Mulombwa are one village is that the men share one net-shelter by the lake; Mulombwa borders on the lake but Mapalassie does not. On the other hand the same net-shelter is also used by the Chinyafwa men (whose village does not border on the lake either) whilst the Kamanga men have their own shelter; only Chiwato (Kam. C 12) occasionally joins the men by KAMISA's shelter but the other Kamanga men usually keep to their own.

KAMISA still talks as if his own village, Mapalassie, and Kamanga are one village. Remember his opening words in 'Meya's Death' in which he pointed out to the emissaries from Bandawe: 'You have arrived in KAMISA's village—not at . . . [and then followed the names of some neighbouring headmen not belonging to Greater Kamisa] . . . This is the country (*charu*) of KAMISA' (para. 25). But in the course of my stay the subdivisions within Greater Kamisa became clearer. There was the fact that although all the kin groups claim some kinship link with KAMISA, there are nevertheless three distinct groups: the founders of Mapalassie who all came from Likoma Island; the Kamanga people who claim patrilateral ties with MANKHAMBIRA and KANGOMA;[1] and KAMISA himself. As for Mtomba in his solitary and comparatively secluded hamlet, I have included him in the village plan of Mulombwa because some say that Mtomba's father (and thus Mtomba, himself, too) was KAMISA's slave. The father is said to have killed somebody in his own village (somewhere north of Nkata Bay and perhaps outside Tongaland) and to have come to KAMISA for protection; KAMISA paid the compensation for Mtomba's crime. At

---

[1] These are two headmen (MANKHAMBIRA holds the Administrative appointment of N.A.) who live a few miles south of KAMISA, at and near Sanga. See 'KAMISA's History', p. 204 above; and also van Velsen (1959*a*), p. 5.

Mapalassie, however, they told me that Donald (Map. B 13) gave some of his own garden to Mtomba. Whatever the facts may be, Mtomba clearly does not count politically either at Mapalassie or Mulombwa. Even socially his presence in the village is barely noticeable partly due to the fact that his hamlet is somewhat set apart whilst Mtomba himself rarely partakes in activities outside his own hamlet.

Nyamwale (Map. C 10 and Chin. F 5) once told me: 'Long ago KAMISA had many houses and there was only one graveyard but now there are three.' The first part of her remark, referring to the past, accords with KAMISA's claim and my own first impression: that Greater Kamisa is one village. But her second observation reflects the present-day reality. Mulombwa has its own graveyard which, so I was told, until a few years ago also served for the kin groups which to-day form Kamanga village, which now has its own graveyard. It is possible that for some time after their arrival from Likoma, Mapalassie people were also buried in KAMISA's graveyard at Mulombwa but Mapalassie now has its own burial ground. This must be comparatively old because as far as I can make out all the people who are said to have come from Likoma and who are now dead seem to be buried at Mapalassie.[1] Those buried at Mapalassie include Tamara (Map. B 7) who married into KAMISA's village[2] and who is considered at Mapalassie, at least by the Mzake group, a pivotal figure since she is said to be the eldest daughter of Mzake.

I mentioned before (p. 115) that villages are reluctant to bury in their graveyard someone from another village. At Mapalassie I was told that when one of Chimuti's (Mul. B 24) wives at Mulombwa died of leprosy some years ago, the Mapalassie people were asked to allow her to be buried in their leper graveyard since the KAMISA leper graveyard had disappeared in the lake.[3] Apparently Mussa was at first reluctant to give his permission since she was

---

[1] Possibly there were others from Likoma who are buried in KAMISA's graveyard and are not remembered or at least not talked about *because* they are buried at KAMISA's. The mention of this fact would be a reminder that the Mapalassie people have not always formed an independent village.

[2] See p. 176. Note that she was not buried at KAMISA's.

[3] There is a small leper graveyard at Mapalassie, a hundred yards or so away from their main graveyard. But I have counted these two as one graveyard, and so by implication did Nyamwale when she mentioned three graveyards although strictly speaking there are four in Greater Kamisa.

only a stranger unrelated to Mapalassie, but he gave in. This reluctance may be taken as a measure of the feeling of corporate independence on the part of Mapalassie. On the other hand when Chagowo's (Kam. C 5) 'brother's' [1] wife died in Kamanga village some years ago, also of leprosy, she was buried at Mapalassie without any difficulty apparently. The difference was, they told me at Mapalassie, that this woman was a relative (not from Mapalassie but from a village a few miles away) so that she was not a stranger but was buried 'on her own land' (*mu charu chaki*).

The importance which the respective villages of Greater Kamisa attach to separate graveyards, combined with the other corporate aspects of these three villages, justify my treating them as three distinct social, residential and political units. At the same time, however, it should be emphasized that the corporate identity and the role of the Tonga village are very vague. Manifold links between individual members of different villages cut across village boundaries and village loyalties. And it is only with this important qualification that one can talk about 'independent' villages in Tongaland. The dispute after Meya's death made it clear that Mapalassie is an independent village in a very limited sense. In spite of Mussa's attempt to act independently of Meya's matrikin from a village a morning's walk away, he eventually submitted to their questioning and people at Mapalassie considered it necessary and worth their while to appease those matrikin. Therefore, the Tonga village is a loose confederation of hamlets made up of extended family groups. And as in any confederation, in the village, too, much of the initiative and many decisions are left to the constituent parts, *viz.* individual villagers or small family groups, each with its own set of extra-village bonds.

Inter-village Groupings

Vague as the identity and the role of the village may be, its corporate identity is rather less ephemeral than that of the hamlet. Hence I have treated the village as the smallest political unit. On the other end of the scale, the largest unit is the Tonga tribe. It is doubtful whether one can call the Tonga tribe in its entirety a 'political' unit. There are no indications that the Tonga as a whole ever acted as a unit. In fact this is very unlikely in the light of the present tribal organization and of what is known of their past.

[1] Chagowo's 'brother' was actually his father's brother's son.

In the modern Administrative system, too, the Tonga are not administered as one unit. Tongaland is divided into a number of N.A. areas and the N.A.'s are responsible to the D.C. whose District contains several other tribal groups beside the Tonga. In the same way as the village lacks a clear identity but shows some degree of cohesion, so the Tonga tribe has an unmistakable identity: the Tonga are widely known as a tribe and the Tonga see themselves as a cultural unit different from non-Tonga. The ultimate cohesion of the Tonga is based upon intricate and overlapping networks of relationships between individuals.

Neither in the village nor in the tribe is cohesion achieved by any kind of hierarchical organization of interests, power or authority. Power and authority are acquired through skilful manipulation of personal relationships on a lateral level and not in a vertical, pyramidal power structure. No display of quasi-power on the part of Ziba (Map. C 3) and Mussa (Map. A 1) could prevent the Mzake group at Mapalassie and the matrikin at Bandawe from having their say in the dispute after Meya's death and re-affirming their respective claims as regards Nyalongwe's (Map. B 12) offspring at Mapalassie. And, paradoxically, it was the four Mzake's women and particularly Nyamwale (Map. C 10) who were instrumental in restoring the peace with Bandawe although in some respects they were Ziba's and Mussa's opponents at Mapalassie. By their skilful handling of the situation and by giving measured doses of support to both Ziba and the Bandawe emissaries, the four women managed to create an impression of unity and a common front at Mapalassie, at least *vis-à-vis* Bandawe. Thus Ziba's opponents at Mapalassie, i.e. the Mzake group, did not give the Bandawe emissaries a chance to exploit dissension at Mapalassie for their own ends, *viz.* to get Nyalongwe, with or without her offspring, back to her matrilocality at Bandawe (pp. 168 *seq.*).

Extra-village relationships are an important factor in tribal identity but they decrease village cohesion. Indeed the cohesion of the village is so vague at present that it is difficult to discern whether the village plays a role at all as a territorial political unit. However, Tonga stories and the literature refer to raids and skirmishes between Tonga villages.[1] It seems likely therefore that even if only for purposes of defence there had to be some terri-

[1] See e.g. Elmslie, p. 101; Jack, p. 244; and Livingstone (1921), p. 186.

torial organization beside the bond of diffuse kinship ties. The village had probably a clearer function in those days of armed conflicts than it has now. In fact there are indications that there were territorial groupings including several villages. During the Ngoni wars there were a few large stockaded villages (*malinga*, sing. *linga*) where people of many villages combined for defence against the Ngoni.[1] After the Ngoni menace was over, the inhabitants of the *malinga* spread themselves out again in separate villages but it seems that not all of them returned to their old sites. I do not know what influenced people's choice of *linga* or how a *linga* was organized.[2] This territorial co-operation within the stockades seems to have ceased with their dissolution; at any rate, there is at present no evidence anywhere of association or co-operation between villages which originates from erstwhile stockade association.

There are however some other, very loose associations between villages, or rather between village headmen; these groupings are smaller than those which assembled in the stockades. We saw that in a very informal way the villages of Greater Kamisa (i.e. KAMISA and its offshoots at Mapalassie and Kamanga) are more closely associated with one another than they are with other villages, even Chinyafwa. This association came out in the dispute after Meya's death when KAMISA acted as arbitrator.[3] And it is likely that if a similar situation arose in KAMISA's own village, Mussa or someone else from Mapalassie or Kamanga would arbitrate. The leaders of Mulombwa, Mapalassie and Kamanga villages consider themselves as of one family or 'house' of which KAMISA is the most senior. Headmen of the villages are similarly grouped into 'houses'. Headmen who belong to the same 'house' do not necessarily live as closely together as those of Greater Kamisa happen to do. The only situations in which I have seen this 'relationship' between headmen function are installation ceremonies and the occasional dispute; I will deal with these

[1] See van Velsen (1959*a*), p. 9.

[2] An interesting detail is that KABUNDULI and some of his kinsmen, who are now (and were probably then, too) political opponents of the Kapunda Banda, took shelter together with many Kapunda Banda in CHINYENTHA's stockade on the southern bank by the mouth of the Luweya River; CHINYENTHA is also a Kapunda Banda. KAMISA lived in MANKHAMBIRA's stockade.

[3] I do not know whether KAMISA had been called in especially for this purpose or whether it was taken for granted that he would arbitrate.

presently. Here again, it is likely that associations of related head-men, particularly when they lived together in the same neigh-bourhood, had greater importance and more use in the old days of warfare when villages banded together for purposes of defence or other activities (e.g. trade) which needed a more or less organ-ized and dependable source of manpower. At present, however, the political or other significance of such links between headmen is very slight and, in any case, is a matter of personal relationships between the headmen, that is, between the titles rather then be-tween their villages.[1]

In analysing the political relationships in Tonga society one cannot usefully apply Schapera's criteria for a 'tribe'[2] or his definition of 'political communities'.[3] This would seem to be due to the fact that he implicitly equates 'politics' with 'government'. The author compares the political systems of all tribal groups in South Africa, ranging from the Mpondo to the Bushmen. He concludes that all peoples can be divided into clearly definable 'political communities' each with its own territory and chief. Each community is independent in that 'it alone decides on mat-ters of local concern'.[4] Tonga local communities, however, are not so easily defined. The hamlet can hardly be called a com-munity. The village comes much closer to being a community. But the external influence of kinship ties of individual villagers is such that the village does not have unfettered control over its members and few matters are purely of local concern. This is particularly so with regard to the virilocal residents of a village

[1] Perhaps comparable to the personal relationships between European royalty which do not, at present, necessarily affect their peoples.

[2] Unfortunately Schapera (1956) does not clearly define the term 'tribe' nor does he seem to be consistent in its use. Although he states on p. 9 that 'it is . . . the band, and not the tribe, which constitutes what I have termed the political community', he appears to contradict this in another statement on the same page: 'But although usually referred to in the literature as a "tribe", they [the Bushmen "tribes"] are not united under a single government, nor do they all ever act together.' Here he seems to use the term 'tribe' in the sense of a corporate political unit or political community. Elsewhere, too, the author would appear to use the term with a connotation of 'corporate existence'. E.g.: 'Many other tribes, too, have disintegrated; the great majority, however, still retain corporate existence' (p. 10); likewise on p. 25. Cunnison (1959, pp. 60-1) has similar difficulties in extracting Schapera's precise meaning of the term 'tribe' and applying it to the Luapula situation.

[3] *Op. cit.*, p. 203.   [4] *Op. cit.*, p. 8.

(like Nyalongwe at Mapalassie[1]) and the patrilocal residents (like Nyalongwe's offspring). An association of headmen is not an association or community of villages but rather a matter of co-operation between the headmen concerned.

Finally, even the whole Tonga tribe is not a 'political community'. It never acts corporately (and has probably never done so in the past), it is not an autonomous group, and it has no single leader. Even in the modern Administrative system the Tonga are not administered as a separate unit. Moreover, there are no clear-cut demarcations between the Tonga and neighbouring tribes; the nearer one gets to the surrounding tribes the more difficult it becomes to determine whether one is dealing with a Tonga or, say, a Tumbuka, or a Tonga village or a Tumbuka village. And even near the centre of Tongaland one meets with individuals or groups of people who maintain relationships with non-Tonga— not only formal but effective social relationships. I mentioned (p. 68) how some inhabitants of Chinyafwa who felt dissatisfied went to live in their paternal country, Usiska. There is also Nyali who wants to secure the leadership at Chinyafwa for his own lineage and went to Deep Bay to fetch a pivotal kinswoman (p. 48). The girl had never lived in Tongaland and she spoke broken chiTonga, but once at Chinyafwa her status was that of any other Tonga. Similarly at Mapalassie where the Mzake people suffer from the absence of their authority-bearing men, they now pin their hopes on Albert who has just arrived from Likoma Island, his matrilocality (p. 151, n. 3).

Thus by Schapera's definition the Tonga are not divided into political communities.[2] And even the tribe is a cultural rather than

---

[1] Cf. 'Meya's Death'.

[2] Schapera limits his comparison to the peoples in South Africa, but it is difficult to accept the validity or indeed the usefulness of his comparative method since it seems to be based on the ethnographically fortuitous circumstance of the international boundaries of a modern state which was created not by the original inhabitants but by European immigrants. In support of his argument for this method of comparison the author quotes (1953, p. 361) the editors of *African Political Systems* who also advocate area comparisons. However, the latter's areas are not delimited by international boundaries but rather they are based on ethnic or cultural affinities. No such affinities would appear to exist between, say, the Mpondo and the Bushmen. Consequently, if the concept of the 'political community' can be used for comparative purposes between two such widely divergent social systems, it is difficult to see why its experimental use should not be extended to other peoples.

x

a political unit. But this does not exclude the fact that there are political relationships between Tonga individuals and groups, and that these relationships contribute to some political cohesion and to a feeling of identity. But permanent, structured groups, whether based on territorial or kinship ties, have traditionally no place in Tonga society. After living in this society for a while, I began to see it as a process of situational alignments of individuals or small groups; these groupings are on the whole characterized less by real continuity (as against formal or ideal continuity[1]) than by *ad hoc* loyalties. I have tried to present my analysis in this light because it was only in this way that I could understand the motivating forces in Tonga society and its cohesion.

Village Headmen: Past and Present Sources of Power

We have noted the ambiguous position of the headman and the absence of clear-cut norms of headmanship. The headman is not much more than the first among equals in the village and his position is essentially that of a leader with personal rather than constitutional authority.

One of the reasons for the nominal status of the headman is that he is not in a privileged position to exploit economic resources, such as natural resources or manpower. The main resources which are required for the Tonga subsistence economy, such as garden land, water, firewood and building materials, are all in relatively plentiful supply and their distribution is not controlled by headmen. As for control over manpower, there are at present no activities in Tongaland which require the large-scale exploitation of manpower in which the person who has manpower at his disposal has an advantage over a person who has not. Manpower is now at a premium in the industrial centres but not in Tongaland, which exports a good deal of this 'commodity'. Indeed, most economic activities above the level of the subsistence economy now take place outside Tongaland and well beyond the control of the headmen or, for that matter, anybody in Tongaland.

There are reasons to assume that this has not always been so, and that in the past, in the pre-Administration and perhaps even in the early Administration days, headmanship had greater economic and political significance. In the days of Ngoni raids or

---

[1] See Chapter V, section on succession to titles.

Tonga inter-village fights,[1] control over manpower was important for purposes of defence, and the headman who could offer safe living conditions presumably would attract more followers than a weak headman. But manpower could also be exploited for other purposes, *viz.* trade, which was not unconnected with defence. It seems (from stories I heard about the past) that a headman who through personal qualities and other factors was capable of organizing trading expeditions, would require warriors for the defence of his caravan, whilst the prospects of trade goods would attract followers.

Trade seems to have consisted of ivory and slaves which were exported to the east. This merchandise came from the west, probably as far west as the Luwangwa valley or beyond, from what is now Northern Rhodesia. There are stories which point to contact between Tonga and Bisa[2] but it is not known whether this contact with and acquisition of slaves from the Bisa were direct or through the Ngoni. Judging by the presence in Tonga villages of people who seem to be slaves of Ngoni origin, the Tonga must also have acquired slaves in Ngoniland either by exchange or through capture; there are references in the literature to Tonga raids into Ngoniland.[3] The Tonga traders took their merchandise to *entrepôts* on the north-eastern shores of the lake[4] and on Likoma Island or to Arab trading centres, where they met with Arab traders or at least with traders representing coastal Arab interests. There are no indications that Arab traders had regular, direct contacts with Tongaland itself, nor that Tonga traders regularly reached the Arab trading posts on the East Coast. The Tonga traders exchanged their trade goods for cloth, guns and gunpowder; according to some stories slaves, too, were brought back from across the lake, particularly from Likoma, but the mechanics of this export *and* import of slaves are not at all clear.

[1] It seems that inter-village strife could lead to Ngoni raids; at least Elmslie refers to Ngoni bands being led by members of attacked Tonga villages who wanted to revenge some wrong (cf. Elmslie, p. 98). See also van Velsen (1959*a*), pp. 8–10.

[2] Cf. the reputed Bisa origin of Siddely's mother at Chinyafwa, p. 135.

[3] Cf. van Velsen (1959*b*), p. 11.

[4] The Tonga refer to that direction as Mbwani; it is now part of Tanganyika Territory. It is interesting to note that Mbwani in Yao means East Coast; private communication from Professor Mitchell.

Among the headmen of whom I have any knowledge, most of those who are now of any stature are known from legend and/or the literature to have been traders and/or war-leaders. And, not altogether fortuitously, these headmen are now leaders of large villages, or rather, conglomerations of villages, and they hold Administrative offices. I will call these leading headmen 'chiefs'. I must emphasize, however, that they were not the superiors of other headmen in a formal political hierarchy. Several of these chiefs[1] of the last century have now been given recognition by the Administration and are in the formal Administrative hierarchy the superiors of other headmen of lower Administrative rank. But outside the Administrative context the other headmen and the Tonga in general do not recognize this ranking. In the same way that a headman is *primus inter pares* in the village but may have additional personal authority or power derived from other sources, so, too, a chief held sway over a number of other headmen by reason of greater prestige and influence rather than constitutional authority. I mentioned that in fact (although not in theory) the Tonga definition of the 'dominant lineage' in the village is essentially empirical: a particular lineage is the dominant lineage *because* the incumbent of the headmanship belongs to that lineage (p. 188). Similarly my use of the word 'chief' is strictly empirical and a convenient short-cut phrase to indicate the distinction, past and present, between headmen with exceptional prestige, power, and authority over several villages, and on the other hand the average headman who is and was a leader of a small group of followers. The Tonga have only one word, *fumu*, for headman whatever his influence and authority.

I will briefly sketch the histories and relationships to the Administration, since its establishment in the area, of the following influential headmen who fall within my category of 'chiefs': MLENGA MZOMA, KABUNDULI, NGOMBO, MKUMBIRA, MANKHAMBIRA, KANGOMA, GURU, CHINYENTHA.[2] This list of chiefly headmen is not exhaustive. Historical data are lacking and I did not visit

[1] Here, again, I am not referring to the incumbents but to the titles or positions themselves.

[2] For a more detailed historical account of these titles and their role in the Administrative system, see van Velsen (1959a, 1959b and 1961). Murray (1932, Chapter V) provides a useful historical survey of the Administration in the Protectorate as a whole.

and/or collect information on all headmen, so I do not know who all the chiefly headmen were in the past. Nor do I know which of the present minor titles may have been of greater importance in the past or whether important and influential titles of the past have disappeared. Finally I do not know the history of all those headmen who are now leaders of large villages or who are influential in other respects. However, the histories of the following traditionally important titles give an indication of their position *vis-à-vis* the Administrative system and the way the headmen themselves view their respective positions.

The first Administrator in the then West Nyasa—now Nkata Bay—District arrived in 1897 and set up his H.Q. at Nkata Bay. In the early days of the Administration in Nyasaland there was no clearly defined policy regulating its formal relationship to the political systems of the tribes administered. In this period 'the police were used for all purposes'.[1] The Administration would also appear to have had informal contacts with Tonga headmen and to have made unofficial use of agencies of the tribal political system. The relationship between the Administration and the headmen in the District was put on a formal footing in 1917 with the appointment of seven Principal Headmen. Two of these belonged to, and were put in charge of, two small non-Tonga groups in the District. The five Tonga headmen appointed as Principal Headmen were: KABUNDULI, MANKHAMBIRA, MKUMBIRA, MLENGA MZOMA and GURU. The new ordinance was in no way intended 'to revivify or perpetuate government by native chiefs'[2] nor were appointments restricted to hereditary headmen. This was the theory but in fact hereditary status did play a role in selection.[3] After some minor changes the office of Principal Headman was abolished in 1933 with the introduction of 'Indirect Rule' which explicitly recognized hereditary status as a principle of selection for Administrative Headman. This was *in effect* still the position during the period of my stay in Tongaland.

KABUNDULI's claim to the traditional leadership of the Phiri faction in the hills seems to be undisputed despite the fact that

---

[1] Murray (1932), p. 126. These 'police' were functionaries who would nowadays be called Boma Messengers. I have given a short history of the Administration among the Tonga in van Velsen (1961).

[2] *Annual Report 1912–13*, quoted in Murray (1932), pp. 130–1.

[3] Cf. *Native Affairs Report, 1931*, p. 3.

during the period of the Ngoni raids—some time in the third quarter of the last century—KABUNDULI sought refuge in CHIN-YENTHA's stockaded village by the lakeshore. His traditional political status may explain the selection of KABUNDULI for the Principal Headmanship in 1917. KABUNDULI has ever since held an important post in the Administrative structure; since the abolition of the post of Principal Headman in 1933 he has held the office of Native Authority.

Nearer to the lakeshore but still in the hills lives NGOMBO, another headman of considerable status. He derives his political status from the fact that he lives by the Luweya River where he controls the Chwandama Falls whose 'owner' he is. I heard some stories of fighting over the control of the Chwandama Falls so it is possible that NGOMBO has not always been the 'owner'; but the 'ownership' has been associated with NGOMBO for at least three generations. It is also possible that the title NGOMBO has been in different matrilineages, but this does not alter the fact that it is the NGOMBO-ship which controls the falls. The importance of the falls lies in the fact that normally every year, from July until about September, great numbers of *sanjika* (*barilius microcephalus*, a trout-like fish) run up the Luweya to their spawning grounds.[1] Whilst negotiating the falls they are scooped up with nets. These catches, amounting to many thousands per season, are of great economic value. The *sanjika* provides one of the favourite relishes —fit to offer an honoured visitor—and many people from other areas come to Chwandama to buy or barter *sanjika*.

NGOMBO allows a few other headmen or individuals to fish in return for a proportion of the catch or as a kinship or political obligation.[2] NGOMBO's historical prestige has never been 're-warded' by the Administration with a Principal Headman or Native Authority appointment; NGOMBO has never been more than an Administrative Headman. Although NGOMBO feels some-what aggrieved by this lack of Administrative recognition, at the same time he is aware of and derives satisfaction from the fact that

[1] Cf. Hoole, p. 36.

[2] *Sanjika* are also found in other rivers where they are caught in traps or nets, but no other river has such an advantageous catching place as the Chwandama Falls where several thousand may be caught on a good day. NGOMBO 'owns' only the fishing in the falls; elsewhere in the Luweya fishing is open to others. Cf. PASSO's fishdam, p. 275.

he alone among Tonga headmen still derives his importance from the same source as in the past and is thus much less dependent on Administrative recognition for his economic and political status.

Another chief with great traditional political prestige is MAN-KHAMBIRA. He has always had and still has a large following in the coastal area north of the Luweya River although his leadership has been challenged by the neighbouring KANGOMA. Both titles are widely and prominently associated with the historical struggle against the Ngoni and with external trade in pre-British days. They used to have important trading contacts with Likoma Island in the past,[1] whilst according to one source KANGOMA went as far as the Arab settlements of Lindi and Kilwa on the eastern seaboard.[2] MANKHAMBIRA gained Administrative recognition in 1917 when he was appointed Principal Headman; at present he holds the post of Native Authority. Similar recognition did not come KANGOMA's way: he is only an Administrative Headman. This could probably be explained by the Administrative impracticability of having two headmen of equal senior Administrative rank in close proximity.

The political status of the four chiefs I have just discussed is firmly rooted in the pre-British period. MLENGA MZOMA, near the mission station at Bandawe on the lakeshore, was also a notable chief in the past and he is also said to have been a successful trader. But with the arrival of the British on the scene he acquired another economic and political asset: he became a firm supporter of the mission and was in turn supported by the mission. This gave him a certain advantage over other, neighbouring, chiefs, including his kinsman in the same 'house', CHIWEYO, who would appear to be structurally (*viz.* within the 'house') senior to MLENGA MZOMA.[3] It was, however, the latter who was made Principal Headman in 1917 and thus became CHIWEYO's superior in the Administrative structure. With the abolition of the office of Principal Headman, CHIWEYO and MLENGA MZOMA became Administratively equals again, i.e. both were now Administrative

---

[1] MANKHAMBIRA's trading activities are referred to in Foreign Office file 84/1702: from Consul Goodrich, No. 1, Africa, 19 February, 1885. I am grateful to Dr. Shepperson who drew my attention to this reference. See also p. 205 above and van Velsen (1959*a* and *b*).

[2] *Aurora*, IV, 20 (April), 1900, p. 21.

[3] For their rivalry see also pp. 220 and 302.

Headmen. CHIWEYO and his supporters continued their campaign to get the Boma to recognize his traditional seniority through a senior Administrative appointment. MLENGA MZOMA is one of the leaders of the Kapunda Banda faction who claim the lakeshore area south of the Luweya River as theirs and hold that their opponents, the Phiri and their leader KABUNDULI, belong to the hills where KABUNDULI holds the appointment of Native Authority.[1] Around 1950 the question came up of the appointment of an N.A. for the lakeshore area south of the Luweya. There were several contenders within the Kapunda Banda faction. Among them were: MLENGA MZOMA, CHIWEYO, GURU and CHINYENTHA. Another contender was KABUNDULI who had the support of the Phiri living by the lake (including the influential Milton[2]) and others. A vote was held among the Administrative Headmen of the area. Due to the split in the Kapunda Banda camp KABUNDULI won and thus his N.A. area now covers both the hills and the southern lakeshore. Whilst MLENGA MZOMA and other Kapunda Banda headmen continued to oppose KAPUNDULI's appointment over 'their' area, others including CHIWEYO decided to co-operate with their new N.A. CHIWEYO's attitude, the reverse of that of his fellow Kapunda Banda, is explained by his opposition to MLENGA MZOMA and his desire for a senior Administrative office. This ambition made co-operation with the Administration in general and with the N.A. in particular a necessity. His ambitions were satisfied in 1951 when he was made a subordinate Native Authority under KABUNDULI. As his Administrative senior he could now demand co-operation from MLENGA MZOMA or else the latter might lose his Book. This co-operation, e.g. attendance at CHIWEYO's court, was not forthcoming and when I left the area MLENGA MZOMA's position as Administrative Headman had become very precarious indeed.[3]

Another well-known Kapunda Banda headman was CHINYENTHA, renowned as a war leader in the struggle against the Ngoni invaders. He had a fortified village by the mouth of the Luweya on its southern bank (where he still lives) which became

---

[1] See also van Velsen (1959a and b) *passim*.

[2] See also pp. 223–5 and 245–6.

[3] I understand that MLENGA MZOMA was deprived of his Book and thus of his Administrative Headmanship by CHIWEYO but was later reinstated. I have not been able to confirm this.

the refuge of many people who had left their own villages but later returned to them. Among those who lived in CHINYENTHA's stockaded village were GURU, KABUNDULI, possibly NGOMBO, and many others from the lakeshore area between the Luweya and Kawiya rivers. On these grounds CHINYENTHA claims the historical right to leadership in this area. But in 1917 the appointment of Principal Headman for this area went to GURU and not to CHINYENTHA and thus the latter became Administratively subordinate to GURU, a situation which CHINYENTHA considered a reversal of their historical political relationship. As in the case of NGOMBO, it has always been a grievance with CHINYENTHA that his historical political rights have never been recognized (as he sees it) by the Boma; he has never been more than an Administrative Headman. CHINYENTHA considers GURU as something of an interloper and impostor who with some 'clever' talk impressed the Boma with his own importance and was made a Principal Headman over the head of CHINYENTHA. He would say: 'Who is this GURU? He was only one of CHINYENTHA's underlings in his *linga* [stockade].'[1] As a result of the change in the Administrative system in 1933, GURU became an Administrative Headman and thus CHINYENTHA's equal again. GURU still resents this 'demotion' (see pp. 221 and 307).

However, GURU would appear to have been a headman of some substance, too, who traded in ivory and had regular contact with Likoma Island. And soon after the turn of the century GURU's village, by the mouth of the Kawiya on the northern bank, was apparently sufficiently significant to attract what must have been one of the first Indian stores in the District. Moreover, in 1902 the District H.Q. moved from Nkata Bay to Chinteche, immediately south of the Kawiya. It is clear that GURU owed his appointment as Principal Headman at least in part to his close proximity to and influence at the Boma. This influence may not necessarily have been directly with the Resident (it probably was not) but rather indirectly through key figures among the Resident's staff. It is known that GURU and his villagers had established close ties of friendship with Boma personnel (many of whom were Yao and other foreigners), for instance through beer, food and other

[1] Following Tonga usage, I am identifying the successive incumbents of a title. In 1917 neither of the present incumbents had succeeded to his title but both speak about past events as if they were personal experience.

kinds of solace for lone soldiers. And a sergeant of the Boma *askari* married a kinswoman of GURU.

It would seem that MKUMBIRA, at Nkata Bay, also owed his Principal Headmanship largely to his close contact with the Boma when it was originally established. Even after the District H.Q. moved to Chinteche the Boma still maintained a foothold at Nkata Bay, maintaining a resthouse and a small force of *askari*. I have no evidence that in pre-British days MKUMBIRA was a war leader or a substantial trader, or had acquired political prestige in another way. At present MKUMBIRA is an N.A. subordinate to MANKHAMBIRA.

What all these headmen have in common, with the possible exception of MKUMBIRA,[1] is that they were all prominent leaders before the establishment of the Administration. Although this was never the expressed policy, it is clear that one of the factors in the Boma's selection of headmen for Administrative office was historical status combined with administrative convenience. Clearly, the Administration could not confer 'recognition' on all historically prominent headmen. Consequently, from the Tonga point of view there was an element of chance in the selection for Administrative posts—an element which ambitious headmen have never tired of exploiting whilst at the same time building up their historical reputation.

Control of, or at least access to, sources of power and wealth, are not only the reward of leadership but also a prerequisite to make headmanship effective rather than nominal. In the past a headman with wealth could buy slaves and thus add to his followers. Or he could receive fugitives (e.g. people who had committed a crime in their own village) if he felt strong enough to face retaliation from the wronged party or alternatively wealthy enough to compensate the latter; this was another way of acquiring bondmen.[2] Goods obtained in trade were used to reward followers and a large following would improve the chances of defence and success in trade. This in turn would attract more followers, as evidenced in particular by the large fortified villages (*malinga*) of such chiefs as MANKHAMBIRA, CHINYENTHA and others

---

[1] I do not have much information about the history of this title and the area as I never made intensive enquiries there.

[2] Cf. KAMISA redeeming Mtomba: p. 285. The same is also reported for KANGOMA: *Aurora, loc. cit.*

PLATE 7. (*a*) Chief MLENGA MZOMA standing in front of the church of the Bandawe Mission on its original site in his village, Chituka. Here, too, David Livingstone first set foot in Tongaland

(*b*) Two canoes have just returned with their catch of *usipa* (a kind of white-bait). Women, children sent by their mothers, and others wait with their basins, handkerchiefs and cloths for their share

where a considerable proportion of the Tonga seems to have been concentrated in the period of the Ngoni raids.

It seems clear that such activities as trade and defence, or warfare in general, required the organization and co-operation of units larger than small independent villages. MANKHAMBIRA and other *malinga* chiefs claim that they were the 'owners' of those stockaded villages and that the inhabitants were their subordinates. It would seem, however, that these large villages were in fact conglomerations of small independent villages, each with its own headman, which had all submitted themselves to the effective leadership of chiefs like MANKHAMBIRA. This leadership of groups of villages in a *linga* was presumably not only politically and economically conditioned but also a matter of personal authority and skilful manipulation of relationships.

The formal norm of headmanship is still preserved; but much of the traditional content of headmanship and the necessity for some co-ordinating leadership within the village or a group of villages have largely disappeared. However, it is clear from the dispute after Meya's death that there was still a role for KAMISA, the senior headman of a group of villages, as pacifier assisting the various groups at Mapalassie to present, when necessary, a united front despite internal differences.

When warfare and trade disappeared as factors conducive to intra-village and inter-village integration, other factors with somewhat similar effects had entered Tongaland: the mission and the Administration. As I have described elsewhere,[1] although MLENGA MZOMA may have been an important headman before the Livingstonia Mission settled near him at Bandawe in 1881, his political stature certainly increased through his early association with the mission and his present importance largely derives from it. This association became a new source of political and economic power for MLENGA MZOMA. There were jobs going on the mission station and the mission distributed soap, cloth, beads and other goods. It also provided education. All these goods and services were available for MLENGA MZOMA's followers and he seems to have attracted a good many. These benefits were, naturally, also available for members of other villages but the co-operation between the mission and MLENGA MZOMA seems to have been closer than that between it and other headmen. And it is more than a

[1] van Velsen (1959b), p. 10.

coincidence that it was MLENGA MZOMA who in 1917 was appointed Principal Headman over an area which contained headmen who were traditionally his senior (for instance CHIWEYO) and who had also been leaders of large *malinga* (stockaded villages).

Presently I will show to what extent the Administration offers political or economic incentives—perquisites—which on the one hand make headmanship something worth striving for and give leadership some content, and which on the other hand also provide the headman with the means to attract followers. In other words, I will deal with the factors which may encourage people to seek and submit themselves to the leadership of a headman, and which may thus contribute to intra-village and inter-village cohesion. We shall find that, at present, these incentives are not many. Inter-village warfare has gone and there are no activities at present which make organized, territorial, co-operation a necessity. Acquisition of wealth, too, no longer requires local co-operation since the main source of wealth now lies in the distant towns where Tonga work and no longer in trade caravans.

Traditional Symbols of Political Prestige and their Present Significance

The factors mentioned above have weakened the position of the headman. His office has been stripped of whatever *raison d'être* and content it may have had in the past and in most cases it is now a nominal rather than a substantial office. There is not much evidence about the specific attributes of headmanship in the past. According to tradition there were three customs which were associated with the position of headman, or at least some headmen, and which distinguished them from other people. These customs were: the girls' puberty ceremonies (*nkholi*); a system of arbitration (*ndauza*); and the installation of a headman (*kuvwalika ufumu*) with a red robe (*nkhazu*).

We came across the girls' puberty ceremony in the story of the KAMISA title (p. 206) where Edward of Mapalassie was offered the right to hold his own *nkholi*. The headman who had this right seems to have had a special place (enclosure?) with a hut near his own hut where girls of his village (or group of villages) were secluded during their first menstruation.[1] At their 'coming out'

---

[1] Read (1956, p. 47) reports a similar tradition for the Chewa who adjoin the Tonga in the south: 'Among the Chewa a man could "become a chief" by acquiring . . . the right to own a site . . . on which female initiation rites were

there would be several days of feasting. According to some informants girls went through these rites in groups, but other informants told me that they were performed as and when a girl reached puberty. The latter practice would indicate that the number of people under one *nkholi* headman was small, or there would have been perennial feasting. But the general tenor of the traditions about *nkholi* is that there were fewer *nkholi* sites than villages and that it was only the 'really big headmen' (i.e. those I call the chiefs) who organized these puberty ceremonies on their own *nkholi* sites. The right to hold the *nkholi* rites seems to have been jealously guarded as a mark of superiority over those headmen who did not have the right or the site; their girl initiands had to go to a headman who did have the right. There are stories about armed fights to protect and impose this right. For instance, when some ancestral KABUNDULI died, his sister's son was too young to succeed him and a kinsman from a junior 'house' acted as KABUNDULI and began to organize *nkholi* ceremonies. But when the young nephew had grown up he assumed the KABUNDULI-ship himself and wanted also the title's privilege of the *nkholi*. The acting KABUNDULI, however, continued to organize the *nkholi* and this meant that he challenged the position of his senior kinsman. KABUNDULI proper made war upon the usurper and defeated him (with, so the story goes, the aid of Ngoni). It seems, then, that the *nkholi* rights used to be held by one headman in a group of villages and that this privilege depended on the headman's personal authority and power to enforce it. In other words, the importance and leadership of the *nkholi* headman seem to have been based upon actual control of this source and attribute of political power, in the same way that actual control of resources in matters of trade and defence was the basis of the position of the chiefly headman. There is no reason to assume that these headmen fell into different categories. Indeed, the initiation ceremonies and subsequent feasting may well have called for some munificence from the *nkholi* headman which he would probably be in a better position to bestow if he had been successful in trade. No evidence

---

carried out.' Mitchell (1956, pp. 95 *seq.*) describes the competition among Yao headmen to obtain and to preserve the right to hold initiation ceremonies. In the light of what evidence I have about Tonga initiation ceremonies in the past, Read's and Mitchell's descriptions give some idea of what may have been the situation among the Tonga.

now remains of *nkholi* sites; KAMISA's and others' claims of having had them cannot be verified. Nor are there any traces left of the *nkholi* ritual itself.[1]

Another ceremony associated with headmen is their installation[2] when they are given one or more red robes resembling Arab robes. We saw (p. 204) that KAMISA had an *nkhazu* which he lost but which was later replaced. I am quite certain, however, that he does not possess one at present. He is not exceptional in that respect because the majority of headmen do not possess red robes and have, in fact, never been ceremonially invested with either office or robe. Those who have robes never wear them in everyday life: the only ceremonial occasions on which I saw red robes worn were two installations and a meeting of the Provincial Council when KABUNDULI and MANKHAMBIRA[3] attended the official opening in their red robes.

It is not known how old this custom is nor what the position was in the past as regards installation and red robe. It may be assumed that it was only the substantial headmen, those with prestige, who were installed; and these were probably more or less the same headmen who had established some reputation in trade and/or warfare and/or female initiation rites. In any case, at present the average small headman, even if he has the Book, succeeds to his title without any ceremony. Of the five villages which are the main subject of this analysis, in Greater Kamisa only KAMISA himself claims to have a robe. I very much doubt whether he ever had one or has one now, particularly since there is no evidence of a ceremonial installation of any of the people who are said to have had the KAMISA title after CHACHAMARA (p. 205). It seems certain that the successor to Mussa at Mapalassie will not be ceremonially installed. Nyali does not claim robe or installation for any of the MAKALAMBAS at Chinyafwa (p. 211). The late KAMBAWE at Mzenga had a robe and he was probably ceremonially installed too.

[1] The word *chikholi* (betrothal payment, see p. 80) may have some connection with *nkholi*, but Tonga informants could not explain it.

[2] *Kuvwalika*, to be invested, lit. to be dressed, *viz.* with the *nkhazu* or red robe. Cf. the Swahili word *kanzu*, i.e. robe: *Swahili Dictionary*, p. 13. The red robe would appear to play a role among the Tonga which is very similar to that of the scarlet headband among the Yao: see Mitchell (1956), pp. 91 *et passim*.

[3] These two headmen are members of the Provincial Council in their capacity as Native Authorities.

I attended two installation ceremonies and heard of a few more. The headmen concerned all had one thing in common: they all held titles which in one way or another were titles with prestige derived either from the past or the present, or from both. In short they all belonged to the category of what I have called the 'chief'. CHINYENTHA, who was installed in 1955, has the title of one of the famous Tonga war-leaders. The present CHINYENTHA still carries this prestige, although he has held no Administrative appointment more important than that of Administrative Headman. Other headmen who are said to possess a robe (and who may also have been ceremonially installed) have prestige which rests upon their present status, in some cases combined with historical prestige. To this category belong the following headmen, all of whom have been mentioned before: the late KAMBAWE[1]; GURU[2]; CHISAMBI[3]; CHIWEYO[4]; MALANDA[5]; KABUNDULI[6]; and MANKHAMBIRA.[7]

I cannot, unfortunately, give detailed historical or numerical information on the subject of robes and installation because there are some unavoidable gaps in my historical and present-day data. The occasions for verifying conflicting stories are few: installations and the use of robes are rare. But these, often conflicting, claims regarding robes and installation, and the antiquity which headmen tend to ascribe to them, are in themselves interesting problems. The answer seems to lie in the attempts of ambitious headmen to replace the sources from which prominence and prestige were derived in the past, by sources from which they can derive prominence and prestige in the different conditions of the present. And nowadays it is the Administrative system which confirms traditional political prestige by conferring new political authority; the latter, in turn, is likely to be given historical respectability through association with robe, girls' puberty ceremonies and other traditional aspects of political power.

We may assume that there was some connection between, on the one hand, the position of the chiefly headmen with their prestige in war and trade and, on the other hand, such symbols of political status as initiation sites and the installation with the red robe. But I do not want to suggest that the Tonga distinguished

[1] See p. 195.   [2] See pp. 221, 274, 299.
[3] See Case 19, p. 247.   [4] See pp. 220, 297.
[5] See p. 249.   [6] See pp. 295 *et passim*.   [7] See pp. 204, 297.

formally between two ranks of headmen of whom only the chiefs had, by definition, the right to hold initiation ceremonies or to be installed with the red robe. They did not have this distinction in the past (i.e. from the latter half of the last century onwards) nor do they have it at present. I merely want to point out the actual difference between two categories of headmen: the chiefs with legendary and/or contemporary prestige, and the smaller, relatively unknown headmen leading small groups of followers. As far as I am aware, the titles of the latter category are not associated either with girls' initiation sites or installation. But it seems that these two privileges became the outward symbols of the chiefs who had established their leadership over a group of neighbouring villages. Some of these chiefs, like CHINYENTHA, NGOMBO or MLENGA MZOMA (who once was a Principal Headman), do not occupy at present a position of political superiority in the Administrative structure, but among the Tonga their legendary prestige is still recognized. For instance, all three are leaders, with support from other headmen, in the opposition of the Kapunda Banda faction to the appointment of KABUNDULI as N.A. over the lakeshore area south of the Luweya River. Their prominent leadership in the past is still symbolized by the red robe and the installation ceremony, which are the only symbols of prestige that have survived.

Headmen with legendary prestige (that is, the chiefs of the past) like MANKHAMBIRA and KABUNDULI, who now also hold important Administrative positions, always make a point of stressing that they do not owe their present prestige or their robe to their Administrative appointment. But the symbols of robe and installation have also been adopted by those headmen who, as far as can be ascertained, have not inherited a position of legendary prestige but whose present political prominence is based upon a position in the Administrative system. These 'new men', like MALANDA who is now a sub-N.A., also like to claim legendary prestige to make their present political status seem a natural consequence[1] of historical importance. This point of view can be explained partly by reference to Tonga values. We noticed that ideally claims to titles or sites are based upon historical conti-

---

[1] We have already noted that headmen tend to regard Administrative appointments as nothing more than proper recognition of an ancient right: see p. 253.

nuity, although there is little continuity in fact. Another factor is the present system of Administration which employs traditional tribal agencies. Thus in Tonga eyes the main qualification for an Administrative appointment is evidence of historical leadership, although in reality the Administration's selection is not exclusively guided by traditional seniority. In the main, however, the Administration tries to make its own system of Administrative authority coincide with what it perceives to be the traditional authority structure. In its search for suitable political leaders, who can be incorporated into the Administrative system, it proceeds on the erroneous assumption that the Tonga tribe has traditionally been governed by hierarchically organized chiefs.[1] And periodically officials ask individuals or meetings of headmen for historical information about traditional seniority. The Administration's selection must necessarily have an element of arbitrariness. There are a great number of headmen of equal status but there is only a limited number of Administrative appointments; there is a general lack of clear attributes of traditional office;[2] and the Administration can, therefore, only select a few out of the many potential candidates for Administrative offices. These selected few have then to be fitted into some Administrative hierarchial order, which conflicts with the traditional structural equality of Tonga headmen.

GURU's claims (p. 299) are a striking example of the projection of modern prestige into the past. There is little doubt of the fact that GURU's ancestors came from a place a few miles inland. During the Ngoni wars they fled to CHINYENTHA's stockaded village (*linga*) by the mouth of the Luweya River. After the end of the wars GURU settled on his present site by the Kawiya River. In the pre-Administration period GURU never was the effective leader or chief of all the headmen between the Luweya and Kapeska Rivers. There were several other leading headmen in this area, amongst others CHINYENTHA[3] himself, whilst KAJULA (p. 274) and CHIS-AMBI probably settled in this area before GURU. But in 1917 GURU

---

[1] As one official once expressed it: 'No tribe can exist without chiefs.' Cf. also pp. 76-7, 128.

[2] As I have pointed out, even the installation and the robe of the comparatively few headmen who have these symbols, are not easily observable.

[3] CHINYENTHA's ancestral home is not on his present site either, but in the same area as GURU's; they are said to belong to the same 'house'.

Y

was appointed Principal Headman over this whole area so that CHINYENTHA and others became GURU's subordinates in the Administrative system. With the abolition of the position of Principal Headman in 1933,[1] the area was divided into smaller Administrative units under Administrative Headmen, and GURU lost his ascendancy over his erstwhile subordinates who then became his Administrative equals; they were all Administrative Headmen. GURU has never forgotten his previous Administrative seniority nor his subsequent demotion; he is now inclined to be non-co-operative towards the Administration.[2] He often complains: 'This whole area from the Luweya to the Kapeska was GURU's land. GURU was a really big chief. But then the Europeans came and they took away his power and now they treat me, GURU, as if I were the same as all the other headmen who used to be my subordinates'—with the clear implication that those headmen are really only upstarts.[3] In fact, of course, he owed his ascendancy to the Administration in the first place.

Village Headmen and Jurisdiction

In 'Meya's Death' we saw that KAMISA acted as arbitrator and conciliator. He was not a judge in the sense that he could give a verdict and, if necessary, back it up with sanctions. Although KAMISA could not apply sanctions, his arbitration was possible because he was supported by the parties at Mapalassie, including the four women of the Mzake group who were structurally opposed to Ziba. In the adultery case in GURU's village (p. 263), GURU was quite explicit about his role as conciliator; he said: 'We are all one[4] and we must settle this amicably for the sake of peace [in the village], otherwise we cannot live together.' Nor was GURU a judge with sanctions; he, too, could arbitrate only with the approval of the parties concerned. GURU, like other headmen who want to settle disputes in the village, has to compete with the courts which are sanctioned by the Administration, i.e. the courts

---

[1] It was the present GURU who at that time held the office of Principal Headman.

[2] I understand that after I left the area he even lost his Book and thus ceased to be an Administrative Headman too.

[3] See also van Velsen (1961), pp. 7–10.

[4] This means roughly: 'we are all one lot', or: 'we are all one family'. GURU's actual words were: '*Tose te weneko weneko pe.*' Cf. p. 43.

of the N.A.'s and the sub-N.A.'s. Although these courts are entirely staffed by Tonga and largely apply Tonga law and custom apart from some administrative and tax regulations, people refer to them as Boma courts because their power of jurisdiction and sanctions (*viz.* fines and imprisonment) are derived from the Boma and they are controlled by it. There may be advantages in taking a case to a Boma court rather than to a village headman without a court warrant because the latter's decision has weaker sanctions: the party who wins the case may not receive his due. On the other hand the disadvantages of a Boma court are that the rules of evidence tend to be stricter and, for the loser of the case, damages may be higher: there is also generally a court fine on top of the damages, whereas in a village court there are only damages.

In the adultery case quoted above (p. 263) the complainant, Dolas, threatened to take the case to a Native Authority court if GURU did not give her satisfaction, but she had good reason to keep the case in the village. The quality of her evidence was such that it might not have been acceptable in an outside court, as it was in the village, where the emphasis is more on conciliation than on the strict application of legal rules. The accused, too, had everything to gain from keeping the case in the village. If he had been found guilty in a Boma court, he would probably have been ordered to pay £3 damages and at least £1 fine. In this instance GURU told him to pay 5*s.* as a conciliation gift (*nyoli*[1]) and Dolas accepted this decision.

We saw (p. 198) the opposite happening at Mzenga, where there was no peace in the village; and the only leader there, Kamoti, who had been acting as headman for a long time, did not want to hear the case. Thus a judge or arbitrator in the village has to rely upon his own authority and upon the support of forces within the village, rather than upon constitutional sanctions.

The examples mentioned so far are of intra-village disputes. But I also recorded instances of cases, settled in the village, between people of different villages. On the whole, cases of this category are perhaps more likely to go to the Boma courts. If the parties do not live within the same village there are fewer pressures upon them to be accommodating for the sake of peace and to

---

[1] *Nyoli* literally means 'chicken'. A chicken is the standard gift to express respect, honour or a desire for good relations. Nowadays a *nyoli* gift is often money.

accept the headman's verdict. Moreover all cases involving payment of fines or damages are supposed to go to the Boma courts. And the N.A.'s and sub-N.A.'s, who hold the Administration's court warrants, are jealous of their rights. I recorded several instances of headmen (with or without Administrative recognition) who were either reprimanded or fined for settling disputes which should have gone to the Boma courts.

In spite of the risks involved, headmen do hear such cases and order payment of damages. For example, Rossie (Chin. E 9) of Chinyafwa one day told her mother that she had been raped by a boy from the nearby village of Samala. Siddely (Chin. D 6) went with her and her mother, Sowamo (Chin. E 9), to Samala and laid their complaint before the headman there.[1] The headman ordered the boy to pay £3 10s., the usual damages for seducing a spinster. The boy would have had to pay the same damages if this case had been heard in a Boma court but he would also have had to pay at least £1 court fine. The girl's party did not lose anything, except that they have no means of enforcing the payment of the damages—although damages awarded by Boma courts, too, are frequently not paid at all or only after a long delay. We have, thus, a situation in which headmen, except those with an official court warrant, are prohibited from settling certain cases, but on the other hand the stricter methods of the Boma courts enhance the attraction of headmen as arbitrators.

The Tonga say that in the old, pre-Administration, days there was a system of arbitration called *Ndauza*. The term is no longer used now.[2] According to the description which the Tonga generally give of this custom, a complainant seeking justice would go around neighbouring villages shouting '*ndauza*' until someone would offer to hear his case. This tradition, in its over-simplification, brings out the two salient features of jurisdiction among the Tonga (outside the Boma courts)—features which are observable at present and which were probably equally characteristic in the past. Firstly, disputes between members of the same village or of

[1] Note that it was Siddely who took this case up and thus acted as the girl's attorney, and not Nyali who is the headman at Chinyafwa. The father of Rossie was also informed and he may have been present at the discussion at Samala village, but I am not certain. I did not attend the hearing.

[2] I was not able to discover the derivation of *ndauza*; I never heard it used in any other context.

different villages may be settled by a third person who does not belong to the village of either litigant. 'Meya's Death' is one example and I have recorded and attended several others. Secondly, it brings out the essentially arbitral nature of Tonga jurisdiction; the arbitrator is supported not by constitutional power but rather by the political conditions and alignments prevalent at the time.

It is possible that a headman with a large and strong following, providing him with power and influence, would have been more frequently called upon to arbitrate than headmen without this prestige. It is certainly significant that, nowadays, popularity as an *ndauza* judge is often adduced as evidence of historical prestige. For instance, the supporters of CHIWEYO liked to tell (and wrote letters to that effect to the D.C. and the Secretariat of the Protectorate Government) how CHIWEYO's court used to be 'widely reputed throughout Tongaland as the only court that administered justice without any prejudice', and that his court used to attract 'many cases from other chiefs' areas'.

There are no reliable data available about *ndauza* nor have I found any records of cases settled in the villages before the advent of the Administration. It seems clear, however, that jurisdiction in a certain area or over a certain group of people was not the exclusive and constitutional right of any one person or headman. This, at least, is the position at present in the traditional political structure: that is, if we except the courts which have been instituted by the Administration. I have already mentioned that the headman has no control over the land of his village and that he has, in general, no access to or control over other economic resources.

This lack of jurisdiction is a further indication that constitutionally the office of headman is vague and of little political significance. But an individual leader who, through skilful manipulation of personal relationships, can command the loyalty of a large following can acquire great prestige and political influence. Headmanship, however, is not a prerequisite for a position of leadership and prestige. Sons of the village, too, can achieve it (e.g. Milton[1] and Kamoti[2])—but generally only through the manipulation of a headman's title. Such a title may also help to achieve a position in the Administrative system.

[1] See pp. 223, 245. [2] See pp. 195 *et passim*.

CHAPTER VII

CONCLUSIONS

I MENTIONED at the beginning how the Tonga have acquired a reputation of being difficult to handle, quarrelsome, factious, conceited and truculent, undisciplined, very individualistic, fond of intrigue and so forth. Indeed, one of the most striking features of Tonga society is the apparent lack of system in all fields of action. For instance, the formal norms relating to headmanship, to which the Tonga easily and frequently refer, lack sanctions and are often at variance with the realities of political influence and succession to titles. There are no easily recognizable centres of power and authority, and no clearly defined focal points of social relationships. Hence the impressions just mentioned. On the other hand my quotations also show that these same people were, and are frequently described as, a peaceful people living in a society marked by a lack of violence; such descriptions are supported by the court statistics in the Protectorate's annual reports.

Thus outsiders express two diametrically opposed views: anarchy *versus* orderliness. The explanation is that the observer, be he missionary, government official or anthropologist, is continually confronted by statements contradicted by other statements and by actual behaviour. And he does not have the assistance of even a few clearly discernible structural regularities as starting points in his search for order in this apparent chaos. The aim of this study is to contribute to the understanding of the paradox of this ordered anarchy.

In spite of the many contradictions between norm and practice, the lack of structure, and the ubiquitous factions and jealousies which overwhelm the observer, it is equally apparent that the people go about their business in peace and that there clearly is order, even although he cannot immediately discern the source of this order. This was a solid datum which became the starting point of my approach. It led me to attach great importance to seemingly trivial interactions between individuals and the different groups with which they aligned themselves in different situations. It was in this way that I began to understand the restraints to which individuals are subject. The events, arguments, minor actions and other details connected with Meya's death in particular gave some very important clues to the factors uniting the intensely individualistic Tonga whose 'mutual jealousies and ambitions' and 'incessant quarrelling' [1] and factiousness have often been taken as signs of disintegration.

Some salient features, then, of Tonga society are firstly the diffusion of authority and power; they are not concentrated in particular localities, or in particular structural positions or groups, but spread throughout the population in a great variety of groups. Many groups active in one situation or another are ephemeral. Alignments are continually shifting. Groups thus emerge and disappear with ease because of the predominance of flexible relationships between individuals or very small groups. A person's status is not determined exclusively or even primarily through permanent membership of a corporate group. [2] The Tonga political scene, then, presents a picture of a large number of 'pressure groups', pressing upon one another rather than upon structural authority. Secondly, overall social and political cohesion is achieved through a wide network of relationships between individuals and small kin groups rather than through a structured ranking and co-ordination of clearly defined and permanent local or kinship units. At the same time I have emphasized the fact that it is the kinship group focalized on a particular locality which becomes most effective as a corporate unit.

Thirdly, there is the very noticeable lack of definition and formality which mark most Tonga institutions such as marriage, attorney-ship, headmanship, land-holding; even kinship

---

[1] Livingstone (1921), p. 186.

[2] Fortes (1953) uses the concept of 'corporation sole' for this kind of society. 'The corporate descent group is not found . . . Instead their political organization is based on what Maine called the corporation sole [p. 29] . . . a system of inter-connected politico-legal statuses . . . and not a collection of people organized in self-perpetuating descent groups . . . the generalization throughout a whole society of the notion of the corporation sole as tied to descent but not to a corporate group' (p. 37). He contrasts the society based on the corporation sole with societies such as the Nuer where 'the individual has no legal or political status except as a member of a lineage' (p. 26). If these two types represent the extremes of a continuum, then the Tonga are clearly very much nearer to the 'corporation sole' type.

terminology is very flexible.[1] And the formal norms which govern these aspects of Tonga society have built into them what one might call 'escape clauses' which in practice facilitate, and can justify, evasion of the formal rules of behaviour. It should be noted, however, that these departures from formal norms in actual situations of real life are not in open defiance of these norms, which would invalidate or weaken them, but are rather in terms of generally accepted values and thus appear to support these values. This is particularly clear with regard to the norms relating to headmanship and succession to titles. There are provisions for acting executives (or 'walkers') which make it difficult to distinguish between legitimists and usurpers of titles and authority. Thus rivals for power and office all operate within the same normative system and ultimately strengthen it.[2] Although the exceptions to the rules seemed sometimes more frequent than the compliance, I have tried to analyse both the 'myth' and the 'reality' as two component parts of one conceptual framework.

Similarly, we found that whereas in theory (i.e. in terms of formal norms) marriage among the Tonga is clearly definable, in practice it is very difficult to establish whether a particular union is a 'legal' marriage or not. I have made a distinction between formal and informal marriages. But this distinction is of secondary importance from the point of view of the *relationships* and *links* which are created by a marriage of either kind and which are of primary importance.[3] Thus the distinction affects the size and the direction of the debts involved but not the individuals and the kin groups linked by these marital debts. In this respect the effect of marriage, whether formal or informal, is the same: in either case it establishes relationships which form the basis of the links which give the Tonga their identity as a tribe. Marital debts reinforce not only relationships directly connected with the marriage concerned, but also other relationships and claims, e.g. political claims. And a claim for marital debts is frequently allowed to lie

---

[1] See p. 143, n. 1.

[2] Cf. Gluckman's argument that 'rebellions, so far from destroying the established social order, work so that they even support this order', contrasting them with revolutions which aim at establishing a new social order: see e.g. Gluckman (1955a), p. 28, and (1940), pp. 42–4.

[3] I have indicated that the Tonga view of marriage is essentially empirical. For a similar conception of marriage see Smith (1956) on marriage in British Guiana.

dormant until it can be utilized to support another, not directly marital claim, which is less tangible and less easy to define.[1] The essential indefiniteness of Tonga marriage, in practice, gives rise to many disputes and thus public discussion.

Turner's study of the Ndembu describes how their ritual serves, among other things, to re-enact and emphasize crucial relationships and values.[2] Amongst the Tonga there are practically no ritual or similar formal occasions: instead quarrels, arguments and disputes achieve the same effect. I have rarely attended any meeting for whatever purpose, be it a funeral, wedding or *malepenga* dance, which did not produce at least one dispute. I submit that it is in these (often petty) disputes such as arose in 'Meya's Death', that the Tonga re-affirm and re-analyse the relationships within the village or larger unit, which in the aggregate provide the foundation for their feeling of identity. In the literature it is generally the negative, disruptive effects of disputes and quarrels which are emphasized to the exclusion of their possible positive effects. These latter effects may be found in any society. My point is not merely that they are present in Tonga society but rather that they are a dominant feature. Colson makes a similar observation regarding the Makah Indians: 'The constant criticism, gossip, and back-biting is a reassertion of these values [*viz.* those governing the behaviour of members of the group] which today can be expressed in no other way' [3] and 'Bickering and home-truths can be a uniting bond in a small society'.[4] Marshall reports a custom of the Kung Bushmen, the 'talk', which might be similarly interpreted. Although the author sees the 'talk' as an 'outlet of tension and anxiety',[5] it would appear from the case she gives that it is also a means of publicly analysing and re-asserting personal relationships and values.

Thus the frequency of disputes in Tonga society is far from being an indication of social disintegration; indeed these disputes

---

[1] Cf. Colson (1951*a*, p. 23) for a similar role of cattle among the Plateau Tonga: '. . . the Tonga are interested in ownership of cattle rather than in immediate possession . . . The Tonga are eager to establish a claim to cattle but are prepared to let the claim lie dormant for a long period of years. The claim remains good, and can be inherited . . .'

[2] Turner (1957). For a similar argument see Sommerfelt (1958), pp. 186, 190 *et passim*.

[3] Colson (1953*b*), p. 229.

[4] *Op. cit.*, p. 231.   [5] Marshall (1961), p. 234.

would appear to be an integral part of this kind of society. The disputatious character of this society may be related to the marked absence of serious crime. The Tonga consider physical force fruitless and the least efficient means of attaining one's ends, but they are skilled manipulators of people and situations; indeed, I have always found it most revealing to watch them exercising their skill during and in between their ubiquitous disputes and arguments. There seems little doubt that this skill is an important contributory factor to the influence which Tonga individuals have had (and still have) in political movements and trade unionism not only in Nyasaland but also in the whole of Central Africa and even South Africa, in spite of their relatively small numbers.[1]

I have drawn attention to the fact that as a result of the permanent relationships established by marital debts different individuals in the same village or even in the same hamlet are generally linked to different kin groups outside the village. This emerged particularly clearly in the case of 'Meya's Death'; this case brought out not only the presence but also the importance of such extra-village links. Their importance lies in the fact that they can be used to support the claims of individuals or a minority group within a village who are in a weak position and who fear that their interests may be ignored by the majority. At the same time these links must detract from the independence, the corporate exclusiveness of the village and from the authority of the headman within the village. In addition, neither the succession to headmanship nor the office itself are clearly defined in practice, nor are they supported by sanctions or other attributes which give the office content. Therefore, it would perhaps have been more correct to speak about the 'leadership' of the village rather than the 'headmanship'. However, this might have led to some confusion since the Tonga do recognize the position of headman however ill-defined this position may be. I have therefore continued to use the term 'headman'.

I have considered Tonga political leadership diachronically through varying political and economic circumstances. In pre-

---

[1] The Tonga number 50,000 out of a total population in Nyasaland of about 2,500,000, in Central Africa of about 8,000,000 and in South Africa of some 13,000,000. The Tonga, however, occupy a disproportionately large number of leadership positions.

Administration days Tonga leaders competed for certain perquisites or prizes, the possession of which was perhaps not so
much a constitutional right inherent in the headmanship, but
rather the result of shrewd manipulation of personal relationships.
These prizes included: trade outside Tongaland; strong defence
position against attacks from Ngoni and perhaps other Tonga;
acquisition of slaves as dependants and, less importantly, as
merchandise; and female initiation rights.

Under present economic and political conditions these perquisites and prizes have largely disappeared and with them the necessity for organization and leadership on a territorial basis, so that
extra-village links have now a greater chance to assert themselves
against local loyalties. Whilst in the old days headmen had opportunities for controlling economic resources with which to support
their political authority, at present the main sources of wealth lie
outside Tongaland, beyond the control of headmen and within
the reach of any individual; access to this wealth does not require
organization or leadership. Tongaland itself is still largely unde-
veloped and now offers few political prizes. The Administration
has created a few positions for which headmen can compete, but
the Administrative system and the Tonga political system each
represent political and economic values which are to a great
extent fundamentally different.

The Administration represents a hierarchical structure of political authority and is based upon an industrial cash economy. The
Tonga political system on the other hand represents a strongly
egalitarian society in which political relationships are horizon-
tally rather than vertically organized, and where power and
authority are diffused. Moreover, although Tongaland is now well
within the orbit of the industrial economy where large numbers
of individual Tonga men earn their living for longer or shorter
periods in their adult lives, these men together with those still
resident in Tongaland continue to find their ultimate security in
the tribal subsistence economy where labour has very little cash
value and land has none.

However, cutting across the differences of aims and methods of
the two systems of government, there are a few basic aims which
they have in common. In many respects both groups, Administration and Tonga (both at home and abroad), work actively
towards retaining what each considers the traditional tribal

institutions.[1] Furthermore, both groups are vitally interested in the maintenance of law and order, and in spite of the different premises from which they proceed, and the different ways whereby they want to achieve this aim, this common interest has been a very real incentive for reaching a compromise. In the present study I was only able to touch on this question. Elsewhere[2] I have given a more detailed account of the inter-action between these two systems of government, Tonga and British, and the resulting compromises.

[1] Cf. Bledisloe (p. 33): 'The present [1937] policy recognizes the principle of tribal unity, and the importance of rebuilding the tribal organization on its old constitutional basis . . .' See also p. 295 above. Regarding the role of labour migrants in the preservation of tribal values, see van Velsen (1960).

[2] van Velsen (1961).

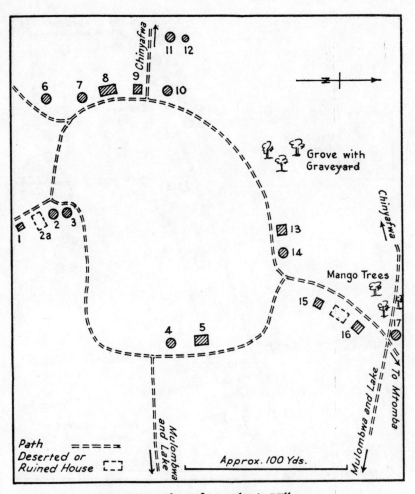

MAP IV.—Plan of Mapalassie Village

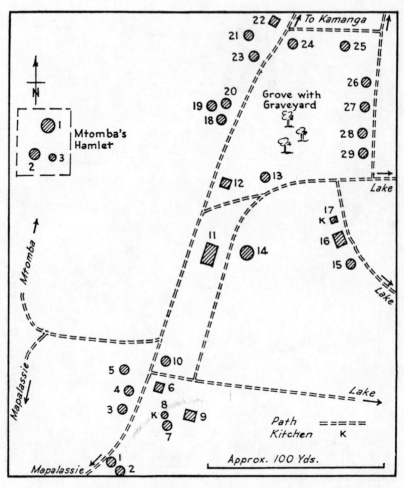

MAP V.—Plan of Mulombwa Village and Mtomba's Hamlet

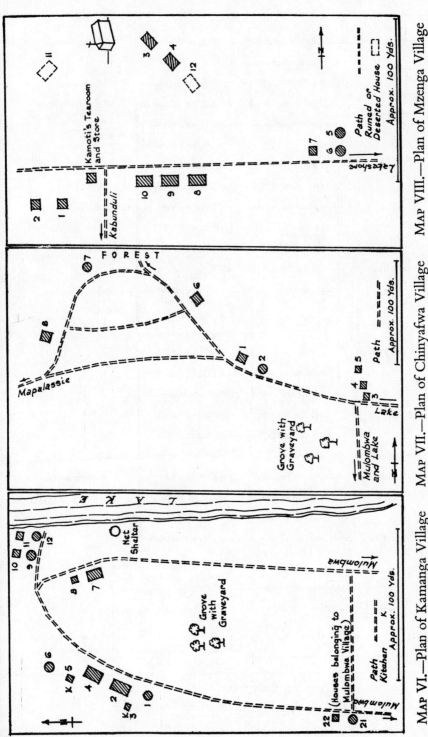

Map VI.—Plan of Kamanga Village Map VII.—Plan of Chinyafwa Village Map VIII.—Plan of Mzenga Village

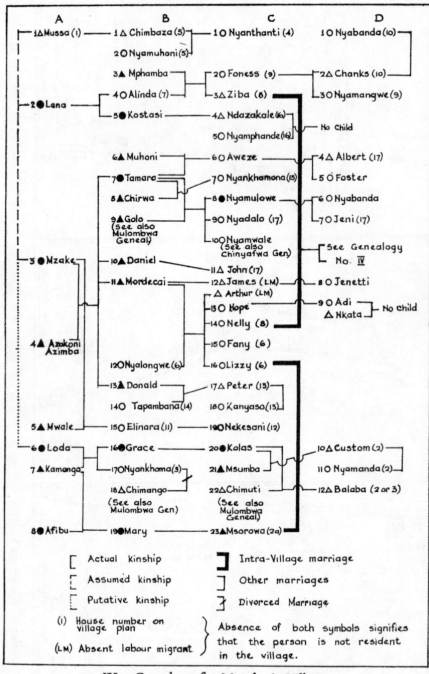

IX.—Genealogy for Mapalassie Village
See also Genealogy IV illustrating 'Meya's Death'

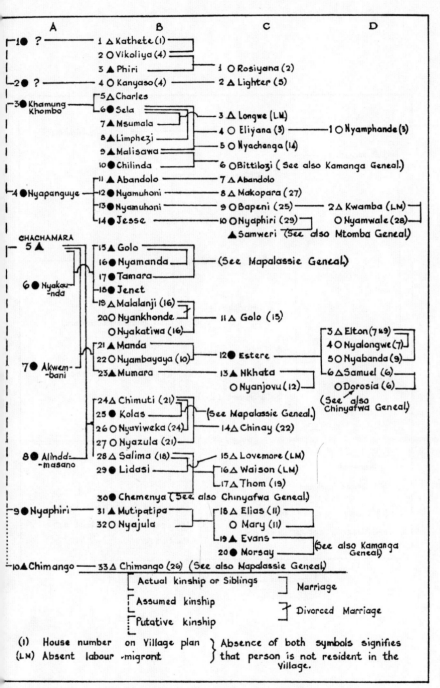

X.—Genealogy for Mulombwa Village

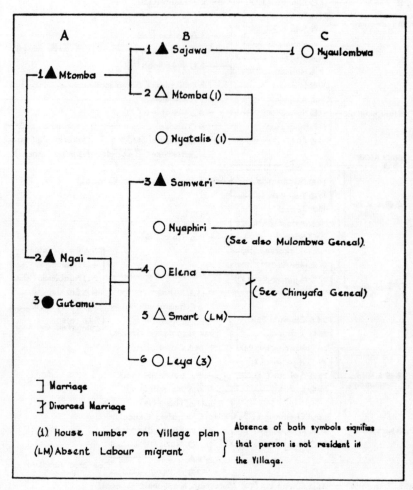

XI.—Genealogy for Mtomba's Hamlet

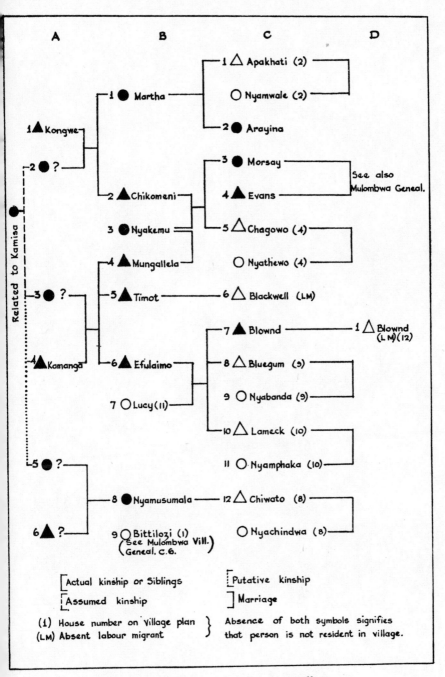

XII.—Genealogy for Kamanga Village

BIBLIOGRAPHY

Works marked * bear directly on the Lakeside Tonga

*Annual Reports
Published by the Government Printer, Zomba:
Annual Report upon Native Affairs for the years 1931 and 1933.
Annual Report of the Provincial Commissioners for the years 1937 onwards.

*Census Reports
Published by the Government Printer, Zomba, 1932 and 1946 respectively:
Report on the Census of 1931 (compiled by the Superintendent of Census, J. C. Abrahams).
Report on the Census of 1945 (compiled by the Superintendent of Census, H. F. Bingham).

ABRAHAMS, J. C., see under Census Reports.
**Aurora, The,* IV, 20 (April), 1900, Livingstonia.
BAILEY, F. G. (1960), *Tribe, Caste and Nation,* Manchester University Press.
BARNES, J. A. (1947), 'The Collection of Genealogies', *Human Problems in British Central Africa,* Rhodes-Livingstone Journal, V, 48–55.
— (1954), *Politics in a Changing Society,* Oxford University Press, London. Now distributed by Manchester University Press.
— (1958), 'Social Anthropology in Theory and Practice: Inaugural Lecture at Sydney University', *Arts, the Proceedings of the Sydney University Arts Association,* I.
*BELL, R. D. (1938), *Report of the Commission Appointed to Enquire into the Financial Position and Further Development of Nyasaland* (Col. No. 152), H.M.S.O., London.
BINGHAM, H. F., see under Census Reports.
*BLEDISLOE (Chairman) (1939), *Rhodesia-Nyasaland Royal Commission, Report of the* (Cmd. 5949), H.M.S.O., London.
BOHANNAN, P. J. (1957), *Justice and Judgement among the Tiv,* Oxford University Press, London.
BUSIA, K. A. (1951), *The Position of the Chief,* Oxford University Press, London.
COLSON, E. (1951a), 'The Role of Cattle among the Plateau Tonga', *Human Problems in British Central Africa,* Rhodes-Livingstone Journal, XI, pp. 10–46. Also in Colson, *The Plateau Tonga, Social and Religious Studies,* Manchester University Press, 1962.
— (1951b), 'The Plateau Tonga of Northern Rhodesia', *Seven Tribes of British Central Africa* (Eds. E. Colson and M. Gluckman), Oxford University Press, London. 2nd edition, Manchester University Press, 1960.

327

COLSON, E. (1953a), 'Social Control and Vengeance in Plateau Tonga Society', *Africa*, XXIII, pp. 199–212. Also in Colson, *The Plateau Tonga, Social and Religious Studies*, Manchester University Press, 1962.

— (1953b), *The Makah Indians*, Manchester University Press.

CUNNISON, I. (1956), 'Perpetual Kinship: a Political Institution of the Luapula Peoples', *Human Problems of British Central Africa*, Rhodes-Livingstone Journal, XX, pp. 28–48.

— (1959), *The Luapula Peoples of Northern Rhodesia*, Manchester University Press.

*DEBENHAM, F. (1955), *Nyasaland*, H.M.S.O., London.

DEVONS, E. (1956), 'Myth and Reality', *The Listener*, May 8, British Broadcasting Corporation, London.

ECKSTEIN, H. (1960), *Pressure Group Politics*, Allen & Unwin, London.

ELMSLIE, W. A. (1899), *Among the Wild Ngoni*, Oliphant, Anderson & Ferrier, Edinburgh.

EPSTEIN, A. L. (1957), *Politics in an Urban African Community*, Manchester University Press.

EVANS-PRITCHARD, E. E. (1940a), *The Nuer*, Oxford University Press, London.

— (1940b), 'The Nuer of the Southern Sudan', *African Political Systems* (Eds. M. Fortes and E. E. Evans-Pritchard), Oxford University Press, London.

FORTES, M. (1938), 'Culture Contact as a Dynamic Process', *Methods of Study of Culture Contact in Africa*, International African Institute, Memorandum XV.

— (1940), 'The Political System of the Tallensi of the Northern Territories of the Gold Coast', *African Political Systems* (Eds. M. Fortes and E. E. Evans-Pritchard), Oxford University Press, London.

— (1945), *The Dynamics of Clanship among the Tallensi*, Oxford University Press, London.

— (1953), 'The Structure of Unilineal Descent Groups', *American Anthropologist*, 55, pp. 17–44.

GLUCKMAN, M. (1940), 'The Kingdom of the Zulu of South Africa,' *African Political Systems* (Eds. M. Fortes and E. E. Evans-Pritchard), Oxford University Press, London.

— (1951), 'The Lozi of Barotseland in North-Western Rhodesia', *Seven Tribes of British Central Africa* (Eds. E. Colson and M. Gluckman), Oxford University Press, London. 2nd edition, Manchester University Press, 1960.

— (1955a), *Custom and Conflict in Africa*, Basil Blackwell, Oxford.

— (1955b), *The Judicial Process among the Barotse of Northern Rhodesia*, Manchester University Press.

— (1961), 'Ethnographic Data in British Social Anthropology', *The Sociological Review*, IX, 1, New Series, pp. 5–17.

*GOODRICH, Letter, F.O. 84/1702, No. 1, Africa.

*HAILEY, Lord (1950), *Native Administration in the British African Territories*, Parts II and IV, H.M.S.O., London.

*Handbook of Nyasaland, The (1910), Wyman, London.

* HANNA, A. J. (1956), *The Beginnings of Nyasaland and North-Eastern Rhodesia, 1859-95*, Clarendon Press, Oxford.

*HOOLE, M. C. (1955), 'Notes on the Fishing and Allied Industries', *The Nyasaland Journal*, VIII, 1, pp. 25-39.

*JACK, J. W. (1901), *Daybreak in Livingstonia*, Oliphant, Anderson and Ferrier, Edinburgh.

*JOHNSON, W. P. (1924?), *My African Reminiscences, 1875-1895*, Universities Mission to Central Africa, London.

*LIVINGSTONE, David and Chas. (1865), *Narrative of an Expedition to the Zambesi and its Tributaries*, John Murray, London.

*LIVINGSTONE, W. P. (1921), *Laws of Livingstonia*, Hodder and Stoughton, London.

*MACALPINE, A. G. (1906), 'Tonga Religious Beliefs and Customs' *Journal of the Africa Society*, XVIII, pp. 188-9, 257-68.

MALINOWSKI, B. (1922), *Argonauts of the Western Pacific*, Routledge, London.

MARSHALL, L. (1961), 'Sharing, Talking, and Giving: Relief of Social Tensions among the Kung Bushmen', *Africa*, XXXI, 3, pp. 231-49.

MARWICK, M. G. (1952), 'The Social Context of Cewa Witch Beliefs', *Africa*, XXII, 2, pp. 120-35.

MITCHELL, J. C. (1954) (1956), *The Yao Village*, Manchester University Press.

— (1957), *The Kalela Dance*, Rhodes-Livingstone Paper, No. 27.

— (1960), *Tribalism and the Plural Society*, Oxford University Press, London.

*MURRAY, S. S. (1932), *A Handbook of Nyasaland*, Crown Agents for the Colonies, London.

P.C. *Report:* See under *Annual Reports.*

*PRYOR, J. W. (1938), *Report of the Agricultural Survey of the Five Most Northerly Districts of Nyasaland*, Government Printer, Zomba.

RADCLIFFE-BROWN, A. R. (1952), *Structure and Function in Primitive Society*, Cohen & West, London.

READ, M. (1956), *The Ngoni of Nyasaland*, Oxford University Press, London.

RICHARDS, A. I. (1939), *Land, Labour and Diet in Northern Rhodesia*, Oxford University Press, London.

— (1950), 'Variations in Family Structure among the Central Bantu', *African Systems of Kinship and Marriage* (Eds. A. R. Radcliffe-Brown and C. D. Forde), Oxford University Press, London.

SCHAPERA, I. (1938), 'Contact between European and Native in South Africa', *Methods of Study of Culture Contact in Africa*, International African Institute, Memorandum XV.

— (1953), 'Some Notes on Comparative Method in Social Anthropology', *American Anthropologist*, LV, pp. 353-61.

— (1956), *Government and Politics in Tribal Societies*, Watts, London.

SCOTT, D. C. (1892), *A Cyclopaedic Dictionary of the Mang'anja Language as spoken in British Central Africa*, Foreign Mission Committee, Church of Scotland, Edinburgh.

SMITH, R. T. (1956), *The Negro Family in British Guiana*, Routledge & Kegan Paul, London.

SOMMERFELT, A. (1958), *Politisk Kohesjon i et Statlost Samfunn: Tallensienne i Nordterritoriet av Gullkysten (Ghana)* (With summary in English: *Political Cohesion in a Stateless Society: The Tallensi of the Northern Territories of the Gold Coast (Ghana)*, Studies Honouring the Centennial of the Universitetets Etnografiske Museum, Oslo.

Swahili Dictionary (1939), *A Standard Swahili-English Dictionary* (under the direction of the late Frederick Johnson), Oxford University Press, London.

TEW, M. (1951), 'A Further Note on Funeral Friendship', *Africa*, XXI, 2, pp. 122–4.

TURNER, V. W. (1957), *Schism and Continuity in an African Society*, Manchester University Press.

TURNER, W. Y. (1952), *Tumbuka-Tonga-English Dictionary*, Hetherwick Press, Blantyre.

*VAN VELSEN, J. (1959*a*), 'Notes on the History of the Lakeside Tonga', *African Studies*, XVII, 3, pp. 105–17.

*— (1959*b*), 'The Missionary Factor among the Lakeside Tonga', *Human Problems in British Central Africa*, Rhodes-Livingstone Journal, XXVI, pp. 1–22.

*— (1960), 'Labor Migration as a Positive Factor in the Continuity of Tonga Tribal Society', *Economic Development and Cultural Change*, VIII, 3, pp. 265–78. Also in A. Southall (Ed.), *Social Change in Modern Africa*, O.U.P. for International African Institute, 1961.

*— (1961), 'The Establishment of the Administration in Tongaland', *Historians in Africa. The Proceedings of the Leverhulme African Inter-Collegiate Conference in History*, University College of Rhodesia and Nyasaland, Salisbury.

WATSON, W. (1958), *Tribal Cohesion in a Money Economy*, Manchester University Press.

INDEX

abduction, 86, 93 *seq.*, 117, 126
See also marriage.
Administration, the 7, 14, 19, 20,
255–6, 261–2, 275, 295, 301, 307–8,
317
Administrative,
appointments, 225, 244, 246 *seq.*,
250, 251 *seq.*, 276, 296–9, 307–8,
317
supports traditional values, 221, 223,
227, 252, 276, 294, 300
system, 6, 225, 251–2, 288, 291
and traditional political status, 20, 22,
44, 220–1, 225, 247 *seq.*, 251–3,
276, 294 *seq.*, 305–7, 318
See also Boma, headmanship, headmen, villages.
adultery, 67, 93, 95, 97–104, 122 *seq.*,
127, 137–8, 169, 173, 198, 263–5,
308–9
See also marriage, Mzenga village.
amnesia,
genealogical, 47, 268
structural, 214
See also genealogies, kinship.
Amuziteni of Mzenga village, 61, 63,
67, 74, 177, 187, 200, 236, 266, 279
Arabs, 17, 204–5, 293, 297
arbitration, 289, 301, 302, 308–11
See also courts, headmen.
Atonga Tribal Council, the, 22
attorneys,
responsible for welfare of his kinsmen, 82–3, 89 *seq.*, 96, 97, 109,
138, 150–1, 157–8, 169, 191, 193,
240–2, 257–8, 310
rights to bridewealth, 82, 86 *seq.*,
101 *seq.*, 117, 135, 137
role in marriage negotiations, 82–3,
84, 175, 249
See also marriage, maternal uncle.

Bailey, F. G., 5
Bandawe, 16, 18, 19, 59, 156 *seq.*, 205,
263, 285, 288, 297
Barnes, J. A., xxiii, xxv, 7, 47
Bell, R. D., 18
Bemba, the, 183

Bisa, the, 64, 68, 135, 293
Bledisloe, 318
Bohannan, P. J., xxv
Boma, the, 21, 23, 57, 220, 223, 247,
249–50, 274, 276, 299–300, 309–10
See also Administration.
Book, the, 26, 196–7, 206 *seq.*, 210,
219 *seq.*, 226, 243, 279, 285, 298, 304
an attribute of headmanship, 219,
221, 223, 226, 246, 252
See also headmanship, headmen.
bridewealth, *see* marriage.
Busia, K. A., 7

Chewa, the, 12, 15, 22, 43, 110, 117, 302
chiefs, 2, 294, 301, 305–7
See also Administration, headmen.
children of the village, *see* sons of the
village.
CHIMBANO, 166, 283
Chinyafwa village, 30, 179, 285
connections with the Siska, 48, 50,
68 *seq.*, 213, 291
graves of, 115, 179, 212
struggle for seniority in, 68 *seq.*,
133–9, 177–8, 188, 192
See also MAKALAMBA, Nyali, Siddely.
CHINYENTHA,
rivalry with GURU, 298–9, 307–8
war leader, 16, 61, 274, 294, 296,
300, 306
See also GURU.
chisoka payment, *see* death.
CHIWEYO,
installation of, 220–1, 305
reputation of his court, 311
rivalry with MLENGA MZOMA, 220–1,
297–8
See also MLENGA MZOMA.
Chizumulu Island, 12, 22, 48, 50, 52,
273
clans, 44–5
See also names.
Colson, E., xxvii, 7, 8, 42, 315
courts, 122, 127, 216, 273
Administrative, 26, 57, 96, 119, 137,
164, 198, 238, 240–2, 243, 248,
251, 257, 264, 276, 298, 309–11

331